First World War
and Army of Occupation
War Diary
France, Belgium and Germany

38 DIVISION
Divisional Troops
Royal Army Medical Corps
131 Field Ambulance
4 December 1915 - 27 May 1919

WO95/2550/1

The Naval & Military Press Ltd
www.nmarchive.com
Published in association with The National Archives

Published by

The Naval & Military Press Ltd

Unit 10 Ridgewood Industrial Park,

Uckfield, East Sussex,

TN22 5QE England

Tel: +44 (0) 1825 749494

www.naval-military-press.com

www.nmarchive.com

This diary has been reprinted in facsimile from the original. Any imperfections are inevitably reproduced and the quality may fall short of modern type and cartographic standards.

© Crown Copyright
Images reproduced by permission of The National Archives, London, England, 2015.

Contents

Document type	Place/Title	Date From	Date To
Heading	WO95/2550/1 131 Field Ambulance		
Heading	38th Division Medical 131st Field Ambulance Dec 1915-1919 May		
Heading	38th Division 13th F.a. Vol. I. Decr 15		
Heading	War Diary Of 131 Field Ambulance 38th (Welsh) Division From December 14th 1915 To Decr 31st 1915		
War Diary	Winchester	04/12/1915	04/12/1915
War Diary	Southampton	04/12/1915	04/12/1915
War Diary	Gosport	04/12/1915	05/12/1915
War Diary	Havre	06/12/1915	06/12/1915
War Diary	Les Tourbieres	07/12/1915	16/12/1915
War Diary	Vielle Chapelle	16/12/1915	23/12/1915
War Diary	Les Tourbieres	20/12/1915	20/12/1915
War Diary	Robecq	20/12/1915	20/12/1915
War Diary	Vielle Chapelle	22/12/1915	24/12/1915
War Diary	Robecq	25/12/1915	25/12/1915
War Diary	Robecq	20/12/1915	31/12/1915
War Diary	Robecq	26/12/1915	31/12/1915
Heading	38th Div 131 F.A. F/202/1 Jan 1916 131th F.a. Vol 2		
Heading	War Diary Of 131 Field Ambulance From January 1st 1916 To 31st January 1916 (Volume II)		
War Diary	Robecq	01/01/1916	22/01/1916
War Diary	Vielle Chapelle	22/01/1916	31/01/1916
Heading	131st Field Ambulance Feb 1916		
Heading	131 F.A. 38th Div Vol 3		
Heading	War Diary Of 131 Field Ambulance From Feb 1st To Feb 29th 1916 (Volume II)		
War Diary	Vieille Chapelle	01/02/1916	29/02/1916
Heading	38th Division No. 131 Field Ambulance March 1916		
Heading	6th Div. 18th Field Ambulance March 1916		
War Diary	Vieille Chapelle	01/03/1916	13/03/1916
War Diary	Bois-De-Pacaut	13/03/1916	22/03/1916
War Diary	Chateau-De Pacaut	23/03/1916	26/03/1916
War Diary	Vieille Chapelle	26/03/1916	31/03/1916
Heading	War Diary 131 Field Ambulance 38 (Welsh) Division For March 1916 131 Fame Vol 4 38th Div.		
War Diary	Vieille Chapelle	01/03/1916	13/03/1916
War Diary	Bois de Pacaut	13/03/1916	19/03/1916
War Diary	Bois de Bacaut	19/03/1916	21/03/1916
War Diary	Bois de Pacaut	21/03/1916	23/03/1916
War Diary	Chateau De Pacaut	23/03/1916	24/03/1916
War Diary	Bois. De Pacaut	25/03/1916	26/03/1916
War Diary	Vieille Chapelle	27/03/1916	31/03/1916
Heading	War Diary Of 131, Field Ambulance From 1st April To 30 April 16 (Volume V)		
Heading	War Diary Of XI Corps Rest Station II From 18-4-16 To 30-4-16 Vol I		
War Diary	Vieille Chapelle	01/04/1916	17/04/1916
War Diary	Merville	17/04/1916	30/04/1916
War Diary	Regnier Le Clercq	19/04/1916	30/04/1916

Heading	War Diary 131. Field Ambulance At Corps Rest Station 38th (Welsh) Division For May 1916		
War Diary	Merville	01/05/1916	21/05/1916
War Diary	Merville C.R.S	22/05/1916	26/05/1916
War Diary	Merville	26/05/1916	31/05/1916
Heading	War Diary 131 Field Ambulance (Regnier Le Clerq XI Corps Skin Disease Depot) for May 1916		
War Diary	Regnier de. Clercq	01/05/1916	31/05/1916
Heading	War Diary 131. Field Ambulance 38th (Welsh) Division June 1916 1st To 30th Inclusive		
War Diary	Merville	01/06/1916	11/06/1916
War Diary	Robecq	12/06/1916	14/06/1916
War Diary	Divion	15/06/1916	15/06/1916
War Diary	Tincquette	16/06/1916	20/06/1916
War Diary	Tincquette	20/06/1916	24/06/1916
War Diary	Tincquette	24/06/1916	26/06/1916
War Diary	Bonnieres	27/06/1916	27/06/1916
War Diary	Recmanil	28/06/1916	30/06/1916
War Diary	Regnier de Clare	01/06/1916	11/06/1916
Heading	War Diary 131. Field Ambulance 38th (Welsh) Division For July 1916 (1-31st Inclusive) July 1916		
War Diary	Recmanil Fme Toutencourt	01/07/1916	01/07/1916
War Diary	Acheux	02/07/1916	03/07/1916
War Diary	Buire Sur L'ancre	04/07/1916	05/07/1916
War Diary	Morlan Court	05/07/1916	07/07/1916
War Diary	Minden Post	07/07/1916	12/07/1916
War Diary	Morlancourt	12/07/1916	16/07/1916
War Diary	Authie	17/07/1916	31/07/1916
Heading	War Diary 131 Field Ambulance 38th (Welsh) Division For August (1/31) 1916 Volume IX		
War Diary	Millain	01/08/1916	03/08/1916
War Diary	Merckeghem	04/08/1916	21/08/1916
War Diary	Map. Sheet 28 A. 28.a. 3.7	21/08/1916	25/08/1916
War Diary	a.28.a.37	26/08/1916	31/08/1916
Heading	38th Div. 131st Field Ambulance Sept 1916		
Miscellaneous	O/C 131st Field Ambulance 38th (Welsh) Division.	30/09/1916	30/09/1916
Heading	War Diary 131 Field Ambulance 38 (Welsh) Division For September 1st-30-1916 (Volume X)		
War Diary	Map Sheet 28 A. 28 a.3.7	01/09/1916	30/09/1916
Heading	War Diary 131, Field Ambulance 38th (Welsh) Division For October 1916 (1st To 31st Inclusive) Volume XI		
War Diary	Map. Sheet 28 A. 28. a 3.7	01/10/1916	31/10/1916
Heading	38th Div. 131st Field Ambulance Nov 1916		
Heading	War Diary 131 Field Ambulance 38 (Welsh) Division For November 1916 (1-30th Inclusive) (Volume VIII) Vol 12		
War Diary	Map. Sheet 28 A. 28.a. 3.7	01/11/1916	30/11/1916
Heading	War Diary 131 Field Ambulance 38th (Welsh) Division For December 1916 (1-31st Inclusive) (Volume XIII) Vol 13		
War Diary	Map. Sheet 28 A. 28.a. 3.7	01/12/1916	13/12/1916
War Diary	Wormhoudt	14/12/1916	16/12/1916
War Diary	Map Sheet 27 Wormhoudt C 16 C 55	17/12/1916	21/12/1916
War Diary	Wormhoudt	22/12/1916	31/12/1916
Heading	War Diary 131 Field Ambulance 38th (Welsh) Division For January 1917 1-31 Inclusive (Volume XII)		

War Diary	Wormhoudt Map 27 C 16.6.55	01/01/1917	14/01/1917
War Diary	A 28 a. 3.7 sheet 28	14/01/1917	31/01/1917
Heading	War Diary 131 Field Ambulance 38 (Welsh) Div For February 1917 (1-28th Inclusive) Volume XV		
War Diary	Map Sheet 28 A. 28.a. 3.7	01/02/1917	28/02/1917
Heading	War Diary 131, Field Ambulance 38th (Welsh) Division For March 1917 (1-31 Inclusive) Volume XVI		
War Diary	Map Sheet 28 A 28.a. 3.7	01/03/1917	31/03/1917
Heading	War Diary 131, Field Ambulance 38 (Welsh) Division For April 1/30. 1917 Volume XVII		
War Diary	Map Sheet 28 A. 28.a.3.7	01/04/1917	05/04/1917
War Diary	Sheet 28 A. 28.a. 3.7	06/04/1917	30/04/1917
Heading	War Diary 131 Field Ambulance 38 (Welsh) Division For May 1/31 (Inclusive) (Volume XVIII) Vol 18		
War Diary	Sheet 28 A 28.a 3.7	01/05/1917	16/05/1917
War Diary	Map Sheet 28 A. 28.a.3.7	17/05/1917	31/05/1917
Heading	War Diary 131. Field Ambulance 38th (Welsh) Division For June 1/30th 1917 Volume XIX		
War Diary	Map Sheet 28 A. 28.a. 3.7	01/06/1917	05/06/1917
War Diary	A 28.a. 3.7	09/06/1917	16/06/1917
War Diary	Sheet 27. L.1.a. 7.7	17/06/1917	25/06/1917
War Diary	Map Sheet 27 L. 1.a.7.7	26/06/1917	30/06/1917
War Diary	Map Sheet 28 A. 28.a. 3.7	06/06/1917	08/06/1917
Miscellaneous	Summary Of Medical War Diaries For 131st F.A., 38th Divn. 14th Corps, 5th Army.		
Miscellaneous	131st F.A., 38th Divn. 14th Corps, 5th Army. Western Front O.C. Lt. Col. R.H. Mills Roberts. June 1917	00/06/1917	00/06/1917
Miscellaneous	Summary Of Medical War Diaries For 131st F.A., 38th Divn. 14th Corps, 5th Army.		
Miscellaneous	131st F.A., 38th Divn. 14th Corps, 5th Army. Western From O.C. Lt. Col. R.H. Mills Roberts June 1917		
Heading	War Diary 131 Field Ambulance 38 (Welsh) Division For July 1/31 1917 Volume XX		
War Diary	Honenghem	01/07/1917	19/07/1917
War Diary	Proven Area	20/07/1917	23/07/1917
War Diary	Sheet 28 A.18.a. 17	24/07/1917	31/07/1917
Heading	War Diary 131, Field Ambulance 38 (Welsh) Division For August 1/31. 1917 (Volume XXI)		
War Diary	Sheet 28 A. 18.a.1.7	01/08/1917	31/08/1917
Heading	No. 131 F.A. 140/2438 Sept 97		
War Diary	Sheet 28 A 18.a. 17	01/09/1917	11/09/1917
War Diary	Eecke	12/09/1917	12/09/1917
War Diary	Morbecque	13/09/1917	13/09/1917
War Diary	Estaires	14/09/1917	14/09/1917
War Diary	Sheet 36 H.7.d. 6.3	15/09/1917	23/09/1917
War Diary	Fort Rompou	23/09/1917	30/09/1917
Heading	War Diary 131 Field Ambulance 38 (Welsh) Division For October 1/31 1917 Volume XXIII		
War Diary	Sheet 36. H.7.d.6.3	01/10/1917	31/10/1917
Heading	War Diary 131. Field Ambulance 38th (Welsh) Division For November 1/30 1917 (Volume XXIV)		
War Diary	Sheet 36 H.7.d.6.3	01/11/1917	30/11/1917
Heading	War Diary 131 Field Ambulance 38 (Welsh) Division For December 1/31-1917 Volume XXIV		
War Diary	Sheet-36 H.7.d.63	01/12/1917	15/12/1917
War Diary	Field	16/12/1917	31/12/1917

Type	Description	From	To
Heading	War Diary 131 Field Ambulance 38th (Welsh) Division For January 1/31. 1918 (Volume XXVI)		
War Diary	Field F9.17.a.8.4	01/01/1918	09/01/1918
War Diary	Map Sheet 36.a. K.22. 6.18	11/01/1918	14/01/1918
War Diary	Map Sheet 36.A. K.22. 6.8.8	15/01/1918	31/01/1918
Heading	No. 131 F.a. Feb 1918		
War Diary	Map Sheet 36.A. K.22.6.88	01/02/1918	15/02/1918
War Diary	Erquinghem	16/02/1918	21/02/1918
War Diary	Waterlands Camp	22/02/1918	28/02/1918
Heading	131st Field Ambulance 140/2849 March 1918		
War Diary	Water Lands Camp. Sheet 36 N.W. B21C 2.2	01/03/1917	03/03/1917
War Diary	Waterlands Camp	04/03/1918	06/03/1918
War Diary	Waterlands	07/03/1918	10/03/1918
War Diary	Waterlands Camp	11/03/1918	15/03/1918
War Diary	Waterlands	15/03/1918	17/03/1918
War Diary	Waterlands Camp	18/03/1918	28/03/1918
War Diary	Waterlands	29/03/1918	29/03/1918
War Diary	Steen Werck	30/03/1918	30/03/1918
War Diary	Haverskerque	31/03/1918	31/03/1918
Operation(al) Order(s)	Medical arrangements issued in accordance with Brigade Order No. 215 Para. 16	28/02/1918	28/02/1918
Miscellaneous	Appendices II & III		
Miscellaneous	Appendix 4	18/03/1918	18/03/1918
Miscellaneous	App V	23/03/1918	23/03/1918
Heading	131st Field Ambulance 140/2900		
Heading	War Diary Of No. 131 Field Ambulance From 1st April 1918 To 30th April 1918 (Volume 29)		
War Diary	Haverskerque	01/04/1918	03/04/1918
War Diary	Clairfaye	05/04/1918	30/04/1918
Heading	No. 131 F.a. May 1918 140/3983 May 1918		
War Diary	Clairfaye	01/05/1918	10/05/1918
War Diary	Hedauville	10/05/1918	11/05/1918
War Diary	Clairfaye	11/05/1918	20/05/1918
War Diary	Herissart	20/05/1918	31/05/1918
Heading	131st F.a. 140/3016 June 1918		
War Diary	Herissart	01/06/1918	05/06/1918
War Diary	St Lot	06/06/1918	12/06/1918
War Diary	Valheureux	13/06/1918	30/06/1918
Heading	131st F.A. 140/3131 July 1918		
War Diary	Valheureux	01/07/1918	24/07/1918
War Diary	O27b8.9	25/07/1918	31/07/1918
Operation(al) Order(s)	38th (Welsh) Division. R.A.M.C. Order No. 55	14/07/1918	14/07/1918
Operation(al) Order(s)	38th (Welsh) Division. Amendment to R.A.M.C. Order No. 55	14/07/1918	14/07/1918
Miscellaneous	38th (Welsh) Division. Medical Defence Scheme For Middle Sector V Corps Front (Mesnil Sector)	14/07/1918	14/07/1918
Miscellaneous	38th (Welsh) Division. R.A.M.C. Order No. 56	17/07/1918	17/07/1918
Miscellaneous	Officer Commanding 131st Field Ambulance. Appendix III	15/07/1918	15/07/1918
Operation(al) Order(s)	38th (Welsh) Division. Addendum To R.A.M.C. Order No. 56	17/07/1918	17/07/1918
Miscellaneous	38th (Welsh) Division. App IV	21/07/1918	21/07/1918
Operation(al) Order(s)	38th (Welsh) Division. R.A.M.C. Order No. 57	22/07/1918	22/07/1918
Operation(al) Order(s)	38th (Welsh) Division. R.A.M.C. Order No. 58	29/07/1918	29/07/1918
Heading	131st F.a. 140/3200 Aug. 1918		
War Diary	O27b8.9	01/08/1918	06/08/1918

War Diary	O 30b 2.8	06/08/1918	24/08/1918
War Diary	W3a 8.7	25/08/1918	26/08/1918
War Diary	XI 6 b.8.2	27/08/1918	31/08/1918
Heading	131st F. Amb. 140/3259 Sept 1918		
War Diary	X16 b.8.2 (57D)	01/09/1918	02/09/1918
War Diary	T8 C 6.1 (57c)	03/09/1918	10/09/1918
War Diary	P31 C 7 7	11/09/1918	11/09/1918
War Diary	Lechelle	12/09/1918	17/09/1918
War Diary	Near Equancourt VII a 2.2	18/09/1918	18/09/1918
War Diary	Equancourt	18/09/1918	19/09/1918
War Diary	Lechelle	20/09/1918	29/09/1918
War Diary	Sorrel Le Grand	30/09/1918	30/09/1918
Heading	131st F.a. 140/3401 Oct 1918		
War Diary	Sorel. Le Grand	01/10/1918	02/10/1918
War Diary	Ronssoy	03/10/1918	06/10/1918
War Diary	Honnecourt S. 14a. Sheet 57 B.	06/10/1918	08/10/1918
War Diary	Aubencheuil	09/10/1918	09/10/1918
War Diary	Walincourt	09/10/1918	10/10/1918
War Diary	Bertry	10/10/1918	11/10/1918
War Diary	Troisvilles	12/10/1918	24/10/1918
War Diary	Forest	25/10/1918	26/10/1918
War Diary	Moulin de Harpies	27/10/1918	31/10/1918
Heading	131st F.a. 140/3401 Nov 1918		
War Diary	Moulin de Harpies	01/11/1918	07/11/1918
War Diary	Berlaimont	08/11/1918	13/11/1918
War Diary	Aulnoye	14/11/1918	29/12/1918
War Diary	Poix Des Nord	30/12/1918	30/12/1918
War Diary	Trenches	31/12/1918	31/12/1918
Heading	38 Div Box 2357 No 131 Field Ambulance Jan 1919		
War Diary	Longeau	01/01/1919	08/01/1919
War Diary	Longeau Chateau	09/01/1919	31/01/1919
Heading	No 131 Field Ambulance Feb 1919		
War Diary	Longueau	01/02/1919	28/02/1919
Heading	131st F.a. 140/3551 Mar 1919		
War Diary	Longueau	01/03/1919	31/03/1919
Heading	131st F.a. 140/3550 April 1919		
War Diary	Longueau	01/04/1919	30/04/1919
Miscellaneous	Reference 38 Div No. 540 of 3/4/19	03/04/1919	03/04/1919
Miscellaneous	A.D.M.S. No. M. 122/44	22/04/1919	22/04/1919
Miscellaneous	February		
Heading	131 Field Ambulance War Diary For Month Of May 1919 Vol 42		
Miscellaneous	G.O.C. British Troops in France ?	22/05/1919	22/05/1919
War Diary	Longueau	01/05/1919	19/05/1919
War Diary	La Motte Brilan	19/05/1919	27/05/1919

WO95/2550/1
131 Field Ambulance

38TH DIVISION MEDICAL

131ST FIELD AMBULANCE
DEC 1915 - DEC 1918 1919 MAY

131.ᵗ 2.a.
tot: I

12/7809

38ᵗʰ Kurans

Keck 15

Dic/15

Dec 15
Dec 18

Confidential

War Diary
of
131 Field Ambulance
38th (Welsh) Division

From Decbr 14th 1915 to Decbr 31st 1915

Army Form C. 2118.

WAR DIARY
or
INTELLIGENCE SUMMARY. of 131st Field Ambulance
38th Welsh Division Dec 1915

(Erase heading not required)

Place	Date	Hour	Summary of Events and Information	Remarks and references to Appendices
Winchester	4/12/15	7.A.M	In accordance with orders received from Headquarters 38th Welsh Division, the 131st Field Ambulance — complete according to War Establishment Part VII. New Army 1915 — moved in column of route, with two days' rations, one carried by the men and one carried in a wagon — from FLOWER DOWN CAMP WINCHESTER at 7.A.M on Saturday Dec 4. 1915. Passing the Infirmary Starting Point — Junction of SOUTHGATE St. and HIGH St. WINCHESTER at 7.40 A.M it proceeded on its journey to SOUTHAMPTON. The weather was threatening and a drizzle commenced about 8.A.M — one mile SOUTH of WINCHESTER — this gradually increased to heavy rain which continued for the remainder of the day. Ground sheets were worn as Capes. Great Coats were carried on Gamesholes. The pockets being filled with men's kits. In addition to the usual halt of a route march a halt of ¾ an hour was made near SOUTHAMPTON COMMON; Haversack rations were consumed here. The starting point — The Electric Depôt Supply — was passed at 12.45 P.M and Dock No. 2. SOUTHAMPTON was	
SOUTHAMPTON	4/12/15	1.30 P.M	reached at 1.30 P.M in a clean form of rain. Everybody was very wet. No one fell out. The R.A.M.C. method of carrying kits in the pockets of Great Coats worn "En Banderole Seems", to me very unsatisfactory and company very rough. M^rMille Joseph Lt. Col	

Army Form C. 2118.

WAR DIARY
or
INTELLIGENCE SUMMARY.
(Erase heading not required.)

131. Field Ambulance
Dec. 1915

Place	Date	Hour	Summary of Events and Information	Remarks and references to Appendices
SOUTHAMPTON	4/12/15		very unfavourably with the pack of the Infantry man. The great coat cannot be called properly – and when it rains the contents of the pockets get wet. On the other hand if the great-coat is worn the bulging pockets look very ugly and unsoldier like – and moreover when it rains the contents soon get wet. There is no reason that I know of why the R.A.M.C. should not carry packs or say neck sacks. I respectfully beg to recommend this important matter to the consideration of the authorities. The arrival of the unit at Dock No. 2 was immediately reported to the Embarkation Officer. From him general instructions were received as to what to do during the voyage. The several guards of the unit was 44. and it is said by the S.S. HUANCHACO and her is gusted to be on board with Transport and equipment complete by 3.0 o'clock P.M. This was easily done. In addition to the 131st Field Ambulance the Ship, troops on board the HUANCHACO were the 77th Sanitary Section under the command of Captain Llewellyn Williams R.A.M.C. Three officers on the French Red Cross Society and two M.O's for the Welsh Division. The O.C. 131 Field Ambulance (Lt Col R.H.Mills D.Ph.O. C.M.G.) being senior officer, was informed by Embarkation Officer	O.H.M.S Mills Lt Col 4/12/15

Army Form C. 2118.

WAR DIARY
or
INTELLIGENCE SUMMARY.
(Erase heading not required.)

131 Field Ambulance

Dec. 1915

No. 3

Place	Date	Hour	Summary of Events and Information	Remarks and references to Appendices
Off GOSPORT	4/12/15	6 P.M.	that he was O.C. troops on board the Ship. Instructions were received from the Chief Officer of S.S. HUNCHACO as to passengers on board — as to posting of men to boats in case of necessity. Life belts were issued to all ranks. It was intended to sail at 8 o'clock P.M. 4/12/15. but owing to the boisterous weather the Captain decided not to proceed to sea to avoid damaging the hunk. He therefore nearly steamed as far as GOSPORT, and anchored off that Port for the night. At 11 A.M. Dec 5. 1915 an inspection	
"	5/12/15	11 A.M.	of Ship took place. Chief Officer complimented the men on clean state of Ship. At 11.30 A.M. the alarm was sounded as an experiment. The result was good. Every man stood to his boat with life belt on. The weather having moderated he weighed anchor and steamed to HAVRE off that PORT after a smooth passage	
HAVRE	6/12/15	2 A.M.	at 4 P.M. 5/12/15, arriving off that PORT, after a smooth passage aboard. 2 A.M. 6/12/1915. The Ship was brought up alongside the Booth S.S. Coy's Quay at 9 A.M. after disembarking a guide took us to No. 5 Rest Camp. The road were atrociously bad. The Officers had dinner and the men partook of their rations at the rest camp and left at 7.30 P.M. accompanied by another guide arriving at the GAR. DU NORD station at 8.15 P.M.	

O'Donnell O'Keeffe
Lt. Col.

Army Form C. 2118.

WAR DIARY
or
INTELLIGENCE SUMMARY.

(Erase heading not required.)

131st Field Ambulance Dec 1915

Instructions regarding War Diaries and Intelligence Summaries are contained in F. S. Regs., Part II. and the Staff Manual respectively. Title pages will be prepared in manuscript.

Place	Date	Hour	Summary of Events and Information	Remarks and references to Appendices
HAVRE	8/12/15	11.50 P.M	After entraining time and Transport, the men were supplied with coffee. The train – with unit complete and undamaged – left HAVRE at 11.50 P.M for St. OMER. The following were the Officers:– Lt. Col. R H Mills-Roberts, C.M.G, T.D (joined May 9, 1915) Combatants Major 2nd in command (5th Batt: R.W.F) Major J. C. Davies, Transferred from Captain 4 Batt: R.W.F May 15, 1915 Capt. J. S. Ireland — joined 15/1/1915 " J. W. David " 8/4/1915 " Granny Sons " 20/8/1915 " G. Wynne Jones " 5/10/1915 " L. M. Fisher " 12/10/1915 " G. D. Latting " 12/11/1915 Sent to Chorlemont to Singleton " 1/10/1915 Sergt. Major G. B. Lee. We left Winchelsea short of one Officer (Lieut M. Indian) who was posted to the 14. Welsh Regiment.	

O Mills Roberts
Lt Col

Army Form C. 2118.

WAR DIARY
or
INTELLIGENCE SUMMARY

131. Field Ambulance, Dec 1915

Place	Date	Hour	Summary of Events and Information	Remarks and references to Appendices
HAVRE	6/12/15	11.50 PM	The 77th Sanitary Section and form details from the 17th R.W.F. travelled by the same train.	
			We arrived at ST OMER at 6.30 P.M. 7/12/15 and onward there at 7.40 P.M. 7/12/15. Instructions to proceed to AIRE and onward there at 7.40 P.M. 7/12/15. We were ordered to detrain and proceed to LES TOURBIERES billet quarters in an empty Chateau close by, the Caretaker of which had been regularly to receive us. The details of 17th R.W.F. were going in same direction — to BLESSY — and then the guide was to show us the way. We left AIRE station at 11.30 P.M. to the accompaniment of wind, rain, and darkness. Detraining at AIRE had taken a long time owing to lack of facilities and circumlocution.	
LES TOURBIERES	7/12/15	12.40 AM	Marching through the village of St QUENTIN we arrived and on our further west opposite a gateway that apparently led to private grounds. Having halted, a reconnoitring party was sent to investigate and reported an empty Chateau. The Caretaker informed us that we were not expected there. The night being wet and dark and did it seemed an opportune occasion to bet the saying that "possession is nine tenths of the law". We accordingly made ourselves comfortable for the night and were delighted to hear half morning from the Caretaker, left that her husband had misinformed us, we were in our right billet — the CHATEAU BLESSIL near LES TOURBIERES. Wm In Walsh Lt Col	

Army Form C. 2118.

WAR DIARY
or
INTELLIGENCE SUMMARY.
(Erase heading not required.)

131 Field Ambulance
6
Dec 1915

Place	Date	Hour	Summary of Events and Information	Remarks and references to Appendices
LES TOURBIERES	7/12/15		Wagons were parked in accordance with instructions on the grass in front of the Chateau. The horse lines were arranged on a disused drive. The whole arrangement was not satisfactory, the ground was very soft after the heavy rain, so that the heavy Transport sank into it.	
	8/12/15		This day was given to fatigue work.	
	9/12/15		An O/S Batman was posted to the unit, to make up complement of officers. Owing to overcrowding at the Chateau I was desired to billet the section going to overcrowding. C section was accordingly removed to the farm on opposite side of Chateau. During our stay at the CHATEAU BLESSIE in addition to general work, having a good deal of time was given to fatigue work, especially sanitary work. The latter was difficult owing to sodden state of ground. Wagons were frequently mud axle deep.	
	10/12/15		The 131 Field Ambulance was not opened as an Ambulance at LES TOURBIERES — but collected sick from the 115th Brigade. Whilst in the adjoining villages — BLESSE, WILTERNESSE, QUERNES, ENGUINEG-ATTE and SQUENTIN and took them to the 129 Field Ambulance Ward which opened out at CLARQUES. A Motor Ambulance left for this purpose every day at 9 o'clock in the morning	
	11/12/15			
	12/12/15			
	13/12/15			O Kennedy Lt Col

Army Form C. 2118.

WAR DIARY
or
INTELLIGENCE SUMMARY.

(Erase heading not required.)

131 Field Ambulance Dec 1915

Place	Date	Hour	Summary of Events and Information	Remarks and references to Appendices
LES TOURBIERES	14/12/15		On Dec 14 instructions were received that the unit would be ready to move in succession by sections for 7 days instruction with the 19th Div.	
"	15/12/15		Instructions received that 3 M.O, 3 N.C.O's and 18 men were to fetch A section tomorrow at 1.30 P.M. and take it to VIEILLE CHAPELLE for instruction with the 57th Field Ambulance	
"	16.12.15	1.30 P.M	In accordance with yesterdays instructions A section consisting of 3 M.O. 1 Quartermaster 1 W.O. and 61 men were taken by 3 omnibuses to VIEILLE CHAPELLE arriving there at 4.30 P.M. They travelled via BETHUNE and LES TOURBIERES and ambulance continued to Gilbert Road & C sections unarmed at 115th Brigade and to take them to the 125th Field Ambulance	
VIEILLE CHAPELLE	16.12.15	4.30 P.M	The O.C of 115th CLARQUES. At VIEILLE CHAPELLE the Officer of A section were the guest of the Officer mess of the 57th Field Ambulance and were billeted in the village. The men were quartered in the barn of the local pharmacien. Patron. The men were drawn locally.	
"	17.12.15		Lieut Davis with one Sergt one Cook and 18 bearers proceeded to advanced dressing station at St VAAST POST for 3 days instruction. They returned to VIEILLE CHAPELLE with Lt.	M. Taylor Lt Col O.C. CHAPELLE Lt.W

Army Form C. 2118.

WAR DIARY
or
INTELLIGENCE SUMMARY.
(Erase heading not required.)

131 Field Ambulance Dec 1915

Army Form C. 2118.

Place	Date	Hour	Summary of Events and Information	Remarks and references to Appendices
VIELLE CHAPELLE	22/12/15		On the 20/12/15 Capt Wynn Jones was replaced at the A.D.S by a similar party under the command of Capt Wynn Jones, who returned to VIELLE CHAPELLE on the 22/12/15. In the meantime Capts were receiving instruction at the excellent hospital established by the 57 Fld Amb. under the command of Major Paul at the village school. The Nursing Orderlies were also given one day, in rota, into the working of the A.D.S.	
"	23/12/15		While A section was receiving instruction at VIELLE CHAPELLE, B & C sections were ordered to leave CHATEAU BLESSY &c. and to take up their Quarters in	
LES TOURRIE-RES	20/12/15		a new area. This was done on 20/12/15 by route march – reaching ROBECQ at	
ROBECQ	20/12/15	1.30 P.M.	1.30 P.M 20/12/1915. A Field Ambulance was immediately got ready at the Yum Mill. Outbuildings were also made to deal with S.O. Cases of Scabies in Farm Outbuildings about 200 yards from the Field Ambulance Hospital. An Officer Hospital – to take 4 patients- was also got ready in a house.	
VIELLE CHAPELLE	24/12/15 23/12/15		A section at VIELLE CHAPELLE received orders to join B & C section at ROBECQ on 24/12/15 – by route march.	
	24/12/15		A section left. VIELLE CHAPELLE at 9.30 A.M. and marching via HINGES reached ROBECQ at 12.30 P.M. 24/12/1915	

OKM Monagh Lt Cl

Army Form C. 2118.

WAR DIARY
or
INTELLIGENCE SUMMARY.
(Erase heading not required.)

131 Field Ambulance
Dec 1915

Place	Date	Hour	Summary of Events and Information	Remarks and references to Appendices
ROBECQ	25/12/15		Xmas day.	
	20/12/15 To 31/12/15		Motor Ambulance left ROBECQ every morning at 9 o'clock to collect sick from:-	
			10. Sw B. billeted at ROBECQ. M.O. Lieut. T.B. Evans R.A.M.C.	
			11. Sw B. " " P.20./Sect. E. Evans "	
			16. Welsh Regt. " " P.21/36.A A.D. Los "	
			17. R.W.F. " " P.24 Thomas "	
			Div. Cavalry & Cyclists billeted at P.17.3	
			119 Artillery Brigade billeted from ST VENANT to BERGUETTE. M.O. Lt Lamming R.A.M.C.	
			120 " " " at HAVERSKERQUE. M.O. Lt Weston R.A.M.C.	
			121 " " " from HAVERSKERQUE to LE SART. T.30. M.O. Lt Pepper "	
			122 " " " East of HAVERSKERQUE T.29. M.O. Lt Phillips "	
			Div. Amm. Col. West of HAVERSKERQUE T.27 M.O. Lt Herbertson "	
			Shut 36.A	
			also Jordan Div. & Ind. Cavalry	
			41. Bd. billeted at RINCQ. M.O. Capt. Macrae R.A.M.C.	
			11. Bd. " doing duty with Scotch Div.) M.O. Lieut Randle R.A.M.C.	
			(3). Bd. " doing " 19 Div) M.O. Lieut MacKinnon R.A.M.C.	
			(3)1. Bd. billeted at GLOMENGHEM M.O. Captain Rutherford R.A.M.C.	
			10 Div. Amm. Col. Div. T. billeted at WARNE. M.O. Lieut Hunt R.A.M.C.	
			O'Neill O'Neill Lt Col	

2353 Wt. W2544/1454 700,000 5/15 D.D. & L. A.D.S.S./Forms/C. 2118.

Army Form C. 2118.

WAR DIARY
or
INTELLIGENCE SUMMARY.

(Erase heading not required.)

10 131 Field Ambulance Dec 1915

Instructions regarding War Diaries and Intelligence Summaries are contained in F. S. Regs., Part II. and the Staff Manual respectively. Title pages will be prepared in manuscript.

Place	Date	Hour	Summary of Events and Information	Remarks and references to Appendices
ROBECQ	29/12/15 to 31/12/15		During this time 92 Patients were admitted	
			74 " " evacuated to C.C.S. & Rest. Camp	
	28/12/15		In accordance with orders B. Section - Ambulance under Command of Major J.C Davis to undergo 7 days instruction with Punts Mades for LA GORGUE to undergo 7 days instruction with an Ambulance in the Frénels Division	
ROBECQ	31/12/15		Extract from A.D.M.S.' orders today: "Under instructions from the D.D.M.S. XI. Corps the following moves will take place." "B. section will rejoin their HeadQuarters on 2nd Jan 1915" "C. Section 131 Field Amb will join No 57 Ambulance of the 19th Division on Monday 2nd Jan and rejoin their HeadQuarters on 10th Jan. 1916." "The move will take place by route march. 1 G.S. wagon will be sent for Fd. Amb. to Ottron Katis and blankets of the ranks. Return will be drawn up to and for the 3rd January 1916."	

131st F.A.
vol 2

38th Div
131 F.A.
F/202/11

Jan 1916

Confidential

War Diary

of

131 Field Ambulance

from January 1st 1916 to 31st January 1916

(Volume II)

WAR DIARY
or
INTELLIGENCE SUMMARY

Army Form C. 2118.

Place	Date	Hour	Summary of Events and Information	Remarks and references to Appendices
ROBECQ	1916. Jan 1		This was practically a "dies non"	
	Jan 2		The A.D.M.S. bought the G.O.C. 38th (Welsh) Division - Major Gen Phillips D.S.O to visit the Hospital. The General was good enough to say that he was very pleased with what he saw. Major Davies rejoined the unit from LA B. Section under command of Major Davies arriving about 2.00 P.M. The unit is rarely together as a whole. GORGUE. among to sections going away for instruction. Being all together today has any to sections going away for instruction. There was added two lorries by Major Plum Puddings or an exhibit. of Regimental and Divisional funds. Davies and Pend Pm (Ero) out a kind of potato grate dining. was a kind of	
	Jan 3.		Section C. under command of Lieut Oulands in residence with A.D.M.S. near word of at 1 PM to join the 57th 2nd Ambulance at VIEILLE CHAPELLE on 7 days instruction. The move was made by route march via LOCON. S. Sgt. Pearce began to Locke and give instruction in weaving Straw Matiuss - after Indian fashion - to be used as bedding. These Straw Matiuss are very comfortable and are today. They are up a good deal of Straw.	

O Kenneth Roberts Lt. Col.

Place	Date 1916	Hour	Summary of Events and Information	Remarks and references to Appendices
ROBECQ	Jan 4		The O.C's 129, 130 & 131 2nd Ambulance met the A.D.M.S. by request at his office at ST VENANT. The 129 & 130 are to send a section to A.D.S's on the 6th inst. The O.C. 129 130 127212 being short of officers asks me if I can lend him one to a to enable him to send a full complement to his A.D.S. I agree. An unofficial letter sent by Sug. Gen. Pike to various C.O's was discussed — I agreed to the alleged dissatisfaction among Civilian M.O's serving in the army and how to remedy this feeling. It appeared that there was no disinfector in this 3 Brit. ol Ambulance. A reply to war sent to Sug. Genl. Pike to this effect (independently)	
	Jan 5		We received 5000 inches to make him standings of a very interior quality. Nevertheless they were any useful but only in making from standings. But also to make foot-paths in the ground behind the Hospital. NMM 130 O.C 129 2nd ambulance Capt. Bateman was sent to help Lt Col. Davis O.C. Jan 4. 1916 in accordance with previous notice.	
	Jan 6		Bad news received that Capt. Bateman who in leg last night whilst going to 130 F.A. His truck became unmanageable & jolted him against a cart. Nasmyth A.D.S Lt Col	

Army Form C. 2118.

WAR DIARY
or
INTELLIGENCE SUMMARY.
(Erase heading not required.)

Place	Date	Hour	Summary of Events and Information	Remarks and references to Appendices
ROBECQ	Jan 6		Visit Batman was taught to Hospital and evacuated direct to CCS at ST VENANT. We are trying to find new Quarters for the Officers Hospital. We have little we can try but during the absence of the 10th S.W.B. to a week at the wet war they leaf. My wish to ask to it. We take trenches, It was they men of Head Quarters. My wish to ask to it. We take one visited a farm in the yard and stalls of which our A.S.C. (detaches) has been installed since our arrival at ROBECQ. The house lends itself for a hospital. There are 4 bedroom opening into a central room. The late dining room is an Officer common room. There is another room opening out of it which will do very well for orderlies. The O.C. No. 3 A. is asking me to help him by taking in 26.0[?] as he was crowded out owing to damage of Cav. in his ambulance. That he would be occupying the 114 Brigade Sick me morning. I agreed. We have today 49 in patients the trenches.	
	Jan 8		The A.D.M.S. visited the Hospital. He is very pleased with our arrangement— especially the sanitary—. He complains that we have to many (Approvals?) — [?] cases. Many of them are due to the damaging of these made in French trenches. A.D.M.S. impressed upon us the necessity of march with them Battal[?].	N Kenneth McCulloch Lt Col

Place	Date	Hour	Summary of Events and Information	Remarks and references to Appendices
ROBECQ	1916 Jan 8		On sending motor Cars to the Rest Camp at MERVILLE and these to the C.C.S. at St VENANT. It is very difficult to draw the line. Cars that cannot look after themselves are not to be sent to Rest Camp and on the other hand Cars sent to C.C.S. are liable to be sent to the Base and on transfer not to their unit. Owing to difficulty of dealing with patient in tents/Apparent M.O.'s may be rather apt to find them to Field Ambulance.	
	9			
	10		The G.O.C. 118 Brigade (Brig. Gen. Evans) visited the Hospital and was very complimentary. He said he would bring the G.O.C. 11 Army Corps to see the place in the afternoon. He had the time; Gen. Hoking had a conference of Officers at ROBECQ this day — unfortunately Gen Hoking did not come round.	
	11		I had all the Quartermasters and Sergt. Majors to see the Rest Camp at MERVILLE under the Command of A Col Probyn D.S.O. He picked up several useful tips. A telegram was received from the A.D.M.S. to say that the 118 Bicycle was missing as the 13th and 15th and that on each occasion 3. Horse Ambulance would accompany the unit from this 13th Field Ambulance.	

Normans Roberts Lt Col

WAR DIARY
or
INTELLIGENCE SUMMARY

Army Form C. 2118.

Place	Date	Hour	Summary of Events and Information	Remarks and references to Appendices
ROBECQ	Jan 12		Orders received from A.D.M.S. 1st R. Section — 2 Officers, 50 other ranks and 9 + SC attached were to march to GREEN BARN on 14/1/16 at 9 A.M. accompanied by 2 Mule Ambulances, 1 water cart, 1 limbered wagon, 1 G.S. wagon, & three Wheeled Stretchers with action for two days. Orders were also received Organising spleniday telegram shop. The 131 the 116 Brigade is being relieved by the 115 Brigade commencing on Jan 13. The 115 Brigade joining at Field Ambulance will send 3 horse Ambulance to accompany the 115 Brigade 8/1/1916. LA MARQUOIS at 7.45 A.M. on 13/1/16 and 7.30 and 18/1/1916. Commenced building a new incinerator to burn faeces and to boil water.	
	13		Yesterday's orders carried out. The Horse Ambulance returned at 3.30 P.M.	
	14		Major Davis and R. Section marched off to GREEN BARN in accordance with instructions of A.D.M.S. A.D.M.S. visited us and reported that the D.D.M.S. Col Britt was very pleased with our Hospital arrangements. 115 Brigade Ambulance arrived about 3 P.M.	
	15		Orders of Jan 12 carried out at 6 115 Brigade 116 Brigade Head Quarters arrived at ROBECQ. The G.O.C. (Brig Gen Hadow) sends for me to tell him my arrangement for collecting the sick. This is the summary of this visit	
	16		Brig Gen. Hadow (116 Brigade) called at our mess ask that an M.O. might be sent to his Head Quarters to examine and treat his Interpreter.	

N.K.Mulholland Lt Col

Army Form C. 2118.

WAR DIARY
or
INTELLIGENCE SUMMARY.
(Erase heading not required.)

Place	Date	Hour	Summary of Events and Information	Remarks and references to Appendices
ROBECQ	Jan 17		We learn unofficially that the 131st Field Ambulance will exchange with the 57th Field Ambulance. — The 131st going to VIELLE CHAPELLE and the 57th coming to ROBECQ, also that Major Davis moves from GREEN BARN to St VAAST dressing station on the 21st.	
"	18		One of our Water Carts, which is fitted with a pump on Either side, is converted into new pattern, that is with one pump only — in front. The new pattern is much neater, and more compact. The Cart to hold contents is behind. It now has a chance of remaining dry. Previously I used to get sent from the side pumps. Today Quartermaster and Sergt Major went to VIELLE CHAPELLE to see if we could transfer stores & exchange some articles with the 57s so as to avoid transport. A good idea seems not to the 57s to form when Officers body. The 131st S.A. at ROBECQ or Captain McKenzie. Capt Davis and the Quartermaster. We hope to include an exchange to our mutual advantage. In preparing our billeting Certificate we find the One of the farms where we established our Officers Hospital and where our A.S.C. are quartered say grazing. A bill for 75 francs changes has been sent in. This is absurd. We have vastly improved the farm yard & stable, making new horse standings &c & greatly repairing and cleaning the place. N.Kitchen A.M.P. Lt Col	

Army Form C. 2118.

WAR DIARY
or
INTELLIGENCE SUMMARY.
(Erase heading not required.)

Instructions regarding War Diaries and Intelligence Summaries are contained in F. S. Regs., Part II. and the Staff Manual respectively. Title pages will be prepared in manuscript.

Place	Date	Hour	Summary of Events and Information	Remarks and references to Appendices
NOEEUX	Jan. 18		A.D.M.S.' order 18/1/1916. (Extract) The 33rd Division takes over the 19th Divisional area. "The section of 131 Field Ambulance at GREEN BARN will proceed to M.32.d.8.4 & take over the St.VAAST A.D.S. from the 57 Field Ambulance arriving there at 12 noon and relieving the bearer in their aid post the same evening. They will hand over GREEN BARN to an advanced dressing station party from the Guards Division."	
	Jan. 19		A.D.M.S.' order 19/1/1916. (extract) "The 131st Field Ambulance will proceed on the 22nd inst via DOUCE CRÊME FME. Q.32.C.6.9. & Q.32.C.9.7 & LE CORNET.MALO. R.20.C.6 & 2. ZELOBES VIELLE CHAPELLE. To Pam R.20.28.2 at 11.40 A.M & VIELLE CHAPELLE. To pam R.20.28.2 at 11.40 A.M & superseding any previous instruction where they carried. — To start at 9.30 A.M. & (this ship was cancelled)	
	20		On the 20th further instruction concerning the above more were received —	
	21		O.C. 131 Field Ambulance accompanied A.D.(M.S on tour of inspection round the new location of the Ambulance — 120.3.A at MESPLAUX 131.7.A at VIELLE CHAPELLE and 129.3.A at ZELOBES. O Kennelly A/Lieut	

Army Form C. 2118.

WAR DIARY
or
INTELLIGENCE SUMMARY.
(Erase heading not required.)

Place	Date	Hour	Summary of Events and Information	Remarks and references to Appendices
ROBECQ	Jan 22.		An advance party consisting of 1 Offr, 2 N.C.O's & 3 men left ROBECQ at 8.30 A.M. in accordance with A.D.M.S. instructions in order to reach VIEILLE CHAPELLE about 9 o'clock to "take on" from the 57 Field Ambulance. The unit less 1 section at GREENBARN. - moved out at 9.30 in accordance with instructions already given and following the route given. Patients passed through the Ambulance during our stay at ROBECQ 337. No deaths. 26 Officers and 311 Other Ranks. The 33 days spent at ROBECQ had been most instructive. Officers, N.C.O's and men were happy and cheery and worked with a will. The Mill in which we established a Hospital was an admirable building for that purpose - and all ranks worked hard to make it a success. And they succeeded. Behind the Hospital much work was done, when he arrived it was a morass of mud between two streams. This was drained and paths made with bricks. Several wood & Canvas buildings were put up. (1) Bathroom (with flannel curtains) 6 tubs. (2) Cook House (brick floored) took into itself an Armstrong hut, a roof incinerator for field cooker (3) Ablution room (with flannel) Latrines and urinals also an Armstrong hut. A urinal incinerator was arranged on the top of which a large boiler was fixed - gun supplied O'Connell Welch Lt Col	

WAR DIARY
or
INTELLIGENCE SUMMARY.

Army Form C. 2118.

Place	Date	Hour	Summary of Events and Information	Remarks and references to Appendices
ROBECQ	Jan 22		Supplied us with a large quantity of Hot Water. In Goggles, on two doses of the incinerator there were openings lined by a biscuit tin. These acted as shorts down which faeces etc were shot into the fire. Shortly after the oct. there was no smell.	gone to ROBECQ
VIELLE CHAPELLE	Jan 22		The 87th Field Ambulance was met near CORNET MALO and R.20.c.8.2 was passed at 11.40. A.M. VIELLE CHAPELLE being reached at 12.15. P.M. The 131st Field Ambulance took possession of the Quarters recently occupied by the 87th Field Ambulance. The Hospital was established at the school and contained 11 Patients on our arrival. The Officers Hospital adjoining the Barracks had one patient. The Officers mess was established at the Presence. The men were quartered in the Barn. The A.S.C. & Horse Transport were in an old building near the Canal Bridge, and the Horse Standings were close by. The Motor Transport had its Headquarters in an old house at the entrance to the Hospital. On Saturday afternoon St VAAST A.D.S was visited by the O.C. 131. F.A.B. section was established there and all going well.	

N. Smith Nkerts Lt-Col

Army Form C. 2118.

WAR DIARY
or
INTELLIGENCE SUMMARY.
(Erase heading not required.)

Place	Date	Hour	Summary of Events and Information	Remarks and references to Appendices
VIEILLE CHAPELLE	Jan 23, 24, 25, 26, 27		Most of the time is spent in fatigue work — cleaning up, relaying paths, making new latrines, making huts taxi ship &c. On the 26th B Section was relieved at St VAAST A.D.S. by C Section, with huts for Fisher and Latrines. The 13th 9 p.m. Clean St VAAST and Divl. Area N of a line running through LA PANNERIE (W.4) — LA COUTURE (exclusive) and Paizoole (Willed in this area — and all units EAST of the Canal.	
	28		The A.D.M.S. visited the unit and expressed satisfaction at the work done. I visited St VAAST A.D.S. with the A.D.M.S. and the Regimental posts at RUE DE BOIS and FACTORY CORNER as well as GREEN BARN A.D.S. at the later place we discussed that an M.O. visited the Regimental posts every day. On the 27th Captain Pursell returned from Latrines at St VAAST in order that the later ought return to VIEILLE CHAPELLE to establish a Canteen.	
	29.		The A.D.M.S. brought the D.M.S. to see the Hospital. He was good enough to consider the view expressed by the A.D.M.S. satisfactory.	
	30.		A new tetanus ("Victor") Stitches received from D.D.M.S. It is	

N Kenneth Polak Lt Col

A.D.S.S./Forms/C. 2118.

WAR DIARY
or
INTELLIGENCE SUMMARY.
(Erase heading not required.)

Army Form C. 2118.

Place	Date	Hour	Summary of Events and Information	Remarks and references to Appendices
NIELLE-CHAPELLE	Jan 30		to be sent to the 3. Regimental and Bn H.Q. at STIRLING CASTLE. MOGGS HALL & RUE DE BOIS. that evacuation to St V.F.T. via BREEN. R.T.N. Each M.O. will keep of for 24 hours and will issue a report conerning it to the A.D.M.S. Wrote to C.R.E. Divisional Headquarters yesterday to ask if he would be good enough to send an officer to give us the benefit of his advice in connection with a new Medical drain behind the Stronghold. An R.E. Captain came today promising to execute out a drain across the Road to the Canal — to to be evacuated the Stagnant material objected to. Work to commence on Feb 1. 1916. Plan is good. Order received from A.D.M.S. 30.1.1916. replacing a person not understood respecting a attacking the two Ramp Stretcher abreast, refused to allow to the stress and parts refused to an issue of the 2-3 Batt" on the left. At present 14 W, 13 W & 15 RWF at STIRLING CASTLE. MOGGS HALL & RUE du BOIS. It is suggested that the Sketch be taken first to STIRLING CASTLE. via GREEN BARN under the direction of a man from there who knows the route — The M.O. will return it one day and hand it on to M.O. at Warwick, next Inn'gs Hall Lt Col	

Army Form C. 2118.

WAR DIARY
or
INTELLIGENCE SUMMARY.
(Erase heading not required.)

Place	Date	Hour	Summary of Events and Information	Remarks and references to Appendices
VIEILLE CHAPELLE	Jan 30		"MOBBS. ITALL not day and so on back to ST-VAAST where will be retained" "pending further instruction." A copy of this order was sent to O.C. at ST-VAAST A.D.S. Copies of other orders issued by A.D.M.S. are:— 29.1.16 "As M.O. from the A.D.S. [Factory corner] (RUE DU BOIS) it is essential that very close touch should be kept between the M.O's at A.D.S's and that M.O's at A.D.S. should be absolutely familiar with Aid Posts & A.D.S's and with the conditions at the Aid Posts. The 2 M.O's at A.D.S. should "the ground & with the conditions at the same time each should be up for a fortnight — one "will be changed each week. (The first to go back will of course only have been up one "week) in the first instance. This will insure some continuity in system & "going down each week." "work at the A.D.S. and will make it easier for everyone." 30.1.16. "Enfy the O.C. ST-VAAST will tell the O.C. GREEN BARN. A.D.S. and "will arrange to station one of his Inch at GREEN BARN. — The Ford "will take cases straight from GREEN-BARN to VIEILLE-CHAPELLE" N Smith White Lt Col	

WAR DIARY or INTELLIGENCE SUMMARY.

Army Form C. 2118.

Place	Date	Hour	Summary of Events and Information	Remarks and references to Appendices
VIELLE CHAPELLE	31.1.16		I visited St VAAST. A.D.S. to see if the last orders of the A.D.M.S. were thoroughly understood, and found they were understood. All was going well at the A.D.S. Since the arrival of the unit at VIELLE CHAPELLE 1627 Patients have been admitted and evacuated. 18 Officers 1627 Other ranks. 18 Officers There have been no deaths in Hospital. On the whole the cases have been slight. The serious ones here are all evacuated to C.C.S. (No 2. Stationary & No 7) at MERVILLE and No 32 - C.C.S. at ST VENANT	

J Knuthowch. Lt Col

131st. Field Ambulance

Feb 1916

131. F. A.
98th Div
Vol 3.

― Confidential ―

War Diary

of

131. Field Ambulance

From: Feby 1st   To: Feby 29th 1916

(Volume II)

WAR DIARY
or
INTELLIGENCE SUMMARY.
(Erase heading not required.)

Army Form C. 2118.

Place	Date	Hour	Summary of Events and Information	Remarks and references to Appendices
VIEILLE CHAPELLE	1.2.16		Motor drivers on their return are to report to orderly room the C.C.S. to which Pts. have been evacuated. This is necessary owing to difficulty experienced in tracing a Pt. who may have been sent to one C.C.S. where I may be unwilling to admit him and is then forwarded to another. An order received from A.D.M.S. today, to report to him all officers admitted with diagrams — also when evacuated. I hear that all the artillery have come up the M.O. of heavy artillery will attend the sick of the two Minor Batts at BOUT DEVILLE which has been done by an O.O.a. of the Mise Field Ambulance.	
	2/2/16		G.O.C. holds Division's congratulation received. He hopes that the Division will continue to carry out policy dressing of Communication from Commander in Chief.	
	3/2/16		Three acetylene lamps received from M.D.M.S. to replenish and POST CHIMNEY CRESCENT. M.O.C.'S HOLE and FACTORY CORNER. Men camp on the property of A.D.M.S. guest. Can not be taken of them. They will not be replaced. Only scene accidental self inflicted wounds are to be sent to BUSNES. Whilst all self inflicted wounds here sent. A note received from A.D.M.S. to say that 5% rate of Corps per day should be raised to all R.A.M.C. men from date of embarkation unless previously granted. Neville Welsh Lt. Col. O.C. 131 British Ambulance	

Army Form C. 2118.

WAR DIARY
or
INTELLIGENCE SUMMARY.
(Erase heading not required.)

Place	Date	Hour	Summary of Events and Information	Remarks and references to Appendices
VIELLE CHAPELLE	4/2/16 5/2/16		General routine work.	
	6/2/16		(continued) Orders received from A.D.M.S. on the medical arrangement in case of a sudden move forward. Also duty of M.O's at and Posts. Rw J. to return joint charge from R.M.O. but Gunner was sent to 14:F Rw J. to return joint charge from R.M.O. b.t.c. and Opl detail firm (present) ordered the unit. Storm Down c.B. and Opl detail firm (present) ordered the unit.	
	7/2/16		Went with A.D.M.S to ST VAAST. A.D.S and GREEN BARN. A.D.S and until the Regimental aid Posts at STIRLING CASTLE and MOG HOLE. Then had once forth evacuated to 131. Dental Ambulance through ST VAAST. via GREEN BARN — This route being more convenient than the PLUM ST & FACTORY CORNER.	
	8/2/16		I went to ST VAAST again. A photograph was expected in connection with ST John's Ambulance Association. The appointment was cancelled by Telegram. 9ul Ow. Oran. Senitary With Army Corps Called on the unit. A Horse Ambulance left at 3 A.M. to had HQ. 16 R.F at RICHBOURG. 4.30 A.M. to convey to their billet at VIEILLE CHAPELLE. Thence men made to march.	
	9/2/16		All the old straw cleaned out of men's billet at BRASSERIE BARN, at VIEILLE CHAPELLE. It was disinfected in manner in yard. It acted as a filter, and cleaned the smell to a great extent. Into ST VAAST. again with 9ul D.w.Oran and went round him via FACTORY CORNER. PLUM. ST. STIRLING CASTLE. MOGITOLE to GREEN.BARN A D S	

A.D.S.S./Forms/C 2118.

WAR DIARY
INTELLIGENCE SUMMARY
(Erase heading not required.)

Army Form C. 2118.

Place	Date	Hour	Summary of Events and Information	Remarks and references to Appendices
VIEILLE CITAPELLE	10/2/16		R.E. Officer visited St VAAST to advise as to repairing dug outs. There is a good deal of water in some of them and others want general repair. Officer hopes it has turned — There are only 6 huts and they are all occupied. Officer had no accommodation for officers at Corps Rest. Camp — so that he have to share with men who are not well enough for C.C.S and not well enough for duty.	
	11/2/16		There is a lot of water in men's dug out at St VAAST A.D.S. Apparently the flow is below the level of the ditch close to. The junction of the latter with EUSTON CANAL seems however, so that if the ditch is & well cleaned the dug out may drain.	
	12/2/16		Went to St VAAST again with the A.D.M.S. Good progress has been made in repairing the approaches and cleansing the dug outs. The Originated and post at FACTORY CORNER was visited, also GREEN BARN A.D.S.	
	13/2/16		Heat Qary O.A.M.C. transferred to this unit from the 129th F Amb.	
	14/2/16		A new incinerator made to burn accreta and to heat water in an old district water Cart Tank. It promises to be a great success.	

O'M(illegible) Lt Cn
O.C. 131 Field Ambulance

WAR DIARY or INTELLIGENCE SUMMARY

Army Form C. 2118.

Place	Date	Hour	Summary of Events and Information	Remarks and references to Appendices
VIEILLE CHAPELLE.	15/9/16		Called at A.D.M.S. Head Quarters at LESTREM. Was informed that the Division is taking up a new line — The Brigade on the left is going over to the Right Flank — then extending the line further South. The 19th Division will occupy the space left on the left Flank. 129 & 130. F. Amblces establish A.D.S. at LONE FARM. and MARAIS and evacuate to ZELOBES and MESPLAUX. On the present 131. F.A. sleep at VIEILLE CHAPELLE but only deals with one battn on the front instead of three a fortnight ago. Going to the CORPS. LAUNDRY. having been knocked down at LA GORGUE — a company is being arranged in one of the Brewery buildings etc. VIEILLE CHAPELLE — Close by Gun Men's Quarters. Major Mackie R.A.M.C. (61st Division) in command of a F.A. at home (2nd Line 3. (2/1st F.A. 61st Div T.F) days instruction.	
	16/9/16		Showed working methods &c of the unit to Major Mackie. Took him to ST VAAST A.D.S. and Jadem Comr. Represented aid post. The latter is much improved at general appearance. Things are much smarter & cleaner. Lieut McMillan is in Command of. Lieut David rejoined unit at VIEILLE CHAPELLE and was replaced at first David rejoined unit. A.D.M.S. had St VAAST. ST VAAST. A.D.S. by—Post. Peke grew. 131st. F.A. returns. FACTORY CORNER Regimental Aid Post Orders received today from A.D.M.S. that ST VAAST is to be handed on to 59' F.A. O(Multbonnel) Lt. Capt. O.C. 131. Ditch Ambulance	

WAR DIARY
or
INTELLIGENCE SUMMARY.

Army Form C. 2118.

Place	Date	Hour	Summary of Events and Information	Remarks and references to Appendices
VIEILLE CHAPELLE	17/2/16		Telegram received from M.O. 10' S.W.B. that Ambulance is required at CROIX BARBEE - to carry 8 men to new destination. Telegram from 113 Brigade (last night) to return 1 N.C.O. & 1 man in charge of divisional Ambulance they will be returned by Hon Freeman's stores after Thursday night. In event of the minimum Ambulance finds Wynn Pass a Pettigrew minor from ST VAAST via RICHBOURG ST VAAST with 40 Mr ranks to RUE DU BOIS. A.D.S. relieving the 130 F.A. at that post. 1 M.O. Car will be stationed at RUE DU BOIS & 1 Motor Cart with two Mrs and other 1 Motor Car will remain at the ST VAAST to bring wounded from FACTORY CORNER. The Regimental and Post feeding RUE DU BOIS. A.D.S. is at CHOCOLATE MENIER CORNER — PRINCES ROAD runs in a Southerly direction from this Corner and is an F an hrs. and prob. DEAD POST. Post and TUBE STATION — Tm must also detach 2 men to each of their posts including Approach and post — B.H. all. There is a Tram used running from TUBE STATION to RUE DU BOIS A.D.S. until it is Cannibals repaired. I cannot be utilized to carry patients. There are three "Island" in few. and hr each of which Tm must also detail one man — also long patrol at night — at BOAR'S HEAD from FACTORY CORNER and two — FARM CORNER one at BOAR'S HEAD from FACTORY CORNER and ROPE KEEP - from RUE DU BOIS. I visited RUE DU BOIS. A.D.S. with Major Mackay (in instructor) and took him afterwards to 130 F.A. at LES MESPLAUX. We visited Scabies Hospital 129 F.A. at ZELOBES and left him in charge of this day. In the morning of this day. O.C. 130 F.A.	O.C. 1/3 Field Ambulance O/Lieut.Col.Ash Lt.Col.

Army Form C. 2118.

WAR DIARY
or
INTELLIGENCE SUMMARY.
(Erase heading not required.)

Instructions regarding War Diaries and Intelligence Summaries are contained in F. S. Regs., Part II. and the Staff Manual respectively. Title pages will be prepared in manuscript.

Place	Date	Hour	Summary of Events and Information	Remarks and references to Appendices
VIEILLE CHAPELLE	17/9/16		We are to attend an M.O. to incl. Pioneers every day at LA COUTURE (A.D.M.S. order) also an officer to FACTORY CORNER, to relieve Lieut Soden (RAMC) who the Welsh — Lieut Soden St. Temp 102° tonight ill. Sent Soden (RAMC) who the Welsh — Lieut Soden St. Temp 102° tonight ill. Hosp. at VIEILLE CHAPELLE.	
	18/9/16		Telegram received to send an Fd. Ambulance to follow 10th S.W.B. from CROIX MARMEUSE. 9.45 a.m. in lorries — they are going down South. Pte. men at LA COUTURE. Hut latrines in detail for duty with 19th Pioneers at LA COUTURE.	
	19/9/16		A.D.M.S. & D.A.D.M.S. visit the unit and inform that Surgeon General will inspect unit on 21st. Lt. Col. Davin (19th Div.) called — he wanted permission to feed 500 men tomorrow (on their way to trenches) in our barn. I reluctantly declined from an men occupy the barn) and have their own mess there. It would mean an output men.	
	20/9/16		G.O.C. Division called at Head Quarters with M.S. Murad M.R. expressed pleasure with what he saw. I visited RUE DU BOIS — and the Aid Posts attached. Work is going on satisfactorily at the A.D.S.	
	21/9/16		Surgeon General Pike D.D.M.S. 1st Army & A.D.M.S. accompanying him inspected the RUE DU BOIS. A.D.S. at 11 a.m. and VIEILLE CHAPELLE Head Quarters in afternoon. Lt. Col. O. C. 1st Gold Ambulance

Army Form C. 2118.

WAR DIARY
or
INTELLIGENCE SUMMARY.
(Erase heading not required.)

Place	Date	Hour	Summary of Events and Information	Remarks and references to Appendices
VIEILLE CHAPELLE	21/2/16		The Brigdr General was pleased and congratulated us. He said "Nothing could be better!" This is very satisfactory. All ranks have worked hard and I think deserve the General's congratulations. Unfortunately Sergeant Pike had to run to hosp on stores & Transport. (Commanding 1st Army Corps)	
	22/2/16		Lt. Gen. Sir R.E.B. Haking K.C.B. and Col. Smith D.D.M.S came to see the Hospital — They also saw the horse and transport. General Haking congratulated us. Orders received from A.D.M.S. to go and inspect the CHATEAU at the BOIS. DU PACQUOT with the view of moving on into there. We went and found a very "septic" place. We are all tired of the idea of leaving the little Hospital where all have worked so hard and satisfactorily. Short again in such unsavoury surroundings. Later on, a telegram arrives cancelling the scheme. We are all delighted!	
	23/2/16		Orders received from A.D.M.S. that 131 Field Ambulance will in future attend for Post Corps Station at MERVILLE also Eye and Dental cases, to commence on the 24/2/16. — In view of 129 Field Ambulance going to Lt. Col. from men van concealed same day — 136. will do the casualties! D.H.M. Murrhett Lt. Col. O.C. 131 Fld Amb	

Army Form C. 2118.

WAR DIARY
or
INTELLIGENCE SUMMARY.
(Erase heading not required.)

Instructions regarding War Diaries and Intelligence Summaries are contained in F. S. Regs., Part II. and the Staff Manual respectively. Title pages will be prepared in manuscript.

Place	Date	Hour	Summary of Events and Information	Remarks and references to Appendices
VIEILLE CHAPELLE	23/2/16		CHATEAU DU PACQUAT. This unit is to take all Cons—Scabies on until further No. 129. Order received from A.D.M.S. complimenting Medical Units on display at inspection by Surgeon General and Dy on good work done. This, as regards us, was not on parade.	
	24/2/16		B. Section under Command of Capt Parry relieved A section at RUE DU BOIS (latter returned under Command of Lieut Wynn Jones to Head Quarters. Genl Philips (G.O.C. 61st Division) visited the A.D.S. at RUE DU BOIS and in addition to him he [was] moved with Sandbags to protect buildings & to pump out dug out — He has a lot of water in it— he has not included the 10,000 Sandbags and a pump some days ago.	
	25/2/16		Order from A.D.M.S. that 131 Field Ambulance will take over the baths in the front area from No. 129. J.A.— First begun Jns. and 3 N.C.O's to be up at LOCON tomorrow morning to Sanitary Office to receive instruction re baths attached to	
	26/2/16		I visited A.D.S. RUE DU BOIS— and then Send Capt Lt William Sanitary officer— With Lieut Wynn Jns & 3 N.C.O's I went with them to Bath Head Quarters. O.C. 131 Field Ambulance	

WAR DIARY
or
INTELLIGENCE SUMMARY.
(Erase heading not required.)

Army Form C. 2118.

Place	Date	Hour	Summary of Events and Information	Remarks and references to Appendices
VIEILLE CHAPELLE	26/2/16		Headquarters Depot at KING'S ROAD. Captain Lt Witham informs me that 1 N.C.O. & 3 men to each bath is not nearly enough. I regret him to let me know in writing through the A.D.M.S. what he does want, so that I can comply with his wishes if possible.	
	27/2/16		Order from A.D.M.S. to supply for the Baths — [in attendance with suggestions of Sanitary Officer Capt Lt Witham]	
			1 Officer in charge	
			1 Cpl. & 5 men for LE TOURET.	
			1 " 4 " " GORB. ST.	
			1 " 4 " " RICHEBOURG.	
			1 Batman ⎫	
			1 Cook ⎪	
			2 men i/c rations & clths ⎪	
			1 Trained man ⎬ for headquarter depot in KING'S ROAD	
			3 A.S.C. men ⎪	
			1 G.S. wagon ⎪	
			1 Water Cart ⎪	
			4 Horses ⎭	
			Rations will be supplied from VIEILLE CHAPELLE. M.P. Smith O/Lt. A.S.	
			O.C. 131 Company	

WAR DIARY or INTELLIGENCE SUMMARY

Army Form C. 2118.

Place	Date	Hour	Summary of Events and Information	Remarks and references to Appendices
VIEILLE CHAPELLE	27/2/16		A Section (62 old ranks) was expected today for the week's instruction (106 Field Ambulance)	
			Two Section arrived. One from 105 Field Ambulance as well as from 106 FA	
			This was a mistake & discovered on enquiry. The Section from 105 FA were processed	
			Should have gone to the 130 at MESPLAUX. They returned there later in the day after dinner.	
	27 28/2/16		Instead of 62 other ranks there were only 57 with three officers — Captain Ryan — Lieut Jenna — & Lt. Qualtrali Smith.	
			Lt Qualtrali Smith to take charge of Lt Qualtrali Smith. See.	
			I took him all three in to show him Captain Ryan & omit senior armd.	
			I took Captain Ryan and dispersed into 3 parts — 19 in each	
			57 other ranks 19 mile forward at 9 a.m from us to RUE DU BOIS	
			party, 19 mile instruction at End of third time they will	
			rts to VIELLE CHAPELLE and will be relieved on Wednesday	
			return to 2nd party of 19. & Sundays 2nd & 3rd party on Tuesday	
			by 2nd party of 19 & 3rd party on Tuesday.	
			D.M.Williamson Lt Col	
			O.C. 131 Field Ambulance	

Army. Form G. 2118.

WAR DIARY
or
INTELLIGENCE SUMMARY.
(Erase heading not required.)

Instructions regarding War Diaries and Intelligence Summaries are contained in F.S. Regs., Part II. and the Staff Manual respectively. Title pages will be prepared in manuscript.

Place	Date	Hour	Summary of Events and Information	Remarks and references to Appendices
VIEILLE CHAPELLE	28/2/16		Party proceeded at 9. A.M. to RUE DU BOIS A.D.S. an arrangement yesterday. They marched with the Bath Party via KING'S ROAD. Balls chosen under Charge of Sergt-Sutcliffe. Captain Evan & Orderly Seaman were taken to the RUE DU BOIS A.D.S. Orders from O.M.S. that this unit will not do general Advising in the present instead from O.M.S. will do it instead. Captain Evan is attached an "not on duty" for orderly Officer, that is he	
	29/2/16		will be orderly Officer tomorrow at VIEILLE CHAPELLE. First Seaman proceeded by the Relief Car at 2 o'clock P.M. for two days instruction at RUE DU BOIS. At end of that time he will return to VIEILLE CHAPELLE, that is on Thursday March. 2. when he will be relieved by Captain Swan who will similarly do two days at RUE DU BOIS. Returning to VIEILLE CHAPELLE. on Saturday March 4.1916. Attaching O.C. 151 Welsh F.O.C. 131 British Ambulance memo from Ambulance Wagon to be at RICHEBOURG ST VAAST (S.2.a.4.5) two horse Ambulance Wagon to be at RICHEBOURG ST VAAST (S.2.a.4.5) at 1.15 P.M. tomorrow to accompany 15 Welsh Regiment to LA PANNERIE. ROUTE. C. RICHBOURNE will be via C. ROIX BARBEE & ST VAAST. A.D.S. End of Narration Fund is being drawn to provide dinner for St. David's Day tomorrow. N.H. Mulberall Lt Col O.C. 131 Ambulance	

J.I.S 2353. Wt. W2544/1454 700,000 5/15 D.D.&L. A.D.S.S./Forms/C 2118.

Army Form C. 2118.

WAR DIARY
or
INTELLIGENCE SUMMARY.
(Erase heading not required.)

Place	Date	Hour	Summary of Events and Information	Remarks and references to Appendices
VIEILLE CHAPELLE	29/2/16		Two ambulances 1½ motor & 1 horse to be at 10" Welsh H.Q. King's Road X.11.a at 9.30 a.m. 1/3/16 to convey I.S. men unable to walk to LES CHOQUAUX.	
	29/2/16		The A.D.M.S. & D.A.D.M.S. called at the Hospital today and warned us as to the possibility of having to leave VIEILLE CHAPELLE — It be remain ad VIEILLE CHAPELLE — we are left in ambulance division's area or our division goes much further south. R H M R	O K Smith Webb Lt-Col O.C. 131. Field Ambulance

38th Division

No. 131 Field Ambulance

March 1918

March 1918

L/Cpl Fred Ambedare

L/C Dixon

WAR DIARY or INTELLIGENCE SUMMARY

Army Form C. 2118.

Place	Date	Hour	Summary of Events and Information	Remarks and references to Appendices
VIEILLE CHAPELLE	1/3/16		St. David's Day. I visited RUE-DU-BOIS A.D.S and Regimental Aid Post at PETIT HOUSE and Aid post at DEAD COW and TUBE STATION. B.O.R. dug out on fair day. The new pump is working well in the dug out. There appear to be several springs in it. — The water was not rain water —. The ground is very sodden. I went to carefully flooded all trench water. I went out to accompany him to two billets. S: Ambulance (3 km x 2 mls) was sent out to collect an ana-flea from an R.A.P. Sent out Davis with some arrivain to collect no one LES CHOQUES. On return LE PANNERIE, LES CAULDRONS, and LES CHOQUES. Gro Offr. being absent, but being accurate. Gro Offr. very difficult to find among LE HAMEL and ESSARS — with care.	
	2/3/16		Men for Collection near LE HAMEL and ESSARS — with care. Plan run for appts award. Walk the may appts award.	
	3/3/16		Went to LOCON to draw money 2700 francs to pay NCO's & men. Went down RUE-DU-BOIS A.D.S and paid men the first afterwards went to KING'S ROAD BATH DEPT. Paid men there & returned to VIEILLE CHAPELLE where remainder of went was paid.	

WAR DIARY or INTELLIGENCE SUMMARY

Army Form C. 2118.

Place	Date	Hour	Summary of Events and Information	Remarks and references to Appendices
VIEILLE CHAPELLE	3/3/16		Sent (Stages) R.F.M.C. was staying at RUE DU BOIS A.D.S. (on being relieved Today) (Night Lieut LOW. 16 Welsh inh Hospital suffering from Influenza — and relieved by 16" Welsh H-Q- and LOW's week. Pending instructions from A.D.M.S. our Staff is now comd released (K 3/4) at VIEILLE CHAPELLE.	
	4/3/16		Order received from A.D.M.S. to send a party to take possession of BOIS DU PACAUT — CHATEAU and farm. Sent David twenty two rank and file. Took Red X spare on one Ref. with 2 G.S. wagon and 2 Tanks of water. No suitable accom. for spare by Part. unhappy situation. Party returned became CHATEAU was occupied by three out. Str. This observation was reported to A.D.M.S. Lieut Lees (Banting) no refused to move out 106.FA Wh. Party for instruction from 106.FA Wh.	
	5/3/16		Another note is received from A.D.M.S. to say that present party 200 men leaving the CHATEAU-DU-RAE AUT. on 6/3/16 after which the 131 Fars Amb will take possession. I am to go then with O.P.M. to examine the place then D/S(?) man — and if the farm is vacant to take it over. A.D.M.S. (Col Peaks) D.A.D.M.S (Major Dennison) and A.A.Q.M.G. of 35" Division nil Str Hospital with the object of looking at accn in a few days. Very are very pleased at VIEILLE CHAPELLE a section from 107. F.A. amount for instruction	

WAR DIARY or INTELLIGENCE SUMMARY

Army Form C. 2118.

Place	Date	Hour	Summary of Events and Information	Remarks and references to Appendices
VIELLE CHAPELLE	5/3/16		Visited BOIS DU PACAUT this afternoon. CHATEAU is still occupied but farm is empty. The whole place has very bad. No roof on barn and inundated with water. The place is very dirty and urging a great deal of tidying took before a Field Ambulance can be established there.	
	6/3/16		Sent S/Sgt Peara and 20 men to take over the farm at BOIS DU PACAUT with 2 G.S. wagons. O.C. D.M.S. 35" Divin called & brgt Major Pritchard the O.C. 106 Fd Amb. VIELLE CHAPELLE. They will — the ambulance is to proceed with 1/2 a section of men for in a day or two for — proceed on an 2 officers with 1/2 a section of men for in a day or two for inspection before taking over. A.D.M.S. & D.D.M.S. 38. Divisin called this afternoon. I spoke to A.D.M.S. & D.D.M.S. when sent down there the episode at CHATEAU DU PACAUT when held by the Brigade with stood evacuation. I also on 4/3/16 and was told by the Brigade with stood empty, I also apoke the necessity of map references — the command definitely in writing that causes much unnecessary labour & waste of time. Major Pritchard O.B. J.F. called again to see Hospital & Billets. They take over VIELLE CHAPELLE & ST VAAST A.D.S.	
	7/3/16			

WAR DIARY or INTELLIGENCE SUMMARY

Army Form C. 2118.

Place	Date	Hour	Summary of Events and Information	Remarks and references to Appendices
VIEILLE CHAPELLE	7/3/16		Major Fairbairn A.T.M.C. O/c 107 F.A. called. They are establishing themselves at ZELOBES and are taking over RUE DU BOIS A.D.S.	
			Order received from A.D.M.S. - in Case of a sudden move forward.	
			Copy of extract from A.D.M.S. order 6/3/16	
			No. 131 Fld Ambulance to hand over the A.D.S. Sit at KINGS ROAD (X11.6.4.3) and the two armoured cars at X16.a.S.S and S2a89 to a party from 2 F.A of 2S Division both at X16.a.S.S and S2a89. On arrival Lt Wynn for R.A.M.C and party will on the morning of the 8 inst. Or arrival Lt Wynn for R.A.M.C. and party will be allotted to billeting stations under the orders of the O C Sanitary Section. On the morning of the 8" instant a section of the 131st F.A. will proceed to BOIS de PACAUT and take on the Chateau and farm there from a tent of the 114 Brigade and will proceed to prepare them for F.A. S.B. No 131 F.A. with Charrock turn all stock west of the BETHUNE–LESTREM Road in to win.	

WAR DIARY or INTELLIGENCE SUMMARY

Army Form C. 2118.

Place	Date	Hour	Summary of Events and Information	Remarks and references to Appendices
NEILLE CHAPELLE	8/3/16		Letter received from A.D.M.S. to say that he is probably going on leave shortly. Am to hold myself in readiness to act as A.D.M.S. during his absence. 1 Officer and 15 men 106.3 F.A. joined our section at SIVAST. A.D.S.	
	9.3.16		Ordered to meet A.D.M.S. shortly after 2. This afternoon at BOIS DE PACAUT. Went there as arranged, and waited until 4 P.M. — Shirley & D.M.S. Sat [?] there — but then a [?] and came J up. The party had come back before I left. There is a great deal more to be done before work at BOIS-DE PACAUT. But there is quite a place. The place is ready for a quite an aeroplane. Field Ambulance Bearers at an A.D.S. extract from A.D.M.S. order. Inspected medical O.H.Q. and ordered to the order of the R.P. wanted, the indoor pool, washing paths to it, standings to wheels, stretcher men and under the orders, informing him, post, making his informing his post, employed by him in informing his parties connected with him and posts, stretchers and any other parties connected with him and posts.	
	10.3.16		Went to LOCON to act as A.D.M.S. during absence of Bt major A.M.S. order received from G.H.Q. " Jailor Punishment No. 1 to Administration unit", will be carried out in the Divisional Detention Room under the A.P.M.	
	11.3.16		Visited LONE FARM A.D.S. and the and posts and WINDY CORNER of GIVENCHY with Major Shener. D.A.D.M.S.	

Army Form C. 2118.

WAR DIARY
or
INTELLIGENCE SUMMARY.
(Erase heading not required.)

Place	Date	Hour	Summary of Events and Information	Remarks and references to Appendices
VIEILLE CHAPELLE	12.3.16		An advance party from the 108. F.A. arrived at RUE DE BOIS A.D.S with the view to taking it over.	
	13.3.16		Handed over VIEILLE CHAPELLE MAIN DRESSING STATION to the 105. F.A. also handed us RUE DE BOIS A.D.S. and not parts to the 108. F.A. 131. F.A. proceeded to CHATEAU DE PACAUT, BOIS DE PACAUT. The Chateau was arranged for as Officers Hospital and the Span room used as a men. The barn was arranged as his wards. The Other buildings were used to administer purposes, and the loft will be used as a Barack of harmony. The Personnel & Horse Transport have their headquarters at the farm. M.T. are parked near Chateau. The surroundings in their present condition, were most depressing. The Chalet was bare of furniture & not a triple pane in any fireplace. A friendly neighbour lent the Quarter-Master a dining table and not a triple pane in any fireplace. Upon our arrival the large Barn was arranged as him hospital wards, with & half a dozen old chairs. Upon our arrival the large Barn was arranged as him hospital wards, with hot water, left fully equipped. The Loops room on the right of the main entrance was converted into an Officers ward with two beds & furnished with Pallaises, Blankets, table and all articles necessary. Another loops bed room was fitted to receive. Pack-Horse, Stretchers, Rations, Park Stores, Medical, Stores, Nose, Wounds,	

WAR DIARY
or
INTELLIGENCE SUMMARY.

(Erase heading not required.)

Army Form C. 2118.

Place	Date	Hour	Summary of Events and Information	Remarks and references to Appendices
BOIS-DE-PACOUT	13/3/16		and preparations commenced. Within an hour of our arrival at BOIS-DU-PACAUT, we were crested by the S.O.C. 38th Division, the minutely inspected the station and informed on opinion that the road was totally unsuited as a site for a Field Ambulance. He laid great stress upon the want of accessibility and of the road leading to it from the main COLONNE – HINGES road. He pointed that it would be hopeless to attempt to evacuate any both or wounded men over it, in its present condition. He promised that the road should be repaired at once.	
	14/3/16		All this day was spent in "fatigue work". The guard in front of the Chalet was cleaned up to mud upon it, in places were a foot deep, a floor of trench boards was also laid for the Inspection Station.	
	15/3/16		From S.S. Hoppin's herd of Indian Coolies were obtained & they & men used to even lift the road in front of the Chalet and apparently to put standing for the Motor Cars & their Motor Ambulances which are retained here for night work. A large amount of fatigue work was put upon the Horse Standings and a Harness-Room was constructed.	
	16/3/16		This day, the Divisional Transport Officer called to inspect the vehicles, Covers, Harness & personnel of the A.S.C. attached. He informed us & approved of their condition, Sanitation, and state of repair. He passed especial attention to the Harness-Room and made a note of it for future reference.	
	17/3/16		Owing to the small numbers of patients in Field Ambulance, opportunity was taken & result evacuation of the Service of all morning orderlies, except those that were absolutely required, to clean & repair the road leading to the station.	
	18/3/16		This day was spent in building a new Officers Latrine, mens latrine, & enlarging & repairing the incinerator in field behind Chalet. Owing to the wet condition of the ground numerous trench boards were used.	

Army Form C. 2118.

WAR DIARY
or
INTELLIGENCE SUMMARY.
(Erase heading not required.)

Instructions regarding War Diaries and Intelligence Summaries are contained in F. S. Regs., Part II. and the Staff Manual respectively. Title pages will be prepared in manuscript.

Place	Date	Hour	Summary of Events and Information	Remarks and references to Appendices
BOIS-DU-PACAUT	19/3/16		When the order the following orders were received from A.D.M.S. 38th Division. The 131st Field Ambulance will, on the 20th inst., send advanced parties and convoying of 1 Officer and 20 other ranks, will arrive at their advanced H.Q. at RUE DE BOIS. The advanced parties, each consisting of 1 Officer and 20 other ranks, will arrive at their destinations by 3.30 p.m. and will relieve the advanced parties of those coming. On the 21st inst. BOIS du PACAUT will be evacuated and 131 Field Ambulance will take over VIEILLE CHAPELLE Dressing Station from No. 105 Field Ambulance, the movement to be completed by 11 a.m. An advanced party of 1 Officer and 15 men will arrive at VIEILLE CHAPELLE by 9 a.m. ST VAAST and RUE de BOIS Advanced Dressing Stations will be taken over from Nos. 105 and 106 Field Ambulances respectively, movement to be completed by 11 a.m. on the 21st inst. Take on the evening of this date the following message was received from the A.D.M.S. "Move will probably be delayed 48 hours. You will be notified later. Enquire at intendency S.S. Mafferne what was ready to move according to orders.	
	20/3/16		A.D.M.S orders :— The arrangement for taking over ST VAAST are :— That you take it over completely in the afternoon of the 22nd. The party of the 105 Field Ambulance will leave the Farm evening. A car of the 35th and of the 19th Divisions will be stationed there to evacuate their own cases. These cars will not be thrown in your books. RUE du BOIS Advanced Dressing Station. An advanced party will arrive in the afternoon of the 23rd and will take over completely on the 24th inst. The taking over of VIEILLE CHAPELLE remains unaltered. You will please arrange to return 8 n.c.o's & men R.A.M.C. of the 19th Division at KINGS ROAD from the 25th inst. A.D. in S. returned from leave — 11.00 rode about, revised his visit 131 F.A. at CHATEAU DE DIEPOT the A.D.M.S. instructions were carried out and all preparations made for the different moves. Return @ was actually en route when a telegram was received all moves cancelled.	
	21/3/16			
	22/3/16			

Col Elliot — A.D.M.S. 47th Division with D.A.D.M.S. 38th Division & O.C. 130 F. Ambulance

Army Form C. 2118.

WAR DIARY
or
INTELLIGENCE SUMMARY.
(Erase heading not required.)

Place	Date	Hour	Summary of Events and Information	Remarks and references to Appendices
CHATEAU DE PACAUT	23.3.16		Visited 131 F.A. at CHATEAU DE PACAUT. Unfortunately the day was very wet and the place dismounted for the anticipated move to VIEILLE CHAPELLE to-morrow was nothing much to show. Col. Elliot expressed himself as well pleased with the activity shown & the general character of the various buildings such as cook-houses, latrines and incinerators. The men themselves the different units and were to-day pleased with their cleanliness.	
	24/3/16		Going on two days' leave. On this day the following was received from a D.M.S. 38 Division:- In accordance with instructions just received I must leave a man will meet the VIEILLE CHAPELLE as previously decided to-morrow there by 10 a.m. 25/3/16. Please leave a party behind & clear up and leave the place clean. Orders as to taking over of RUE DE BOIS will be issued subsequently. The received this message at 7.30pm. Later the farm work the following message was received :- VIEILLE CHAPELLE the afternoon. Main body to arrive at VIEILLE CHAPELLE advanced party will proceed to RUE DE BOIS 25th inst. taking over RUE DE BOIS 26th inst. 10 a.m. 25th inst. Advanced party to RUE DE BOIS 25th inst. taking over RUE DE BOIS 26th inst. Later the following message was received:- The move is again delayed from advanced party will remain at VIEILLE CHAPELLE but the main body will remain at BOIS du PACAUT until further orders. This may be in 2 or 3 days, but you will be informed immediately anything is known. On 24th the following instructions were issued:- Please send an advanced party to RUE de BOIS abreast of Running Bridge the afternoon to arrive there by 3 p.m. They will relieve the advanced bearers at TUBE STATION and PATH HOUSE POST. There is one med. & first bearers in the team vacated parts, unless this is arrived for by the 19th Division. AVE de BOIS. A.D.S. will be taken over completely by 10 a.m. to-morrow. Left BOIS de PACAUT at 12 mid-day 25/3/16. This order was carried out. Staff Capt. Paris & 15 other ranks.	
	25/3/16			
	26/3/16		The main body of 131" Field Ambulance left BOIS de Pacaut at 7.30 a.m. and arrived at VIEILLE CHAPELLE at 9.30 a.m. At 1.30 p.m. the main body of Section B under the command of Captain Y.P. Brand R.A.M.C.	

J.C. Bisson Major

Army Form C. 2118.

WAR DIARY
or
INTELLIGENCE SUMMARY.

(Erase heading not required.)

Instructions regarding War Diaries and Intelligence Summaries are contained in F.S. Regs., Part II. and the Staff Manual respectively. Title pages will be prepared in manuscript.

Place	Date	Hour	Summary of Events and Information	Remarks and references to Appendices
VIEILLE CHAPELLE	26/3/16		Left VIEILLE CHAPELLE to take over the Advanced Dressing Station at RUE de BOIS from a Section of the 106 Field Ambulance. A small party was left behind at BOIS de PACAUT, consisting of 1 NCO + 12 men with a few medical comforts and one motor ambulance until dusk in case patient should arrive. The place was left perfectly clean and a certificate signed by the proprietor, was obtained stating that no damage had been done to the property by the Field Ambulance during its occupation.	
	27/3/16		The day was spent in arranging the equipment in wards, filling palliasses with fresh straw, white washing walls, & making wooden stands for patients kits. Early this morning the following instructions were received:- 121st Bde RFA & take over Medical charge for 5 days from Lieut Rupfen RAMC. Please send a Medical Officer to HQ 121 Brigade RFA & take over Medical charge of this duty from Lieut Rupfen. It will be necessary for 121st Bde HQ are at F.10.6.w.1. He will obtain full particulars of his duty from Lieut Rupfen before he leaves. On probable return to his duty at Left VIEILLE CHAPELLE at 10 a.m. Lieut J.D. Lutmers R.A.M.C was detailed for this duty and left from Bde HQ's. No divine service, in any intimation of such from Bde H Q's.	
	28/3/16		The Knowsley and Bearnsion Wards, whitewashed. The floors washed & scrubbed. Clean palliasses & filled with fresh straw. At 10 a.m. a motor reparation arr'd, & was found that the Field Ambulance was left without a single Motor Ambulance. The establishment number is Seven (7). and on this date they were disposed as follows.	
			1. Aquines (small trip Evres)	
			3. Merville (Central Evres)	
			1. Divisional Sanitary Section (on loan for 14 days)	
			1. Retained at Advanced Dressing Station RUE de BOIS.	
			1. Workshop (for repairs)	
			/7/	
			In the event of a rush of cases we have no Motor Ambulances available.	
				J.P.Davis Major

2353 Wt. W2544/1454 700,000 5/15 D.D. & L. A.D.S.S./Forms/C. 2118.

WAR DIARY
or
INTELLIGENCE SUMMARY.
(Erase heading not required.)

Army Form C. 2118.

Place	Date	Hour	Summary of Events and Information	Remarks and references to Appendices
VIEILLE CHAPELLE	28/3/16		Graded advanced dressing Station at RUE du BOIS. Captain J.N. Baird R.A.M.C. Captain Parry R.A.M.C. Staff Sgt Pinci and the men of Section B had put in a lot of work since Sunday 26th inst. The old arrangement had been removed in very few cases had been put in force since their arrival, opportunity was taken of this lull to improve and clean up the present surroundings.	
	29/3/16		A good beginning was made this day in clearing the Nissen Huts & Horse Standings of all movement & litter. Arrangements were made with a farmer within 200 y[a]rds of VIEILLE CHAPELLE Sgt Major Patrick A.S.C. attached made arrangement with R.E. for wire (Lenk of Grid) to extend and improve the So. Wh. ale before on the land. The above obtained through R.E. Sam. Lenk of Grid to extend and improve the present Standings. Instructions were received from A.D.M.S. to detail one officer for permanent duty with the 10th WELSH BATT. Lieut R.C. McMillan named was put in attempt at present doing duty at A.D.S. RUE du BOIS, there leaving 2 Officers only at the Field Ambulance. Captain J.N. Baird and Captain S.N. Parry left this evening for England on 10 days leave granted to them when asking renewal of their contract. D.A.D.M.S. & 19 Division called to enquire of the Motor Ambulance obtained this morning and to see if an RI. The men attended pure satisfaction.	
	30/3/16		Lieut Colonel E.D. Thomas was notified, he arriving as suffering from latest germs. In the afternoon O.D.M.S. and Sr.D.M.S. / Sanitary Officer called to make enquiries. Work was continued all day on the transport lines and in securing to remove & set up going form, extension of the horsing of the Horse Standings & Paving Yard at the Stables.	
	31/3/16		In accordance with A.D.M.S. verbal instructions, all transport and nursing staff was undertak[en]. Separate cooking utensils & castles to be supplied. Separate Latrines provided. All new medical cases to be placed in Emergency Ward. A large amount of work was put in to day in improvise the surface of the Ambulance yard. A new hut was erected in rear of working room for articles to clean boots in.	

J.C. Brown Major.

131 F Amb
Vol 4
38th Div

COMMITTEE FOR THE
MEDICAL HISTORY OF THE WAR
Date 9 – JUN. '15

Confidential
Copy.

War Diary

131 Field Ambulance
38 (Welsh) Division
for
March 1916.

A March 1916

Certified to be a true copy.
O H Mills Roberts
LIEUT. COL. R.A.M.C.
o/c 131st FIELD AMBULANCE
38TH (WELSH) DIVISION.

Army Form C. 2118.

WAR DIARY
or
INTELLIGENCE SUMMARY.

(Erase heading not required.)

Instructions regarding War Diaries and Intelligence Summaries are contained in F. S. Regs., Part II. and the Staff Manual respectively. Title pages will be prepared in manuscript.

Place	Date	Hour	Summary of Events and Information	Remarks and references to Appendices
VIEILLE CHAPELLE	1/3/16		St. David's Day. I visited RUE. DU. BOIS A.D.S and Regimental Aid Post at PATH HOUSE and Aid Posts at DEAD COW and TUBE STATION. Both dug outs are fairly dry. The new pump is working well in the dug out nearest the road. There appear to be several springs in it. The water was not rain water. The ground is very sodden – and must be carefully floored with French Boards 5 ambulances (3 horse and 2 motor) were sent out to accompany hoops to new billets	
	2/3/16		Sent Lieut. David with Horse Ambulance to collect new area- places given were:- LE. PANNERIE. LES. CAULDRONS. and LES CHOQUES. The hoops were difficult to find owing to map references not being accurate. Two other Places given for collection were LE. HAMEL and ESSARS – in neither case was the map reference accurate.	
	3/3/16		Went to 10 CON to draw money 2700 francs to pay N.C.O.s and men. Went down RUE. DU. BOIS A.D.S. and paid men there first- afterwards went to KING'S ROAD BATH DEPOT paid men there and returned to VIEILLE CHAPELLE where remainder of unit was paid	

A H Millward Lt Col
O/C 131 Field Ambulance

Army Form C. 2118.

WAR DIARY
or
INTELLIGENCE SUMMARY.
(Erase heading not required.)

Instructions regarding War Diaries and Intelligence Summaries are contained in F. S. Regs., Part II. and the Staff Manual respectively. Title pages will be prepared in manuscript.

Place	Date	Hour	Summary of Events and Information	Remarks and references to Appendices
VIEILLE CHAPELLE	3/3/16		Lieut. Pettigrew, R.A.M.C. now stationed at RUE-DU-BOIS A.D.S. (on being relieved today) brought Lieut. Low, 16 Welch into hospital suffering from Influenza – and returned to 16 Welch to do Lieut. Low's work. Pending instruction from A.D.M.S. our staff is now much reduced (to 3) at VIEILLE CHAPELLE.	
	4/3/16		Orders received from A.D.M.S. to send a party to take possession of BOIS-DU-PACAUT – CHATEAU and farm. Lieut. David and twenty two other ranks were sent with a G.S. wagon and a tank of water. No water cart to spare, as one is undergoing alteration. Party returned because CHATEAU was occupied by Fanc. Fusiliers (Bantams) who refused to move out. This adventure was reported to A.D.M.S. Party for instruction from 106 Field Amb. left. Another note is received from A.D.M.S. to say that present party - 200 men are leaving the CHATEAU. DU. PACAUT on 8/3/16 after which the 131 Field Ambulance will take possession. I am to go there with Q.M. to examine the place this afternoon – and of the farm is vacant to take it over.	
	5/3/16		A.D.M.S. (Col. S. Tozer) D.A.D.M.S. (Major Davidson) and A.A. & Q.M.G. of 35 Division visit the hospital, with the object of taking it over in a few days. They are very pleased with it. A section of 107 Field Amb. arrived for instruction	

O.N. Mills Abbott
O.C. 131 field Ambulance

WAR DIARY
or
INTELLIGENCE SUMMARY

Army Form C. 2118.

Place	Date	Hour	Summary of Events and Information	Remarks and references to Appendices
VIEILLE CHAPELLE	5/3/16		Visited BOIS-DU-BACAUT this afternoon. CHATEAU is still occupied but farm is empty. The whole place lies very low. The roads are bad and inundated with water. The place is very dirty and requires a great deal of fatigue work before a Field Ambulance can be established there.	
	6/3/16		Sent S. Sergt. Pearce and 20 men to take over the farm at BOIS-DU-BACAUT with 2 G.S. wagons. D.A.D.M.S. 35 Division called and brought Major Richards the C.O. 106 Field Ambulance. His ambulance is to succeed us at VIEILLE CHAPELLE. They will send over 2 or 3 Officers with half a section of men in a day or two for instruction before taking over. A.D.M.S. and D.A.D.M.S. 38 Division called this afternoon. I reported the episode at CHATEAU-DU-PACAUT when Lieut. Davis went there on 4/3/16 and was treated by the Brigadier with scant courtesy. I also reported the inaccuracy of War references — the consequent difficulty in finding units — causing much unnecessary labour and waste of time.	
	7/3/16		Major Richards, 106 Field Ambulance called again to see Hospital and Billets. They take over VIEILLE CHAPELLE and ST. VAAST A.D.S.	

D.R. Smith Wsmb Lt Col
OR 131 Field Ambulance

Army Form C. 2118.

WAR DIARY
or
INTELLIGENCE SUMMARY.
(Erase heading not required.)

Instructions regarding War Diaries and Intelligence Summaries are contained in F. S. Regs., Part II. and the Staff Manual respectively. Title pages will be prepared in manuscript.

Place	Date	Hour	Summary of Events and Information	Remarks and references to Appendices
VIEILLE CHAPELLE	7/3/16		Major Fairbourne, R.A.M.C. O/C 107 Field Ambulance called. They are establishing themselves at ZELOBES and are taking over RUE DU BOIS A.D.S. Orders received from A.D.M.S. in case of a sudden move forward. Extract from A.D.M.S. order. 6/3/16. "No. 131 Field Ambulance will hand over the A.D.S. site at KING'S ROAD (X.11.6.4.3) and the two advanced baths at X.18.a.5.5. and S.8.a.8.9 to a party from a Field Amb. of 35th Division. On the morning of the 9th inst. In relief of Wynne Jones, R.A.M.C. and party will be allotted to bathing sections under the orders of the O.C. Sanitary Section. On the morning of the 8th instant a section of the 131 Field Ambulance will proceed to BOIS de PACAUT and take over the Chateau and farm there from a Unit of the 114 Brigade and will proceed to prepare them for a Field Amb. site. No: 131 Field Amb will clear sick from all units west of the BETHUNE - LESTREM Road inclusive."	

N.K.McIlmurch, Lt Col
O/C 131 Field Ambulance

Army Form C. 2118.

WAR DIARY
or
INTELLIGENCE SUMMARY.
(Erase heading not required.)

Instructions regarding War Diaries and Intelligence Summaries are contained in F. S. Regs., Part II. and the Staff Manual respectively. Title pages will be prepared in manuscript.

Place	Date	Hour	Summary of Events and Information	Remarks and references to Appendices
VIEILLE CHAPELLE	8/3/16		Letter received from A.D.M.S. to say that he is probably going on leave shortly am to hold myself in readiness to act as A.D.M.S. during his absence.	
	9/3/16		Officer and 13 men 106 Field Amb. joined our section at ST. VAAST A.D.S. Ordered to meet A.D.M.S. Thattyafter 3 this afternoon at BOIS DE PACAUT. Went there as requested and waited until 4 p.m. Thinking A.D.M.S. had been detained as he did not come I left. The party has done good work at 301S. DE PACAUT, but there is a great deal more to be done before the place is ready for a Field Ambulance. Extract from A.D.M.S. orders Field Amb. Bearers at Adv. Pos.- "These men are under the orders of the Regimental Medical Officer and should therefore be employed by him in improving his post, making paths to it, standing for wheeled stretchers, and any other purpose needed such as aid post."	
	10/3/16		Went to LOCON to act as A.D.M.S. during absence of Col. Morgan A.M.S. Order received from L.H.Q. "Field Punishment No 1 for administrative punish will be carried out in the Divisional Detention Room under the A.P.M."	

O.W. North Webb. Lt Col
O/C 131 Fld Ambulance

Army Form C. 2118.

WAR DIARY
or
INTELLIGENCE SUMMARY.
(Erase heading not required.)

Instructions regarding War Diaries and Intelligence Summaries are contained in F.S. Regs., Part II. and the Staff Manual respectively. Title pages will be prepared in manuscript.

Place	Date	Hour	Summary of Events and Information	Remarks and references to Appendices
VIEILLE CHAPELLE	8/3/16		Visited LONE FARM A.D.S. and the Aid Posts round WINDY CORNER at GIVENCHY with Major Shenen, D.A.D.M.S.	
	12/3/16		An advanced party from the 106 Field Amb. arrived at RUE DE BOIS A.D.S. with the view to taking over.	
	13/3/16		Handed over VIEILLE CHAPELLE MAIN DRESSING STATION to the 105 Field Amb. also handed over RUE DE BOIS A.D.S. and Aid Posts to the 106 Field Amb. 131 Field Amb. proceeded to CHATEAU-DE-PACAUT-BOIS-DE-PACAUT. The Chateau was arranged for an officers' Hospital and the spare rooms used as a mess. The barn was arranged as two wards. The other buildings were used for administrative purposes, and the loft-wide to be used as a ward if necessary. The Personnel and Horse transport have their headquarters at the farm. M.T. are parked near CHATEAU. The surroundings, in their present condition, were most depressing. The chalet was bare of furniture and not a single grate in any fireplace. A kindly neighbour lent the dwarts master a dining table and half a dozen old chairs. Upon our arrival the large barn was arranged as two hospital wards, 1 right side - medical - left side - surgical	O'Neille, No lab. Lt Col Capt 101 2nd Ambulance

2353 Wt. W.2514/1454 700,000 5/15 D.D. & L.   A.D.S.S./Form/C. 2118.

Army Form C. 2118.

WAR DIARY
or
INTELLIGENCE SUMMARY.
(Erase heading not required.)

Instructions regarding War Diaries and Intelligence Summaries are contained in F. S. Regs., Part II. and the Staff Manual respectively. Title pages will be prepared in manuscript.

Place	Date	Hour	Summary of Events and Information	Remarks and references to Appendices
BOIS DE PACAUT.	13/3/16		The large room on the right of the main entrance was converted into an officers ward with two beds and furnished with halliases, blankets, tables, and all articles necessary. Another large bed room was held in reserve. Pack stores, kitchens, boot stores, mess room, latrines, urinals and incinerator constructed. Within an hour of our arrival at BOIS-DU-PACAUT we were visited by the G.O.C. 38th Division. He minutely inspected the station and expressed an opinion that the spot was totally unsuited as a site for a field ambulance. He laid great stress upon the want of accessibility and the bad state of the road leading to it from the main (ALONNE-HINGES) road. He said that it would be simply cruel to attempt to evacuate any sick or wounded men over it, in its present condition. He promised that the road should be repaired at once.	
	14/3/16		All this day was spent in "fatigue work". The yard in front of the Chalet was cleared of the mud upon it. In places over a foot deep. A floor of sand bags was also laid for the hospital kitchen.	
	15/3/16		Two seven G.S. Wagons' load of hoten ricks were obtained today and were used to cover half the yard in front of the Chalet and affording a good standing for the water cart and two motor ambulances which are retained here for nightwork.	O.R. Mills DSO Lt Col O/c 131 (Iste) Ambulance

WAR DIARY
or
INTELLIGENCE SUMMARY.

(Erase heading not required.)

Army Form C. 2118.

Place	Date	Hour	Summary of Events and Information	Remarks and references to Appendices
BOIS DE PACAUT	15/3/16		A large amount of fatigue work was put upon "the Horse Standings" and a Harness Room was constructed	
	16/3/16		This day the Divisional Transport Officer called to inspect the vehicles horses harness and personnel of the A.S.C. attached. He expressed his approval of their condition cleanliness and state of repair. He paid special attention to the "Harness Room" and made a sketch of it for future reference.	
	17/3/16		Owing to the small number of patients in Field Ambulance opportunity was taken to avail ourselves of the services of the running orderlies, except those that were absolutely required, to clean and repair the road leading to the Station.	
	18/3/16		This day was spent in building a new officers latrine, and enlarging and repairing the incinerator in field behind chalet, owing to the wet condition of the ground numerous trench boards were used.	
	19/3/16		Upon this date the following orders were received from A.D.M.S. 38 Division. "1. 131st Field Ambulance will on the 20th inst. send advanced parties to the Advanced Dressing Station at ST AAST.	O Kniblibul? Lt Col O/C 131 Fld Ambulance

WAR DIARY
or
INTELLIGENCE SUMMARY.
(Erase heading not required.)

Army Form C. 2118.

Place	Date	Hour	Summary of Events and Information	Remarks and references to Appendices
BOIS-de-BACAUT	19/3/16		"and RUE. DE. BOIS. The Advanced parties, each consisting of 1 Officer and 20 other ranks will arrive at their destinations by 3.30 p.m. and will relieve the advanced parties the same evening. On the 21st inst. BOIS. de PACAUT will be evacuated, and No: 131 Field Ambulance will take over VIEILLE. CHAPELLE Dressing Station from No: 105 Field Ambulance, the movement to be completed by 11 a.m. An advanced party of 1 Officer and 15 men will arrive at VIEILLE. CHAPELLE by 9 a.m. ST VAAST and RUE. DE. BOIS Advanced Dressing stations will be taken over from No: 105 and 106 Field Ambulances respectively. Movements to be completed by 11 a.m. on the 21st inst. Late in the evening of this date the following message was received from the A.D.M.S. "Moves will probably be delayed 48 hours. You will be notified later."	
	20/3/16		Day spent in unloading G.S. wagons which were ready to move according to orders.	
	21/3/16		A.D.M.S. Orders:- "The arrangements for taking over ST VAAST are:- That you take it over completely on the afternoon of the 22nd inst. The party of the 105 Field Amb. will leave the same evening. A car of the 35th and of the 19th Divisions	

O. Wallis ODlets Lt Col
OC 131 field Amphlan

WAR DIARY
or
INTELLIGENCE SUMMARY.
(Erase heading not required.)

Army Form C. 2118.

Place	Date	Hour	Summary of Events and Information	Remarks and references to Appendices
BOIS de PACAUT	21/3/16		"will be stationed there to evacuate their own cases. These cases will not be shewn in your books". "RUE DU BOIS advanced Dressing Station" An advanced party will arrive in the afternoon of the 23rd, and will take over completely on the 24th inst. "The taking over of VIEILLE-CHAPELLE remains unaltered" "You will please arrange to ration 8 N.C.O.s and men "R.A.M.C. of the 19th Division at KING'S ROAD from the 25th inst". A.D.M.S. returned from leave. – Lt. Col. R.A. Wells Roberts rejoined his unit. – 131 Field Amb. at CHATEAU-DE-PACAUT	
	22/3/16		The A.D.M.S.'s instructions were carried out and all preparations made for the different moves. Section "C" was actually en route when a telegram was received "all moves cancelled."	
	23/3/16		Col. Elliot A.D.M.S. 47th Division with D.A.D.M.S. 38 Division and O.C. 130 Field Ambulances visited 131 Field Amb. at CHATEAU-DE-PACAUT. Unfortunately the day was very wet and the place dismantled for the anticipated move to VIEILLE-CHAPELLE so that there was nothing much to show. Col. Elliot expressed himself as well pleased	

M. Smith Roberts Lt. Col.
O.C. 131 Field Ambulance

Army Form C. 2118.

WAR DIARY
or
INTELLIGENCE SUMMARY.
(Erase heading not required.)

Place	Date	Hour	Summary of Events and Information	Remarks and references to Appendices
CHATEAU DE PACAUT.	23/3/16		with the utility and temporary character of the various buildings, such as cook-houses, latrines, and incinerators. He was shown the different wards and was highly pleased with their cleanliness.	
	24/3/16		Going on ten days leave. On this day the following was received from A.D.M.S. 38 Division "In accordance with instruction just received you will move to VIEILLE-CHAPELLE so thoroughly directed to arrive there by 10 a.m. 25/3/16. Please leave a party behind to "clean up" and leave the place clean. Orders as to the taking over of RUE-DE-BOIS will be issued subsequently." We received this message at 8.30 p.m. Later the same night the following message was received:- "Advanced party will proceed to VIEILLE-CHAPELLE this afternoon. Main body to arrive at VIEILLE-CHAPELLE 10 a.m. 25 inst. Advanced party to RUE-DE-BOIS 25th inst. Taking over RUE-DE-BOIS 26th inst." Later the following message was received:- "The moves to VIEILLE-CHAPELLE &c main body today will remain at BOIS, &c. PACAUT until further orders. This may be in 2 or 3 days. Please be prepared to immediately anything is known."	A. Huthwoek Lt. Col. ONC 131 2nd Division

WAR DIARY or INTELLIGENCE SUMMARY

Army Form C. 2118.

Place	Date	Hour	Summary of Events and Information	Remarks and references to Appendices
BOIS. DE. PACAUT.	25/3/16		On this day the following instructions were received. "Please send an advanced party to RUE. de. BOIS advanced Dressing Station this afternoon to arrive there by 3 p.m. They will relieve the advanced Bearers at TUBE STATION and "PATH HOUSE POST." "There is no need to put Bearers in the three isolated posts unless this is asked for by the 19th Division" "RUE. DE. BOIS A.D.S. will be taken over completely by 10 a.m. tomorrow." This order was carried out. Staff Sergt. Pierce and 15 other Ranks left BOIS. DE. PACAUT at 12 mid-day 25-3-16	
	26/3/16		The main body of 131 Field Ambulance left BOIS. du. PACAUT at 9.30 a.m. and arrived at VIEILLE CHAPELLE at 9.30 a.m. At 1.30 p.m. the main body of section 'B' under the command of Captain T.W. David. R.A.M.C. left VIEILLE CHAPELLE to take over the advanced Dressing Station at RUE. de. BOIS from a section of the 106 Field Amb. A small party was left behind at BOIS. de. PACAUT consisting of 1 N.C.O and 12 men with a few medical comforts and one motor ambulance until such in case patients should arrive. The place was left perfectly clean and a certificate signed by the historian [?] C.O obtained stating that no damage had been done to the property by the F.A. Amb. during its occupation.	

O.K. [signature] Lt. Col.
O/C 131 Field Ambulance

Army Form C. 2118.

WAR DIARY
or
INTELLIGENCE SUMMARY.
(Erase heading not required.)

Place	Date	Hour	Summary of Events and Information	Remarks and references to Appendices
VIEILLE CHAPELLE	27/3/16		This day was spent in arranging the equipment in wards filling palliasses with fresh straw, while washing walls and making wooden hands for patients beds. Early this morning the following instructions were received:- "Please send a Medical Officer to H.Q. 121 Bde. R.F.A. to take over Medical charge for 5 days from Lieut. Rippon R.A.M.C. 121 OC Bde. H.Q. are at F.10.b.4.1. He will obtain full particulars of his duty from Lieut. Rippon. It will be necessary for him to submit inoculation returns of the unit before he leaves. Lieut. J.D. Skinner R.A.M.C. was detailed for this duty and left VIEILLE-CHAPELLE at 10 a.m. to drive serve or any instruction from Brig. Han. 20 attendance, whatever."	
	27/3/16		The Emergency and Evacuation wards. Clean palliasses and bed floors washed and scrubbed. Clean palliasses and fresh straw. At 10 a.m. a novel relaxation arose, with fresh straw. At 10 a.m. a novel relaxation arose, it was found that the Field Ambulance was left without a single Motor Ambulance. The establishment numbers seven (7) and on this date they were disposed as follows :- 1. ARQUES (with Eye cases) 3 MERVILLE (Dentalcases,) 1 Divisional Sanitary Section (on loan for 14days) 1 Returned at Advanced Dressing Station RUE. DE. BOIS. 1. Workshop for (repair) (SSD) J. B. Davies. Major O/C [British]	O/C (3) British Ambulance

Army Form C. 2118.

WAR DIARY
or
INTELLIGENCE SUMMARY.
(Erase heading not required.)

Instructions regarding War Diaries and Intelligence Summaries are contained in F. S. Regs., Part II. and the Staff Manual respectively. Title pages will be prepared in manuscript.

Place	Date	Hour	Summary of Events and Information	Remarks and references to Appendices
VIEILLE CHAPELLE	28/3/16		In the event of a rush of cases we have no vehicles available. Visited Advanced Dressing Station at RUE DE BOIS. Capt. J. W. David R.A.M.C, Capt. Parry R.A.M.C, Staff Sergt. Pierce and the men of Section B had put in a lot of work, since Sunday, 26 Xtant. The old arrangements had been reverted to. Very few cases had been sent in since their arrival, opportunity was taken of this lull to improve and clean up the general surroundings.	
	29/3/16		A good beginning was made this day in clearing the wagon lines and horse standings of all manure and litter. S/-Major Edwards A.S.C. attached made arrangements with a farmer within half a mile to lift all refuse on his land. Re also obtained through R.E. seven S.S. loads of brick to spread and improve the present standings. Instructions were received from A.D.M.S. to detail one officer for permanent duty with the 14/F Welsh Batt. Lieut. R.C. McMillan name was sent in although at present doing duty at A.D.S. RUE DE BOIS. Thus leaving 2 Officers only at the Field Ambulance.	

(SE?) J.C. Davies, Major
O/C 131 Field Ambulance.

O. Newill, Lt. Col.
O/C 131 Field Ambulance

Army Form C. 2118.

WAR DIARY
or
INTELLIGENCE SUMMARY.
(Erase heading not required.)

Place	Date	Hour	Summary of Events and Information	Remarks and references to Appendices
VIEILLE CHAPELLE	29/3/16		Capt. J.W. Davidson and Capt. G.W. Parry left this evening for England on 14 days leave granted to them upon resigning renewal of their contract.	
	30/3/16		D.A.D.M.S. of 19th Division called to enquire if the Motor Ambulance stationed here was of any use to us and if the men attached gave satisfaction. Lance Corporal E.F. Thomas was notified this morning as suffering from Enteric Fever. In the afternoon A.D.M.S. and D.A.D.M.S. and Sanitary Officer called to make an enquiry. Work was continued all day on the transport lines such as renewing the manure to an adjoining farm. Extension of the having of the Horse Standings and having of yard at the stables.	
	31/3/16		In accordance with A.D.M.S. verbal instructions all contacts and nursing staff were isolated. Separate cookery utensils and cutlery to be supplied. Separate latrines provided. All new medical cases to be placed in "Emergency Ward". A large amount of work was put in today in improving the surface of the Field Ambulance yard. A shed that was erected in rear of washing room for orderlies to clean boots in. (Sgd) J.C. Davies, Major O/C 131 Field Ambulance	

Confidential

War Diary

of

131 Field Ambulance

from 1st April to 30 April '16

(Volume V)

Confidential

War Diary

of

XI Corps Rest Station

From 18/6 to 30/6

Vol I

"A Section" 131 Field Ambulance

COMMITTEE FOR THE
[ME]DICAL HISTORY OF THE WAR
Date   9 - JUN. 1916

Army Form C. 2118.

WAR DIARY
or
INTELLIGENCE SUMMARY.
(Erase heading not required.)

Instructions regarding War Diaries and Intelligence Summaries are contained in F.S. Regs., Part II. and the Staff Manual respectively. Title pages will be prepared in manuscript.

Place	Date	Hour	Summary of Events and Information	Remarks and references to Appendices
VIEILLE CHAPELLE	1/4/16		Great difficulty arose this morning on account of absence on duty of 5 motor ambulances, the remaining two of our complement being at Workshop for repairs. This was put out by making use of the horse drawn vehicles. A large Fatigue Party engaged all day in removing manure and litter from transport lines in rear of the dressing station. The boundary of the Field Ambulance was cleaned out, the mud thrown on the trench and the ditch near the boundary of the Field Ambulance. Will probably not extend to close. Will probably not extend until warm completed. New pavement outside waiting room completed. A case of influenza having occurred in the Field Ambulance, acting on the A.D.M.S.'s orders the whole ward, orderlies, & nursing personnel were isolated & inoculated with 0.5 cc mixed vaccine.	
	2/4/16		Provision was made today for dealing with a large number of sick and wounded in the event of a rush. Clerks and orderlies were detailed and their special duties explained to them. Work was continued on the refuse and manure heaps. Instructions received for Lieut R.C. Macmillan to report himself at A.D.M.S. office at 10 a.m on the 3rd inst for special duty, and he is struck off from strength. NAME Lieut S.B. Lechmere R.A.M.C. proceeded this morning & assumed Divisional Station RUE du BOIS & replaces Lieut R.C. Macmillan R.A.M.C.	
	3/4/16		The following order was received from the A.D.M.S.: Under orders from XI Corps Wages each Field Ambulance will send two able bodied medical officers to attend lectures by the Chemical adviser, first meeting at 10.30 a.m. and 2.30 p.m. on the 8th & 9th April at the Factory AIRE (near to the Zinc Works Canteen.) This officer will take the medical officers when available to enable them & instruct all the other medical officers of the Division. Three officers must assemble at the 130th Field Ambulance at 9 a.m. each day for conveyance.	
	4/4/16		Lt Colonel A.H. Nutt, Robert returned this day from leave. 1 Person and 2 Officers 130th Field Ambulance were attached this day for purposes of instruction.	

J.C. Barnes Major
O/C 131 Field Ambulance

Army Form C. 2118.

WAR DIARY
or
INTELLIGENCE SUMMARY.
(Erase heading not required.)

Instructions regarding War Diaries and Intelligence Summaries are contained in F. S. Regs., Part II. and the Staff Manual respectively. Title pages will be prepared in manuscript.

Place	Date	Hour	Summary of Events and Information	Remarks and references to Appendices
VIEILLE CHAPELLE	5/4/15		One Officer and 15 men of 131 Field Ambulance was attached to the section at the advanced Dressing Station at RUE DE BOIS for instruction. Work continued on transport field — horse standings being erected to enable to take all the horses of the unit which have been in Stables.	
	6/4/15		Orr Sham LH℞ handed the men & Officer (on his return) back with the men & horses and marched round to a field abt 200 yards North. Met by A.D.M.S. D.A.D.M.S. & Capt Paxye Balch as Inspecting Sec g District & no screen put up along side of horse standings or protection against wind.	
	7/4/15		One Officer and 15 men of 134 F.A. returned from RUE DE BOIS and relieved by a similar party from the same unit. A.D.M.S. D.A.D.M.S. that army who mainly inspected the field ambulances on Saturday & visit Sec'ns & said were a being fitted to works. A new water trough made along side of B.H.Q. — work very satisfactory — permits 9 company horses to S.T.	
	8/4/15		The D.D.V.S. 1st Army inspected the lines and informed pleased. Church Parade at 11.15 a.m.	
	9/4/15		Section 9 134 Field Ambulance having completed their period of instruction attended to the wounded. The large proportion & minimum type of Stanroe yard affected with 1 foot of soft. Snowing (4 men ht.) unable to carry Sh'd from	
	10/4/15		New test Shed and Tanks and Carbos Ships erected. O.C. Divisional Team unit inspected on Triumph in	(1) K. Williamson Lt Col O/C 13' F.A.

Army Form C. 2118.

WAR DIARY
or
INTELLIGENCE SUMMARY.
(Erase heading not required.)

Instructions regarding War Diaries and Intelligence Summaries are contained in F. S. Regs., Part II. and the Staff Manual respectively. Title pages will be prepared in manuscript.

Place	Date	Hour	Summary of Events and Information	Remarks and references to Appendices
VIEILLE CHAPELLE	10/4/16		Captain Simpson R.A.M.C. O/C 131st Field Ambulance had received his Sister — there are no Field Ambulance reports. Bacteriological reports came in regularly. He in ordering of the Corps Car is managed return during to Béthune to Antiphone Serum. One of the cars had Dope of Anti-Tetanus Serum, for need Chareiclic STN. A spy rested as Spain and informed that the 131 FA will take over the CORPS REST STATION at MERVILLE at an early date and will run a Scabies and Skin Hospital at MERVILLE. REGNIER LE CLERCQ & Co F.E. Pard. O/C reported that the place is clean. There are great possible them.	
	12/4/16		Attended a letter by Capt. Page R.A.M.C. on "Gamias" & treatment at 130th F.A. MESPLAUX. We are to take over CRS at MERVILLE on 17 inst. Report from Divn. quite weak at an inspection of the lines of the Division on the 6th, 7th & 8th ints. by D.D.M.S. — The health & condition of the horse was on the whole acceptable. " good " — " good " — " the other units of the Division were quite satisfactory — The "131st Field Ambulance parked out very good" — "131 Field Ambulance"	

J.H. Morris Haney picked out very good.
This is very gratifying.

(J) O. H. Miller. D.S.O. Lt. Col
O/c. 131. F.A.

WAR DIARY
or
INTELLIGENCE SUMMARY.

Army Form C. 2118.

Place	Date	Hour	Summary of Events and Information	Remarks and references to Appendices
VIELLE CHAPELLE	13/4/16		"Inspection of Transport by O.C. & Asst Amm. Park is cancelled". A D M S: Order	
	14/4/16		On team of men to MERVILLE on 17/4/16 - Amm.[?] picking up Corps. David and O.M. touching to MERVILLE on advance party consisting of 1 O.M. & 20 men from 105 F.A. Cam & VIEILLE CHAPELLE on arrival	
	15/4/16		One Officer & 20 men from 105 F.A. Cam & VIEILLE CHAPELLE today. An advance party left for MERVILLE today. Our advance party left for MERVILLE today. One Officer & 20 men from 108 F.A. Cam & RUE DE BOIS A.D.S.	
	16/4/16		An advance party arrived & took over the A.D.S. from RUE DE BOIS A.D.S.) Lieuts LATIMER & LOWE with section B. relieve the VIEILLE CHAPELLE Handed over VIEILLE CHAPELLE to advance party of 105 F.A. who arrived yesterday. Just began Mrs Office next to LA CROIX to take charge of the laundry (Corps).	
	17/4/16		The unit moved from VIEILLE CHAPELLE at 9 A.M. Keep, and reached the Convent on the Southern side of MERVILLE at 10.30 A.M. A section under command of O.C. 131 Brit Ambulance. Proceeded to the C.R.S. in MERVILLE - to take charge of it. O/(omitted)Litt. Lt Col. OC 13 F A	

Army Form C. 2118.

WAR DIARY
or
INTELLIGENCE SUMMARY.
(Erase heading not required.)

Instructions regarding War Diaries and Intelligence Summaries are contained in F.S. Regs., Part II. and the Staff Manual respectively. Title pages will be prepared in manuscript.

Place	Date	Hour	Summary of Events and Information	Remarks and references to Appendices
MERVILLE	17.4.16	whole	B & C Sections under Command of Capt Mortland (OC C Section) – Paraded and went to REGNIER LE CLERCQ to man the Scabies Hospital.	Diary sent in as 11th Report Not Rect here to April 16
	18.4.16		This unit (131 F.A.) is divided into two: (1) 1st Lieut Col. Mills with ambulance Capt. ... David } first detailed (temporarily, during duty) ... in part when this unit takes in charge of LA COULGUE-Laundry) with personnel and equipment of A Section take charge of C.R.S. at MERVILLE and detail an Officer i/c of Town Sanitation and Officer i/c of Corps Baths at MERVILLE. and Major Davis run B Section. (2) Captain Rowland } with personnel and equipment of B & C Section take on the Scabies Captain Parry } and Skin Hospital at REGNIER LE CLERCQ. An M.O. is detailed from REGNIER to M.O. i/c FORET DE NIEPPE Hutments to be visited by him every morning – from other is under jurisdiction of C.R.S. All the transport of the unit will be stationed at REGNIER except two Motor Ambulances with the able to kept at MERVILLE in readiness for emergencies. One Man is on ample water supply at C.R.S. the three water carts will be stationed at REGNIER.	

D.H.Mill Osb.h. Lt Col
O/C 131 F.A.

WAR DIARY
or
INTELLIGENCE SUMMARY
(Erase heading not required.)

Army Form C. 2118.

Place	Date	Hour	Summary of Events and Information	Remarks and references to Appendices
MERVILLE	18/4/16		The C.R.S. in MERVILLE is situated in the RUE DE BETHUNE — about the middle of the town. It is entered from the main street by a long passage — There are, unfortunately, in this passage public urinals — leaving a bad impression on a visitor in spite of all the care that is taken to clean and disinfect them. The passage leads to a large room which in peace time is used as a Gymnasium & Theatre. This, about 120 patients sleep in this room. There is a surgical dressing room at one end and a Pack Store at the other end of the Pack Store are the Quarter Masters Stores. Running parallel with the "Theatre" is another long room — in peace time a skittle alley — This room is used as a dining room. About 170 OR can sit down. Behind the main buildings are the usual outbuildings — (latrines, ablution room, cookhouse) taken in use as well as a B Company hut in each of which 30 OR can sleep. There is a plot of land about behind the ORS in length planted. It is to be regretted that this piece of land cannot be acquired for the use of the C.R.S. It would afford convenience. Thus, the space is rather cramped — and this will be felt more when the weather is too hot. The C O S with accommodate 295 OR. These new "annexes" 181 when the 13'" F. A. took over.	
	19.4.16		Captain David is detailed Officer i/c Town Sanitation. First taking to detailed Officer i/c	D (M? with ODMh Lt Col O/C R.S Corps
				O/C F Corps Bakks.

Army Form C. 2118.

WAR DIARY
or
INTELLIGENCE SUMMARY.
(Erase heading not required.)

Instructions regarding War Diaries and Intelligence Summaries are contained in F. S. Regs., Part II. and the Staff Manual respectively. Title pages will be prepared in manuscript.

Place	Date	Hour	Summary of Events and Information	Remarks and references to Appendices
MERVILLE	19.4.16		A.D.M.S. & D.A.D.M.S. 38" British Division visited and inspected C.R.S. — went with them afterwards to inspect R & C section 131 F.A. at REGNIER LE CLERCQ. Commenced wrote washing — baths and enlarging facilities, by running screen &c	
	20.4.16		The open drain behind Pack Store & Guards QM Store closed up with mud obtained unloading faction Wood Work white washed. H/Huts. New doors swing on closed with old blankets. No pack Store is now much lighter. Good Sunday Service in dining room by S.C. of Corps Revd O'ROURKE. It does not seem to be generally understood that the Corps baths are primarily for the use of Corps troops — and that they are only allotted to the troops in and around MERVILLE when not required by Corps troops. The baths are in a Brasserie in the South End of the Town close to the railway station. They are open from 8 p.m to 12 noon & 1 p.m to 5 p.m. 25 men are bathed each half hour making a total of 9.40 pr diem. There is no bathing on Sundays. There are 24 tubs & a good supply of clean warm water and a cold shower bath. Men are supplied with changes of clean clothing & towels. There are 5 P.B. men on the permanent staff of the baths. They draw rations from railhead and the Town Major is responsible for pay & clothing.	
	22.4.16		The men are working hard with white wash &c. There is a great deal to do. Orders received from A.D.M.S. re arrangements in case of Cholera outbreak	

O.H. Whitwell Lt. Col.
O/C C.R.S.
11" Corps Trps.

WAR DIARY
or
INTELLIGENCE SUMMARY.

Army Form C. 2118.

Place	Date	Hour	Summary of Events and Information	Remarks and references to Appendices
MERVILLE	23/4/16		Sunday. C of England Service 11.30 am in dining Room. 3.30 PM HC in same room. (Major Davies-arrived with him to be spot inspected K.24.C.8.2. Map 36A.)	
			Visited by A.D.M.S. + D.A.D.M.S. – Went with them to see spot inspected K.24.C.8.2. Map 36A. Visited Hos. spot yesterday and was not satisfied with it. Copy of D.D.M.S. note received saying "In the event of an outbreak of Cholera a site has been chosen in open area K.24.C. 8.2. Map 36A.	
			Please attend Temp Capt. F.S. Ardern D.A.D.C. forthwith the Personnel and Equipment of a Tent Subdivision of 131 Field Ambulance for the administration of the Camp. Captain Ardern to ensure inocul. himself thoroughly acquainted with Anti-Cholera arrangements and "Cholera Bath" by Dyson."	
			(Please investigate & report on this F.E.)	
			A Copy of "Cholera bath" has been applied for and will be sent you on receipt.	
			Signed H.S. Flower Col. A.D.M.S	
	24/4/16		— We were not satisfied with site.	
	25/4/16		Early Sunday. Went to Memorial Service at R.C. Cathedral.	
			The work is progressing satisfactorily – W.J. is going to take some from before the C.R.S. is up to the standard of our field Ambulance near Quadri just left at VIEILLE CHAPELLE.	

Army Form C. 2118.

WAR DIARY
or
INTELLIGENCE SUMMARY.
(Erase heading not required.)

Instructions regarding War Diaries and Intelligence Summaries are contained in F. S. Regs., Part II. and the Staff Manual respectively. Title pages will be prepared in manuscript.

Place	Date	Hour	Summary of Events and Information	Remarks and references to Appendices
MERVILLE	25/4/16		A.D.M.S. & D.A.D.M.S. 3₹ (Lilt) Division met the C.R.S. They are anxious to both as many Dismissed (SC) from a panish in neighborhood of MERVILLE. I explained that the bully was eventually Corps Battn - and that Divisional I referred to me when not required by Corps Troops, and only to me when not required by Corps Troops. A.D.M.S. says he would see the D.D.M.S. about it. The "Jolleys" of 19ᵗʰ Division gave an enjoyable entertainment at C.R.S. in the evening.	
	26/4/16		Several lectures around. Gallery at rear of large sleeping room constructed into an (a candle & pedals) orderly room by partitioning off from sleeping room. This will enable me to use the present orderly room as a … dining room. Watch an up to mid dinner in a part of large room screened off in large room. Am in every duty & dainty. Wrote REGNIER - with a proposal Staff going to bask of weekend for seconds from A.D.M.S. (2ᶠ) tubth. Divn. asking me to allow 2 days to Sad. Batt. of 2ᶠ Divn. Conduit near MERVILLE	
	27/4/16		Went to HINGES to see D.D.M.S. to consult him, D.A. ?+ A.D.M.S. 2ᶠ Divn. re argent - as it is not compatible with Corps Order upholding Corps Battn. D.D.M.S. unfortunately was away. Saw his Asst. Major Potts.	

Army Form C. 2118.

WAR DIARY
or
INTELLIGENCE SUMMARY.
(Erase heading not required.)

Instructions regarding War Diaries and Intelligence Summaries are contained in F. S. Regs., Part II. and the Staff Manual respectively. Title pages will be prepared in manuscript.

Place	Date	Hour	Summary of Events and Information	Remarks and references to Appendices
MERVILLE	27/4/16		Went to A.D.M.S. at 36 Armin Believing a copy of Corps orders regarding Corps Bath.	
	28/4/16		Pay day. Went to LOCON to draw money. Paid A section CRS at 12 o'clock noon and paid B & C section of REGNIER at 2.30 P.M.	
	29/4/16		Visited the FORET DE NIEPPE. The M.O. I/C is detached from R & C section of 131 Field Ambulance at REGNIER. LE CLERCQ and at 10 o'Clock at A MOTTE AU BOIS. The cells of C.R.S. every morning at 9 o'clock on his way thro' Imperial Road, Black and hours has and found Sanitation in FOREST. Men are generally Satisfactory. The men get baths weekly and a change of clothing at each bath. On excellent arrangement exists for men in base camp by 13th R.W.F. The Sanitation of MERVILLE — An Officer (Captain Dean R.A.M.C.) is detailed from C.R.S. to Superintend the Sanitation of the Town. (1) **Personnel** The Sanitation is in the charge of the Town Major and is carried out by the M.O. I/C (above referred to) and 14 men under a Corporal. Defects are reported by the M.O. I/C to the Town Major and are remedied by the Maire and the French Commission.	

Army Form C. 2118.

WAR DIARY
or
INTELLIGENCE SUMMARY.
(Erase heading not required.)

Place	Date	Hour	Summary of Events and Information	Remarks and references to Appendices
MERVILLE	29/4/16		Sanitation of MERVILLE continued	

(2) Scheme. The Betheric district consists of the Town itself and the surrounding country to a distance of 1 kilometre (approx). It is divided for inspection into 4 areas by the RUE D'ORSEE – RUE DE BETHUNE, on one direction and by RUE DE CAPUCINES & RUE DU PIERRE in the other.

(3) Sanitary arrangements
A. Military Town latrines are provided in some places for Polish troops. They are permanent and latrine pans are used. Each is provided with an incinerator and all refuse is burnt. Latrine pans are also fitted with Croot filter an permanent sanitary men attached to each. They latrines are kept in excellent condition.

B. Civilian
(1) Water supply from Artesian strength mains to every street. Water is reported good.
(2) Drainage. There is no drainage system.
(3) Latrines. Practically all town them are cleaned out on fit - mostly in an unsanitary condition. They are cleaned by a French Contract on payment of 9.5 fr. liquid. It is difficult to get the inhabitants to empty these.
(4) Midden pits in many farms and no provision are made to drain off seepage daily.
(5) House Refuse is carried into the streets and collected daily.

2353 Wt. W2514/1454 700,000 5/15 D. D. & L. A.D.S.S./Forms/C. 2118.

WAR DIARY or INTELLIGENCE SUMMARY

Army Form C. 2118.

Place	Date	Hour	Summary of Events and Information	Remarks and references to Appendices
MERVILLE	29/4/16		4. State of Sanitary Squad. These men are attached to each of the Town areas. They look every house in the area daily and disinfect latrines, middens and surface drains. They also clear away accumulation of rubbish and from circuits formed in open places. They visit and report to Sanitary Corporal anything that they wish the Sanitary Officer to inspect. They also disinfect and clean the Town Slaughter House. The Sanitary Medical Officer inspects one of the 4 areas daily with the Sanitary Corporal and also visits any places reported to him by the Sanitary Squad. He sends in a weekly report to the Town Mayor on the Sanitary Condition of the Town.	
			5. Scavenging. Refuse is placed in the streets and is collected	
			(1) In the main streets by a squad of men R.E. Thus sweep the streets and the rubbish is collected by British carts and taken to the Town dump and incinerated.	
			(2) In bye streets by a French Contractor. This rubbish is spread over fields at some distance from the Town.	
	30/4/16		Int by C.R.E. XI CORPS and D.D.M.S. – to admin re drainage of C.O.S. farms. 11.30 A.M. re D.H.Q. area. R.E. Sans. from in MERVILLE Church also N.C.Os. 3 P.M. in dining room	

Army Form C. 2118.

WAR DIARY
or
INTELLIGENCE SUMMARY.
(Erase heading not required.)

Instructions regarding War Diaries and Intelligence Summaries are contained in F.S. Regs., Part II. and the Staff Manual respectively. Title pages will be prepared in manuscript.

Place	Date	Hour	Summary of Events and Information	Remarks and references to Appendices
REGNIER-LE-CLERCQ.	19.4.16		The Head Quarters of the Unit is at C.R.S. MERVILLE and M.O. detached for duty at REGNIER ^ now at FOREST DE NIEPPE will report himself every morning at orderly at 9 O'clock — on his way to the Forest. Parade for Motor ambulances to travel against the enemy are cancelled for the present. It is noted in standard orders that it has come to knowledge that hostile agents (especially female) are making use of Conspicuous Prussperts admirable to avoid intended of value to the enemy. Officers and men are warned against this Spy system. Lieut T.B. Bean R.A.M.C. attaches himself for duty with the 131 F.A. and is posted to C section.	
	20.4.16		During the first 3 days the weather was very bad. It was practically impossible to do much outside work of a permanent kind. Squads of men were detailed	
	21.4.16			
	22.4.16		to remove the liquid mud covering the Surface of Hospital Camp and Surroundings of huts.	
	23/4/16		R & C section marched to Church Parade at C.R.S. MERVILLE. A.D.M.S. & D.A.D.M.S. visited the Camp in the afternoon —	O.K. Miller W/Sgt L. Col. O/C 131st F.A.
	24/4/16		Weather much better and ground getting dry.	

WAR DIARY or INTELLIGENCE SUMMARY

Army Form C. 2118.

Place	Date	Hour	Summary of Events and Information	Remarks and references to Appendices
REGNIER LE CLERCQ	24/4/16		A new incinerator has been built for detritus. A tower & also a large well have been dug. Men will supply Detachment Hot Water to have all the Stew Cans. Men have been made an enormous Drinker Line to the one we built at VIEILLE CHAPELLE	
	25/4/16		Sent one detail as M.O. to 11 S.W.R. during Temporary absence of Capt. S. Davis. Sent T.R. Evans detail as M.O. 1/C (FOREST DE NIEPPE) instead of Pvt Bove	
	26/4/16		General Health of Batch unused. Work is proceeding Satisfactory – a new Bath attached. Orders has been made with draining & Medical Inspection room. This will enable us to whitewash the huts – each accommodating 20 – Tin Patients to sleep in. Half of the huts was Given up to bathing & during Patrols. Both huts and billets have been whitewashed. The camp is looking much better.	
	27/4/16 28/4/16		Whole work continues – an outside latrine. Pay at 2 o'clock P.M.	

O.H. Millwood Lt. Col.
O/C 131 F.A.

WAR DIARY
or
INTELLIGENCE SUMMARY.

Army Form C. 2118.

Place	Date	Hour	Summary of Events and Information	Remarks and references to Appendices
REGNIER LE CLERCQ	29/4/16		Inspector of Camps by A.D.M.S. & D.A.D.M.S. — They arrived shortly after 2.30 P.M. & admitted him J. — I stayed until 3.45 when I had to return to C.R.S.	
	30/4/16		Usual Sunday duty. Wrote in the back area, our collecting area, to the clinic west of LA GORGUE occupied (North of 38th Field Service the clinic west of) LA GORGUE. occupied (North of 38th Field Service the clinic west of) the units (2 Batts) in the immediate vicinity of a horse ambulance with the units — an Indian up MERVILLE. and hope the 5ch to C.R.S. when they are taken up by a Moto Ambulance at 10.30 A.M. — and taken to 130 F.A. — The Ambulance meeting other ths units on its way there.	

J H Mulholland. Lt. Col.
O/C 131 F.A.

Confidential 131 Funds Vol 6

War Diary
131 Field Ambulance at Corps Rest Station
38th (Welsh) Division
for
May 1916

COMMITTEE FOR THE MEDICAL HISTORY OF THE WAR
Date 26 JUN. 1916

REST STATION
No. May 1916
Date 31 : 5 : 16
11th CORPS

Army Form C. 2118.

WAR DIARY
or
INTELLIGENCE SUMMARY.
(Erase heading not required.)

Instructions regarding War Diaries and Intelligence Summaries are contained in F. S. Regs., Part II. and the Staff Manual respectively. Title pages will be prepared in manuscript.

Place	Date	Hour	Summary of Events and Information	Remarks and references to Appendices
MERVILLE	1-5-16		General fatigue work. Continued with drains and outbuildings at C.R.S. Visited by Lt Col Little, A.A. Q.M.G. 38th Welsh Division. He was pleased with work done at C.R.S. He wanted to know how many 38th Wild Division Troops located near MERVILLE could be dealt with at the baths and was not certain that the baths at MERVILLE are for Corps Troops and only to be used by other Units when not required by Corps Troops. This was explained while the bath with the A + Q.M.G. 38th Division.	
	2.5.16		Another bath Concert in the unit given by Personnel A.T.M.S. in charge of C.R.S. assisted by Patients.	
	3.5.16		Order received from A.D.M.S. for inspection at MERVILLE of 131 F.A. personnel attached to C.R.S. at 5.30 P.M on 5/5/16.	
	4/5/16		Work on drains continued — sent out buildings. Special a preliminary inspection of personnel at 5. P.M. proof of the clothing is good.	
	5/5/16		Inspection by A.D.M.S. in full marching order. A.T.M.S. informed great pleasure with turn out.	

WAR DIARY
or
INTELLIGENCE SUMMARY

Army Form C. 2118.

Place	Date	Hour	Summary of Events and Information	Remarks and references to Appendices
MERVILLE	6/5/16		Corps order that all sents to HQrs Cavalry and Artillery on roll call sharper bright clear to C.R.S. from REGNIER. MERVILLE Town is not supplied in Said Centeon R. Cotis in abundance. L/C Chadwick English + Sin. La. go on leave 2 A.M. from LA BOURSE. Cpl. Began Jnr. appointed acting Q.M. and S/Sgt Peach acting S.M. — is bright down from REGNIER to C.R.S. at MERVILLE	
	7/5/16		Routine work	
	8/5/16			
	9/5/16		Inspection by Bakker Triggen (R.E.) on NEW ZEALAND disinfector by Lantern Slides.	
	10/5/16		Visit by D.M.S. – Surg Genl Pike. He was pleased with what he saw and was specially brought to say that Hosp. (C.R.S) was first rate.	
	11/5/1916		Order from D.D.M.S. to "Please note that the O/C 1st Labour Coy R.E. has been asked to arrange with you for the medical attendance of B Company, 1st Labour Bn. R.E. in MERVILLE during the absence on leave of the Officer in Medical charge of that unit for 14 days from the 10 inst.	

Army Form C. 2118.

WAR DIARY
or
INTELLIGENCE SUMMARY.
(Erase heading not required.)

Instructions regarding War Diaries and Intelligence Summaries are contained in F. S. Regs., Part II. and the Staff Manual respectively. Title pages will be prepared in manuscript.

Place	Date	Hour	Summary of Events and Information	Remarks and references to Appendices
MERVILLE	11/5/16		Qasgas note on Cholera received from A.D.M.S. 38 Division. Wrote major POOE (A D.D.M.S) asking him to let me see at his convenience to get to benefit of his views.	
	12/5/16		Paid surprise visit C.R.S at 12 o'clock noon. Sergt. Pruitt David (R.A.M.C.) detached to take medical charge not by A.D.M.S. 12 Labour Bn. R.E. He will also take over duties of Town of B. Company 17/5/16 owing to present sonas going on leave Sanitation 17/5/16 incite a kiddly inspection DAC 38 with him ready Capt Daniel will also week of A.D.M.S. 38 Div with him	
	13/5/16		Main drain at back of C.R.S. completed & covered in.	
	14/5/16		Sergt Major returned from leave. C. of S. parade as usual at 11.30 A.M. R.E. " " 11.30 N.C. " at 10.45 A.M.	
	15/5/16.		asked N.C. chaplain if a fixed hour could be arranged for Service.	
	16 5/16		Routine work	

Army Form C. 2118.

WAR DIARY
or
INTELLIGENCE SUMMARY.
(Erase heading not required.)

Place	Date	Hour	Summary of Events and Information	Remarks and references to Appendices
MERVILLE	17/5/16		Met by D.D.M.S. accompanied him to REGNIER LE CLERCQ. Scabies Hospital. A.D.M.S. 38 Division noted C.R.S. — accompanied him to REGNIER LE CLERCQ. He inspected the Camp.	
	18/5/16		Accompanied Major P.M.L. D.D.M.S. and Town Major to REGNIER LE CLERCQ. The DDMS has apparently decided to convert REGNIER divisional Scabies Hospital into CORPS Scabies Hospital.	
	19/5/16		Tents + Conveyances in arrear to make wash up room for being extra things + drums. N.C. Chaplain (Mr Evans) called from 38 held division — has arranged N.C. service on 2 P.M. on Sunday at C.R.S. discussed with him the possibility of having a field from every Sunday.	
	20/5/16		Captain Nurland — O/C REGNIER LE CLERCQ — taken for duty at C.R.S. and is relieved at REGNIER by Captain David.	
	21/5/16		D.D.M.S. today Inspector C.R.S. had a consult with him + Town Major concerning proposed Scabies Hospital at REGNIER — decide to meet premises to west 1/2 field adjoining present camp. Church of S. Service 11.30 a.m. + N.C. service from N.C. at 2 P.M.	

Army Form C. 2118.

WAR DIARY
or
INTELLIGENCE SUMMARY.

(Erase heading not required.)

Instructions regarding War Diaries and Intelligence Summaries are contained in F.S. Regs., Part II. and the Staff Manual respectively. Title pages will be prepared in manuscript.

Place	Date	Hour	Summary of Events and Information	Remarks and references to Appendices
MERVILLE C.R.S.	22/5/16		M.O. from 3rd Armie Cating with the use of Ambulant Medical arrangements at FORET DE NIEPPE. Other M.O. having gone I instructed him to go to LA MOTTE. They met at medical inspection room there and arranged matters in accordance with instruction from respective A.D.M.S.'s. Sgt. Major not well — 3 cases of nicolate. Corps order to have medical Board on Friday at 10 A.M. O.C. C.R.S. President.	
	23/5/16		Ordered to send 4 men & 2 Sergt. Instr. to 6 P.M. relay to Railway Station for convenience of troops passing through. — 61st Division. Communication from A.D.M.S. that Co. at E. Evan. 2/3 light field Ambulance will arrive T.N. & must tomorrow 24th for and will be attached 5-4/5 a day - T/c is C.R.S. etc	
	24.5.16		M.Co. Evan and not turn up.	
	25.5.16		M.Co. Evan 2/3 light field Ambulance & Ofc 125 field Ambulance arrived though them now C.R.S. & RESISTED E CLERICQ Stores Station — had reference to no. 7 C.C.S. and late L 29 field Ambulance at LA GORGUE	
	26/5/16		In accordance with Corps Order letter 824 a board under Manchney of O.C. C.R.S. Mervin Corps P.M.C. — fact from A.M.C.	

2353 Wt. W5141/1454 700,000 5/15 D.D.&L. A.D.S.S./Form/C. 2118.

WAR DIARY
or
INTELLIGENCE SUMMARY.
(Erase heading not required.)

Army Form C. 2118.

Instructions regarding War Diaries and Intelligence Summaries are contained in F. S. Regs., Part II. and the Staff Manual respectively. Title pages will be prepared in manuscript.

Place	Date	Hour	Summary of Events and Information	Remarks and references to Appendices
MERVILLE	26/5/16		Examined all "P.B." men in MERVILLE — Total examined — 145 — Others F.D. 22 — and P.O. 122 — 1 Sheet of Wool was not received.	
	27/5/16		A.D.M.S. & D.A.D.M.S. 38 Divn. on visit. C.R.S. & REGNIER. and reported much satisfaction. A.D.M.S. goes on leave on 29.5.16. I am to go to LA GORGUE during his absence to act in his stead. Odr. from A.D.M.S. to send M.O. to duty at Divisional Ammunition Column during absence of their M.O.	
	28/5/16		Asst. Major Gray proceeds in accordance with A.F.W. 3405 order of yesterday to relieve M.O. at D.A.C. Major Dann & Major Osmer Dann arrive from leave.	
	29/5/16		Lieut. Col. A. N. Mills. Relieved Lt. Col. Corps Rest Station, & takes over duties of A.D.M.S. 38 Division at LA GORGUE. Major Potts O.D.M.S. visited Corps Rest Station, expressed his approval of the newly instituted "mess tent" and washing up Pantry. He also proceeded to REGNIER and inspected the additional Convalescent Rest estb. I was honored out to him the difficulty of providing an adequate supply of blankets; twenty new watr. units in the Field Ambulances, one of which is at the Corps Rest Station, and there at only three watr. units in the totally inadequate to provide water for personnel of three REGNIER, the hrs at REGNIER, ... A.S.C. personnel, bathos, and troops. He promises to supply another watr. cart to here Section.	

2353 Wt. W2514/1454 700,000 5/15 D. D. & L. A.D.S.S/Forms/C. 2118.

WAR DIARY or INTELLIGENCE SUMMARY

Army Form C. 2118.

Place	Date	Hour	Summary of Events and Information	Remarks and references to Appendices
MERVILLE	29/5/16		60 Sutton performed tanks.	
"	30/5/16		Went hurriedly round to the 1st Field Ambulance. Visited RESNIER and found the Hospital marques erected, part of the instruments not in hand. Observed the new system of enumeration of patients at Corps Rest Station. Affords a greater spirit of "Privacy" and works smoothly. Received wire from D.M.S. that Scabies and infectious skin cases will be received at RESNIER between the hours of 2 & 4 p.m. subject in doing call almost completed. The victim of yesterday for hospital permission to visit the "Peel depôt" RESNIER. I took Captain McPhee, Bacteriologist, Merville asked permission to visit the "Peel depôt" at HAESBROUCK run by Col Clay. He informed me that there was an army "Peel depôt" at HAESBROUCK and the Knights that it would be a most valuable experience if the Time am the Knight that it would be a most valuable experience if the 58th C.C.S. NORTHUMBERLAND. T.F. and Captain Davis and Captain Parr, Senior Officers in charge of RESNIER could visit it. Accordingly I had Captain Parr and HAESBROUCK. They returned in the evening deeply pleased with their visit. They were well received by Col Clay & were shown over the hospital, had the arrangements for bathing & treatment explained to them. Working up of Poultry completed.	
"	31/5/16		This morning Col J Salbury A.M.S., Consulting Physician to the 1st and 2nd Armies visited the Corps Rest Station. I took him round & he expressed himself as very well pleased with all arrangement. He then informed one that he had been requested by General Pike D.M.S. 1st Army to visit RESNIER and report as to the arrangement for treating Scabies and infectious skin diseases and as to the possibility of greatly the accompanied him to RESNIER. He made a most minute examination of the whole camp. He inspected a batch of patients (16) which had been admitted this morning and went over the treatment of each. Very valuable hints were obtained and he pointed out that the infection but a very small percentage of cases admitted as Scabies were really such. I pointed out to him the difficulties that we had to encounter regarding the water supply. He agreed that their water can't been totally inadequate. He also impressed on the disinfecting of contaminated clothing. He	

Army Form C. 2118.

WAR DIARY
or
INTELLIGENCE SUMMARY.
(Erase heading not required.)

Instructions regarding War Diaries and Intelligence Summaries are contained in F. S. Regs., Part II. and the Staff Manual respectively. Title pages will be prepared in manuscript.

Place	Date	Hour	Summary of Events and Information	Remarks and references to Appendices
MERVILLE	30/5/16		informed prob Carpenter that all the clothing was sent to LA GORGUE, promising that to avoid family recommend to General Peter that a "fixed" should be applied. J.C Bavius Major R.A.M.C. 131st Field Ambulance. for Moenspank O/C N. Carpenter	

2353 Wt. W2544/1454 700,000 5/15 D. D. & L. A.D.S.S./Forms/C. 2118.

131 ȝ amb
Afor to vol 6

Confidential

War Diary
131 Field Ambulance
(Regnier Le Clerq.
XI Corps Skin Disease Depot)
for
May 1916

COMMITTEE FOR THE
MEDICAL HISTORY OF THE WAR
Date 26 JUN. 1915

Army Form C. 2118.

WAR DIARY
or
INTELLIGENCE SUMMARY.
(Erase heading not required.)

Instructions regarding War Diaries and Intelligence Summaries are contained in F. S. Regs., Part II. and the Staff Manual respectively. Title pages will be prepared in manuscript.

Place	Date	Hour	Summary of Events and Information	Remarks and references to Appendices
REGNIER LE CLERCQ	1.5.16		Miss Lafosse completed. Miss Rathbone + medical inspection + cleaning rooms preceding well. Staff Sergt Dodd upon C section of REGNIER from C.D.S. MERVILLE	
	2.5.16		Order received from A.D.M.S. to check medical and other stores at end of every month and to send a return to him on the 1st of each month and up to date as soon as possible. Issued order accordingly to O/C section to check medical + other stores at once.	
			Orders received from A.D.M.S. to send 1 N.C.O. + 2 men to LA GORGUE to loading. (The firsts are to proceed + relieve 4) 130 F.A.) Firemen to arrive there 2.30 p.m.	
	3.6.16		8 men + one N.C.O. proceeded as directed to LABOGUE. Order received from A.D.M.S. to inspect 9 F.A. at REGNIER LE CLERCQ on Friday 5. at 6.15 p.m.	
	4.5.16		Visited REGNIER. Were hard worried in the morning and again at 6 P.M. He had a preliminary inspection for fineness. Some of the clothing + his bed prided to 2 in 3 was bad on enquiry apparently indent sent to him from later (C camp in advance) was not sent to him. He clothing his bed + great amount of kit was in great need of further wash down at various ones (cleaning up) M.O. received from A.D.M.S. to evacuate 15 cases of Scabies to No. 7 C.C.S Inspection by A.D.M.S. in accompanied me — He was very pleased	
	5/5/16			

Army Form C. 2118.

WAR DIARY
or
INTELLIGENCE SUMMARY.
(Erase heading not required.)

Instructions regarding War Diaries and Intelligence Summaries are contained in F. S. Regs., Part II. and the Staff Manual respectively. Title pages will be prepared in manuscript.

Place	Date	Hour	Summary of Events and Information	Remarks and references to Appendices
REGNIER LECLERCQ	6/5/16		Walk out to C.D.S. MERVILLE. Two manuals Complete at Home from to him Brennan. General route walk entered but latere detached to 101 Bde. R.F.A at MAZINGHEM.	
	7.5.16		Notified by A.D.M.S that FOREST-CONTROLL - NIEPPE an 11th Army Troops, and that no men outside the 11th CORPS are to be sent to C.D.S. MERVILLE	
	8.5.16		At D. of S. Orders — So supply following Ambulance Wagons as per 9th inst. (i) On the 10th Welsh at FORK R.D M 76 2.2 at 9.00 a.m (ii) On the 13 Welsh at ROUGE CROIX Cross Roads at 9 P.M (iii) On the 15th Welsh at Battalion H.Q. M.21.a.55 at 8.30 a.m Sent Group Ambulance Wagons Bearers in accordance with yesterday instructions	
	9.5.16		Ordinary Routine work	
	10/5/16		Both groups of bearers are employed — except on cementing the hill floor.	
	11/5/16		Received March at 2 P.M.	
	12/5/16		Lieut David in detail from REGNIER Dressing Station to C.D.S MERVILLE	

Army Form C. 2118.

WAR DIARY
or
INTELLIGENCE SUMMARY.
(Erase heading not required.)

Instructions regarding War Diaries and Intelligence Summaries are contained in F.S. Regs., Part II. and the Staff Manual respectively. Title pages will be prepared in manuscript.

Place	Date	Hour	Summary of Events and Information	Remarks and references to Appendices
REGNIER LE CLEREQ	12/5/16		To obtain that Evans D'Arc (who is going on leave tonight) as Town Sanitation officer. Capt. Dawson will also act as M.O. of 1st Lahore Div. R.E. in accordance with DDMS instructions during absence of in leave of the M.O. (had malaria)	
	13/5/16		Inspection of Transport at REGNIER by D+DOS – afford satisfaction	
	14/5/16		N.C. Service at 3 P.M. Pont. Latham attend from 121 R.F.A at MAZINGHAM. He will return for our in Permanent duty K R F A headquarters	
	15/5/16		Order from HQ M.S 3o held Down is to attend 1 Officer & 5 men for duty at PONT RIQUEL – near LESTREM on Wednesday.	
	16/5/16		A.D.M.S asks to send one horse Ambulance to follow 15 "B" with Pages to K. 24 a & b at 10.30 AM Tomorrow.	
	17/5/16		Complied with A.D.M.S order of 15/5/16 & 16/5/16 and by D.D.M.S – Camp Inspected with view of enlarging it, to convert into CORPS Scabies Camp. I apply in afternoon to DDMS. that he can run it	

WAR DIARY or INTELLIGENCE SUMMARY

Army Form C. 2118.

Place	Date	Hour	Summary of Events and Information	Remarks and references to Appendices
REGNIER LE CLERCQ	17/5/16		ADMS inspects the Camp	
	18/5/16		Major Potts (DDMS) Tom Many accompany me round camp. Attends to arr. CMDS Scabies Hospital. Decide to ask for 1/3 of adjoining field. 3 Hospital Marquees will be put up. I am to find a lot of material necessary for necessary accommodation.	
	19/5/16		Decide to send Captain David to run REGNIER Camp instead of Captain Pollard — The latter will return to C.R.S. MERVILLE	
	20/5/16		Captain Pollard return to CRS and accompanying Captain Perry to FORÊT DE NIEPPE to learn duties so as to take over from Captain Perry, latter will remain at REGNIER. LECLERCQ to help Captain Denio who is now O.C. Scabies Hospital there. "D.M.S. 2nd Army has instructed DDMS Anzac Corps which medical arrangement to make. located Hdr— Camp 181. 7A L and nd LE FORET. T.25C T.7C. T.3C SA (Army 36A)" Completion of the FORÊT in tree felling.	
	21/5/16		Instruction from ADMS 35th Division has been requested to find an M.O. to take over from the Brow2 tents at T1. 7.25d + T.26.a. We are to consult as to the test possible of vacancy. It is decided a/k account the whole with DDMS Anzac. Met it will be best to combine Medical Inspection Room at LAMOTTE	

WAR DIARY
or
INTELLIGENCE SUMMARY.
(Erase heading not required.)

Army Form C. 2118.

Place	Date	Hour	Summary of Events and Information	Remarks and references to Appendices
REGNIER LE CLERCQ	22/5/16		Some medical arms for attending cases of sick of Army Corps Scotia Camp. Good progress is being made with a new field sta — the one hitherto used behind the Balmoral lynes the Scots Camp is too small and insanitary an insanitary.	
	23/5/16		Visits REGNIER again. Hôpital Marjon have arrived — We are not able to pitch them because permission has not yet been obtained to utilize the adjoining field. Capt R.E. are short of tools — we have succeeded in getting a loan from the front good progress is being made with stables of Rest room, Cook Shop and Latrines. Cinemas "Catching" the troops.	
	24/5/16			
	25/5/16		evacuation of sick of horse division still compares favourably with the division of XI Corps Three Ambulances supplied to follow one for 13" Bat RWF at K.24.d.7.7 at 9 a.m. 18" RWF at K.29.d.2.2. at 9.15 a.m.	
	26/5/16		The following present establishment of 131 Field Ambulance @ A.S.C. (H.T.) 36 (B) (M.T.) 13 Total Motor Ambulance 2+2 (A.D.M.S) Telegram from D.D.M.S. "Be prepared to receive 60 cases of sick returns from CALONNE	

Army Form C. 2118.

WAR DIARY
or
INTELLIGENCE SUMMARY.
(Erase heading not required.)

Instructions regarding War Diaries and Intelligence Summaries are contained in F. S. Regs., Part II. and the Staff Manual respectively. Title pages will be prepared in manuscript.

Place	Date	Hour	Summary of Events and Information	Remarks and references to Appendices
REGNIER L.F. CLERCQ	25/5/16		from D.D.M.S. — daily return of Scabs Corps depot — 9 a.m. — 9 p.m.	
			discharged — admitted — Remaining	
			33 dis	
			35 "	
			38 "	
			39 "	
			61	
			The 4 stop. hangars one of + "Artisha" — 3 out of 6 centre ones + puncho's coming today to fence off No.3 adjoining field in which hangars are pitched.	
		27/5/16	from today to meet. Tele Army fork cars of depot which were in attn of the above division.	
		28/5/16	A.D.M.S. & A.D.V.S. 3rd division accompanied me to Scabs Corps depot.	

WAR DIARY or INTELLIGENCE SUMMARY

Army Form C. 2118.

Place	Date	Hour	Summary of Events and Information	Remarks and references to Appendices
REGNIER as CLARE	29/5/16		Work was recommenced in extension of buildings used as pack transport camp.	
	30/5/16		Major Potts D.D.M.S. II Corps visited REGNIER. He informed himself as well pleased with the progress of new work. He inspected the pump recently erected Mangan, was pleased with the manner the "Patching" had been carried out. He inspected pack panns and clothing store shed. The water difficulty was promised but I him and he promised to procure for Major a large 300 gallon tank and if possible another water cart. Had informed to find out that the water was transported from NASHVILLE, and that we were not only supplying the post itself, but also the civilians in proximity to the depôts but also the troops (probable) supplying the pump by the well.	
	31/5/16		Col. Galloway A.M.S. Consulting Physician 1st & 2nd Army visited and inspected REGNIER. He entered minutely into the working arrangement of the depôt. He took detail of patients admitted, spoken to numerous sick parallel before him. With the officers in charge, Captain Speed and Capt Murry, he went into each and permit to to them what to him best method of treatment. He remarks were highly appreciated by the officers present. He expressed himself as highly pleased with what he had seen. In leaving he expressed to the two Returns at REGNIER, Visitors was carried out. The afternoon an loading the equipment of the have been packed, ready to move the two S.S. Waggons and london-cart. Action B, and Section C. the hour and Section were packed, ready to move the various moments.	

J.C. Lewis Major R.A.M.C.
It. G.C. 2.H. Matt. Patient
O.C. 131st Field Ambulance

1317 Vol 7
June

Confidential

War Diary

131 Field Ambulance

38th (Welsh) Division

June

1st to 30th inclusive

WAR DIARY or INTELLIGENCE SUMMARY

Army Form C. 2118.

Place	Date	Hour	Summary of Events and Information	Remarks and references to Appendices
MERVILLE	1/6/16		Lieut Col R.H. Mills-Roberts, ADMS, 38th Division visited Corps Rest Station this morning.	
	2/6/16		In the afternoon, accompanied by the A.D.M.S., 38th Division and myself, he held a medical board on men considered by the Medical Officer Corps Rest Station as not likely to derive further benefit from treatment at Corps Rest Station. 14 men were examined, 5 were found to be P.B., 3 T.D. at duty, 2 Casualty Clearing Station. Captain Baker, Officer in charge of Motor Ambulance Convoy requested me to supply him with 2 orderlies for "Hospital Train" at MERVILLE Station. Complied with the request. The men in charge of Sgt Moore were tightly adapted with their experience and much information was gained by them. Commenced white-washing the huts, inside and saving outside.	
	3/6/16		Sent a communication to a.D.M.S. 33rd & 39th Division informing them that men of their respective Divisions were at present at Corps Rest Station. Had in the opinion of the Medical Officer they were cases which would not derive any benefit by a further stay and asking them how they wished to have them disposed of. Completed the white-washing of No.1 & 2 huts. The floors scraped out thoroughly disinfected. When application to Secretary Officer, 35th Division for C Station we were informed that it was unattainable, to supplied in, with 6 Manchester Brigade the Tromalleville Station, and recommend it use as a solution ½ in 20. Commenced the erection of a meal tent behind the Corps home for the men of our regiment and was intended to be entered the following morning. Visited the Officer Iman-Verten and Party at the Piscerie: Fiscetel as men next left here. Also visited the Corps Baths and found them clean & tidy. The Clothing Stores were especially well arranged and Inspected the Corps Baths and found the dry heat the tunnel of the tubs at Corps Rest Station etc.	
	4/6/16		Yesterday in General Orders a certificate was put the day that the turning of the tubs at Corps Rest Station now completed. Tested "Rat Inspection" was held this afternoon. All particulars found in an unsatisfactory condition were replaced. The weekly "Rat Inspection" numbering 4.7.5. and was inoculated daily into the most successful exploited. Small proofs of the personnel numbering 4.7.5. and was inoculated daily into the most successful exploited and Paratyphoid. Subsequently little reaction was found. Parade hours: Church of England 11.30 a.m. ADMS visited Corps Rest Station.	

O H Mills Rest Lt Col
OC 131 Field Ambulance

WAR DIARY
or
INTELLIGENCE SUMMARY.

(Erase heading not required.)

Army Form C. 2118.

Instructions regarding War Diaries and Intelligence Summaries are contained in F. S. Regs., Part II. and the Staff Manual respectively. Title pages will be prepared in manuscript.

Place	Date	Hour	Summary of Events and Information	Remarks and references to Appendices
MERVILLE	5/6/16		Map of sewers of Tour Morin from M.H.7.12.15. On attempts was made today to find out if the ditch in CRS grounds communicated with the Tour sewer. Found that it did not. Apparently a similar attempt was made about 3 months ago but without success. It does to lead to under the Tobacco Factory and then empties itself into the Canal. Captain J.S. Arkland detailed to take medical charge of 121 Major R.F.A. when just taken O.H.M.C. going on leave. Finished cleaning the sewers. Medical board held on patient of 39 Division by me & O.M.S & Clarke. Man hem J P B of I.T.C. Men reported medically unfit —	
	6/6/16		Opened drain leading from B.I.Ch. Had interview with Town Major concerning the condition of the ditch. He decrees a letter report to him to forward to MAIRIE.	
	7/6/16		Report offered to in cal. forms sent to Town Major. Works of Jackson Ironwork cleaning up continued. O/c 129 J.A. + Major Madan 2/1 J.A. 61. division (on instruction) to Med C R S	

D Hamilton, Lt Col
O/c 131 Field Ambulance

WAR DIARY or INTELLIGENCE SUMMARY

Army Form C. 2118.

Place	Date	Hour	Summary of Events and Information	Remarks and references to Appendices
MERVILLE	8/6/16		Completed the white-washing of huts & praying of floors. All opens out clean and fresh, drains flushed & new lamp-form. Had visited Dr Harris, Bolls. Completed the Survey of Latrines.	
	9/6/16		A Major & a NCO Battalion and a D.C. Surveyed General called at Headquarters but night requesting permission to hold a Cinematograph Show in our front Hall on the 9'. and 10' inst for men of the two Battalions in Rest at MERVILLE, performance to be from between the hours of 5 & 8 p.m. This was agreed. 8/9 Maj. Lee our pinor inspections & clean the main hall & all articles of bedding, kit, and the interpreter & others as many shown as tenable. As the performances are for the benefit of troops in Rest, Patients and Personnel would remain in the Front Hall & huts, and if the Hall would not be inconvenienced by troops a few patients are to be admitted. On 9' day at 12 met Dep: Robert returned to Capt Ray Returns from LA SORGUE having from A.D.M.S. 2nd Lt R.H. Mills during the absence on leave of Col F J Morgan. No 38th Division showing the absence on leave of Col F J Morgan.	
	10/6/16		Inspected the Cinematograph ambulance arriving to order permission to proceed South. C R S at MERVILLE & Corps Sion Depot at REGNIER LE CLERCQ handed over to - 2/L Bidel Ambulance 61st Division - (Arth. Mueller). This Ambulance has not been in France long. In D.D.M.S. 11 Army Corps reports O.C. C. LoS - to instruct this intensity Ambulance in the method adopted to run C.P.S. and new 3rd Field D.E.P.S.T. O.T.C. C.R.S with Quickest & Regt. War & Regt Club.	

O Knightly Lt. Col
O/c 131. Field Ambulance

Army Form C. 2118.

WAR DIARY
or
INTELLIGENCE SUMMARY.
(Erase heading not required.)

Instructions regarding War Diaries and Intelligence Summaries are contained in F. S. Regs., Part II. and the Staff Manual respectively. Title pages will be prepared in manuscript.

Place	Date	Hour	Summary of Events and Information	Remarks and references to Appendices
MERVILLE	10/6/16		Unit therefore stays a few days at MERVILLE to instruct mounin.	
	11/6/16		Lt J R Swan OMC with an Crpnal and 5 men proceed as an advance party to ROBECQ at 9 am to take over baths and to prepare to billet men of the Brigade opening a bath any time after 11 am.	
			A section from C.R.S. MERVILLE and B.O.C section from Corps Shoe depot REGNIER LE CLERCQ — Move (in 6 lengths units (once lomes)) with 115 Musicale to ROBECQ — and assume its organisation on a complete brigade Field Ambulance	
ROBECQ	12.6.16 / 13.6.16		Unit remains in act at ROBECQ. This was the first place where the unit opened out for an Ambulance in since 1915.	
	13.6.16		One officer – 2 N.C.O's 6 men proceeded on an advance party to TINCQUETTE to take over SIC from 77 field Ambulance. A horse ambulance sent to Hy Donal Brigade ST VENANT to accompany storm and artillery on theme of march. Motor Ambulance sent to A.D.M.S office at 2.15 pm. detail left with C.O at MERVILLE again unit in the evening at ROBECQ.	

A M Nicholson Lt Col
O/C 131 Field Ambulance

Army Form C. 2118.

WAR DIARY
or
INTELLIGENCE SUMMARY.
(Erase heading not required.)

Instructions regarding War Diaries and Intelligence Summaries are contained in F.S. Regs., Part II. and the Staff Manual respectively. Title pages will be prepared in manuscript.

Place	Date	Hour	Summary of Events and Information	Remarks and references to Appendices
ROBECQ	14/6/16		Unit left ROBECQ at 9.30 AM and 115 Inf Brigade. Arrived at DIVION at 3 PM. None fell out through [illeg]. [illeg] [illeg] walk to train, were evacuated to No 9 C.C.S. 7 Cases from [illeg 17,267] [illeg 11,5013] 20 Cases [9 with [illeg]] admitted at CALONNE who also evacuated to C.C.S. (No 9) [illeg] [In SMB. 13]	
DIVION	15/6/16		Unit left DIVION at 8 AM and arrived TINCQUETTE at 3 PM. No sick checked on unit. None admitted. Motor Ambulance [illeg] followed unit about one hour late.	
TINCQUETTE	16/6/16		Visited A.D.M.S. at his office with O/C's 120 & 129 Field Ambulances to discuss [illeg] [illeg] at TINCQUETTE. All had to inspect training area. Training programme of unit is to be drawn out & applied to A.M.S. A daily programme [illeg] [illeg] [illeg]	
	17/6/16		Unit to training area. Called to see G.O.C. 115 Brigade to learn training area again. Brigade informed me that he was leaving Brigade. Training programme [illeg] in a few days — and brigade [illeg] to brigade [illeg]. 7A. O/C 120 called, we go together towards H.Q.M.S. & O/C 129 on training area.	
	18/6/16		Routine work.	
	19/6/16			
	20/6/16			

N.H. Williamson Lt Col
O/C 131 [illeg]

Army Form C. 2118.

WAR DIARY
or
INTELLIGENCE SUMMARY.
(Erase heading not required.)

Instructions regarding War Diaries and Intelligence Summaries are contained in F. S. Regs., Part II. and the Staff Manual respectively. Title pages will be prepared in manuscript.

Place	Date	Hour	Summary of Events and Information	Remarks and references to Appendices
FINCHVILLE	20/9/16		A.D.M.S. told camp Colonel sent in very complimentary from as to the work done by them in ambulance with a letter from D.D.M.S. 11th Army Corps to G.O.C. 38 divn.	
	21/9/16		Took unit for route march this morning and orders received from A.D.M.S. a.b. divisional field day on 29/8/16	
	22/9/16		Routine work — Inspection of equipment (Nos 1,2,9)	
	23/9/16		Received orders from G.O.C. 115 Brigade that I am to assist Lar Timmins. Called on Brigadier to ask if he may satisfy the same scheme that has been arranged for divisional memory on 25/6/16 — C.E. to have an A.D.S. at MONCHY BRETON and main army station at BRIAS	
	24/9/16		Orders from 115th Infantry Brigade Operation order no 52 :— dealing with medical arrangements on to Manning Relay "Regt and posts will be established by units in the 1st German line" 131 Intl Ambulance will form an advanced dressing station at O.31.d 66 (MONCHY BRETON) and a main dressing station at LA THIEULOYE G.O.C. allowed us to fix main station a stage farm her BRIAS	

O.T. Mulholland Lt Col
O/C 131 Fd Ambulance

WAR DIARY
or
INTELLIGENCE SUMMARY.
(Erase heading not required.)

Army Form C. 2118.

Place	Date	Hour	Summary of Events and Information	Remarks and references to Appendices
TINCQUETTE	24/6/16		Md GOC with other OC's visited at 6.2.a.10.10 at 8 A.M. Medical arrangement worked very satisfactory. ASM. Orders 131. F.A. for Jun 24, 1916. Received 4:45 A.M. Hand on marker S.U.S. in ready track of at 6 A.M. At 131. F.A. An C. Section & Keven Subdivision of A & B Section under Lt Davis will proceed to N 24.a.0.5 and there open command of Major During Station. 1. (2) C. Section with Rear Subdivision of A & B Section under command of Captain Davis will form an AP at 0.21 d.66 (3) Captain Pany will get in touch with Regimental Aid Post in left sector and despatch 6 bearers to each Post with 1 Medical Corporal. Surgical transport under Lt White. Kohl Dentist was attached in orders 2 horses, he did not evacuate 104 Dentist was attached in orders 2 horses - Arid Car to main Dressing Station (in order to save petrol & tyres) - works satisfactorily 3 miles away - being satisfied that things were going satisfactorily	
	25/6/16		Divisional Field day - Medical arrangement of 131. F.A. were the yesterday, the only casualty to A.D.S. 67 Cars between Gas Batt. time duration for wounded men to rejoin their units. Medical Scheme the satisfactory was quite satisfactory.	

Army Form C. 2118.

WAR DIARY
or
INTELLIGENCE SUMMARY.
(Erase heading not required.)

Place	Date	Hour	Summary of Events and Information	Remarks and references to Appendices
TINCQUETTE	25/6/16		Orders received to move South. The Brigade will move in two Columns. One horse ambulance to accompany each Column. Ambulance following about 2 hour after Column it picks up stragglers.	
	24/6/16		Batgs took charge of Camp at TINCQUETTE. Made in marches S.P.M ready to march off at S.15 at M.4. HAUT in LE HAUTRAIEF FAG. On line of march as far as Starting Point. One Packhorse in harness. By head of Column (3rd) at 6 o'clock P.M. The journey was mainly wet. We detailed on BONNIERES at 3 am 27/6/16 - horse fell out, rested on distraction Harassed return. Battn's had field Cookers. All ranks carried one shough of opinion that field ambulances one per company. I am thought field Cookers - one per unit. The presence of Army Service had been preferable to the comfort of all ranks. A 2nd order would add very materially to the starting Pt. 131. F.A. in his of head and during marches. At the Standing Transport was brigaded behind. Joined the rear of Column.	
BONNIERES	27/6/16		Stayed the night at BONNIERES. All ranks rested this day, and marched in marches at 7.45 P.M ready to march of at 2 P.M	Melville Alph tlc OPC 191 8 tol Amlu

WAR DIARY
or
INTELLIGENCE SUMMARY.

Army Form C. 2118.

Place	Date	Hour	Summary of Events and Information	Remarks and references to Appendices
BONNIÈRES	27/6/16		Coll. H.Q. at starting point (Convoy) about 1½ mile South W.of [?] to BEAUVOIR. Convoy at RECMANIL about 12.30 midnight 27/28. and took prisoner hut near Red Cross Head Quarters. We are to run a CORPS Divisional Rest Camp here. There are 5 splendid huts &c. The place has been occupied by a French Field Ambulance. The accommodation is very good but there is no equipment such as tables &c &c and clearly a first rate C.R.S. of material in Sanitary picks a tinker corrugated iron canvas &c to make the various accessories Shed an enclosed field a Cookhouse, path-Store room, washhouses, latrines &c.	
RECMANIL	28/6/16		Went to see A.D.M.S. to obtain plans and to organizing a C.R.S. I am tonight billeted at Red Cross Head Quarters. In the evening a telegram was received from + D.M.S. k collect men from 9 11st. Anzac who by some mistake had been left and not called — he sent an Ambulance & G.S. wagon and brgt 4 in 1St. Cons. The marching of the 11.S. Brigade has been very good. 68 men brght. [?] in ambulance [?] by Ambulance [?]	

Army Form C. 2118.

WAR DIARY
or
INTELLIGENCE SUMMARY.
(Erase heading not required.)

Instructions regarding War Diaries and Intelligence Summaries are contained in F. S. Regs., Part II. and the Staff Manual respectively. Title pages will be prepared in manuscript.

Place	Date	Hour	Summary of Events and Information	Remarks and references to Appendices
REMAISNIL	28/6/16		The Column March Ambulance following 242 from late	
			The Brigade moved to have continued its journey today to TOUTENCOURT. M/c Ambulance to accompany it. The yesterday, but the move was cancelled. Unit did fatigue work most of the day, clearing surroundings of new camp.	
	29/6/16		O.C. Bn. S. & D.A.D.M.S. visited us to inspect the 151 men of 114 Brigade and were billeted by us last night. These men were left on line of march also Bn. Medr. Ambulance from 130 T.A. and were billeted up 130 T.A. Stations.	
			I. et qe work continued at new Station. Bn. Medr. Ambulance from 130 T.A. collected from our unit 129 of the 151 men that were collected night before last - & were sent to them unit. Remainder will be collected tomorrow.	
	30/6/16		Another week. Division continues its move towards today, Code from A.D.M.S. Please added we have Ambulance to follow the Divisional Artillery on the march tomorrow. We arrived to at the Starting Point, @ used motor bs and E.S.E of MACFER at 9 p.m. today t accompany the Divisional Artillery to the PIERREGOT and MIRVAUX AREA. The will be completed with	M.Walker ALC. A Lt. Col O/C 3 3rd Ambl.

Army Form C. 2118.

WAR DIARY
or
INTELLIGENCE SUMMARY.
(Erase heading not required.)

Instructions regarding War Diaries and Intelligence Summaries are contained in F. S. Regs. Part II. and the Staff Manual respectively. Title pages will be prepared in manuscript.

Place	Date	Hour	Summary of Events and Information	Remarks and references to Appendices
REGNIER & CLARE	1/6/16.		Accompanied by A.D.M.S. visited field hospitals. Pack Horse veterinary, and new clothing stores nearly completed. 350 fallen tents arrived from R.E. depot, La SORGUE.	
	2/6/16.		Captain T.D. Baird R.A.M.C. reported this morning that the bags under tents obtained from R.E. depot La SORGUE and delivered yesterday were not provided with a top, I also had a cask on it. Sent Sgt Puffett to La SORGUE to endeavour to obtain a top. A top was obtained and the casks in the top repaired.	
	3/6/16.		Commenced the erection of new "Medical Inspection Room". Erected pipes to be placed on the different buildings.	
	4/6/16.		A.D.M.S. visited REGNIER. Free Church Parade at 2.30 p.m.	
	5/6/16.		Large water tank fixed into position. This is a great boon in the camp, but the filling of it outside proves arduous on the water duty men, its tank requiring just water and travel to fill it.	
	6/6/16.		Visited REGNIER LE CLERC. Captain T.D. Baird briefed on the inadequate supply of tents. Two periods only are left over from the previous day for cutting & braking water for Battn. The following morning belonged to a Servs. I cont. & obtained the terms. Kindled M and equally between the two i.e. Sgt Dipot and Corpls. Rect. Battn. Hu aftn sun shewn me with tubercular plants in a breaking down condition. This was a portion of the Coy of motion was shewn me on the 5th June 1915.	
	7/6/16.		Men's delivered on the 6 day by Lt/Col Simon 129 Field Ambulance and Major Mentier 3/c Lift Midland Field Ambulance. The Matron was visited by the left Col Simon also especially interested in the treatment of certain infection. Regem. Ram affection. 61 Dioxide. Major Marshal was especially interested in the filling of the tops under tents. One water cart is kept continually In my opinion the meaning labour is invariable to use in this dusty city.	
	8/6/16.		Post Room, Clothing Room, and extension of Medical Inspection Room completed.	

O.K. Smith A.B. LT.Col
6/4 1914 Inter. Amb.

Army Form C. 2118.

WAR DIARY
or
INTELLIGENCE SUMMARY.
(Erase heading not required.)

Instructions regarding War Diaries and Intelligence Summaries are contained in F. S. Regs., Part II. and the Staff Manual respectively. Title pages will be prepared in manuscript.

Place	Date	Hour	Summary of Events and Information	Remarks and references to Appendices
REGNIER LE CLERCQ	9/6/16		Day at 2 p.m. The white camp looked well. The huts and various buildings were very clean, especially the kitchens and mess billets. Its A.S.C. transport wagons were inspected & found to be in excellent order, especially the Horse Ambulance Waggon. 3 Horse Ambulance sent to A.D.M.S. Office to bring in 113th Infantry Brigade. Corps Rest Station Corps Plain defect handed over before 12 noon to Field Ambulance of 61st Division.	
	10/6/16	11 a.m.	Summons 11 a.m. — A Section left MERVILLE (12 noon) B + C Sections left REGNIER LE CLERCQ (1 o'clock) to follow the 113th Infantry Brigade to ROBECQ via CALONNE B + C Sections left to 131st Field Ambulance. to march in the middle of the column, ie between the Scout and 3rd Battalions. The Resting Point was the Brick bridge over the canal at MERVILLE. The Resting Point was LA GORGUE arriving at its Resting Point 13 minutes earlier. In one of the Infantry Battalions were obliged to follow to 3rd Battalion instead of the before the appointed time. The 131st Field Ambulance was detailed to march in rear of the 1, 2, 3 & 4 Battalions in order. One Horse drawn Ambulance was attended according to the appointed Time. A Horse & pick up Supplies + Ash. The march was accomplished according to the appointed Time. A Horse & pick up Supplies + Ash. The march was not during the march but owing to the fact that men carried to prevent dehydration men not sick during the march but owing to the fact that men carried to prevent The men reached the billets that they are destined And all arrived at ROBECQ in a dry condition. The men reached the billets that they and destined The Ambulance's first Hq. at ROBECQ had tea and rested before cooperating to the night. The Ambulance's first Hq at ROBECQ had tea and rifled them cooperately to the night. Captain S. N. Ivory R.A.M.C. with 2 nursing orderlies, 1 orderly-room clerk, and 1 Ash Time Clerk remained at REGNIER. Lieut. Col. P. H. Mills Roberts C.M.S. T.D. and Lieut & Quart Mr Crighton, with 2 orderly-room clerks, 1 Pack Store Corporal, 2 nursing-room orderlies, 1 cook, 1 dining hall orderly remained at MERVILLE to form temporary Horse Ambulance as the method adopted is run the C.R.S. at MERVILLE and Corps Store depot at REGNIER LE CLERCQ	

2353 Wt. W2514/1454 700,000 5/15 D. D. & L. A.D.S.S./Forms/C. 2118.

Confidential

War Diary

131 Field Ambulance

38th (Welsh) Division

for

July 1916
(1 - 31st inclusive)

COMMITTEE FOR THE
MEDICAL HISTORY OF THE WAR
Date -9 OCT.1916

WAR DIARY
or
INTELLIGENCE SUMMARY

Army Form C. 2118.

Place	Date	Hour	Summary of Events and Information	Remarks and references to Appendices
RECMANIL FME TOUTENCOURT	1.7.16		In accordance with A.D.M.S. (telegram) orders the 131 F.A. less 2 Officers/Major Davis & Lieut (R.A.M.C.) proceeded by lorries at 4.30 P.M. to Quartermarle. 30 R.A.M.C. personnel (and regimental numbers of F&C) arriving there and reporting to G.O.C. at 6.30 P.M. Soon learnt from 115 Brigade at TOUTENCOURT arriving the unit and refilling park, that 2 ACHEUX. Head of Column left TOUTENCOURT that the unit was bound for a new area. Refilling park, but 2 ACHEUX. Head of Column left TOUTENCOURT at 9.30 P.M. 131 F.A. (following in rear) arrived ACHEUX at 1.30 A.M. 2.7.16, bivouaced in a wood	
ACHEUX	2.7.16		Several great casks and old artificers were left behind at RECMANIL FME to be in running continued work which wanting to be relieved by a C.C.S. Ambulance and no time ambulance was left at RECMANIL FME. The D.R.S. at later 2 Mob Ambulances on the Hare Ambulance, place was to be maintained as an extract going concern, exports of dealing with large numbers of transit cases. Gain evening (1.7.16). 75 cars here admitted from the 38 Division – Chiefly Jan pits. Strong night (1–2.7/16). 210 wounded were admitted from 29 C.C.S. much to hand, with instructions to take over RECMANIL FME – Major Davis a N.C.O. from 7 F.A. arrived with instructions to take over RECMANIL FME. There was probably some declined to hand over – not having received orders to that effect. Facilities were given to Modden arrived & midnight. The 7. F.A. – been to billet in adjoining farm. Faults were given to Modden arrived & midnight. There was some difficulty in Morning – Subaltern orders to the assistance of 29 C.C.S. 210 Ph. The difficulty was overcome with the assistance of 29 C.C.S. on 2" & 3" & 4/7/16	
	3.7.16		The unit rested in the wood NE of ACHEUX. Relieving officers sent to 115 Brigade H.Q. also 30 Pr. order received to move. Head of Column to pass X Roads N.J. ACHEUX STATION at 8.30 P.M. – F 131. F.A. following in rear arriving at 1.30.A.M. 4.7.16. at BUIRE SUR–ANCRE. – billets had been procured. Lt.Col. Stephens 2/1 C.C.S. S.M. Division arrived at RECMNIL FME and took over the running, opening up as a C.C.S. at 5 P.M. the personnel of 131 F.A.	

O.H.Williams, Lt.Col
O/c 131 Field Ambulance

Army Form C. 2118.

WAR DIARY
or
INTELLIGENCE SUMMARY.
(Erase heading not required.)

Place	Date	Hour	Summary of Events and Information	Remarks and references to Appendices
ACHEUX	3.7.16		131 F.A. left behind at RECMENIL under Command of Major Davis proceeded to join the ( ) unit at ACHEUX arriving there about 11.30 P.M. The Unit having as already stated ( ) ACHEUX for BUIRE. Major Davis' party noted above the night at ACHEUX – moving to BUIRE next morning	
BUIRE SUR L'ANCRE	4/7/16		131 F.A reached BUIRE at 11.30 A.M. including the Recmenil Contingent joining the rest there (via ACHEUX) at 1.30 P.M. The unit is together as a whole once again. A very wet day during which we rested at BUIRE. The Chaplain of the Brigade reports that they are attached for rations etc. during the scarcity of room to No 2 men is being arranged for them but	
	5.7.16		A Conference of O.C's 129. 130 & 131 F.A & A.D.M.S. Opps at TREUX. Extract from A & M S' orders July 5th 1916. "Information. The 38 (Welsh) Division will relieve the 7 Division in the line to-night." "The 113 Brigade will hold the front of the line" " " 114 " " " " " in Support " " " 115 " " " " " in reserve " "No. 131. Field Ambulance less Bearer Division will be in reserve of MORLANCOURT (K.8.a.9), & the Bearer Division will take over the A.D.S at MINDEN POST. (F.18.C.3.8)" "Evacuation of Casualties. The bearers of Nos. 130 & 131 F.A's will clear the front of casualties the former in the left sector and the latter in the right sector – Sick & wounded officers will be sent to No 21 Field Ambulance	

2353 Wt. W2544/1454 700,000 5/15 D. D. & L. A.D.S.S. Forms/C. 2118.

Army Form C. 2118.

WAR DIARY
or
INTELLIGENCE SUMMARY.
(Erase heading not required.)

Instructions regarding War Diaries and Intelligence Summaries are contained in F.S. Regs., Part II. and the Staff Manual respectively. Title pages will be prepared in manuscript.

Place	Date	Hour	Summary of Events and Information	Remarks and references to Appendices
BUIRE SUR L'ANCRE	5/7/16		"Sick Transport. Ambulance Wagons of No 130 & 131 F.A's will be temporarily handed over to the Bearer division of 129 F.A at Divisional Collecting Station at L.g.a." "The trolley tram line from MINDEN POST via the CITADEL to the Divisional Collecting Station will be utilised for lying down cases and for the carry of walking Ambulance Cars can proceed to the Divisional Collecting Station, the CITADEL and MINDEN POST, moving by the route indicated in the hostile maps issued." "The Offrs of the A.S.T.M.S will clear at TREUX at 4 P.M. and will open at MORLANCOURT at the same time to which all reports will be sent. There is a Telephone station at MORLANCOURT."	
MORLAN-COURT	5/7/16		The 131 F.A. moved this day to MORLANCOURT. Capts David & Penny with Bearer Subdivision of C. section proceeded by Motor Ambulance to MINDEN POST & took over from the 92 F.A. The advanced Post at MAMETZ and the rear relay Post near the cross roads in MAMETZ village were also taken on by this party. The advanced Post was in an old German dug out and was well equipped & heavily used. Surgically. Late in the evening Captain Lowe and Lieut Taylor R.A.M.C. left MORLAN COURT with Bearer Subdivision & equipment of A & B sections and arrived MINDEN POST at midnight (5-6/7/1916). Lieut Taylor with 20 bearers was sent to BRIGHT ALLEY (MAMETZ) and 12 men Bearers were left at Bearer relay Post. #22. F.A Chief Instrt Lieut MINDEN POST until 6 A.M. 6/7/16. The heading over being [than place at midnight] (12 men again S-6/7/16	M. Mulqueed Lt Col O/C 131 Field Ambce

2353 Wt. W3544/1454 700,000 5/15 D.D. & L. A.D.S.S./Forms/C. 2118.

WAR DIARY or INTELLIGENCE SUMMARY

Army Form C. 2118.

Place	Date	Hour	Summary of Events and Information	Remarks and references to Appendices
MORLANCOURT	6.7.16		O/C's 129, 130 & 131. F.A's had Conference with A.D.M.S at his Office at 2.45. P.M. (6.7.16) Covering General arrangements for tomorrow — in scheme to attack on MAMETZ wood. O/C 131 F.A is to meet A.D.M.S at 8.20 A.M. tomorrow and proceed with him to MINDEN POST. Extract from A.D.M.S's orders 6.7.16 {115. Inf. Brigade is attacking eastern end of MAMETZ WOOD II {113. " " " " " holding the line South of the wood." No 131. Field Ambulance less two Tent Subdivisions and one Officer will remain at MINDEN POST. The O/C No.131. F.A. will take Command of the two Bearer Divisions at the A.D.S and will collect wounded from the MAMETZ & CATERPILLAR WOOD area. The motor Ambulances of No.21. & 130. F.A's will report at MINDEN POST at 9.30 A.M on 7th inst. The two tent Subdivisions will remain at MORLANCOURT in Reserve. The Bearer Division of 130. F.A. with 4 Officers will report to the O/C. 131. F.A. at MINDEN POST at 9.20 A.M on the 7th inst. A small retaining party only being left at the CITADEL. O/C. 131. F.A. Visited MINDEN POST. and reconnoitred the district with Capt. Parry R.A.M.C. (including RELAY POST) Reinforcements. 18. O.R. have gone to MAMETZ Advanced Post making a total of 50 Bearers at MINDEN POST. All the team remained at MINDEN POST.	
	7.7.16		Met A.D.M.S. as arranged at his Office at 8.30.A.M and went with him by motor car to MINDEN POST. At 9. A.M. 2 N.C.O's and 40. O.R. went to the triangle and opened an Aid Post inside O.L. 8. A.M. 2 N.C.O's and 40. O.R. went to the triangle and opened an Aid Post inside Capt. David. R.A.M.C. Lieut. 4 Officer and	

Army Form C. 2118.

WAR DIARY
or
INTELLIGENCE SUMMARY.
(Erase heading not required.)

Instructions regarding War Diaries and Intelligence Summaries are contained in F. S. Regs., Part II. and the Staff Manual respectively. Title pages will be prepared in manuscript.

Place	Date	Hour	Summary of Events and Information	Remarks and references to Appendices
MINDEN POST	7/7/16		4 Officers and 94 bearers reported for duty from 120 F.A. in accordance to A.D.M.S. instructions. The force already referred to incld. Capt. David at the Triangle — and 34 other ranks who formed the Sanitary Section 94 stayed in reserve collecting wounded from the right sector of the attack — 30 bearers remained from 129 reported at MINDEN POST. Divided Sanitary Section 38th division plus one M.O. formed a new Collecting Station at MINDEN POST in accordance with A.D.M.S instruction — had late in the day O/c Sanitary Section 38th division plus one M.O. at the Triangle. The carry from R. trenches to with his Section formed a relay of bearers at the Triangle. The carry from R. trenches to 'Jali' on 7 Mt 20 ^ bearers from 129 reported for duty. Fifty Triangle was very heavy, 129 were in charge of and working the carry road from MINDEN POST to via CITADEL to Divisional Collecting Station at L.9.a. Relative thereafter —Six M.O's were at work at MINDEN POST — each in his own tent or dug out. Two in the main dug out — two in the smaller dug outs and one in each of the opening tents of A. & B. Tent Subdivisions (the tent of which were backed along side MINDON POST dug out. So that men were as stream of patient being dealt with at any given time — at 6 different dressing rooms. A.D.M.S. was present during the whole day — he was relieved about 10 P.M. by D.A.D.M.S.	

D.H. Smithwick Lt Col
O/c 131 British Ambulance

2353 Wt. W2544/1454 700,000 5/15 D. D. & L. A.D.S.S./Forms/C. 2118.

Army Form C. 2118.

WAR DIARY
or
INTELLIGENCE SUMMARY.

(Erase heading not required.)

Instructions regarding War Diaries and Intelligence Summaries are contained in F. S. Regs., Part II. and the Staff Manual respectively. Title pages will be prepared in manuscript.

Place	Date	Hour	Summary of Events and Information	Remarks and references to Appendices
MINDEN POST	8/7/16		About 2.30 A.M. – S.B. team (from 129 & 131. F.A.) reinforced those at the Triangle and CATERPILLAR TRENCH. Many cases had but been admitted to MINDEN POST during the night. About 6 A.M. O/c 131 Field Ambulance visited the TRIANGLE and had a consultation with Captain Spooks and Gong who were in charge. Captain Daniel had returned to MINDEN POST after spending the opera a team to there post. Things were going very well, but I was not possible to remove the wounded by day. They were therefore placed in CATERPILLAR TRENCH to safety to be brought away following night. All the bearers were very tired. The carry is very heavy. At 6 P.M all the bearers except 1 Cap & 2 men left in CATERPILLAR TRENCH were withdrawn the patients were completed, and were turned after by the M.O's Capt. Peterson & Capt. Brown Esau. About 8 P.M. 120. 5yards with R.A.M.C. guards removed all the wounded placed in CATERPILLAR TRENCH. I am told so many became the team was exhausted. At 10. P.M. all team 130. F.A. (except 3. finally) returned to their unit by M/Br. Fitkia. All 129. team returned via Tram Lane to their unit. During the day O/c 131. F.A. also visited MAMETZ secured Post and found all in order.	
	9/7/16		1. N.C.O & 30. team sent to reinforce MAMETZ POST. – 1. Cap & 6 men only remained at TRIANGLE during the day. All from 131. F.A. New plan of attack on MAMETZ WOOD between 113 & 114 Brigades are to attack	

2353 Wt. W2544/1454 700,000 5/15 D. D. & L.   A.D.S.S./Forms/C 2118.

Army Form C. 2118.

WAR DIARY
or
INTELLIGENCE SUMMARY.
(Erase heading not required.)

Instructions regarding War Diaries and Intelligence Summaries are contained in F. S. Regs., Part II. and the Staff Manual respectively. Title pages will be prepared in manuscript.

Place	Date	Hour	Summary of Events and Information	Remarks and references to Appendices
MINDEN POST	9.7.16		Sent to F.A's 129 & 130 Tn on much as possible Tn tomorrow. (2) Tn Officer from 129 F.A and Fire (5) from 130. F.A came. I held a conference (10 P.M.) with these Officers, the D.A.D.M.S & O/c Sanitary Section being also present — and as a result issued the following orders. (1) O/c Sanitary Section will form an advanced rest station at Cross Roads N.W. of CARNOY Village. (Tent cloth & comforts to be supplied him) (2) 3 Bearer Subdivisions with two officers of 130 F.A. will rendezvous at CARNOY Cross roads, tonight. They will reach the right sector tomorrow 10/7/16 tonight (3) One Bearer Subdivision from 129 F.A with two officers will rendezvous at MAMETZ advanced post and will reach the left sector tomorrow (4) Fifty bearers from 131 F.A will be in reserve with two M.O's Chateau at MAMETZ. (5) Fifty bearers from 131 F.A. will be in reserve of A.D.S. MINDEN POST (6) 4. Horse Ambulances will be at X roads N.Y. of CARNOY. VILLAGE at 7.A.M. 10/7/16 (7) 3. Motor Ambulances will take up a forward position near MAMETZ POST — on the MAMETZ — MINDEN POST ROAD. N. Smith-Marsh Lt-Col O/C 131 Field Ambulance	

Army Form C. 2118.

WAR DIARY
or
INTELLIGENCE SUMMARY.

(Erase heading not required.)

Instructions regarding War Diaries and Intelligence Summaries are contained in F. S. Regs., Part II. and the Staff Manual respectively. Title pages will be prepared in manuscript.

Place	Date	Hour	Summary of Events and Information	Remarks and references to Appendices
MINDEN POST.	10/7/16.		The above orders were carried out & the Scheme worked well. At 4.15. A.M. Stretcher bearers in great request and all ranks were called on to MAMETZ. This by 6 o'clock A.M. All ranks worked splendidly, especially the bearers — Private Cunningham & B.E. Shuker both of 131. F.A. were recommended to the A.D.M.S. for official recognition for their gallantry and devotion to duty. Unfortunately Capt. David @ A.T.T.C. (131. F.A.) was wounded whilst accompanying the bearers from ROSE Cottage — MAMETZ — Capt. @ Laurie. R.A.M.C. and 3 others being killed at same time. David @ was struck by a piece of the shell. He was the death to all c.c.s. at cess was fractured and he had blood splitting. 2. M.O.'s from another Ambulance came to help in about 6. P.M. and stayed on duty the whole night. All ranks very tired. The same method of working as on the 7' inst. — I.S. B. clearing rooms going at the same time. The plan worked well. Cases were evacuated by Motor Ambulance — 6. of 131 F.A., 5. from 130. F.A. and 4. from 129. F.A. The 21. F.A. also sent 4. Motor Ambulances and the M.A.C. sent 10. Cars. 1. Motor Lorry from Sanitary Section. 38. Divn. was also employed and 2. Char-a-bancs. An Advanced Rest Station was established at FRICOURT. N.C.O. & 4 men were stationed there with hot drinks & medical comforts.	Willcock Lt. o/c 131. 3rd October

WAR DIARY
or
INTELLIGENCE SUMMARY.
(Erase heading not required.)

Army Form C. 2118.

Place	Date	Hour	Summary of Events and Information	Remarks and references to Appendices
MINDEN POST	11/7/16		Work slackened off very considerably today. A.D.M.S. issued orders today (part was cancelled subsequently afterwards). He is to hand over MINDEN POST to 23rd F.A. and on to return to MORLAN COURT & BUIRE tomorrow. O/c 23rd F.A. visited 131 F.A. at MINDEN POST. I was arranged to hand over at 12 noon tomorrow. S.O. Cavalry details appointed to help bearer bring in wounded. In the event of the night bearer division of 129 & 130 F.A. relieving MINDEN POST not in order to again their units tomorrow.	
	12/7/16		A.D.M.S. & D.A.D.M.S. visited MINDEN POST about 2.A.M and informed me that orders issued last night were cancelled. We are to entrain at MALAN COURT at 1.P.M tomorrow. J upland to A.D.M.S impossibility of doing this – as we were not handing over until 12 noon, but that he would do MINDEN POST on best. The night 11—12. Was a busy one. MINDEN POST was heavily shelled by German – 7. men were killed in road Clr by.	

O. McIlraith Lt/Col
O/c 131 Fd Ambce

Place	Date	Hour	Summary of Events and Information	Remarks and references to Appendices
MINDEN POST	12/7/16		Sent message to OTC 23. F.A. requesting him to take over as soon as possible in order to enable us to employ with 4 Coys. August to be at MORLANCOURT at 1 P.M. August proceeded his assault — at 11 A.M. a train was running my Adjutant & myself proceeded on foot to MORLAN COURT. We were held up near FRICOURT by heavy German shelling and did not reach MORLANCOURT until 2 P.M. The unit had a very strenuous time at MINDEN POST during its stay there — @ Wounded passed through as follows:—	

July 6.
Officers. b. Other Ranks
7   3   101
8   13   170
9   4   100
10   52   123
11   25   1194
12   9   963
     ___   296
     112   ____
          2947 — Total 3059

All ranks worked very hard and did their best — and everything worked very smoothly.

O.K. Willoughby. Lt Col
O/C 131 Field Ambulance

WAR DIARY
or
INTELLIGENCE SUMMARY.

(Erase heading not required.)

Army Form C. 2118.

Place	Date	Hour	Summary of Events and Information	Remarks and references to Appendices
MORLANCOURT	12.7.16		On reaching MORLANCOURT I found that plans were again changed as follows:— "Brear Division to return by Motor Ambulance in batches from MINDEN POST to MORLANCOURT and rest there for the night, and proceed 8 A.M. tomorrow to VAUCHELLES-LES-QUESNOY N.W. of AMIENS." "All the personnel at MORLANCOURT to entrain at EDGEHILL at 6 P.M. (tonight)." "All transport (except Mot Ambulance) to go by road at 2 P.M. (12.7.16)." (Extract from A.D.M.S's. order. #2.7.16) Personnel at MORLANCOURT — new tent as ordered. Transport did not arrive from MINDEN POST until late in day — too late for the column. About 9 P.P. the following telegram was received from 38' Division. "The 131 Field Ambulance will march tomorrow with 115 Inf. Brigade to WHARLOY, BAILLON area. Orders will be issued direct to 131 Field Ambulance by G.O.C 115 Inf. Brigade acquiring 115 Inf. Brigade Director (131 Field Ambulance)." Later orders received O/C 131 F.A. — "You should join the column of 115 Inf. Brigade at road junction E.26.c.9.0. at 7.45 A.M. tomorrow morning." H.I Swan Commanding 115 Inf. Bgde. F.A.	

Army Form C. 2118.

WAR DIARY
or
INTELLIGENCE SUMMARY.
(Erase heading not required.)

Place	Date	Hour	Summary of Events and Information	Remarks and references to Appendices
MORLANCOURT	13.7.16		The last note referred to from G.O.C. 115 Infantry Brigade was complied with. Received WARLOY at 10.45 A.M.	
	14.7.16		Under G.O.C. 115 Brigade to report at 6 P.M. Brigade proceed to COIN this evening by train. 131 Field Ambulance stays the night at WARLOY and proceed to THIEVRES by train 16 hours.	
	15.7.16		Proceeded to THIEVRES — by horse lorries at 3 P.M. Transport followed independently by road. Arrived THIEVRES at 6 P.M.	
	16.7.16		Ambulance did not open up. Orders at THIEVRES.	
			Sent an advance party in accordance with A.D.M.S. orders to take over D.R.S. and C.O.S. at AUTHIE.	
AUTHIE	17.7.16		The unit proceeded to AUTHIE. The Divisional rest station is situated in the wood, has accommodation for about 200 N.Cs in huts. Officer line in Tents & personnel in huts. The situation is excellent. The huts are poor. The roofs are not rain proof. They are evidently meant for summer only.	

Army Form C. 2118.

WAR DIARY
or
INTELLIGENCE SUMMARY.
(Erase heading not required.)

Instructions regarding War Diaries and Intelligence Summaries are contained in F. S. Regs., Part II. and the Staff Manual respectively. Title pages will be prepared in manuscript.

Place	Date	Hour	Summary of Events and Information	Remarks and references to Appendices
AUTHIE	17.7.16		21 of the personnel are detailed for duty at C.O.S. The C.O.S. is run by an operating Surgeon and Anaesthetist — there are 6 Nursing Sisters, he detail two M.O. to assist. The C.O.S. deals with abdominal cases only, (latterly head injury cases have also been admitted) 1 N.C.O. + 8 men proceeded to Dist Baths COIN (A.D.M.S. order)	(Signed) [illegible] Lt. O/C 1st 2nd Cumbria
	18.7.16		Routine work.	
	19.7.16			
	20.7.16		30 Other ranks with detach from 129 & 130 report to O/C 123 Field Co R.E. at T.16.b.6.2 at 6 A.M. for large clipping (A.D.M.S. order) A.D.M.S. hrgts. G.O.E. 28 Division to the C.O.S. and D.R.S. (B.Gen Woodcock)	
	21.7.16		1 N.C.O. + 29 men proceeded to duty with C.R.E. at T.16.b.6.2 (A.D.M.S. order) 4 abd. cases admitted to C.O.S. 2 died. All cases admitted on this date one mortality is about 50%. D.A.D.M.S. visited unit A new Corporal appointed for duty	
	22.7.16		4 Sisters left C.O.S. in accordance with A.D.M.S. order. 3 to New Zealand Hosp (AMIENS) 1 to WARLOY	

2353 Wt. W2544/1454 700,000 5/15 D.D. & L. A.D.S.S./Forms/C. 2118.

Army Form C. 2118.

WAR DIARY
or
INTELLIGENCE SUMMARY.
(Erase heading not required.)

Place	Date	Hour	Summary of Events and Information	Remarks and references to Appendices
AUTHIE	23.7.16		Sunday. C of E. Service at 4 P.M. N.C. Chaplain made an unexpected visit. It was explained to him that it was not possible to get the men together for Service without notice. This was regretted.	
	24.7.16		Visit by A.D.M.S. Discussed organisation of C.O.S. with him.	
	25.7.16		A.D.M.S. & D.A.D.M.S. visited d.D.S. to examine S.B.D. men. I visited OC. 129. to say good bye. A.D.M.S. informed me this morning that Lt Col Simmond is leaving this afternoon. [struck]	
	26.7.16		Routine work	
	27.7.16		Extract from A.D.M.S. orders 27.7.16 "The 38 (Welsh) division will be relieved by the 20th division on the "25th & 29th inst." No. 131 Field Ambulance will hand over the Corps Operating	

O/C Muirhead Lt/Col
O/C 131 Fond Ambulance

WAR DIARY
or
INTELLIGENCE SUMMARY.

Army Form C. 2118.

Place	Date	Hour	Summary of Events and Information	Remarks and references to Appendices
AUTHIE	27.7.16		"Station and Divisional Rest Station at AUTHIE to be a Field Ambulance of the 20th Division on the afternoon of the 28th inst. The Ambulance will remain at the Divisional Rest Station until ordered to entrain." Advance Parks from the 3 Field Ambulances, 20th Division are being sent to each Ambulance of the 38th (Welsh) Division today, 27th instant to make themselves familiar with the forward area. Every ambulance and information will be given to them. Order for time of march for entrainments will be issued later. Field Ambulances will be associated with Brigades as on previous occasions on the line of march in order of march billeting and latrines. Accommodation may be available in the hands by which Field Ambulances will travel for some patients able to proceed to the bus area. O/C 131 Field Ambulance will select so slight cases able to march now at the D.R.S who also will be held in readiness to	McMurtrie Lt Col O/C 131 Field Ambulance

Army Form C. 2118.

WAR DIARY
or
INTELLIGENCE SUMMARY.
(Erase heading not required.)

Instructions regarding War Diaries and Intelligence Summaries are contained in F. S. Regs., Part II. and the Staff Manual respectively. Title pages will be prepared in manuscript.

Place	Date	Hour	Summary of Events and Information	Remarks and references to Appendices
AUTHIE	27/7/16		to proceed. All men should have baths and clean underclothing.	
			S.D.M.S. VIII. Corps and A.D.M.S. XIV Corps visited C.O.S & D.R.S	
			A.M.S. + D.A.D.M.S. XV also visited C.O.S + D.R.S	
			Apparently the Sanit. Ambulance from XV. Corps is not going to run	
			C.O.S. and D.R.S. An advance party from 16. 60. F.A. Came to inspect	
			the C.O.S. and an advance party from 61st F.A. Came to inspect the	
			D.R.S.	
	28/7/16		1 Man on Sanitary orderly sent to Offr attached Advance Depot. C.A.V.D.H.S. (A.S.M.S. order).	
			1 N.C.O. & 5 men taking from 35 C.C.S. - 2 Men doing fatigue work with 44 C.C.S	
			and also late Offr (Lt Col MacDougall) 35 C.C.S drawn attention to the excellent bearing	
			in which Lt Corp Brown and his party carried out their duties at C.C.S.	
			at 12 noon handed over C.O.S. to 61st F.A. (20th division)	
			copy	
			40/c 131 Field Ambulance	
			"a gun will be attached to 115 Brigade for the move". (A.S.M.S. order 28.7.16)	
			N. Kenneth White Lt Col	
			O/c 131 Field Ambulance	

WAR DIARY
or
INTELLIGENCE SUMMARY

Army Form C. 2118.

Place	Date	Hour	Summary of Events and Information	Remarks and references to Appendices
AUTHIE	29/7/16		"Commanding 131 Field Ambulance" to arrange to evacuate sick from 115 Brigade trains and evacuate to "COIN" (received 29.7.16)(copy A.D.M.S. note). — Sent on M.O. to see Capt. Swan from M.O. 11 S.W.B — he has Phlemosi Tonsilitis" — late diagnosed by A.D.M.S. he sent him to F.A. as too unwell he is still enough to take with us! — I applied to send him to C.C.S. — am sending him to F.A. at COIN. belonging to 20 division. Handed over to R.S. to Co. 9 A. (20 division). 115 Brigade report 4 Ambulance to follow this their Regt's early tomorrow morning. Am sending 3 Motor Ambulance wagons and one Mule Ambulance. Along of Motor Ambulances been afterwards round (M.A. & M.S) to follow & pick up dumped stragglers as on previous occasion.	
	30/7/16		Complied with 4 D.M.S. orders concerning milk & Horn Ambulances following Rgts; things looked satisfactorily, although we only have G.S. M. Ambulances and ...	Dunmall Lt Col O/c 131 Field Ambulance

WAR DIARY
or
INTELLIGENCE SUMMARY.

Army Form C. 2118.

Place	Date	Hour	Summary of Events and Information	Remarks and references to Appendices
AUTHIE	30/7/16		Went to CANDAS to inspect G.O.C. 115 Brigade as to any instruction after reaching detraining station St OMER. G.O.C. gives me permission, if I am satisfied all is well, to take away M.Tm ambulance in a much as we only have three. That is him and the three M.A's O/out trains for St OMER with sent love as M.O. in charge, to deal with "stragglers" at the Stn. Sec.	
	31/7/16		Breakfast 4 A.M. March in marches 5.30 A.M. march out to CANDAS at 5.45 A.M. arrive CANDAS 12.30 P.M. A very hot day so that marching was easy with numerous halts. In addition to unit we brought with us. 50. "markers" to join their units from D.R.S. We are to entrain at 13.51. for St OMER from CANDAS.	

Confidential Vol 9
Aug. 1916.

War Diary
131 Field Ambulance
38th (Welsh) Division
for
August (1/31) 1916

(Volume IX)

COMMITTEE FOR THE
MEDICAL HISTORY OF THE WAR
Date -5 OCT. 1915

WAR DIARY
or
INTELLIGENCE SUMMARY.
(Erase heading not required.)

Army Form C. 2118.

Place	Date	Hour	Summary of Events and Information	Remarks and references to Appendices
MILLAIN	1.8.16		After leaving CANDAS yesterday at 13.51 reaching HAZEBROUCK at 7.20 P.M. on supposed destination then ordered to continue our journey by train to ST. OMER. arrived there at 8.30 P.M. Tea provided in station. After detraining. Proceeded to march to MILLAIN and arrived there at 1.30 A.M. 1/8/16. After a few hours rest — field ambulance opened up — patients accommodated in our small houses in main street — and tents in rear. Visit by D.A.D.M.S. in afternoon.	
	2.8.16		Extract from A.D.M.S. order Aug 1. 1916. No. 131. Field Ambulance will move from MILLAIN to BOLLEZEELE on the 3rd August and will take over the ambulance site there. Orders also received from Brigade to march out to it on 3/8/16. Advanced party of billeting party sent to BOLLEZEELE. They return being unable to find an ambulance site there. Similarly there is no available site at VOLKERINCKHOVE. There was reported to A.D.M.S. he are unable to "endeavour to find a site in the area BOLLEZEELE — MERCKEGHEM — VOLKERINCKHOVE area — as soon a possible". In distribution of areas this F.A. must have been forgotten. Inform Brigade H.Q. that we shall not move with them tomorrow as no ambulance site has been provided. Brigade agrees.	
	3.8.16		Sent intelligence & billeting office to hunt for a site — They report a fairly suitable site at MERCKEGHEM. but had much been used as a F.A. before. Asked A.D.M.S. if we might establish ourselves there. He agrees.	O. Hanthworth Lt. Col. O/C 131 Field Ambulance

WAR DIARY or INTELLIGENCE SUMMARY

Army Form C. 2118.

Place	Date	Hour	Summary of Events and Information	Remarks and references to Appendices
MERCKEGHEM	4/8/16		Move to MERCKEGHEM. Personal kitbags in three fairly good barns. Officers' billets are inferior. Tents are put up for reception of patients. Horse & M. Transport are placed in a large field, the nearby being fair. The ground is dry & level. The site is essentially a fine weather site. It will not do for the units without considerable expenditure of money & labour on huts etc. It is not worth the expense. O/C 2nd in command and one other M.O.'s who were on duty at MINDEN POST from 1-4 P.M. on 11/7/16, attended a C.M. at 7.27 head quarters of 15' R.W.F to give evidence in a case of desertion where the accused alleged that he was at MINDEN POST A.D.S. at that time. He failed to accompany either of the M.O.'s — and neither of them accompanied the prisoner. A.D.M.S. & D.A.D.M.S. visit the unit.	
	5/8/16		Chaplain & Jackope work in general cleaning up.	
	6/8/16		Sunday. C of E service at headquarters @ 16 held at 10.30 A.M also N.C. at same place at 11.15 A.M.	
	7/8/16		Published an order that Petrol & fats are not to be used for cleaning or...	J Howells Roberts Lt. Col O/c 131 Field Ambulance

Army Form C. 2118.

WAR DIARY
or
INTELLIGENCE SUMMARY.
(Erase heading not required.)

Instructions regarding War Diaries and Intelligence Summaries are contained in F. S. Regs., Part II. and the Staff Manual respectively. Title pages will be prepared in manuscript.

Place	Date	Hour	Summary of Events and Information	Remarks and references to Appendices
MERCKEGHEM	8/8/16		A.D.M.S. orders that all pools in billeting area are to be sprinkled with Paraffin or the mineral oil.	
	9/8/16		Daily gas helmet drill commencing. A.D.M.S. orders that all pools in billeting area are to be examined for mosquito larvae & if so to be sprinkled with mineral oil.	
	10/8/16		Converted the large barn at H.Quarters of the unit into a ward - I will hold 30 Pts. Completed. Pts. are evacuated into it from Manges and for other Officers and Manges well for Officers (this was done in Nt 7.) men & high fever. Another similar barn has been found for personnel.	
	11/8/16		A.D.M.S. & A.D.M.S. visit 131 Field Ambulance to inspect P.B. & T.Sh men from 115 Brigade. A.D.M.S. inspects records of unit and express satisfaction. Divisional (Belgian) Troops, 131 F.A. win by 7 goals to nil. 131 F.A. play football against	
	12/8/16		Unit bathed at ROLLEZEELE BATHS. Lieut. LOWE R.A.M.C. relieve Lieut. PETTIGREW as M.O. to 16 Welsh during latter's absence on leave. 131 3 A. play 16 Welsh Regiment at Cricket & lose by 3 runs.	
	13/8/16		Sunday Church Parade at Headquarters. 16 Welsh C of E. 11:15 A.M. N.C. 11:30 A.M.	
	14/8/16		Sent report to A.D.M.S. concerning early history of up to march 1915 of 131. 3 A. H. Müller Roberts Lt Col. O/C 131 Field Ambulance	

Army Form C. 2118.

WAR DIARY
or
INTELLIGENCE SUMMARY.
(Erase heading not required.)

Instructions regarding War Diaries and Intelligence Summaries are contained in F. S. Regs., Part II. and the Staff Manual respectively. Title pages will be prepared in manuscript.

Place	Date	Hour	Summary of Events and Information	Remarks and references to Appendices
MERCKEGHEM	14/8/16		As I only joined the unit in May 1915 — I did not know much about it. Staff Sergt Davies — who has been in the unit since its start — supplied the necessary information. Orders received to make unit "hire standings" — I have already reported that this site (MERCKEGHEM) is not suitable for the unit. Am seeing A.D.M.S. tomorrow and will talk the matter over with him.	
	15/8/16		Routine work.	
	16/8/16		Met A.D.M.S. at Officers Corps Rest Camp at 10.15.A.M at WORMHOUDT and attended a conference with him at D.M.S Office PROVEN. Subject Sanitation. A.D.M.S. could not help me as to hire standings — nor could he say when he was likely to leave MERCHEGHEM	
	17/8/16		} Routine Work	
	18/8/16			
	19/8/16		An order received from A.D.M.S "Please send an advanced party to take over Herzeele Ostalts Lt.Col O/C 131 Field Ambulance	

2353 Wt. W2544/1454 700,000 5/15 D.D. & L. A.D.S.S./Forms/C 2118.

Army Form C. 2118.

WAR DIARY
or
INTELLIGENCE SUMMARY.
(Erase heading not required.)

Place	Date	Hour	Summary of Events and Information	Remarks and references to Appendices
MERCKEGHEM	19/8/16		Received Draining Stations from no 10 Field Ambulance A.28.a.37 hdqrs no 28.4 today. Please arrange with the G.O.E 115th Brigade for this party to proceed in the train going to POPERINGHE today. The main body will proceed forward by train. "Transport will go by road tomorrow morning completing the journey in one day and starting at 6 a.m. Further instructions for main body will be issued later." Complied with above order — but formed G.O.C. 115. Brigade head qrs & H.Q. thought arranged to send advanced party by 21 train of 10's W.R.! A.B. Consisted of 3 Officers and 19 other ranks. After this party had left — further orders were issued him on being among them. "Please send one Ambulance Car to A.28.a.3.7 at once with one Corpand and two men to take over Ambulance Stand at REIGSBURGH CHATEAU. You will also put two men in LA BELLE ALLIANCE Aid Post tonight and two men in MOROCCO Post." FARM Canal Bank and Post tonight. You will also send one officer and 26 O.R tomorrow morning to A.28.a.3.7 — 2 officers and 11 men at OUTSKIRT FARM A.D.S." 1.2.62.8 "You should then have at least — 2 officers and 11 men at OUTSKIRT FARM A.D.S." "1. Capt & 2 men at REIGSBURGH CHATEAU H.6.6.5.7." "1. Officer & 25 men at main dressing station" "4 men at Aid Post."	O H Mullerstele Lt Col OfC. 131. Field Ambulance

WAR DIARY or INTELLIGENCE SUMMARY

Army Form C. 2118.

Place	Date	Hour	Summary of Events and Information	Remarks and references to Appendices
MERCKEGHEM	19/8/16		Moved from LA BELLE ALLIANCE — had apparently been taken over by the 129.74 Ambns. A/S M.S. wire "O/C's F.A. are warned that there is a great shortage of Petrol."	
	20/8/16		Yesterday's orders for today complied with. Major DAVIES & 2 b. O.R. sent off by ration lorry with 2 b. O R. to S.a.28.a.3.7.	
			A.D.M.S. orders. No. 20. Copy no. 3. dated Aug. 19 received today — That " No. 131. Fld. Ambulance will move on the morning of the 21." to S.28.a.3.7 taking on the Fld. Ambulance Set from the 10th Fld. Ambulance. Transport to move by road starting at 6 a.m.; personnel by train, to arrive at 12 midday on the 20th inst — an advanced party will take over the A.D.S. at LABRIQUE. (The A.D.S. went last night) ASMS from Ham leave MERCKEGHEM at — Extract of ambln. orders from POPERINGE.! "There is no station at 9 A.M. on Monday for POPERINGE. — BOLLEZEELE is the nearest. MERCKEGHEM. — BOLLEZEELE & the nearest.	
	21/8/16		The unit marched en masse at 7.30 A.M. ready to march off at 7.45 A.M. to BOLLEZEELE to entrain by the 9 A.M. train to POPERINGE. Reached latter place 12.30 Noon. Marched to S.A.28.a.3.7. Map 28. Arrived there 1.30 p.m.	Handed over to Lt.Col. J. Hurd. bred. owner O/C 131 Fld. Ambulance

WAR DIARY
or
INTELLIGENCE SUMMARY.
(Erase heading not required.)

Army Form C. 2118.

Place	Date	Hour	Summary of Events and Information	Remarks and references to Appendices
Map Sheet 28 A.28.a.3.7	21/8/16		Have Transport left MERCHTEM at 6.30 a.m. by road. A.T.M.S. unclm to present 6 a.m. yesterday has not carried out — omissi ldrs return later. "main body" to stores fast-pending further relief and awtn. "you" "main body" with move early on Sunday. Transport by road — personnel by "rail". The 10: J.A. do not hand on until noon tomorrow 22/8/16 — although the A.D.S. at Gutschut Farm, the Ambulance Stand at REIGSBURGH. CHATEAU¹ Map 28 and the outlying post at B.28.6.0.2 where heavier are, last night. The 131: J.A. will deal with all cars admitted to A.28.a.3.7. — The main dressing station taking with them. Recovery away a good deal of material such as Tables, bunks, bath or Kittle stores. I shunt on the multi up to A.D.M.S. The instructions of him (131) J.A. are to leave all equipments on the site, turn him to him he has made a great number of "tent stag" — & leave them which for the benefit of the incoming Unit. — So we reach a new side light! & begin once again to include Table, bunks & so on. I visit the A.D.S. this evening. Can go here every evening at 9 o'clock to evacuate the sick & wounded. As for a finish all movement must be made at night, so as not to attract the notice of enemy aircraft.	H. Hamilton [?] Lt. Col. O/C 131st Field Ambulance

2353 Wt. W2544/1454 700,000 5/15 D. D. & L. A.D.S.S./Forms/C. 2118.

WAR DIARY or INTELLIGENCE SUMMARY

Army Form C. 2118.

Place	Date	Hour	Summary of Events and Information	Remarks and references to Appendices
Map Sheet 28. a.28.a.37	22/8/16		"Jack on" J.A. Sit. from 10" J.A. at a.28.a.3.7. – L.E. main dressing station. Visit by A.D.M.S & D.A.D.M.S. Sent Major Davis to 129 J.A. to take charge during absence of O/C (Major Edwards). The 10" J.A. had an outbreak of Glanders among their horses. The field occupied by them is out of bounds. As a precautionary measure he was ordered to hand over all our horses to the 10" J.A. in return to take away their transport. But they are to use them for work. Their men-horses are to be left with their A.S.C. in charge in quarantine. If we want them to work he was to borrow from the 129 J.A. About 15 minutes after our horses (with A.S.C.) left for new site g to "J.A. & late order came to say that each unit is to stick to its own horses. Our horses need not go. Unfortunately they have gone. Visit by D.D.M.S and later by D.A.D.V.S. 38" W[est] Division. Later to inspect horse &c.	
	23/8/16		Routine work.	
	24/8/16			
	25/8/16		Visit by A.D.M.S. & D.A.D.M.S. to examine P.B. & T.U. men from various units. In future the A.D.M.S. will visit this unit every Tuesday & Friday at 10 o'clock A.M. for this purpose.	

N. Harrill Roberts Lt Col
O/C 131 Field Ambulance

WAR DIARY or INTELLIGENCE SUMMARY

Army Form C. 2118.

Place	Date	Hour	Summary of Events and Information	Remarks and references to Appendices
a.28.a.3.7.	26/8/16		First with fly of 7.0.R. relieved Capt. Beaton Evans and similar party at A.D.S. Sanitary Section Officer (Capt. Anthony) visited and to see about pus hive hive. The old one occupied by 10. J.A. having been condemned. Unfortunately the owner is away. I am to interview him tomorrow, and arrange an appointment with Claims Officer.	
	27/8/16		A.D.M.S. & O/C Sanitary Section called and are taking Capt. Percy Pearce as guide to A.D.S. to see. Gen. Prudermon (10 J.A) pointed out to us that this was only to be done at night — so on hat — he attract attention of enemy observer. He reported from 6.A.S.M.S. He is anxious to see the funsord area in day light. Claim Officer calls again. He sees the farm about him standings, he decides to ask the A.D.D.S. if the field lately used by 10 J.A. std. horse guarantee — if not store standings will be made there. Claim Officer will wire me A.D.M.S opinion tonight.	
	28/8/16		Wire received from Claim Officer to say that A.D.U.S. will not guarantee the field referred to utility. It is therefore decided to make standings in a field adjoining the road leading to a.28.a.3.7. attending e.m. to give evidence re some Battery S.M. 122. Dates N.A. was absconding from 131. Field Ambulance at MERCKEGHEM on 19.8.16. visited A.D.S. O/ Hmith Nephews Lt.Col O/c 131. Field Ambulance	

Army Form C. 2118.

WAR DIARY
or
INTELLIGENCE SUMMARY.
(Erase heading not required.)

Place	Date	Hour	Summary of Events and Information	Remarks and references to Appendices
a 26/a.37	29/8/16		A.D.M.S. attended 131. F.A. to inspect P.B. & T.U. men. A.A.Q.M.G. (Sanitation) & O/C Sanitary inspection accompanied A.D.M.S. - & inspected the 131 F.A. all seem very complimentary.	
	30/8/16		Wet day. Gas alert on. A very trying time in which every heavy shower an accumulates an leakings badly - & observed all the huts in which perused an accumulated in barn to a large leak. They are be unroofed. The P.B. are accommodated in the hut meant for P.B. - them sleeping even now empty quite dry - there are too many men unfit before the units set in the same applies to this Unit & will again the intimation on this subj. Stone Standings an flooded -	
	31/8/16		Pay day. Capt. Red Benson Evan R.A.M.C. to visit Unfm from R.A.M.C. Sent in accordance with A.D.M.S. MD's of 9.10 S.W.R. + 16 R.W.J. to them orders which have instruction to return MD's of OXELAENE. on Small box respirators Officers are doing a course of instruction at OXELAENE. Proceeding with times hour Standings	

O H Mulhollands Lt Col
O/C 131 Fd. Ambulance

139/134

38th Divn.

131st Field Ambulance.

Sept 1916

COMMITTEE FOR THE
MEDICAL HISTORY OF THE WAR
Date 30 OCT. 1916

From O/C 131st Field Ambulance.
38th (Welsh) Division.

To D.A.G.
3rd Echelon.

War Diary September 1st to 30th 1916.

The above is forwarded you herewith.

30-9-1916

J. ____ Major
LIEUT. COL. R.A.M.C
O/C 131st FIELD AMBULANCE
38TH (WELSH) DIVISION.

Confidential

War Diary
131 Field Ambulance
38 (Welsh) Division

for September 1st - 30 - 1916

(Volume X)

Army Form C. 2118.

WAR DIARY
or
INTELLIGENCE SUMMARY.
(Erase heading not required.)

Instructions regarding War Diaries and Intelligence Summaries are contained in F. S. Regs., Part II. and the Staff Manual respectively. Title pages will be prepared in manuscript.

Place	Date	Hour	Summary of Events and Information	Remarks and references to Appendices
Mapsheet 28 A.28.a.3.7.	1.9.16		A.D.M.S. 38 (Welsh) Division visited Camp to examine P.B. & T.U. men. In future these examinations will be made every Tuesday morning at 10 o'clock instead of Fridays & Saturdays. O.C. Camp Commandant of D & E Camps D & E. and A. 4 & 5. I made first inspection today.	
	2.9.16		Accompanied A.D.M.S. and O/C Sanitary Section on tour of inspection of Camps.	
	3.9.16		Expected visit of A.D.M.S. to Camp (ostponed) — made visit to two last Camps D & E, which are very bad.	
	4.9.16		The temporary huts standing occupied by this unit are very wet owing to recent heavy rain. They cannot be drained because railway embankment cuts across & there are no culverts. w/ O/C 129. J.A. to ask if we may stand our horses in part of his land — a her in mine average than 129 aspects. Permission cordially given. Had D & E Camps with A.D.M.S. hrs office. Sent Pirie — joined the unit.	
	5.9.16		Huts taken over to standing at 129. J.A. until our new standing are finished. A.D.M.S. not to until to examine P.R. men, owing to some mistake many did not turn up — from 110. Bicycle	
	6.9.16		A.D.M.S. again out. Came to inspect P.O. men that did not turn up yesterday	

① K Mellwater Lt Col
O/C 131 Field Ambulance

WAR DIARY or INTELLIGENCE SUMMARY

Army Form C. 2118.

Place	Date	Hour	Summary of Events and Information	Remarks and references to Appendices
Map sheet 28 A.28.a.3.7	7/9/16		Sent M.O. (Lieut Wynn Jones) to D.A.C. to relieve Lieut Houston on leave. Visited A.D.S. It was subjected to very heavy bombardment yesterday — about 150 shells fell in its neighbourhood — apparently trying to locate batteries in vacinity.	
	8/9/16		Visited Camps of Tranquil 16. welsh 10th welsh + 17th R W F. Sent S.S. Doak to relieve S.S. Pearce at A D S	
	9/9/16		Sent Capt. Perry R.A.M.C to relieve Capt. Lowe R.A.M.C at A.D.S Ethad. from A.D.M.S's order "a recall to be kept of every case of men evacuated to c.c.s". Visited all camps in my area.	
	10/9/16		Sunday. N.C. senr at 129 F.A.; No C. of E. Service Ethad from A.D.M.S' order "Field ambulance will in future be in possession of 150 stretchers". also will now have Standings — also	
	11/9/16		Routine work — good progress is being made with preparations for winter. general repair of huts and "Detail on M.O. to visit Trench Mortar Battery to innoculate men of unit". Ethad A.D.M.S orders.	
	12/9/16		G.O.C 38 (welsh) Division Maj Gen. Blackader DSO visited ASM S. inspected unit. and was good enough to express pleasure & satisfaction with state of affairs at 131 F.A.	

O.H. Milbastutt Lt-Col
O/c. 131. field. Ambulance

WAR DIARY
or
INTELLIGENCE SUMMARY.

(Erase heading not required.)

Army Form C. 2118.

Instructions regarding War Diaries and Intelligence Summaries are contained in F. S. Regs., Part II. and the Staff Manual respectively. Title pages will be prepared in manuscript.

Place	Date	Hour	Summary of Events and Information	Remarks and references to Appendices
Map Sheet 2C A 25.a.37	13/9/16		Lieut. Welph. R.A.M.C. transferred by request of A.D.M.S. to 4 M.A.C. worked (accompanied by Lieut Lowe R.A.M.C.) A.D.S. and near camp in Spectors by daylight of neighbourhood. On a rule an visits are made at night so as not to draw Artillery fire. To-day there were no German aircraft about. Atmosphere being too hazy for observation purposes.	
	14/9/16		Pay day. General routine work.	
	15/9/16		Lieut R.H. Mills, Robert proceeded on leave Monday, his leave commencing on the 16 inst. Large "destyne Party" worked all day in our "Bone Yard/type" at the camp drain cleared. A commencement was made of to a laying of timed Roads.	
	16/9/16		Church Parade: Church of England in Church Army Hut at 11 a.m. Non-conformist at 129# field Ambulance at 10.45 a.m.	
	17/9/16		A.D.M.S. visited field Ambulance & introduced near #A.D.M.S. Captain Waddle D.S.O. (S.M.).	
	18/9/16		A.D.M.S. visited field ambulance to present Ribbons of the Military Medal to Lance Cpl. E.B. Thomas. The A.D.M.S. addressed the Officers and men. In accordance with A.D.M.S. instructions which were as follows. Please inspect all ante-fal arrangements at A.D.S. Dressing Station, Bearer Relay Posts and Blanket, Cushions at Dumps etc, and report to me on their condition. I complied with the order on the night of 18/9/16 and a certificate thereof.	

J. Stewart Major

Army Form C. 2118.

WAR DIARY
or
INTELLIGENCE SUMMARY.
(Erase heading not required.)

Instructions regarding War Diaries and Intelligence Summaries are contained in F.S. Regs., Part II. and the Staff Manual respectively. Title pages will be prepared in manuscript.

Place	Date	Hour	Summary of Events and Information	Remarks and references to Appendices
Map. Sheet 28. A 28. a 3.7.	19/9/16		A.D.M.S. visited Field Ambulance for the purpose of selecting a Guard or men not fit for trench duties. He was accompanied by Captain Tyrell A.D.M.S. 8th corps. A.D.M.S. inspected camp and informed one that it was my duty to visit the R.E. Park of obtain what material required for new Horse standings and constructional work generally. If not able to obtain the same a report in writing was to be made to A.D.M.S. Visited R.E. Park & saw Lieut Bazgill. He kindly promised that he would supply material daily for the next days work. Then proceeded to see steeping kept.	
	20/9/16		The ground of the Field Ambulance area were completed to day and no new Horse-standings obtained from R.E. 150 yards of "Duck boards" were laid & Rubble was obtained from BRIELEN and placed near bridge.	
	21/9/16		Great progress was this day made on the New Horse Standings. Many fatigue parties were detailed to clean drains on each side of the road leading from the Field Ambulance to main road. Captain Sir Parry R.A.M.C. was detailed in accordance with A.D.M.S. orders to attend a class in "Defences for Gas Masons" to be held by Chemical Officer 2nd Army at OXALIANCE; to details will last two and a half days.	
	22/9/16		A.D.M.S. visited this day & a supply team with a change of clothing arrangement were made to bathe 50 men of the unit per day to remove from an officer of the 10th Welsh from the A request was received from A.D.M.S. Wales Div. to remove from an officer of the 10th Welsh from the from McFadden C.C.S. the information could be obtained from the A.D.M.S.'s office but upon enquiring at D.R.S. PROVEN the despite information was obtained.	
	23/9/16		Days amount of work put in on the new Horse Standings. Having completed visited all the Camps and supper lines within Map reference sheet 28. G.S.a.c: A28: A29.A30. Camps D&E.	

J. Kearns Biepan

Army Form C. 2118.

WAR DIARY
or
INTELLIGENCE SUMMARY.
(Erase heading not required.)

Instructions regarding War Diaries and Intelligence
Summaries are contained in F.S. Regs., Part II.
and the Staff Manual respectively. Title pages
will be prepared in manuscript.

Place	Date	Hour	Summary of Events and Information	Remarks and references to Appendices
Map Sheet 28. A.28.a37.	24/9/16		Church Parades, C.E. at Church tent at 11.a.m. R.C. in recreation at 129 Field Ambulance 10.45 a.m. Lieut. J. Mima-Tones R.A.M.C. this day returned to the unit, having been in temporary medical charge of D.A.C. for fourteen days.	
	25/9/16		Spt. Major G.B. Lee returned from R.M: C.C.S. with a certificate that he was unfit for duty. Captain J. Beveren Jones R.A.M.C. returned from A.8. Gen R.A.M.C. at A.B.S. Completed the surgery & nurse Markings. New pit are shafts commenced. New Incinerator nearly completed. Colonel R.N. Mills-Retant returned from leave.	
	26/9/16		Commenced work in addition to time road. Opening of time Bandages commenced. Lieut. Mills said when required addressed to A.D.M.S. office for duty.	
	27/9/16		Colonel R.H. Mills-Retant proceeded to 35 Level Stretchers. New incinerator completed. Intended for winter. S. Mary act 35 Level Stretchers. Lieut. S.B. Mortimer-Land R.A.M.C. proceeded to England on 10 days leave.	
	28/9/16		Commenced new Bandages for rate. tents.	
	29/9/16		Horse Bandages completed. Issued all upright, horns straps wire complete tubes tents. A.D.M.S. & D.A.D.M.S. visited field ambulance.	
	30/16		Drained leaves to new Horse Bandage, erected 5 tents for A.S.C. personnel in field behind farm. Completed the roofing of the period huts.	

J. O'Bacew Major R.A.M.C.
for C.O. 131st Field Ambulance
35 Petit Gevarenne.

Confidential
Oct. 1916

War Diary
131, Field Ambulance
38th (Welsh) Division
for
October 1916
(1st to 31st inclusive)

(Volume XI)

14d/1815

COMMITTEE FOR THE
MEDICAL HISTORY OF THE WAR
Date — 9 DEC. 1916

WAR DIARY or INTELLIGENCE SUMMARY

Army Form C. 2118.

Place	Date	Hour	Summary of Events and Information	Remarks and references to Appendices
MAP. SHEETS 20 ADFa 37.	1/10/16		Chanel Smades.	
		11 A.M.	C.E. Church Parade at 11 A.M.	
		11.30 A.M.	NON-CON. 129 Field Ambulance 11.30 a.m.	
	2/10/16		Accompanied by Capt S.W. DARBY. R.A.M.C. visited No 3 Mobile Laboratory and viewed thrown cases of WIELS disease, photos of the spirochaete and the post-mortem appearances of the organs of a person before autopsy examination. Lieut ADV. SOPHIE allowed Lieut J.W. WYNNE JONES at A.D.S. Lieut J. WYNNE JONES proceeded this day to ENGLAND upon expiration of his contract. Notice proceeded with in the District Courts Martial & addition to leave head. Now received from ADMS's Office instructions that no further cases were to be evacuated to D.R.S. at present. The accommodation having been fully taken up. Drawing of House standings nearly completed.	
	3/10/16		ADMS visited the units this day for the purpose of examining men thought to be unfit for duty in the forward area. Completed the interviewing of Officers Maid. Captain S.W. DARBY R.A.M.C. lectured to the white personnel of the unit on the history & development of the precautions taken to safeguard troops during a "gas attack." The Lecture was admirable in every respect and was listened to with profound attention.	
	4/10/16		Heavy rain interfered with the carrying out of ill. Vespers. Captain SM Darcy gave a practical demonstration to A. Section, in the method of using the Small Box Respirator. Received a quantity of material from BRC in order to complete the furnishing of the Officers Maid.	
	5/10/16		Work continued in the addition to the "Lewin Maid". ADMS & DADMS visited the unit. The showers of the camp were opened for use & cleaned.	

J.C. Bernard Major

WAR DIARY
or
INTELLIGENCE SUMMARY.

(Erase heading not required.)

Army Form C. 2118.

Instructions regarding War Diaries and Intelligence Summaries are contained in F. S. Regs., Part II. and the Staff Manual respectively. Title pages will be prepared in manuscript.

Place	Date	Hour	Summary of Events and Information	Remarks and references to Appendices
MAP.SHEET 28. A 28. a. 3. 7.	6/10/16		Completed the issuing of the Small Arms Respirators. All men of the unit have now been given instruction in their use. Visited the R.E. Depot D'agenal material. CRE very kindly offered to grant the field ambulance an order to me for temporarily what material was required.	
"	7/10/16		Main drain of camp cleaned & repaired. A.D.M.S. return from leave tonight at O/C 131.F.A. (who has been doing duty as A.D.M.S.) return to his unit.	
"	8/10/16		Sunday — Church services as usual. Major J.C. Brown (2nd in command) goes on leave.	
"	9/10/16		Routine work — G.R.O. 1242. re begin republished	
"	10/10/16		A.D.M.S. visited ambulance to inspect P.B. & T.U. men. O/C Sanitary Section accompanied by D.A.D.M.S. 7th. Corps visits the unit.	
"	11/10/16		Small Arm respiration tests. 2nd hand. McFarland against unit in application of leave.	
"	12/10/16		Pay day — Unit (including various outlying details) paid. No. 48899 Pte F. Barry (unsound condition) to leave to be posted to a home unit under instructions from War Office.	
"	13/10/16		One Case ? Cerebro Spinal Meningitis admitted.	

O. Hamilton Smith, Lt Col
O/C 131 Field Ambulance

Army Form C. 2118.

WAR DIARY
or
INTELLIGENCE SUMMARY.
(Erase heading not required.)

Instructions regarding War Diaries and Intelligence Summaries are contained in F. S. Regs., Part II. and the Staff Manual respectively. Title pages will be prepared in manuscript.

Place	Date	Hour	Summary of Events and Information	Remarks and references to Appendices
Map Sheet 2 A.26.a.37	14/10/16		Applied by A.D.M.S. to indent on R.E. for 6 huts to replace wooden framework (previously sent). Huts on acquired for housing personnel. Complied with request. Acting Staff Sergt Major D. Edwards promoted to permanent rank from Sergt W.T. authority received A.S.C. 28.9.16	
	15.10.16.		Capt: T.R. Evan R.A.M.C. taken over medical charge of 15th R.W.F. vice M.O. (Capt ....) Stay is on leave). Sunday, Church Service as usual.	
	16/10/16		Extract from C.R.O. No. 74 dft. 13.10.16. (41) Precaution against Syphilis published.	
	17/10/16		A.D.M.S. unit weekly visit to examine P.B. + T.U. Cases	
	18/10/16		New M case of ? Tetanus admitted to this F.A. 1st one annual in B.E.F.	
	19/10/16		Routine work — Major Davis returned from leave.	
	20/10/16		Corps (VIII) Commander inspected unit today accompanied by D.D.M.S + A.D.M.S. stated He was good enough to say things were very nice.	
	21/10/16		2. More huts arrived	

D Hillcoat Lt. Col
O/c 131 Field Ambulance

WAR DIARY
or
INTELLIGENCE SUMMARY.

(Erase heading not required.)

Army Form C. 2118.

Place	Date	Hour	Summary of Events and Information	Remarks and references to Appendices
Map Sheet 28 A.28.a.3.7	22.10.16		Sunday — Church Parade as usual	
	23.10.16		Extract from A.D.M.S. order:— "The kits of patients in wards, gas helmets and hot respirators will be arranged on the walls &" "floor of each ward in a precisely uniform manner. It both gas helmets and hot respirators" "are not brought by the sick on admission to Field Ambulance officers commanding will" "be informed." "Drainage. The drainage of all ambulance sites will be given particular attention" "and every drain will be traced from its origin to its outfall in the lowest pond in" "the stream within reasonable distance so that at no point will water stagnate." "As regards the drainage of this Ambulance I am [?] out that all surface drainage" "has to pass through a Culvert under a Railroad about 50 yards N of main" "dressing station. Satisfactory drainage cannot be obtained without lowering the" "Culvert 1 — in 2 feet. There is ample fall" on the other side of the railway." "M.T. has been recommenced to the A.D.M.S. approval.	
	24.10.16		Routine work. A.D.M.S. examines P.B's & T.U's.	
	25.10.16		Weather very bad — much work done in connection with drains.	

N.H.Willoughby Lt. Col.
O/c 131. Field Ambulance

WAR DIARY
or
INTELLIGENCE SUMMARY.

Army Form C. 2118.

Place	Date	Hour	Summary of Events and Information	Remarks and references to Appendices
Map Sheet 28 A26.a.37	26.10.16		Pay day. D.D.M.S. visits unit and inspects change &c.	
	27.10.16		Routine work	
	28.10.16		D.D.M.S. & A.D.M.S. had usual & inspect cases of Trench foot	
	29.10.16		Sunday - usual Ad.Com Service. Visited RICKSROOVG CHATEAU to examine dug out, which is taking to pieces	
	30.10.16		Visited C.R.E (with approval of A.D.M.S) to report bad state of road leading from Ambulance to main road & to ask for 2nd dug out for RICKSROOVG CHATEAU &c. C.R.E. infinitely out. A.D.M.S will take matter up	
	31.10.16		A.D.M.S. visits unit to examine P.B's & T.U.S.	

N H Willoughby Lt Col
O/c 131. 3rd Ambulance

140/862

38th Div.

131st Field Ambulance.

Nov. 1916

COMMITTEE FOR THE
MEDICAL HISTORY OF THE WAR
Date −3 JAN. 1917

Confidential   Vol 12

War Diary

131 Field Ambulance

38 (Welsh) Division

for

November 1916
(1 – 30th inclusive)

(Volume XIII)

Army Form C. 2118.

WAR DIARY
or
INTELLIGENCE SUMMARY.
(Erase heading not required.)

Instructions regarding War Diaries and Intelligence Summaries are contained in F. S. Regs., Part II. and the Staff Manual respectively. Title pages will be prepared in manuscript.

Place	Date	Hour	Summary of Events and Information	Remarks and references to Appendices
Map Sheet 28 A 28-a 37	1916 Nov 1.		Captain Buchan joined 131 Bristol Ambulance from 70 F.A. – Took advantage of fine day to open drains and roads. – There is a lot to do owing to bad weather.	
	2.		Attended lecture by Capt: Stratton, instructor of Catering at D. Camp. Took with me Quartermaster, Sergt. Major and Corp. Cook – very instructive lecture. Visited A.D.S in evening. Everything satisfactory.	
	3.		Routine work	
	4.		Capt: Buchan relieving Capt: Low at A.D.S. Capt: Parry went on leave. Capt: Parry's return to last allows latter's return to main army station during Capt Parry's leave. Sent McFarland attached to Cont: mental to D. Camp to give evidence in case of Capt: Evans a patient evacuated through 131 F.A. – a few weeks ago.	
	5.		A.D.M.S. & O/C Sanitary Section 16' Divi: visit the unit. Any case of talk to admission arriving at N0+29 F.A. will be sent to N0 131. – (A.D.M.S. order) 5/11/16	
	6.		D.M.S. notes unit: reported to A.D.M.S. that we can accommodate 99 Publish (comfortably) normal maximum – emergency – 150 patients.	

M. Walrond, Lt. Cl.
o/c 131. British Ambulance

A.D.S.S. Forms/C. 2118.

Army Form C. 2118.

WAR DIARY
or
INTELLIGENCE SUMMARY.
(Erase heading not required.)

Instructions regarding War Diaries and Intelligence Summaries are contained in F.S. Regs., Part II. and the Staff Manual respectively. Title pages will be prepared in manuscript.

Place	Date	Hour	Summary of Events and Information	Remarks and references to Appendices
Maps Sheet 28 A28a.37	6/4/16		"Some cases Conjunctivitis or running from P.U.O. (Trench fever) in this area." "All forwd. to have hot skin. Have jaths. Plus examine all associates" "revacant cases and keep outs of the Total number examined and re-" "admitts of cases affected." (A.D.M.S. ends. 5/11/16). This was done with ____ Nil. ____ In fulm: "Officer requiring evacuation to a C.C.S. will be sent to" "No 46. C.C.S. PROVEN." (A.D.M.S ordr. 6/11/16). "Do enable P.M.O's to give hot food to sick men in the forward area" "For particularly at night, O.C.'s India Ambulances will maintain an" "adequate supply of ten, cocoa, soya, milk & soup Equiag or fins with re-" "adequate supply of ten, cocoa, soya, milk & soup Equiag or fins with re-" "supplied to A.D.M.S., and issued to P.M.O's of Divs (units on demand)" "Complied." (A.D.M.S end. 6/4/16)	
	7/4/16		Weather Continues fine. Got sand bags on dug-out at R.A. and foot and CHATEAU REIGSBOURG and ruttling and long wahner array. Am asking wooden Sone at the CHATEAU. Am fencing in to stop dogs out to office (front out) — we can draftud fatigue parts to latter places to re-ewd. and repair with the enemies consent of work at Head Quarter, apart the men owing to the enemies amount of work at Head Quarter, apart work, cutting drains & putting in new huts, &c	O.Neille Ostoh Lt. Cot O/C 181 Field Ambulance

WAR DIARY or INTELLIGENCE SUMMARY

Army Form C. 2118.

Place	Date	Hour	Summary of Events and Information	Remarks and references to Appendices
Map Sheet 2b A.26.a.37	8/4/16		Captain Donovan Evan O.Mel. of this unit doing Temporary duty with R.w.F brought in at 12.15 AM suffering from Appendicitis — evacuated to 46 C.C.S. Operated on. Same date. (on in-lying M.O. in Major Davis & did same.) Condition satisfactory. Yesterday morning accompanied & reported to duty. First & Quartermaster Cpr reports for duty with the unit. Very heavy rain during last 36 hours. The stream about 100 yds North of the camp rose 6–9 feet. The camp is a veritable Quagmire. With a scarcity of winter camp, drainage will be difficult. ER	
	9/4/16		Still digging out. Taken to REIGSBOORG CHATEAU and fatigue party 6 men to F.J. and Sandbags. 3 men sent to Pontax Sandbaggins at R.A. and post.	
	10/4/16		Pay day — visited A.D.S. — CHATEAU & R.A. and post. Gun Batt. 5 Cans of dynamite sent in by Black Watch Labor Batt: also lab / sub. retired from the Somme and is to be headed at P.Camp.	
	11/4/16		Mortuary work. Made A.S.S. work on dug-out providing satisfactory at REIGSBOORG and R.A. and post. O'Mulleran Lt-Col O/C 131 Field Ambulance	

O'Mulleran Lt-Col
O/C 131 Field Ambulance

WAR DIARY
or
INTELLIGENCE SUMMARY.
(Erase heading not required.)

Army Form C. 2118.

Instructions regarding War Diaries and Intelligence Summaries are contained in F. S. Regs., Part II. and the Staff Manual respectively. Title pages will be prepared in manuscript.

Place	Date	Hour	Summary of Events and Information	Remarks and references to Appendices
Mop Sheet 28 A28a37	12/4/16		Visited A.D.S and CHATEAU REIGERSBOURG and R.A and 105th Sektor today. Program of being ready with new dug out to replace old one.	
	13/4/16		1 N.C.O. & 19 men in ambulance with A.D.M.S instructions sent as working party to R.E. at ESSEX FARM — to be an emergency ghost forward in case repair or these ground having to many of the roads out.	
	14/4/16		A.D.M.S took away to warm P.A. + V.P.M. an advance party, 1 N.C.O & 8 men to establish a Corps Scabies Camp Plus. Major Davis & Quartermaster B.S.M. with he on to establish a Corps Scabies station — he is to proceed to visit the site. Major Davis was instructor to S.O.C.C.S. at HAZEBROUCK. In 3 days instruction I N.C.O & 19 men were in headquarters from Canal Bank (Lieut Aubrey, working party, Major Asten, with Mr. Alden and Mr 25th Army) (On Scabies Major Davis proceeded with first to establish Corps Scabies Party of (proceed yesterday) to WORMHOUDT next to Northants Party at D.D.S. — and on same day he (Major D) went to Northants Station at Ninen first occupied by A section of	
	15/4/16		C.C.S for 3 days instruction — gave general instruction on & headquarters — J in 3 days aquired instruction —	
	16/4/16		Visited D.R.S at WORMHOUDT — on same line, a Smetan instructor was totally establishing Scabies Station in same line, a Smetan instructor was totally at REGNIER LE CLERQUE — Last May (1916) — M. Lt Col 11th Army Corps. O/C 131 Ambulance	

Army Form C. 2118.

WAR DIARY
or
INTELLIGENCE SUMMARY.
(Erase heading not required.)

Place	Date	Hour	Summary of Events and Information	Remarks and references to Appendices
Map Sheet 28 A 22.a.3.7	16/11/16		Captain Parry returned from leave. Lieut — — — — — — left unit and reported for duty at 50 C.C.S.	
	17/11/16		Captain Dunlop reports for duty with 131. F.A. from 50. C.C.S. 1 N.C.O & 12 bearers to 3 wheeled stretcher report temporary to Staff Captain 114th Brigade at Headquarters on Canal Bank for duty there tonight. Visits A.D.S.	
	18/11/16		We evacuate D.R.S. at WORMHOUDT. — 2 Officers and 23 O.R. return to main dressing station — leaving 1 N.C.O + 1 Private in charge of S.R.S. until it is taken over by another division. 1. N.C.O + 12 bearers return to Headquarters from Canal Bank having been on duty during last night's visit.	
	19.11.16		First Pine A 15th C.R. form Party 1 N.C.O + 19 men again report for duty to O/C Machine Gun Farm on wake on Canal Bank.	
	20.11.16		Sergt Major Fee evacuated to 46 C.C.S. (V.D.H) handed over S.R.S. WORMHOUDT to 39th Division — & made Captain Superintendent returning to main dressing station & bringing the N.C.O & O.R. Man left in charge with him. (1) H Smith Auts Lt/Col O/C 131 Field Ambulance	

2353 Wt. W25141/1454 700,000 5/15 D. D. & L. A.D.S.S./Forms/C. 2118.

WAR DIARY
or
INTELLIGENCE SUMMARY

Army Form C. 2118.

Place	Date	Hour	Summary of Events and Information	Remarks and references to Appendices
Map Sheet 21/4/8 26 A.28.a.3.7			A.D.M.S. visited camp to examine P.B. & T.U. men	
	22.11.16		D.M.S. (Surg Gen Pike) accompanied by A.D.M.S. inspected camp — and appeared to be satisfied with what he saw	
	23.11.16		Two large Nissen huts arriving one to be put up in A.S.C. camp and [one] for the other. Worked at A.S. — REIGERSBURG CHATEAU and Ray diary. R.A. and foot and found them quite satisfactory. What from A.D.M.S. orders — "It is hoped to make by end of March that Cavern of Trench Feet have [?]ment of trenches — In future Trench Feet will be charged [?] to each [?] Pime returned. Capt Nugent to C.C.S. a prisoner at J.C.T. [?] needs etc. —	
	24.11.16		Capt. Nugent at 17 R.W.F. — St with troops to visit another [?] to camp and visible inspection of men transferred into 114 & 115 Brigades in another mess with A.D.M.S. orders — instead of leaving from who had been detailed (Senior ones) in accordance with A.D.M.S. Brigade (Afficial orders)	
	25/11/16		Sent Officer (Capt. Parry) to inspect personnel transport of his 115 Brigade attention drawn by A.D.M.S. to shortage of parafin and troops members for tommy	
	26.11.16		Sunday. Sent Capt. Parry to inspect men transferred into 114 Brigade visited A.D.S. — CHATEAU REIGERSBURG and R.A. and foot — was given orders Lt Col [?]	

M M Smith Lt Col
O/c 131. 2nd/1st [?]

Army Form C. 2118.

WAR DIARY
or
INTELLIGENCE SUMMARY.
(Erase heading not required.)

Place	Date	Hour	Summary of Events and Information	Remarks and references to Appendices
Map Sheet 28 A 28 a 37	26/11/16		Are progressing satisfactorily. Attitude two Officers are always forward to A.D.S. at OUTSKIRT FARM — things being very quiet there — and a scarcity of Officers existing in the unit it is desired to leave one other Officer in charge of A.D.S. so as to set the Mr for fit for other duty — find MacFarlane one of the Officers return with me to the fr Manoeuvring Station. He will be details to temporarily take over medical charge of 16th R. Welsh Regiment, tomorrow at R. Camp. Both M.O.'s for England at end of year's contract.	
	27/11/16		Sent McFarlane R.A.M.C. proceeded to 16th Bath Welsh Regiment in accordance with Wednesday Plan. New Quartermasters Stores completed — and stores moved in.	
	28/11/16		P.B. & T.H. men inspected by me owing to A.D.M.S. not being able to come. After inspection I moved with D.A.D.M.S. & O/c Sanitary Section with Interpreter 64th & 39th Division, as immersion foot to be taken up — to inspect new lines about to be held by the French. The 131 Field Ambulance with 38th Division and has hitd by the French. Take over Medical arrangement — orders will be issued tomorrow. Marmite attach to Col. O/C 131 Field Ambulance	

Army Form C. 2118.

WAR DIARY
or
INTELLIGENCE SUMMARY.
(Erase heading not required.)

Place	Date	Hour	Summary of Events and Information	Remarks and references to Appendices
Map Sheet 28 A.26.a.3.7	29/11/16		Extract from A.D.M.S. order — dated Nov 28. 1916.	

2. **Medical arrangements**

1. Medical relief are being arranged between 79th French Regiment and 38th Division. 39. A.D.M.S. - 38th Division will administer the medical arrangements in the new sector on completion of relief.

The advanced Dressing Station at LARRY FARM (FERME 1889 Noord Junction B.9 c.1/2, 2.1/2) will be taken over on 30th November by a party of 1 Officer & 12 other ranks of 131 Field Ambulance 38th (Welsh) Division and will be equipped with necessary Medical, Surgical & general equipment, and will be equipped with necessary Medical, Surgical & general equipment. The Despatched Aid post at BOESINGHE CHATEAU will be taken over on the 30th November by 1 N.C.O. & 4 men of the A.D.S. party until the arrival of the R.M.O. of the Advance Battalion of the 116th Infantry Brigade. Sch of wounded will be evacuated from LARRY FARM every hour, at 11 A.M. by Ambulance Transport of No. 131. Field Ambulance and will be taken to No. 129 Field Ambulance (A.23.e.2.9) from whence they will be removed by 39 Field Ambulance of 39 Division at 2 P.M. daily. Transport of a field ambulance of

Macmullen M.B. Lt Col
O/c 131 Field Ambulance

Army Form C. 2118.

WAR DIARY
or
INTELLIGENCE SUMMARY.
(Erase heading not required.)

Place	Date	Hour	Summary of Events and Information	Remarks and references to Appendices
Map Sheet 28 A 28 a 3.7	29/4/16		Visited A.D.S. — all going on satisfactorily.	
	30/4/16		12. The ranks under Command of Captain Parry R.A.M.C. — proceeded to LARRY FARM — with all necessary equipment — in accordance with A.D.M.S's order of yesterday — at 10.30 AM. Two Officers at Main Station now — M.Os and there are only two Officers at Main Station now — MO and 2·0 in Command. Things are running very smoothly so that there will be no difficulty. Officers doing temporary duty as reported MOs will soon be returning.	

O. Donnell Walsh Lt-Col

O.C. 131 Field Ambulance

Confidential

140/902

War Diary
131. Field Ambulance Vol 13
38th (Welsh) Division
for
December 1916
(1 – 31st inclusive)

Volume XIII

COMMITTEE FOR THE
MEDICAL HISTORY OF THE WAR
Date   31 JAN. 1917

WAR DIARY
or
INTELLIGENCE SUMMARY.
(Erase heading not required.)

Army Form C. 2118.

Place	Date	Hour	Summary of Events and Information	Remarks and references to Appendices
Mon Shut Fee 28 A.28.a.3.7	1.12.16		Captain Parry return to Headquarters (A.28.a.3.7) from LARRY FARM (B.9.c.½.2.½) The M.O. (of John Bull's Mark works) - Batt. of 39 Division that is in support it has established his Regimental aid post at LARRY FARM and will perform the medical arrangements of the A.D.S. there than relieving Captain Parry. He took our personnel - 2.M.C. O+12.O.R + all necessary medical equipment. Noted H.D.S. at LARRY FARM.	
	2/12/16		Capt. Buchan rejoins unit from REIGERSBOURG CHATEAU where he had been along duty for Captain WESTON (or Gan) 4th Artillery. Captain Buchan to proceed on duty with 15th Welsh at LA BELLE ALLIANCE - and Captain Ewan's on duty with has P.O.U. and is at 129 J.A. above date. A.D.S. at LA BRIQUE, LARRYFARM, RA and post at LATRUISTOUR and REIGERSBOURG CHATEAU	
	3/12/16		Captain Parry return and MacHutt at LA BRIQUE - latter again unit.	
	4/12/16		Lieut LIMBERY - 134. J.A. 39 Division reports for temporary duty - he will daily the units at ELVERDINGHE CHATEAU, and the RE Coy of the 39 Division (allotted in the huts west of ELVERDINGHE (A.S.M.S.'mls) of Sanitary Sanitary Arrangements	

WAR DIARY
or
INTELLIGENCE SUMMARY.
(Erase heading not required.)

Army Form C. 2118.

O.H. Mitchell Lt Col
O/c 131 Field Ambulance

Place	Date	Hour	Summary of Events and Information	Remarks and references to Appendices
Mapsheet 28 A.26.a.2.7	5/10/16		A.D.M.S. with unit for inspection of P.B. & T.U. men — he also interviews Lieut Findlay (134 F.A.) — is unit at ELVERDINGHE	
	6/10/16		Routine work. Visited A.D.S. all satisfactory	
	7/10/16		Lieut Smith attended from leave and is posted to 16" with instead of Lieut McFarland who is returning to England at end of 12 months contract. Officer visited unit to inspect A.D.S. both — all satisfactory. 34 D.M.S. 36" Irish Division visited unit to inspect A.D.S. both — all satisfactory	
	8/10/16		Lieut McFarland left for England. Lieut Findlay R.A.M.C. rejoined his unit. 134 F.A. at WORMHOUDT. Lieut Findlay R.A.M.C. attended 1st Army Conference of 2nd Army at HAZEBROUCK — Subject attended 1st Medical Board today of 2nd Army at HAZEBROUCK — Subject "Treatment of # (penetrating) wounds of Skull — introduced by Captain Kennedy R.A.M.C. An unavoidable absence of D.M.S. Chair was taken by Col Smith Weber D.A.D.M.S.	
	9/10/16		Col Forwarded O/cs Field Ambulances at A.D.M.S.'s Office at 3 P.M.	

WAR DIARY
INTELLIGENCE SUMMARY

Army Form C. 2118.

Place	Date	Hour	Summary of Events and Information	Remarks and references to Appendices
Map Sheet 28 A 28 c 3.7	8/12/16		Lieut J.O. Marpurtant proceeded to England upon expiration of contract. Capt. D.B. Bendorf proceeded to take over medical charge of 16th Middx.	
	10/12/16		Church Parade C.E. Church Army Hut 11a.m. Roman - 129 Field Ambulance at 11.30 am.	
	11/12/16		Lt. Col. R.H. Mills Robert proceeded to Divisional Headquarters acting A.D.M.S. during temporary absence of Col. F.J. Morgan A.M.S.	
	11/12/16		Pte. Grant No. 48650 of this unit proceeded to England on 10 days leave.	
	12/12/16		A.D.M.S. orders:- No 131 Field Ambulance will hand over to present site at A 28, A 36, K a Field Ambulance of the 39th Division. No 13th unit and will take over the sites at BOLLEZEELE and WORMHOUDT, at present occupied by a Field Ambulance of the 39th Divn. commencing during the Officers Confer Red Station at WORMHOUDT. The portion of the A.D.S. at OUTSKIRT FARM (T.6. d.S.F.) REIGERSBURGH CHATEAU (M.8.F.2.5?) Artillery Collecting Post (B.25.d.S.3) will open their events on the 12th and after handing over to portion of a Field Ambulance of the 39th Divn. which will arrive there on the 11 inst. No 131 Field Ambulance (main body) will move by train on the 13 inst, 2nd Field Ambn. will make arrangements to hand on advance and Advance Parties. Head on Tuesday 7 a.m. this day. Lieut. A Marteston R.A.M.C and M./Sgt R Coe with 12 other ranks (including 2 clerks) will proceed by motor ambulance at 8 a.m. 12 Dec. to BOLLEZEELE and take over Field Ambulance site there from 130 Field Ambulance, 39 Division. The party will make such tempty preparation as suit the new area and the arrangement connected therewith. The party will not proceed with the 12 new mentioned party and be left at WORMHOUDT. At 9 a.m. R Coe having completed his duties at BOLLEZEELE will proceed to WORMHOUDT and take over the site at WORMHOUDT from a Field Ambulance of the 39 Division. At 1 p.m. H Con will return to Headquarters (A28.c.3.7) this day. Personnel 2 S.S. Mappers with 'C' Echelon 'spearhead', London Cork, and 1 Motor Cock will proceed to BOLLEZEELE this day. Will leave Camp Headquarters at 7.45 a.m. by road conveying Map NAMC Officers Maps NAMC	

2353 Wt. W2541/1454 700,000 5/15 D.D.&L. A.D.S.S./Form/C. 2118.

Army Form C. 2118.

WAR DIARY
or
INTELLIGENCE SUMMARY.
(Erase heading not required.)

Place	Date	Hour	Summary of Events and Information	Remarks and references to Appendices
Map Sheet 28. A 25 c.7	13/12/16		Proceeded to and took over D.R.S., C.R.S. & Field Ambulance Rds. at WORMHOUDT. Lt. A.M.C. Penn R.A.M.C. at L.I.V.A.N. of Cov. was left behind to complete all arrangement concerning the handing over to the incoming Field Ambulance. 133rd Field Ambulance arrived at A.D.S. OUTSKIRT Farm without return or equipment. The party from 133rd Field Ambulance arrived on temporarily to take over the following articles of equipment:- Captain S.N. Perry R.A.M.C. stated were temporarily to take over the following articles of equipment;- 1 Whist. Aprestor (non-pattern) in Metchkin, 20 Blankets & The case of 1 Ehlond of Serno upon the decision 1 Whist. Aprestor understanding that the article should be returned upon the first possible opportunity. A certificate was obtained & forwarded A.D.M.S.	
WORMHOUDT.	14/12/16		Received orders from A.D.M.S. regarding the collection of A.R. 2 Ambulance Cars will proceed to ARNEKE to purpose of collecting sick in that neighbourhood. Intended upon C.R.G. to hand books, plumbing &c. Inspected B 016 Z 66 45 and inspected the out-door works & road. The road is every & was accommodated 50 patients easily, upon company 75s. It and our works was of a very rudimentary description. Lieut S.L. Pall R.A.M.C. reported himself for duty.	
	15/12/16		Took the day to A.D.M.S. regarding instructions for keeping of books at the various Stations. Received a reply concerning the same. Recommended with O.C. North Midland F.C.S. MONT de CAT respecting him to warn to in the number of cases that came to his Staff. He was entitled to his services. Re-arranged the branch branch at D.R.S. as thus turn an account of the difficulty of finding bed rooms. Lieut A.M.K. Price proceed leave to England from 19/12/16 to 26/12/16. Cpl & Private U CUSS- R.A.M.C. proceed leave to England from 16/12/16 to 23/12/16 Received a communication from Headquarters St. ?? 3.5 Hopper assigned study at Hd. ?	
	16/12/16		WORMHOUDT Laundry for transmission of arranging stream clothing & the Bath at BOLGOZELLE and 2 lorry back the Soiled clothing. The instructions having been received, under to A.D.M.S. with respect to the temp. stand of offs. for offs, milk, vegetables & laundry T.C.N.S., Capt J. Brown R.A.M.C. attached temporally to dig & was taken on the strength accordingly.	

J.O.Brown Major R.A.M.C

2353 W. W2544/1434 700,000 5/15 D.D.&L. ADSS/Form/C. 2118.

WAR DIARY
or
INTELLIGENCE SUMMARY.

(Erase heading not required.)

Army Form C. 2118.

Place	Date	Hour	Summary of Events and Information	Remarks and references to Appendices
Hosp Hut 27, WORMHOUDT. O.16.6.5.5.	17/12/16		Church Parade, C.E. CINEMA 11 a.m. A.D.M.S. visited the Position. Received medical arrangements Reserve Area. Communicated with a A.D.M.S. forwarding out the fact that there was no accommodation for sick or wounded officers at the Station.	
	18/12/16		Captain J.E. Evans R.A.M.C. is detailed to take over the duties of Sanitary Officer of WORMHOUDT. He reported himself this day to the Town Major, & requested him to obtain a Sanitary Raft. Received a reply from A.D.M.S. regarding the accommodation for sick & wounded Officers. It only carries that can be adopted at present is to send an Officer to hut No 2 C.C.S., if there is not a vacancy at C.C.S. to send to hut No 12. C.C.S. HAZEBROUCK. Received 2 doz prs. Field Mayor Christmas Cards from A.D.M.S. & same posted to 3/4th dozen ordinary the Contract for 1 doz 3/4 Fed dozen. They were all rather disposed of. The communicated with O.C. 133 Field Amb. appointing them to deliver the equipment. Send one in town to OUTKUIST FARM, visited Field Ambulance at BLEEZEELE. The West End has been benefitted out not white washed. Re partial/total application for promotion of Staff Sgt Pearson as Sgt Major in attendance with Given Orders D.G.M.S. also Cpl Myers to acting Raft Sgt work Hosp, acting Cpl Teebay to acting Sgt with Pay.	
	19/12/16		Capt. C.J.B. Andrews R.A.M.C. reported the day from 15" Motor Pay". Received a communication return from M.A.D.M.S. attending on this the Commander in Chief, will be in the Army area to morrow & following days. Cockburnstown, & the co-ordination of 35" Divisional Supply Column.	
	20/12/16		46058 Pte. A.C. Pryle; 46047 Pte. J.F. Pilmington provided to R.O.D. Depot AUDRUICQ, to be held as firemen. Captain C.J.B. Andrews posted bear to Enfland from 20/12/16 to 3/1/17. Pte. Lut L. B.M.S. were all inspected, and several places where the unfit fell was were replaced by Corporate oatmeal.	
	20/12/16		Visited BOLEEZEELE.	
	21/12/16		Visited Field Cashier, & paid men at Laundry. Pay of the rest at 2 p.m. this day.	

J.C. Band Major R.A.M.C.
Capt.

Army Form C. 2118.

WAR DIARY
or
INTELLIGENCE SUMMARY.
(Erase heading not required.)

Instructions regarding War Diaries and Intelligence Summaries are contained in F. S. Regs., Part II. and the Staff Manual respectively. Title pages will be prepared in manuscript.

Place	Date	Hour	Summary of Events and Information	Remarks and references to Appendices
WORMHOUDT	22/12/16		Four men of the unit proceeded on leave to England from 22/12/16 to 1/1/17. Kit & medical inspection at 2 p.m. Received from A.D.M.S. List of future M. Courses on Past would evacuate all sick & wounded to C.C.S at REMY SIDING. A return audited to A.D.M.S. showing normal accommodation at D.R.S. = 100; Field Ambulance WORMHOUDT = 50; Field Ambulance BOLEZEELE = 50, Total 200. Emergency accommodation :- D.R.S = 150; Field Am WORMHOUDT = 60; BOLEZEELE = 50; = Total = 260.	
	23/12/16		D.M.S. 2nd Army visited Field Ambulance & D.R.S. He drew attention to the brand of Lard Arrack, & the General water supply condition of the D.R.S. site. Major J.C.Bruns & Lieut R Macdadum with the personnel of the Field Ambulance at BOLEZEELE accompanied the 113th Infantry Brigade to VOLKERHINKOVE where they were inspected by the Commander-in-Chief. He was very complimentary and paid special attention to the cleanliness of the units in parade. Received 345 letters of the Corps Commanders Christmas message to the troops. Received message from A.D.M.S. that an issue of a Hard Rocket for men staying under canvas approved, but number of blankets mentioned. The only numbers required - Nil return. Received from A.D.M.S. that an enclosure has been made with the O.C. N.I. C.C.S. that men who are not quite fit for duty at the end of the period at MONT de CAT Rest Cd. but back to the D.R.S. for a few days further rest.	
	24/12/16		Church Parade in Cinema at 11 a.m. Service taken by Captain Mc Pollard for Lieut Arrack, & their material & informing from the Montt A.M.C.C.B respectfully. Mass & DADO's to being in the Ambulance Wagon Wheels. D.M.S. 2nd Army would visit the unit in a few days. Most to special attention to the bare aspect of the wards at C.M.S. etc. D.D.M.S. VIII Corps visited WORMHOUDT. He drew special attention to the bare aspect of the wards & the roof of B.R.C.S	
	25/12/16		Religious Services: Church Parade; "Holy Communion at CINEMA at 11 a.m. The usual schools were kindly lent for the various Christmas dinners. These were followed by a Concert which was patronised by A.D.M.S. D.M.S & other Staff Officers. Captain S.H. Parry proceeded to B.R.C.S at R-OMER and returned with a car load of articles for the extra furnishing of C.M.S, visited the Field Ambulance at BOLEZEELE. A man letter E.S. Brun visited Eno Gall relieved Lieut R Macdadum at BOLEZEELE.	
	26/12/16			
	27/12/16		No further emergency return. Lorry has been received from Et.Col.Arroch 133 Field Ambulance apositing the return of Lieutenant. Major J.C.Bruns visited Em at A 28 a 37, to arranged to meet at took the mid day. Guidemont.	J C Bruns Major RAMC

2353 Wt. W2514/1434 700,000 5/15 D.D.&L. A.D.S.S./Forms/C. 2118.

WAR DIARY
or
INTELLIGENCE SUMMARY.
(Erase heading not required.)

Army Form C. 2118.

Instructions regarding War Diaries and Intelligence Summaries are contained in F.S. Regs., Part II. and the Staff Manual respectively. Title pages will be prepared in manuscript.

Place	Date	Hour	Summary of Events and Information	Remarks and references to Appendices
WORMHOUDT.	28/12/16.		Four men proceeded on leave to England from 29/12/16 to 7/1/17. In accordance with the D.D.M.S's instructions 1 N.C.O. & 11 men reported to the Town Major for duty with the Sanitary Section. 3 T.U. men were also sent from Divisional Head Quarters. Owing to the weather. Urgent condition of The D.R.S. rifle ranges were cut in the morning directions. Lieut. A.W. Rini R.A.M.C. returned from leave.	
	29/12/16.		In accordance with D.M.S. orders: In future no civil patient will be conveyed to an hospital by Motor Ambulance Cars, without a further application from a Mayor to Commune. D.D.M.S. orders; Field Amb. A.T.S. "In a matter of routine all Army cases of frost bite when there is discoloration or sepsis of the Skin will be given an inspection of A.T.S. Medical + V&I Inspection. 20 Fritz I. Ind. Troops tarried over to D.A.C. 38 Division. Return from A.D.M.S. instructions for the Field Ambulance to supply 30 'special School with drinking water. A communication received from A.D.M.S 38 Division in reference to burial trainings. The training to around the Church Spire self up tuf ball matches; Gun country Running; Among it Captain G.R. Perry was appointed to take the matter in hand for the R.A.M.C. (3 Field Ambulances).	
	30/12/16.		Visited BOLEZEELE.	
	31/12/16.		Church Parade C.E. in CINEMA H.A.M.	

J. Bearn, Major R.A.M.C.

Confidential

War Diary

1st Field Ambulance
38th (Welsh) Division

for
January 1917
1-31 inclusive

(Volume XIV)

Army Form C. 2118.

WAR DIARY
or
INTELLIGENCE SUMMARY.
(Erase heading not required.)

Instructions regarding War Diaries and Intelligence Summaries are contained in F. S. Regs., Part II. and the Staff Manual respectively. Title pages will be prepared in manuscript.

Place	Date	Hour	Summary of Events and Information	Remarks and references to Appendices
WORMHOUDT Map 27. C 16.6.55"	1/1/17		Received notification that an inspection of ATS will be given in all cases of "Trench Feet" irrespective of whether there is suspicion of the man or not. In accordance of D.D.M.S. II Army N⁰ W179/6 no Patients will accompany "Motor Ambulances" when sent to Workshops for repair.	
	2/1/17		Visited Field Ambulance Detachment at BOLLEZEELE. A new (with leave & foot cleaning) Hut erected. Sent a M.O. viz R.A.M.C. but no temporary medical charge of 19th M.R.C. (Rouen). New medical arrangement of 3F Division issued from A.D.M.S. for the Reserve Area.	
	3/1/17		Received from A.D.M.S. Circular Memos on Chloroform vapour, at Dumpers, & the best means of undertaking Operating Theatres & Operating Marquees.	
	4/1/17		The A.D.M.S. again founded out the weakness of foundry to time special application for leave. Heard particulars of the 3F (Nth) trainer received from A.D.M.S. A.D.M.S. visited WORMHOUDT. Completed the attached diagram of 8 N.S. Ame. A man admitted at CCS WHL for Sand Arcade, was again informed that none were available.	
	5/1/17		Received a communication from A.D.M.S. drawing attention to the fact that patients were being evacuated to CCS with a diagnosis of J.D.T. fed, expected feet, another fact, trench feet which were showing 2nd feet. and came up found that and be diagnosed as such. Medical & 12st inspection.	
	6/1/17		Received from A.D.M.S. Re Capt Crommelin Carvlin will afternoon to Schooling viâ la BOLLEZEELEN argument with the Chaplain. Enquiries made for landing & unions & accommend the sergt & Pather. Found that the Claims for landing & union were made but all the desired my knowledge of the sergt in France. Sent instructions reminding the day to take medical charge of 13th R.A.M.C.	
	7/1/17		Religion's Service C.E. 11 a.m. at Camera. 12 a.m. at Camera. The non-uniformed chaplain did not put in an appearance throughout. I regretted that arrangement should be made for Service at 5 p.m. No request could not be complied with. J. Graves Major R.A.M.C.	

WAR DIARY or INTELLIGENCE SUMMARY

Army Form C. 2118.

Place	Date	Hour	Summary of Events and Information	Remarks and references to Appendices
WORMHOUDT Sheet 27 C.16.c.6.55"	7/1/17		The queen proceeded on leave to England this day. ADMS visited Proven	
	8/1/17		Colonel Jackson ADMS 55th Division visited Proven, & requested it be known the different branches of the work carried on. He informed us that a Field Ambulance of his Division would in all probability take over from us at an early date. The previous storm in the Division having transmuted was decided this day.	
	9/1/17		In accordance with ADMS's instructions Captain S.E. Bryan & Lieuts. Martin & Wyman erected an old portion of Mays 9.E. A.D.E. A.D.? with a view to what our in or about C. 14 c.d. First difficulty to obtaining supplies of tent for Officers Coffee Rest Station. Sgt Major I.O. En. Late of these Field Ambulances, undertook in gratuitous and application for tents through outside channels, own subscription. Submitted to body orders upon that application for tents through outside channels, own subscription.	
	10/1/17		ADMS visited BOLLEZEELE.	
	11/1/17		Received wire from ADMS to proceed tomorrow Proven", including Jackson's. Lt Col R.H. Mills R.A.M.C. proceeded this day to England on 10 days leave.	
	12/1/17		ADMS: DADMS: visited & inspected the Proven. Lt Col Mord 2/1 West Lancashire Field Ambulance visited & inspected the different departments of the Field Ambulance at WORMHOUDT & BOLLEZEELE, with a view of taking over on the 14 inst. Instruction was received that the Advance party of the 1/5th Corps Lord Care formed at the COLLEGE POPERINGHE, 9 & that the Advance party of the 1/5th Corps Lord Care formed at that Zint SALL NAME was 2 be started to 10. SM B	
	13/1/17		Received orders the Move from ADMS Reserve instruction that Zint SALL NAME was 2 be started to 10 Advanced unit alarm. Visited BOLLEZEELE, 2/1 Lancashire Fd Amb Arr at BOLLEZEELE was landed over to an advanced unit alarm, visited BOLLEZEELE, 2/1 Lancashire Field Ambulance.	
	14/1/17		Early V. the 2/1 West LANCASHIRE Officers Coffee Rest Station was handed over to R.C. Field Ambulance & the 55th Division. Divisional Rest Station. Officers Coffee Rest Station was landed over R.C. Field Ambulance. The Personnel of Proven Stores Party of this Field Ambulance proceeded to LA BRIQUE ADS consisting Party was conveyed in 8 Motor Lorries. An advance party consisting 2 NCOs and Captain S.E. Bryan and 12 other ranks and equipment. An advance party consisting 2 NCOs and 1 the other ranks proceeded to ADS at LARREYS FARM. 2 NCOs & one man remained behind at DES & CORS as WORMHOUDT.	

Lieut A.W. PIRIE R.A.M.C. reported having completed indexed change of 1/19 West Regiment.

J.Cosens Major R.A.M.C.

WAR DIARY or INTELLIGENCE SUMMARY

Army Form C. 2118.

Place	Date	Hour	Summary of Events and Information	Remarks and references to Appendices
A 28 a 3 4 Sheet 28.	14/1/17		Arrived at the Pasture at mid day and took over from a party of the 133rd Field Ambulance. 2 NCOs proceeded to School of Sanitation.	
	15/1/17		Capt C.J.B. BUCHANAN R.A.M.C. and Lieut A.W.R. PRICE R.A.M.C. were detailed to attend a course in Sanitation at HAZEBROUCK commencing the day at 9.30 a.m. and lasting four days. Received new medical arrangements in the Divisional Area from ADMS. Captains A.B. EBBITT R.A.M.C. & F.P.S.T. R.A.M.C. S.R. joined the Field Ambulance for duty.	
	16/1/17		Removed the Enemy & one Corp. NIESSEN HUT. and commenced to visit and view the hospital wounds. Removed the Enemy & one Corp. NIESSEN HUT. from the 13th M.A.C. these casualties were not caused by the shelling of WELSH Farm.	
			ADMS visited the Pasture. He regretted that an inspection should be made of the out buildings at REIGERSBURG CHATEAU, with special reference to the amount of accommodation for sick & wounded.	
	17/1/17		Accompanied by Captains C & W PRICE R.A.M.C. & Sgt-Major Benn proceeded to REIGERSBURG CHATEAU. The out buildings were found to be most convenient & easily accommodate 200 Pasture cases. Visited LARREYS FARM.	
	18/1/17		Proceeded to Field Cashier to draw pay for unit. ADMS and Secretary Officer's Division visited Field Ambulance. ADMS outlined a scheme that was to be adopted to clear the BATTLE AREA in case of an attack on this front. He now attaches to the fact that a large number of which are very inconvenient from the field ambulance to the brigade to C.C.S. endeavour should be made to return men to D.R.S and only Accommodation at Field Ambulance should be worked to 20 M.C. should be kept available for emergency.	
	19/1/17		Attended clinical meeting of 17 C.C.S. at REMY SIDING. Sent medical R.A.M.S. proceeded this day to WISQUES to take up temporary medical charge of 1st S.M.B.	
	20/1/17		Received a memo from ADMS that 20 beds must always be held in reserve and when these beds are encroached upon it was to be notified to that arrangements could be made to transfer patients to other Field Ambulances, visited LARRY FM and LA BRIQUE.	
	21/1/17			J O'Bauns Major R.A. M.C.

WAR DIARY or INTELLIGENCE SUMMARY

Army Form C. 2118.

Place	Date	Hour	Summary of Events and Information	Remarks and references to Appendices
A 28 a 3.7 Sheet 28	21/1/17		Lt Col A Millwarth returned from leave and resumed command 131 Field Ambulance.	
	22/4/17		1 N.C.O. & 20 men proceeded to Corps Baths for duty under Lieut Beachy Roure. Sanitary OM.g in accordance with A.D.M.S. instructions. Noted O.P.S.'s at OUTSKIRT FARM and LARRY FARM. also part of REIGERSBURG CHATEAU and found all working smoothly. Major Bowie 91 Field took on temporarily the command of 130 F.A. during absence on leave of C.O. A.T.M.S. visited unit to examine P.B. & T.U. men. Water hampered there 10 to 15 Regular. — Sanitary arrangements satisfactory.	
	23/4/17			
	24/4/17		Attended an M.O.s attend morning sick of 2 Coys of Infantry 20 Division billeted in & near the Gendarmerie near D.H.Q.S. in POPERINGHE – (A.D.M.S. instructions) – the Walk king from M.O. walk-ridden.	
	25/4/17		Noted OUTSKIRT FARM with A.D.M.S. & investigated best ways to evacuate from A.D.S. – It is a difficult problem.	
	26/4/17		2 A.M.S. visited unit – to see "Trench Feet". Apology to A.D.M.S. that new Sgt Major has Diabetes Gravata nummecht. Did so in the afternoon. attended medical meeting at BAILLEUL Interesting paper on "Some Observation on wounds of the Chest" by Captain S.R. ARMSTRONG Conference of O/C Field Ambulance at A.D.M.S. this afternoon. — A K Millwarth Lt Col O/C 131. Field Ambulance	
	27/4/17			

WAR DIARY or INTELLIGENCE SUMMARY

Army Form C. 2118.

Place	Date	Hour	Summary of Events and Information	Remarks and references to Appendices
A 26.a.37 Sheet 28	28/1/17		Sunday. Routine work	
			Arrived 3rd British F.A. 131 F.A. was by 2 goals to 0.	
	29/1/17		M.O. (Lieut Pond) at OUTSKIRT FARM attended by Captain Poole R.A.M.C. Spent the afternoon trying to find a more suitable spot than A 26.a.37 for a main dressing station — in case of big operation. The road to the present site is very bad and it is a big job to put it in proper repair. P. & T.O. men.	
	30/1/17		A.D.M.S. visited unit to examine P. & T.O. men. Reconnoitred district about ELVERDINGHE with object of establishing A.D.S's in case of attack from LARRY FARM, ESSEX & SUSSEX FARMS & OUTSKIRT FARMS. Inspected the various roads from these places.	
	31/1/17		Visited Regimental aid posts at BOESINGHE CHATEAU and OUTSKIRT FARM. The Regimental aid post that normally consists of the farm evacuated to LARRY FARM. The OUTSKIRT FARM is at present treated as latter. IRISH FARM and evacuated to OUTSKIRT FARM and evacuated to our headquarters. Necessary instructions given to have place owing to obstruction of the new headquarters. Visits made and aid posts properly equipped in accordance with A.D.M.S. instructions.	

M Mulloosack Lt. Col

O/c 131. British Ambulance

Confidential Vol 15

War Diary

131 Field Ambulance
38 (Welsh) Div

for

February 1917
(1 - 28th inclusive)

(Volume XV)

COMMITTEE FOR THE
MEDICAL HISTORY OF THE WAR
Date 4 — APR. 1917

WAR DIARY or INTELLIGENCE SUMMARY

Army Form C. 2118.

Place	Date	Hour	Summary of Events and Information	Remarks and references to Appendices
Sheet 2-A. A.26.a.37	Feb 1. 1917		Noted Order Cashin and chus Cork to 57 [5/7?] Bn personnel. Visited all outlying detachments. LA BRIQUE. LARRY FARM &c and paid personnel their	
	2.2.17		A.D.M.S. (Col Myers) visited unit to say farewell on leaving division to take up duties as D.D.M.S. Lieut Gate struck off strength of this F.A. and attached an M.O. to SW Bn. 9 Cavalry Bde. Submitted and (?) for appointment from Feb 1.M.17. Submitted appd to A.D.M.S. re emergency team parts. Substantial and (?) application for S.S. Pearce to be appointed S. Major.	
	3.2.17		Capt Parry recommends myth (?) wound 9 LARRY FARM re RUSSELL FARM and reeds by which patient can be evacuated. Report seen & Sketch sent to A.D.M.S.	
	4.2.17		Sundaay, Divine Service. Routine work. Sent M.O. (Lieut Parry) to relieve M.O. (Capt Day) 15 R.W.F. while on leave. Capt Buchan relieved Capt Bork at 2nd BRIQUE A.D.S. instruction and received from A.D.M.S. to keep 3 days ration at A.D.S. per 15 personnel and 50 patients. (30 stumen (?))	
	5.8.17		Medical board ammoeld at 131.F.A. in afford of reclassify P.B & T.U. men – Major Rowe & Capt Weston Dist. C.C. Consist of Col O'Millerwell & Lt C. member. Capt Seven & SW B. White on leave. Lieut M'Alsik rejoined 131 F.A. after attending Capt Evans noted unit 1st of him.	
	6.2.17		New A.D.M.S. (Lt. Col. G.H. D.D.M.C.) visited unit. Inspection of P.B & T.U. men by A.D.M.S. A.D.G.S. (Major Gaster) noted & inspected horse lives — very well pleased...	6/12/131 Col

Army Form C. 2118.

WAR DIARY
or
INTELLIGENCE SUMMARY.
(Erase heading not required.)

Instructions regarding War Diaries and Intelligence Summaries are contained in F. S. Regs., Part II. and the Staff Manual respectively. Title pages will be prepared in manuscript.

Place	Date	Hour	Summary of Events and Information	Remarks and references to Appendices
Map Sheet 28 / 3 / A 28 a 5.7	7/2/17		Major J.C. Daw - 2nd in Command - reported unit after being in charge of 130 F.A. during absence of on leave of Lt. Col. Daw O/c 130 F.A. Capt. J.E. Daw proceeded on leave. This unit is relieved of duty of looking after 2. St. detached Coys. of 38th Division at POPERINGHE. Capt Tod (temp attached this unit) relieves Capt. Tate as medical charge of 13th R.W.F.	
	8/2/17		A.D.M.S. order "No man flying in to be used by Medical units to ask gas appliances". Quartermaster with R.R.T. Headquarters at ST. OMER with view of fixing out suitable material for fixing his Nissen hut to be used as a ward.	
	9/2/17		Capt. Tod (temp attached) returns from 13th R.W.F. and sent to adjt on duty with 22 M.A.C.(10/17). R.R.T. + appendages from ST. OMER used used to unpack his large Nissen hut.	
	10/2/17		A.D.M.S. order "All camels evacuated to Div. Ambulance will have their feet examined immediately in common in view of finish F.B. or T.F.	
	11/2/17		Sunday. All fun, pumps, Lent. parades returned Capt. Buchan at L.A. BRQUE. leave stopped indefinitely.	

O.H.Mitchell Lt Col
O/c. 131 Field Ambulance.

Army Form C. 2118.

WAR DIARY
or
INTELLIGENCE SUMMARY.
(Erase heading not required.)

Instructions regarding War Diaries and Intelligence Summaries are contained in F.S. Regs., Part II. and the Staff Manual respectively. Title pages will be prepared in manuscript.

Place	Date	Hour	Summary of Events and Information	Remarks and references to Appendices
Map Sheet 28 A28.a.37	12/2/17		A.D.M.S. held Ambulance. Lecture on "Inhalation and care of wet feet" by Quartermaster. Draft — 5. men — arrive.	
	13/2/17		Inspection of P.O. & T.O. men by E.O.M.C. (Lt.Col. R Rowell A.M.S.) & others went to Corps.	
	14/2/17		attended Conference of O.C.'s F.A. at A.D.M.S. Office. Routine work.	
	15/2/17		Visited Sotd. Cocher and drew cart. K/say Pennant. 1st class of outlying detachments.	
			Spare personnel men. D.D.M.S. VIIth Corps visits unit. Removed from L.A. BRIQUE to LARRY FARM. 2 officers & 100 mes read as Reg. ADS & 50 ad ADS. Staff on personal these unit change of R.M.O. using to a R.A.P.	
	16/2/17		A.D.M.S. visits unit in probability of removing evacuation. Visited Isolat. Coches & Med. messes of BATIEUL District Medical inspection. hut and medical inspection.	
	17/2/17		62. attended Pick Parade. 2 Officers & 107. O.R. unit behind in F.A. Sunday Religions Service. Visited LARRY FARM & inspected with view to putting up "Elephant" dug outs. O'Mulrookh H.Q.	
	18/2/17		Major Davis, went on 10 days leave. O/C Sr. Field Ambulance.	

Major Davis

Army Form C. 2118.

WAR DIARY
or
INTELLIGENCE SUMMARY.
(Erase heading not required.)

Instructions regarding War Diaries and Intelligence
Summaries are contained in F.S. Regs., Part II.
and the Staff Manual respectively. Title pages
will be prepared in manuscript.

Place	Date	Hour	Summary of Events and Information	Remarks and references to Appendices
Map Sheet 28 A.28.a.3.7	19/2/17		4 Officers } under treatment at F.A. 103 O.R. } No. (other units) attended sick parade – 48	
	20/2/17		Rain. A.D.M.S inspected P.O. & T.O. men. 4 Officers } under treatment at F.A. No (other units) attended sick parade 26. 107 O.R. }	
	21/2/17		Capt. J. Ope's Field Ambulance at A.D.M.S.'s Office. Routine work. 2 Officers } under treatment at F.A. No (other units) attended sick parade 41 91 O.R. }	
	22/2/17		10 Officers } under treatment at F.A. Sick parade 62. 87 O.R. } Visited all outlying detachments.	
	23/2/17		1 Officer } under treatment. Sick parade 54. 94 O.R. } 2nd Grand Surround Dustbath Completter V.13.d.135 Corp.A.S.C.—V.30 4 yards 5.1.	
	24/2/17		WSLA LARRY FARM, A.D.S. Improvements & alkaline spray on sick taking also under R.a.d. pit at FM BLEUET and CHÂTEAU ROESINGHE + page L.E.O all in good order. O.C. Mullenholst, (31. Infant Ambulance)	

2353 Wt. W5H/1454 700,000 5/15 D.D.&L. A.D.S.S./Form/C. 2118.

WAR DIARY or INTELLIGENCE SUMMARY

Army Form C. 2118.

Place	Date	Hour	Summary of Events and Information	Remarks and references to Appendices
Map Shut 28 A 26 a 3.7	25/9/17		Sunday. Church service as usual. Routine work. Sent M.O. to relieve M.O. 17 R.W.3 Employed at BLEUET FARM first Diva beyond mud after doing company duty above M.O. 15 R.W.3	
	26/9/17		Personal + equipment arrived from LA BRIQUE + A.S — (1 N.C.O. + Old medical equipment held relieved by men of another division.) 4 men remain at Pn's instruction. A.D.M.S may now be done without sub - Evacuation of infection cases (A.D.M.S) "Isolation Inspection of O.R. Sanitary Section (on hentrying) — (order — melting same morning sick parade. 46. attended morning sick treatment in hospital. 2-officers men on treatment. 7: O.R.S	
	27/9/17		A.D.M.3 inspected Tw. + P.B. men Demands of personnel + medical equipment arrived from L.A. BRIQUE. The A.D.S. handed us to 3 + 9 SS'ton in. We mv'd evacuated from our A.D.S. only — LARRY FARM	
	28/9/17		70 officers of D.A. C/o + at ADMS office. Routine work	

O M Millwaite LtCol
O/C 131. Field Ambulance

Confidential

War Diary
151, Field Ambulance
38th (Welsh) Division
for
March 1917
(1-31 inclusive)

Volume XVI

No. 2/6

140/202

3rd Div

COMMITTEE FOR THE
MEDICAL HISTORY OF THE WAR
Date 11 MAY. 1917

Army Form C. 2118.

WAR DIARY
or
INTELLIGENCE SUMMARY.
(Erase heading not required.)

Instructions regarding War Diaries and Intelligence Summaries are contained in F. S. Regs., Part II. and the Staff Manual respectively. Title pages will be prepared in manuscript.

Place	Date	Hour	Summary of Events and Information	Remarks and references to Appendices
Map Sheet 28 28.a.37	1/3/17		St. David's Day. © 3rd Corps Tug of War Competition. 131.9 A. W.m. by 2 - 4 - 1 against 2/121 R.F.A.	
	2/3/17		Pay day. Routine work	
	3/3/17		O C 2nd Col R H Mills Roberts proceeded to Headquarters as acting A.D.M.S. during absence on leave of Col J S Gill. Captain J N Danny acting O.C. 3 Officers and 68 Other ranks under treatment at this ambulance	
	4/3/17		Religious Services. Routine Training. Semi-Final in Army Football competition played this day. 131st Field Ambulance — v — 3/8 B.2.O Scorer = D&C 4 goals - nil. Captain J B Buchan took over medical charge of 13 Batt North Reff Lieut R.C.A Reynolds R.A.M.C. joined this unit from 13 Bath North Reff Lt v Dundee wanted & Cox provided to 132 Field Ambulance for duty 3 Officers and 75 Other ranks under treatment.	
	5/3/17		Major J C Barnes joined on leave. Captain G N Parry proceeded on leave 4/3/17 to 20/3/17 proceeded to England Lt Col J Heist reported for duty from 132 Field Ambulance. 2 Officers and 65 Other ranks under treatment	
	6/3/17		Proposed P.B and T.U areas inspected by A D M S at the Field Ambulance. 3 Officers and 69 Other ranks under treatment.	
	7/3/17		O C proceeded to LARCH FARM A.D.S. now work of Strengthening room to more front. Wagon Station down and outlet. All ranks well acquainted with their several duties. 4 Officers and 75 Other ranks under treatment.	

J C Barnes Major R.A.M.C.

WAR DIARY
or
INTELLIGENCE SUMMARY.

(Erase heading not required.)

Army Form C. 2118.

Instructions regarding War Diaries and Intelligence Summaries are contained in F.S. Regs., Part II. and the Staff Manual respectively. Title pages will be prepared in manuscript.

Place	Date	Hour	Summary of Events and Information	Remarks and references to Appendices
Map Sheet 28 A.27.a.37	8/3/17.		Orders published in Brigade Orders :- No NCO or men will leave this area in which he is billeted without being properly dressed. Passes for POPERINGHE will be thoroughly scrutinised. 1 Officer and 75 Other ranks under treatment.	
	9/3/17.		Medical, Foot, and Kit Inspection. O.C. visited LARRY FARM A.D.S. 2 Officers and 66 Other ranks under treatment.	
	10/3/17.		Published order in Bn. orders, case of O.R. not to be placed in amb. for the infantry who are obliged to find their own bretten when away to the trenches being trench stretcher in full — all ranks warned of the danger of this practice. 3 S.B.'s & 3 gym provided to BLUETT FARM with Elephant top 0.22 fm 17 R.M.F. Foot-ball match 109.131. v. 130' field ambulance Score 130' F.A.- 6 points — 3 points. 2 Officers and 53 other ranks under treatment. Religious Service.	
	11/3/17.		Published orders in Orie in Bn. Orders :- Brigade Rifle & Bomb. 113 Infantry Brigade received to fall in disposed 2 men from hospitals. Baths unable to have them Foot-ball field. The field & adjoining farm where football used to be played must not be used in future for recreation purposes. All cases of measles to be evacuated daily at 4 p.m. by B. U.M.C. Pte Jnn. J.E. Barnes returned let 2 handcarts at LARRY FARM A.D.S. 2 Officers and 52 other ranks under treatment.	

J.C. Bowen Major R.A.M.C.

Army Form C. 2118.

WAR DIARY
or
INTELLIGENCE SUMMARY.
(Erase heading not required.)

Instructions regarding War Diaries and Intelligence Summaries are contained in F.S. Regs., Part II. and the Staff Manual respectively. Title pages will be prepared in manuscript.

Place	Date	Hour	Summary of Events and Information	Remarks and references to Appendices
Trap. Sheet 28 A.28 a.3.7.	12/3/17		A.D.M.S. and D.A.D.M.S. visited Unit.	
			2 Pent frames 15' in length x 20. 6x3' Pent trampings were drawn from R.E. yard and conveyed to LARRY FARM A.D.S. This material will complete the intended improvements.	
			3 Officers and 71 Other ranks under treatment.	
	13/3/17		Inspection of proposed P.B. & T.U. men by A.D.M.S. 1 Officer and 82 Other ranks under treatment.	
	14/3/17		D.D.M.S. VIII Corps visited unit.	
			D.D.M.S. orders:— Coward Forman wards need not be evacuated, arrangements should be made for Isolation at Field Ambulances. Contacts should be inspected by M.O's, but need not be segregated.	
			D.D.M.S. inspected Isolation Arrangement, expressed his approval of work done, by the various U.S. 2 Canadian Dents. 3 Officers and 78 Other ranks under treatment.	
			Lieut. A.M.R. Paine, R.A.M.C. took over medical charge of 16th Welsh. vice Captain R. Hamilton, the latter reporting for duty with this Unit.	
	15/3/17		Major J.C. Davis proceeded to Field Castries for 6 days for treatment. District Laundry Baths and A.D.S. LARREY TOE. 2 Officers and 81 Other ranks under treatment.	
	16/3/17		17/3/17 Medical and Anti-infection. Post Inspection the day. Inspection of Clothing Field Ambulance Personnel. 3 Officers and 67 Other ranks under treatment.	
	18/3/17		Relieve. Armee Field this day. 2 Officers and 73 Other ranks under treatment.	
	19/3/17		A.D.M.S. visited unit. 1 Officer and 77 Other ranks under treatment.	
	20/3/17		Inspection of P.B. and T.U. men by A.D.M.S. 1 Officer and 85 Other ranks under treatment. O.C. reprimanded from HdQrs A.D.M.S. — and assumed command of 131 Field Ambulance.	
	21/3/17		1 M.O. (Lieut. Reynolds) went on leave and another M.O. Captain Parry returned from leave. Monica — Ott Warren to be carted to B.13.E.5.5 when followed down to the Army. (Extract A.R.O 16.3.17)	

2353 Wt. W25H/1454 700,000 5/15 D.D.&L. A.D.S.S./Forms/C. 2118.

WAR DIARY
or
INTELLIGENCE SUMMARY.
(Erase heading not required.)

Army Form C. 2118.

Place	Date	Hour	Summary of Events and Information	Remarks and references to Appendices
Map Shul 2F A 28.a.3.7.	22/3/17		Short run only. The gradual recovery must be assumed in the case of horse Shrs. No. 5 1 Other. 92 O.R.) made treatment.	
	23/3/17		Reserve attack of horses for medical exam at MINDEN POST Lat. July. – 5 Sgt. Mayo, Rennie. Sgt. Pirritt and La. Cpl. Tunnah. Attack on Pte. W. J. Davis decd. and Pte. T. D. Wickham (dec'd) to be sent to the parents. (forms. note) — Uncomplicated cases of measles are to be treated at Dilot Ambulance. Medical, Foot and Kit inspection. Per respirator drill. First J. P. Ryan reports for duty. inter A.D.S. at LARRY FARM.	
	24/3/17		Summer Time — Clocks put on an hour. O/C sections in conjunction with Q.M. to make detailed arrangements by sections for cleaning and clothing the equipment of their respective sections. 2 Other. (L.nco. treatment.) ST. O.R.	
	25/3/17		Sunday. Religion Service and routine work	

O.K. Millinelach Lt. Col.
O/C 131 Field Ambulance

WAR DIARY
INTELLIGENCE SUMMARY.
(Erase heading not required.)

Army Form C. 2118.

Place	Date	Hour	Summary of Events and Information	Remarks and references to Appendices
Map Sheet 28 A.28.a.3.7	26/3/17		Traffic from 22nd March 1917 inclusive which will not be allowed to pass Eastwards from VLAMERTINGHE until 6.30 P.M. 2 Officers	
			& other ranks 81.O.R.	
	27/3/17		A.D.M.S. visited and for inspection of R & T.U. men — 16 for expection. 2 Officers & other ranks 73.O.R.	
	28/3/17		In future all dental cases admitted to hospital or CCS will be shown at D.D. back. D.D.M.S. concurs in that A.D.M.S. 2nd Army would inspect the C.A. at or about 30/3/17. Visited A.D.S. at LARRY FARM.	
	29/3/17		Very heavy rain. Pay day; paint personal est head quarters and in outlying detachments. Found R.A. and foot practically destroyed by still — no camels. Petitioned to other "that evening aged men be found in pumas & basketball outlet for Struckung glands especially in Cavalry Units" Football Semi Final Cup ½ for Winners Competition R.A.M.C. v A.S.C. Result R.A.M.C. — 11 pts — to nil	O.K. Truth O.C.Atub Lt Col O/C 131 Field Ambulance

Army Form C. 2118.

WAR DIARY
or
INTELLIGENCE SUMMARY.
(Erase heading not required.)

Place	Date	Hour	Summary of Events and Information	Remarks and references to Appendices
Hop Stack St ABEAT	30/3/17		A.M.S. 2nd Army accompanied by D.A.M.S. VIII Corps inspected the Unit this day and was good enough to say that he was very pleased with all he saw.	
	31/3/17		Visit A.D.S. at LARRY FARM. with T.A. and post & wounded for a new post. 4 officers under Lieutenant 92 O.R.	N.Prinneauloote Lt Col O/c 151 Field Ambulance

Confidential

Vol17

War Diary
131. Field Ambulance
38(Welsh) Division
for
April. 1/30. 1917

Volume XVII

COMMITTEE FOR THE
MEDICAL HISTORY OF THE WAR
Date -6 JUN.1917

Army Form C. 2118.

WAR DIARY
or
INTELLIGENCE SUMMARY.
(Erase heading not required.)

Instructions regarding War Diaries and Intelligence Summaries are contained in F. S. Regs., Part II. and the Staff Manual respectively. Title pages will be prepared in manuscript.

Place	Date	Hour	Summary of Events and Information	Remarks and references to Appendices
Mapshed A 28 a 3.7	1/4/17		Sunday — Religious Services. 4 Officers & 96 O.R's went to treatment. 2nd Army. Official inspection from D.D.M.S. 17th Corps that D.M.S. was unpired pleased with it. He was at this unit during his inspection on 30th ult.	
	2/4/17		Guard Mounted — Bns and inol 3 Officers under treatment 90 O.R's	
	3/4/17		A.D.M.S. took out 6 nipot P.O. & T.O. men. Fully equipped. Walk out past R. ELVERDINGHE CHATEAU possibly demolish by the 77 Cad with. Decided to abandon R.A.M.D. POST (now TROIS TOURS).	
	4/4/17		Visit and inspected LARRY FARM (A.D.S). 2 Officers under treatment 77 O.R's	
	5/4/17		Preston & Protection in Belgium by British troops in Palestine. Comm: Rect. for temporary command in 8 Infantry regnal on Ap. 1 Coy + 9 men joined the unit. N Smalldwitch Lt Col O/C 131 Field Ambulance	

Army Form C. 2118.

WAR DIARY
or
INTELLIGENCE SUMMARY.
(Erase heading not required.)

Instructions regarding War Diaries and Intelligence Summaries are contained in F. S. Regs., Part II. and the Staff Manual respectively. Title pages will be prepared in manuscript.

Place	Date	Hour	Summary of Events and Information	Remarks and references to Appendices
Shot 2E	6/4/17		Good Friday — ath inspection postponed till tomorrow	
#FA 37			Band Rugby match } R+A+M+C 17 p/b } R+A+M+C Played a very good (in group) v s/b } game. 122 Int Bgd s/b	
	7/4/17		General hat inspection. Post officials still a That should have taken place yesterday took place today. Capt Ramsden R+A+M+C returned from leave. 3 officers } under treatment S+O+R }	
	8/4/17		Sunday Church Service attended. Airfield Capt C.S. Intel admitted at A+M+S Oftic Roy of M.O.'s at LARRY FARM (+D.S).	
	9/4/17		Routine work 2 officers } under treatment S+O+R }	
	10/4/17		R+A+M+C inspection of P.B. + Th. men attended. Inspection of O/c's F.A's at HILLHOEK D.R.S. — D.O.M.S. 0th rendered O.Trench Mortar 4Col Ti/c 131 Field Ambulance	

2353 Wt. W25/4/1454 700,000 5/15 D. D. & L. A.D.S.S./Forms/C. 2118.

WAR DIARY
or
INTELLIGENCE SUMMARY.
(Erase heading not required.)

Army Form C. 2118.

Place	Date	Hour	Summary of Events and Information	Remarks and references to Appendices
Sheet 28 A 28 a 37	11/4/17		Visited LARRY FARM A.D.S. met A.D.M.S. by request of 180 B Division recently of nearing accumulation at BOESINGHE CHATEAU - ordered to put up two dug outs close to present one. items have been forward in case to Division - Surgeon from amb to attend.	
	12/4/17		Pay day. Visited nursing to pour ale outlying detachments Visited + inspected A.D.S. LARRY FARM and went to proposed A.D.S. past a BOESINCHE CHATEAU, discussed with Captains Parry & Van Ryan to place one new dug out parallel + quite near present one. The 2nd new dug out will be placed behind the present one. Afterwards I went to be R.E. Officer at CARDON FARM and arranged to him to take of LARRY FARM A.D.S. at 10 A.M. tomorrow morning for Capt. Parry - 13th with then proceed to BOESINGHE CHATEAU (proposed A.D.S. post and Capt. at extension of proposed A.D.S. Post - Returned by telephone to ADMS what had been done.	
	13/4/17		Visited LARRY FARM in morning - Everbody warned to dress in Elephant dug outs 5,000 sand bags - for BOESINGHE - material + working party sent to LARRY FARM. Authorised by a Lieut. S. to arrange an elephant dug out near ELVERDINGHE. D. Methebetts Lt. Col OC 131 Field Ambulance	

WAR DIARY or INTELLIGENCE SUMMARY

Army Form C. 2118.

Place	Date	Hour	Summary of Events and Information	Remarks and references to Appendices
Shell 2E. A 28.a.3.7	13/4/17		Men all to clean by labour party and taken to BOESINGHE for erection. Sgt. Major J. O'Brien, Captains J.E. Bacon & Hamilton attended meeting at BAILLEUL.	
	14/4/17		2/Army Medical Society. Lieut. Ryan R.A.M.C. proceeded to LARREY FARM for duty. 72 other ranks under treatment. Catering Officers Report: 131" Field Ambulance. Very good exit. Clean cook-houses. A.D.M.S. instructions by telephone. Admit no sick for 4 days. All sick and wounded will be kept at D.R.S. Men under our command during the day. 131" Field Ambulance to act as a D.R.S. 131" Field Ambulance to move the "Elephant" dug-out at ELVERDINGHE CHATEAU and take all the day. A.D.M.S. also to move the "Elephant" dug-out at ELVERDINGHE CHATEAU and take all Advised to A.D.S. LARREY FARM. Instructions received from A.D.M.S. that the Sanitary Supervision V.D.E. X Camps & 114" Brigade transport lines would be under O.C. 131st Field Ambulance. Test for alarm received. O.C. proceeded on 10 days leave to England. Captain & A.E. Reynolds promoted to D.H.Q. for temporary duty. An Officer and 70 other ranks under treatment.	
	15/4/17		Return forwid. Capt S.N Parcy R.A.M.C returned HQt. being released at A.D.S by Capt. J.E.Burns R.A.M.C. Visited LARREY FARM A.D.S.	
	16/4/17		1 Officer and 76 other ranks under treatment. O/I/C visited D.E. X Camps and 114 Brigade Transport. Lines for Sanitary Inspection of same. Received telephone message from O.C. 130 Field Ambulance that they were taking over RIGERSBURG CHATEAU and for us to withdraw our 2nd Ambulance Car. There was complied with although no instructions were received by us from the ADMS. Instructions from ADMS to hand over to 130 Field Ambulance the Elephant dug-out & shelters at LARREY FARM. Capt Hamilton to take on temporary medical charge of 10 S.M.B. Self proceeded on leave.	

J O'Brien Major R.A.M.C.

Army Form C. 2118.

WAR DIARY
or
INTELLIGENCE SUMMARY.
(Erase heading not required.)

Instructions regarding War Diaries and Intelligence Summaries are contained in F.S. Regs., Part II. and the Staff Manual respectively. Title pages will be prepared in manuscript.

Place	Date	Hour	Summary of Events and Information	Remarks and references to Appendices
Sheet 28 A 28 & 37	17/4/17		1 Officer and 87 Other ranks under treatment. Inspection of proposed R.B. and T.U men by A.D.M.S. Received notification from A.D.M.S. that Lieut. & med Cree was returning to the unit, Lieut & O.M. Shute to return to 132nd Field Ambulance. O/I/C attend conference V.O.of Field Ambulances at 130th Field Ambulance.	
	18/4/17		1 Officer 103 Other ranks under treatment. Belgian telephonists found their work for duty.	
	19/4/17		1 Officer and 111 Other ranks under treatment. Received instruction from A.D.M.S. that ROUSSEL FARM to be a very bad Sanitary condition and that Rooms would be under Supervision of the 131st Field Ambulance.	
	20/4/17		1 Officer and 109 Other ranks under treatment. O/I/C visited ROUSSEL FARM and found the place in a very bad Sanitary condition. Reported on and forwarded same to A.D.M.S. 1 N.C.O. and 3 men of the unit that I can not the necessary improvements. O/I/c visited LARREY FARM.	
	21/4/17		103 Officer and Other ranks under treatment. Received notification from A.D.M.S. that the arrival of the Field ambulance will be fed through the info in infantry mess 25ins commencing 3.30 p.m. Indent forwarded for approval for material required for ROUSSEL FARM. 3 Officers and 112 Other ranks remaining under treatment.	
	22/4/17		O/I/c visited LARREY FARM and inspected the new Repairment and Med under construction at BOESINGHE village. Belgian Lorries.	

J.Crews Major N/am e

WAR DIARY or INTELLIGENCE SUMMARY

Army Form C. 2118.

Place	Date	Hour	Summary of Events and Information	Remarks and references to Appendices
Shut 2F. A 25 a 3.7	23/4/17		O/C/C inspected D.E. & X camps. 1/C "A" Brigade transport lines and ROUSSEL FARM.	
	24/4/17		O/C 151 Bates Ambulance returned from leave. (from S.) inspection of P.B. & T. U men. Weather reports show that the wind will probably be favourable for the [?] on the night. two nights [?] [?] and/or [?] meantime meant to take [?] [?] under treatment. 2 Officers } under treatment 108 O.R.S	
	25/4/17		All hours of this ambulance put through two (Corps) dipping baths. O.S. [?] sent pte of exchange from 25/30 April and to 27 for - 25 a.b. for [?] Dent. [?] Nursing Cadet (India element) at Hazebrouck R.M.C. seen. 2 Officers } under treatment 108 O.R.S	
	26/4/17		Pay day. — Work went including ordery detachment, parade, squads REGIMORT CHATEAU orm BILLET FARM [?] and parks. will.	
	27/4/17		Capt. Reynolds reported out from D.H.Q. Medical & Foot inspection Post Infantry drill. 2 Officers } under treatment. 95 O.R.S	

O. H. Mullaly Lt. Col.
O/C 151 2nd of Ambulance

WAR DIARY
or
INTELLIGENCE SUMMARY.

(Erase heading not required.)

Army Form C. 2118.

Place	Date	Hour	Summary of Events and Information	Remarks and references to Appendices
Shed 28 A 28 a 37	28/4/17		John Funnel Proxy Competition - R.A.M.C. v D.+C - later won. Rugby match 38 Division R+ M.C. v R.A.M.C. - R.A.M.C. SS Brigade team won. This was the final match. In 38 division + has hardly played SS match. All took part by 130 an to be admitted to 131 F.A. (from S. Hulpline role) - 2nd in temporary mess. W.O. temporary & made tentants. 2 Other & made tentants. T.C. O.R's	
	29/4/17		Sunday. Ablehpen funeral. M.O. detached to be attended with Q/17, H.F. Army show a lain of Plain air M.O. will transport him at 15 ohld to D+E camp. D. camp to-morrow multiplely. O/C Sanitary Section required the M.O. to report circumstances to R.A.M.S. + informed him he 2 should find a bed report in to-morrow. Than anything Capt Hamilton who had been relieving him but Est infant from leave than anything to all - to this truck. 3 Other & master tentant. F.O.R	
	30/4/17		Visited and inspected A.A.S at LARRY FARM and R.A.P at good BLEVET FARM and BOESINGHE Chateau. Everything satisfactory good work being put in, in relation of R.A.P at BOESINGHE O	

O. Mulholland Lt.Col
O/C 131 Field Ambulance

O.H. Ded/H91

1911/1918

Vol 18

War Diary
131 Field Ambulance
38 (Welsh) Division
for
May 1/31 (inclusive) 19

(Volume XVIII)

COMMITTEE FOR THE
MEDICAL HISTORY OF THE WAR
Date 10 JUL. 1917

Army Form C. 2118.

WAR DIARY
or
INTELLIGENCE SUMMARY.   /31 Fld Ambulance   38 DW

(Erase heading not required.)

Instructions regarding War Diaries and Intelligence Summaries are contained in F.S. Regs., Part II. and the Staff Manual respectively. Title pages will be prepared in manuscript.

Place	Date	Hour	Summary of Events and Information	Remarks and references to Appendices
Shrul 2E A 28 a 3.7	May 1 1917		A.D.M.S. inspects P.B. + T.U. men O/C visited & inspected Z1 Z1. Battery & Bleuelyp Station and Larry Farm. Officers Mil. } unde treatment O.R. 255 }	
	2/5/17		Captain Henry Stokes No.10 Canadian C.C.S. takes him out to form ambulance on approaches of B.T.P. h that septic wound. It was offered to Septic come – & water. The cars were not Smyth as I am myself, when an ambulance to go up & get at – what expected. Officers Mil } I am 5 & 6 days under heavy painful in am any O.R. 255 } ade in not well to shewing such changing. I am very sorry as to under — tunnigu appreau crudi. O/C inspected Sanitary arrangts. Round Farm. "Gas Alarm", at night. Officers Nil. 79 O.R. under treatment.	
	3/5/17		O/C + Major Davis D.A.M.C. visited No 12 Canadian C.C.S. — Capt. Henry Stokes very kindly Shewed some good case treated by B.I.P. – The would, mean a deep empyema in knap Saw & O/C. Received typhus innoculation from A.D.M.S. to say that 20 men of 114 J.F. Donyos, were details on fatigue duty at Round Farm. Gas alarm. Officers Nil. } under treatment. S.I. O.R. } O) P. Willimsleth Lt. Col O/c 131 - British Ambulance	

2353 Wt. W3144/1454 700,000 5/15 D.D.&L. A.D.S.S./Form/C. 2118.

WAR DIARY
INTELLIGENCE SUMMARY

Army Form C. 2118.

131 Field Amb. 38 Division

Place	Date	Hour	Summary of Events and Information	Remarks and references to Appendices
Shel 28 A.28.a.37	4/5/17		Attended Medical meeting at 2/HAZEBROUCK (So. c.c.s) — Subject Trench Feet and Gassing by Thomas (Gas) Splint. 1 Offr. } under treatment 81 O.R. }	
	5/5/17		Visited 2 & 10 C.C.S & saw Capt. Henry 38th Div. Gas[?] spec[?] and Capts. B.9.P. & new cases. Am satisfied as to their good will on our due to strong spring & cleaning that application of R.I.P. method and not to B.I.P itself. Many of cases that were treated by Capt. Stirh with B.I.P. at the unit did not do well and during heart been removed. 1 Offr } under treatment 77 O.R } Sent M.O. to take on temporary medical charge of 122 Bde R.F.A.	
	6/5/17		Medical Board assembled at 131. Entd Andrews admitted & [...] H.G.O. Medicale[?] members Major Dawn & Capt Parry, N.S. to [?] details attached to 38 Divn. 26 arrived. 1 Offr } under treatment 62 O.R } Airgun Room on road. Hotel Long Jean	

O.H. Muhroh[?] Lt Col.
O/C 131 [?] Ambce

Army Form C. 2118.

WAR DIARY
or
INTELLIGENCE SUMMARY
(Erase heading not required.)

131 F. Amb 38 Division

Instructions regarding War Diaries and Intelligence Summaries are contained in F. S. Regs., Part II. and the Staff Manual respectively. Title pages will be prepared in manuscript.

Place	Date	Hour	Summary of Events and Information	Remarks and references to Appendices
Shul 28 Area 07	7/5/17		Commenced making a new incinerator, Drying room & Washing room will be attached. 1 Officer & O.R's made treatment.	
	8/5/17		A.D.M.S. inspected P.B. & T.O. mess water. LARRY FARM. ROUET FARM and ROEINGHE CHATEAU. The new R.A.P. at Lister under Canosby. 2 bus Dugout dug out into BOESINGHE village for R.A.P. a suitable place for an advanced R.A.P. & Man Gun intra a Dugout. 2nd M.O. to the company sick with Sgt Sutherland Searles Went Home M.O. get a leave. 80 O.R's made treatment.	
	9/5/17		Visited & inspected Camp. It has received by 13" Labour Batteln. (Queen's) 1 Officer made treatment. 88 O.R's made treatment.	
	10/5/17		Pay day O/c attended Conferance of M.O.'s F.A. Commanders Officers at Roustaen 2 Officers made treatment. 63 O.R's made treatment	

Mitchell Roberts Lt Coll
O/c 131 Field Ambulance

Army Form C. 2118.

WAR DIARY
or
INTELLIGENCE SUMMARY.   131 Fd Ambulance. 38 Division

(Erase heading not required.)

Instructions regarding War Diaries and Intelligence Summaries are contained in F.S. Regs., Part II. and the Staff Manual respectively. Title pages will be prepared in manuscript.

Place	Date	Hour	Summary of Events and Information	Remarks and references to Appendices
Shtt 28. A 28 a 27	11/9/17.		O/C attended lectures on Nephritis at No 2 C.C.S. Perry Siding. Two dug outs at BOESINGHE completed. 2 Officers } under treatment 28 O.R } Inoc. & inspected Transport lines 114. Fd Bgde.	
	12/9/17.		Capt. Hamilton R.A.M.C. proceeded on 14 days leave ahead of yearly contract. 2 Officers } under treatment 59 O.R }	
	13/9/17		Sunday Nelgm Service. Route walk. Visited A.D.S. LARRY FARM.	
	14/9/17		D.D.M.S. visited und & inspected a/c accommodation. visited & inspected X Camp & ROUSSEL FARM 3 Officers } under treatment 59 O.R }	
	15/9/17		A.D.M.S. inspected P.B. & T.U. – only 2 appeared 4 officers } under treatment 63 O.R }	
	16/9/17		Capt. Davis returned to unit from LARRY FARM Rennes. leaving Lieut Ryan R.a.m.c. in charge. 3 Officers } under treatment 65 O.R } O/C Hrs inspected Lt Col O/C 131 Fd Ambulance	

2353 Wt. W2314/1454 700,000 5/15 D.D. & L.   A.D.S.S./Form/C. 2118.

Army Form C. 2118.

WAR DIARY
or
INTELLIGENCE SUMMARY.
(Erase heading not required.)

131 Fd Amb   38 Division

Instructions regarding War Diaries and Intelligence Summaries are contained in F. S. Regs., Part II. and the Staff Manual respectively. Title pages will be prepared in manuscript.

Place	Date	Hour	Summary of Events and Information	Remarks and references to Appendices
Proposhut 28 A.28.a.3.7	17/5/17		Horse Ambulance detached to proceed to 28.L.2.a.5.6 on 19 x 20. A S.T.S. inspection. 2 other ranks to hospital. 61 O.R.	
	18/5/17		Visited & inspected Transport lines 114 Infantry Brigade — Considerable improvement. 2 M.O's attended medical meeting at No.2 C.C.S. 2 other ranks to hospital. 65 O.R.	
	19/5/17		Semi-final Rugby match (Inter-Divisional Sports) 16 Welch v 13 Welch } Latter won in extra time 13 R.W.F v RAMC } v 13 RWF. Ambulance wagon detached to report to OPC 13 RWF. 4 other ranks to hospital. 58 O.R.	
	20/5/17		Sunday. Adjm Sanitary Section visited Capt Parry attending front party of A.D.S. - one officer in charge to "aan" A.D.S. in that divas only. to take Ambulance wagons to Ope 14 RWF at BOESINGHE CHATEAU are completed.	
	21/5/17		Visited and inspected ROUSSEL FARM 0 other ranks to hospital. 65 O.R.	O.K. Williamson Lt Col OPC 131 Fd Ambulance

WAR DIARY
or
INTELLIGENCE SUMMARY. 131 Fd Amb 36 Division

Army Form C. 2118.

(Erase heading not required.)

Place	Date	Hour	Summary of Events and Information	Remarks and references to Appendices
Map Sheet 28 A 26 a 37	22/5/17		A.D.M.S. inspected P.O. & T.U. men. Visited & inspected H.Q.S. LARRY FARM & BOESINGHE-CHATEAU. Regimental A.P. in situation receiving from A.D.M.S. that X. Camp will henceforth be made Supervisor of O/c 130 F.A. 1 Other } under treatment. 66. O.R } Pat. McAlistic returned from leave.	
	23/5/17		Stone Initial Dirty match (intra divisional Competition) R.A.M.C. v 13 Welsh — latter won by 1 try. New J. medical cards will be brought into use 1st June. 2. Other } under treatment. 63. O.R }	
	04/5/17		Pay day — Visited LARRY FARM (A.D.S.) and BOESINGHE-CHATEAU — also outlying detachments. Priest Ryan attached for temporary duty, with Div Train during absence on leave Capt McMillan. 1 Other } under treatment. 75. O.R } 1 allot.d 1 horse gun to be sent to 46. C.C.S. A.D.M.S. order. No new dental cases to be sent to 46. C.C.S. A.D.M.S. order. Re Inspection of P.H. helmets not to be withdrawn from packs or issued to C.C.S. 200. P.H. helmets to be kept at F.A.	
	26/5/17		Inspection Transferred him Mc Donald O/c Brigade to RUSSEL FARM. Capt McDonald O E o R attached this F.A. to do Divisional Anaesthetical work (Sanders) 1 Other.a } under treatment. 73. O.R } O/C 131 Field Ambulance	

2353 Wt W2544/1454 700,000 5/15 D.D.&L. A.D.S.S./Forms/C. 2118.

Army Form C. 2118.

WAR DIARY
or
INTELLIGENCE SUMMARY.
(Erase heading not required.)

131 St Amb 3rd Division

Place	Date	Hour	Summary of Events and Information	Remarks and references to Appendices
Map Sheet 28 A 28 c 3.7	26/5/17		Visited ELVERDINGHE CHATEAU with A.D.M.S. re Sanitary T.U. men. Inspected Sanitary arrangements at ROUSSEL FARM. Received authority from Corps to draw Material for Construction work at Round Farm & Elverdinghe. 1 Other } Under Treatment. 79 O.R. }	
	27/5/17		Sunday. Division Service & Parade Work. CARDOEN FARM and MOUTON FARM to be made Sanitary Superior of the Unit (A.T.Inc note.) 2 Officers } Under Treatment. 71 O.R. }	
	28/5/17		Completion of dug out at BOESINGHE CHATEAU with other Depts. Spiral patrol A.D.M.S. obtained Officer & O.R. on leaving the Division for France. 2 Officers } Under Treatment. 67 O.R. }	
	29/5/17		Inspection of P.B. & T.U. men by acting A.D.M.S. Captain R. Hamilton proceeded to S.S. Division for duty. 1 Officer } Under treatment. 71 Other ranks }	
	30/5/17		Fuel progress made in the construction of new bays - trams & accessory buildings. Attention was this day paid to all drainage in encampment. 1 Officer } under treatment 66 Other ranks }	
	31/5/17		Visited A.D.S. at LARREY FARM. Further hut under construction in field & dressing room & ward. 1 Officer & 62 other ranks under treatment	N. Brown Major R.A.M.C.

Confidential Vol 19

140/2230

War Diary
of
131 Field Ambulance
38th (Welsh) Division
for
June 1130th 1917

Volume XIX

COMMITTEE FOR THE
MEDICAL HISTORY OF THE WAR
Date -7 AUG. 1917

Army Form C. 2118.

WAR DIARY
or
INTELLIGENCE SUMMARY.   131 Field Ambulance

(Erase heading not required.)

Instructions regarding War Diaries and Intelligence Summaries are contained in F. S. Regs., Part II. and the Staff Manual respectively. Title pages will be prepared in manuscript.

Place	Date	Hour	Summary of Events and Information	Remarks and references to Appendices
Map Sheet 28 A 28 a. 3.7	1/6/17		O/c attended 131 F.A. office during temp. duty during absence of A.D.M.S. (Lt. Col. B. Indies) and proceeding arrival of new one. New A.D.M.S. Col. Thompson joined H.Q. Medical & Dent. inspection - bed inspection - Boot inspection abode. Visited LARRY FARM A.D.S. 1 Officer } 57 O.Rs } under treatment.	
	2/6/17.		A.D.M.S. (Col. Thompson) visited unit. Acting Sanitary (Division) Officer (Capt. M: Donald) proceeded in boat. Relieved by Capt. Rand 129 F.A. (attached this unit). Sent M.O. (Capt. M: Clark) to relieve 130 F.A. Emergency duty. 2 Officers } 63 O.Rs. } under treatment.	
	3/6/17.		Sunday. Religion Services. Heavy enemy shelling. Several shells exploded near F.A - sent Curis killed & 5 wounded hospl in to F.A. M.O's attended at LARRY FARM (Capt. Agnew) relieved Capt. Parry. (Rg. Sn. 2nd hospl in gunned left site.) 1 Officer } 68 O.Rs } under treatment.	
	4/6/17.		Inspection around Mort o Tim camp on stretchers able and not fit to be sent Base. Summoned band played at 130 F.A. 1 Officer } under treatment. 63 O.Rs }	
	5/6/17.		A.D.M.S. visited Unit to inspect P.B. & P.U. men. Medical Board met at 131 F.A. to actuality P.B. men attached 85 Divisn. Present Lt. Col. Hubbold members maj. Davis, R. Shine & Capt. Parry R.A.M.C. Limiard Cinema shows at 121 F.A. Visited LARRY FARM A.D.S. and optined evacuated Tractors. 1 Officer } under treatment. O/c Willoughby Lt. Col. 90 O.R. } O/c 131 Field Ambulance	

Army Form C. 2118.

WAR DIARY
or
INTELLIGENCE SUMMARY of 131 Field Ambulance
(Erase heading not required.)

Instructions regarding War Diaries and Intelligence Summaries are contained in F. S. Regs., Part II. and the Staff Manual respectively. Title pages will be prepared in manuscript.

Place	Date	Hour	Summary of Events and Information	Remarks and references to Appendices
A16 a 3.7	9/6/17		4 Officers } Under treatment. 66 Other Ranks } Parcel received & various number of "Riding Horses" in a Field Ambulance by 9. (2) Refitan horse ambulances by Motor Ambulances. Major J.O'Bairi visited Campil - Canichery bridge etc.	
	10/6/17		4 Officers } Under treatment 5 E Other Ranks }	
	11/6/17		4 Officers } 5.9 Other Ranks } Under treatment. Practised in Daily Orders an order in which - timing form available times & water is required on this day, districts during the summer months.	
	12/6/17		4 Officers } 69 Other Ranks } Under treatment. In position of T.V. & P.B. men by O/A.D.M.S. Col Gerrard D.D.M.S. VIII Corps visited Camp.	
	13/6/17		3 Officers } 69 Other Ranks } Under treatment. Received R.A.M.C. order No. 29. Moves:- No 131 Field Ambulance will hand over its present site at 28. a 3.6 to No 9 Field Ambulance M.G Grande division on the 16th inst and will on the same day take over its present site at ST JEAN. TERBIEZEN: 27 L. I. a. 7. 7. The parties at LARRY FARM B. 9 c. ½. 2½ will, after handing over upon their unit on the evening of the 15th inst after handing over to parties of No 9 Field Ambulance.	

J. O'Beirne Major R.A.M.C.

Army Form C. 2118.

WAR DIARY
or
INTELLIGENCE SUMMARY of 131 Field Ambulance
(Erase heading not required.)

Instructions regarding War Diaries and Intelligence Summaries are contained in F.S. Regs., Part II. and the Staff Manual respectively. Title pages will be prepared in manuscript.

Place	Date	Hour	Summary of Events and Information	Remarks and references to Appendices
28.A.a.3.6	13/6/17		An advance party - Sgt Coles and 9 Other ranks have been detailed to proceed by Cars at 9 a.m. on this morning to the 15th Fld. A take over from No.9 Field Ambulance. Major Davies and Captain Parry proceeded to see the new site.	
	14/6/17		3 Officers } under treatment 65 Other ranks } Evacuated 27 O.R. to D.R.S. Officers of No.9 Field Ambulance visited Camp. Officer of No.29 General n none. R.A.M.C. order No.29 Received in none.	
	15/6/17		3 Officers } under treatment 40 Other ranks } Major Davies visited Camps - Sanitary Instruction. Major Davies visited No.9 Field Ambulance with our ADS. LARRY FARM at 12 noon this day Most: A party from No.9 Field Ambulance returning to Headquarters Captain F.C.A. REYNOLDS and personnel returning by Cars at 9 a.m. this dy & take over from No.9 F. Ambulance. Advance Party, 1 NCO & 9 Other Ranks Proceeded by Cars at 9 a.m. this dy & take over from No.9 F. Ambulance. at ST JAN TERBIEZEN A.D.S. A.3.6. Col BROWN and Col BRAZIER CREAGH A.D.M.S. 39 Division visited Camp at A.25. a.3.6.	
	16/6/17		2 Officers } under treatment 40 Other ranks } Main Dressing Station of the Field Ambulance at A.28 a.3.6. was handed over to No.9 Field Ambulance this morning and our site at L.1.a.77. Sheet 27. Km dry Field ambulance not opened up, in 131. Field Ambulance took over site at L.1.a.77. Sheet 27. Km dry Field Ambulance. Evacuate 23 patients landed over to No.9 Field Ambulance.	
Sheet 27. L.1.a.77.	17/6/17		Marched Off at 11 a.m. Sharp, very hot dy. All ranks paraded at 9 a.m. this day for Inoculation. Relieves known - Noon & 6 E at 6 p.m. Lieut. J.D.Ryan. R.A.M.C. took over temporary medical charge of 76 Army Brigade R.F.A.	

JCDavies Major RAMC

Army Form C. 2118.

WAR DIARY
or
INTELLIGENCE SUMMARY.

(Erase heading not required.) of 131 Field Ambulance

Instructions regarding War Diaries and Intelligence Summaries are contained in F. S. Regs., Part II. and the Staff Manual respectively. Title pages will be prepared in manuscript.

Place	Date	Hour	Summary of Events and Information	Remarks and references to Appendices
Sheet 27. L.I.4. 7.7.	18/6/17		No parades. Usual routine after inoculation. Drew 4. H.D. horses from W. 330 Coy. A.S.C.	
	19/6/17		Training. Route March at 6.30.a.m. No tennis to be worn. Course of Reveille. Stretcher drill 6 – 7 p.m. Captain E.A.O. REYNOLDS took over medical charge of "H" Camp. O.C. inspected and passed from Divisional Kent grenades.	
	20/6/17		Yesterday's training repeated.	
	21/6/17		Pay day — 2nd Cashier was at St. Sixte. Pte. Perry Davis awarded military medal.	
	22/6/17		1. N.C.O. & 30.O.R. detailed to be to report to O.C. 130 F.A. on duty on canal bank. 2. G.S. wagon to report daily by 7 a.m. at the Laundry COSTROVE. Capt. Sewn a 2.O.R. with one push car detailed to duty at XIV Corps Court of ROLEZEELE.	
	23/6/17		2 N.C.O. & 42. men detailed to ance Commandant of A.O. 2.69 (St. SIXTE) on fatigue work — marched off at 5. A.m. 2 Officer & 30. O.R. detailed as advanced party to new Site — CANADA FARM in accordance with A.D.M.S. instruction — Rest of unit to follow as soon as possible — Body moved off at 4.30 P.M. — at 8.30 P.M. — instructions O.A.Millbank. Lt. Col. O/C 131 Field Ambulance

2353 Wt. W2544/1454 700,000 5/15 D.D.& L. A.D.S.S./Forms/C. 2118.

Army Form C. 2118.

WAR DIARY
or
INTELLIGENCE SUMMARY

(Erase heading not required.)

of 131 Fld Ambulance

Instructions regarding War Diaries and Intelligence Summaries are contained in F.S. Regs., Part II. and the Staff Manual respectively. Title pages will be prepared in manuscript.

Place	Date	Hour	Summary of Events and Information	Remarks and references to Appendices
Shed L.A.20/7/7	22/6/17		Instructions received from A.D.M.S. - That H.Q. of unit will not move to CANADA FARM in view of early move of division. - The party of 2 Officers & 30 O.R. will remain there and will be augmented by the 50 O.R. who were rest today to L.S.M.S. as fatigue party. The L.S.M.S. wishes this party to clean up the camp in readiness for a medical unit to move in during the course of next week. Every assistance will be given by the Sanitary Controlation [Sanitary Section]	
	24/6/17		Noted CANADA FARM not practical - also A.D.M.S. & D.D.M.S. It is intended that Bt F.A. who relieve 15 CANADA FARM after 2 or 3 weeks in training area. Noted H.Q. 115 Brigade on instruction in Army that Raincy area. Move to take place on Wednesday 27/6/17 - by LORRY. Stay the night at CAESTRE night that 27 & 28. Arrival. Thursday S. follow stay to HONDEGHEM near LAIRES.	
	28/6/17		Joined H.S.M.S. & D.A.D.M.S. at 8 a.m. at Divisional Headquarters and proceeded with them to Divisional Train(area in neighbourhood of LAIRES. After attending District Establishment of XV Corps School at BOLLEZEELE	

O/C McDonald Lt Col
O/C 131 Fld Ambulance

Army Form C. 2118.

WAR DIARY
or
INTELLIGENCE SUMMARY.
(Erase heading not required.)

Of /31 2nd Ambulance

Place	Date	Hour	Summary of Events and Information	Remarks and references to Appendices
	26/6/17		The M.O. (Major Brown) & seven O.R. proceeded by Motor Ambulance to CAESTRE to meet Brigade Billeting Officer, to make arrangements for tonight.	
a.a.77			One N.C.O. will be left there. M.O. & remainder proceeding to POPERINGHE.	
			2 Officers & detachment from CANADA FARM and 130 F.A. report unit.	
	27/6/17		The unit complete less (8 M.O.s) with Transport marched under Brigade orders to CAESTRE. left LA 16.77 at 7.15 a.m. arrived CAESTRE at 11.a.m. En route for bus training area — Billets for night at BOESCHEPE. Transport arrived 2 hrs. & the proceeded to this area. The unit stayed the night at CAESTRE — Sheet 27. W. 3 Central	
	28/6/17		Unit examined for bus training area (NONENCHEM) at 6.30 a.m. & arrived at destination 1 p.m. Transport marching independently arrived at 3 p.m. Opened to 9 O.R. 115 Pongees at LHIRES.	
	29/6/17		Unit established at CHATEAU MOULINEL. General Police & Routine work	
	30/6/17		Fatigue & Routine work	

(signed) A.S. Humphreys? Lt Col
Comm'g

O/ H. McIntosh Lt Col
O/C 131. 2nd Ambulance

Army Form C. 2118.

WAR DIARY
or
INTELLIGENCE SUMMARY.

131. Field Ambulance

(Erase heading not required.)

Instructions regarding War Diaries and Intelligence Summaries are contained in F.S. Regs., Part II. and the Staff Manual respectively. Title pages will be prepared in manuscript.

Place	Date	Hour	Summary of Events and Information	Remarks and references to Appendices
Map Sheet 28 6/6/17 A 28 a 3.7	6/6/17		Occupied A.D.M.S & D.A.D.M.S. at 5.30 am to LARRY FARM A.D.S. and BLEUET FARM to BOESINGHE CHATEAU. Opened aid post, on way back walked along our route (No. 12 input) had to CARDEON FARM. h demolished. Came way for evacuation to h. avoid ELVERDINGHE. Motorcycles received that No. 12 C.C.S. will receive patients or abidute days with 46 CCS. 1 MO (Lieut RYAN) & 10 OR. forwarded to refit to ADMS 2d Division. Received instrs for temp. Elephant dug out @ to be erected at BLEUET FARM. Drew 16 section for 130. F.A. & 15 for 131 F.A. Commenced Casualty ws & hourly. 4 Officers) under treatment 91 OR)	
	7/6/17		Pay day — Field Cashier attended at 3rd Corps School. Head Quark & attachment paid. Under BLEUET FARM & two armed with MO (Capt Ryan) but portion for him Elephant dug out. 3 Officers) under treatment 79 OR)	
	8/6/17		Great many received successful practice at MESSINES Ridge. Erection of additional elephant dug out commenced at BLEUET FARM. OR. proceeded to SHQ on temp, acting ADMS, and Lieut on leave. 2 Officers) under treatment 79 OR)	

D H Mitcholal, Lt Col
O/C 131 Fld Ambulance

B.E.F.

SUMMARY OF MEDICAL WAR DIARIES FOR
131st F.A.,38th Divn. 14th Corps, 5th Army.

WESTERN FRONT JUNE 1917.

O.C. Lt. Col. R.H. Mills Roberts.

SUMMARISED UNDER THE FOLLOWING HEADING.

Phase "D" Battle of Messines June 1917.

B.E.F. 1.

131st F.A., 38th Divn. 14th Corps, 5th Army. WESTERN FRONT
O.C. Lt. Col. R.H. Mills Roberts. June 1917.

Phase "D" Battle of Messines June 1917.

1917.	Headquarters. At A.28.a.3.7. Sheet 28.
June 10th.	Transfer. Unit transferred with 38th Divn. from 8th Corps, 2nd Army to 14th Corps, 5th Army.
	Medical Arrangements: Unit ran M.D.S. at A.28.a.3.7. A.D.S. at Larry Farm B.9.a.0.2. (Sheet 28)
15th.	Medical Arrangements: A.D.S. Larry Farm handed over to 9th Field Ambulance Guards Divn.
16th.	Medical Arrangements: Main Dressing Station handed over to 9th Field Ambulance.
	Moves: To L.1.a.7.7. (Sheet 27)
21st.	Decoration: Pte Davies P. awarded M.M.
23rd.	Moves Detachment: 1 and 2 to 14th Corps School at Bollezeele.
	2 and 30 to Canada Farm (advance party) Rejoined unit 26th.
27th- 28th.	Moves: To Honenghem Training Area.

B.E.F.

SUMMARY OF MEDICAL WAR DIARIES FOR
131st F.A., 38th Divn. 14th Corps, 5th Army.

WESTERN FRONT JUNE 1917.

O.C. Lt. Col. R.H. Mills Roberts.

SUMMARISED UNDER THE FOLLOWING HEADING.

Phase "D" Battle of Messines June 1917.

B.E.F. 1.

131st F.A., 38th Divn. 14th Corps, 5th Army.   WESTERN FRONT
O.C. Lt. Col. R.R. Mills Roberts.   June 1917.

Phase "D" Battle of Messines June 1917.

1917.	Headquarters. At A.28.a.3.7. Sheet 28.
June 10th.	Transfer. Unit transferred with 38th Divn. from 8th Corps, 2nd Army to 14th Corps, 5th Army.
	Medical Arrangements: Unit ran M.D.S. at A.28.a.3.7. A.D.S. at Larry Farm B.9.a.0.2. (Sheet 28)
15th.	Medical Arrangements: A.D.S. Larry Farm handed over to 9th Field Ambulance Guards Divn.
16th.	Medical Arrangements: Main Dressing Station handed over to 9th Field Ambulance.
	Moves: To L.1.a.7.7. (Sheet 27)
21st.	Decoration: Pte Davies P. awarded M.M.
23rd.	Moves Detachment: 1 and 2 to 14th Corps School at Bollezeele.
	2 and 30 to Canada Farm (advance party) Rejoined Unit 26th.
27th- 28th.	Moves: To Honenghem Training Area.

Confidential MV 20

War Diary

5/1/31 Field Ambulance
38 (Welsh) Division

for

July 1st 31 1917

Volume XX

COMMITTEE FOR THE
MEDICAL HISTORY OF THE WAR
Date 10 SEP. 1917

WAR DIARY or INTELLIGENCE SUMMARY of 131. Field Ambulance

Army Form C. 2118.

Place	Date	Hour	Summary of Events and Information	Remarks and references to Appendices
HONENGIFEM	1·7·17		Sunday. Routine work and Religious Services. MO detailed to visit morning Sick of 124. Field. Coy. R.E. at BONCOURT. O/c visited Field Cashier at NORRENT-FONTES to draw Pay money for next Thursday. This being — apparently — the only duty of F.C. to this neighbourhood for some time. 3. O.R. under treatment.	
	2·7·17		A.D.M.S. inspected P.B. & T.U. men at this unit. One tent subdivision of this unit is to be held at readiness for disposal by D.M.S. 1st Army. "D.D.M.S." XIV Corps instructions.	
	3·7·17		Training ground in the immediate vicinity is difficult to obtain on all the land practically is under cultivation. Proceeded in earmarking a good field — about ½ miles away. Training consist of Route marching. Stretcher drill & lecture in addition to ½ hour close order Company drill every day — & foot inspection drill. { 1. Officer } under treatment. { 8. O.R. }	
	4·7·17		Visited { Brigade } training area — also 130 F.A. at LA-TIRNAND. Sent M.O. to take medical charge of 11 S.W.B. during absence on leave of Regimental M.O. (Capt. S. Swan) another M.O. Lieut. Ryan struck of strength of unit in order to replace M.O. 122 Bde. F.A. 2. men transferred to 6.S. Labour Coy. { 1. Officer } under treatment. { 10. O.R. }	

D.H. Smith Oakeley Lt. Col.
O/c 131. Field Ambulance

Army Form C. 2118.

WAR DIARY
or
INTELLIGENCE SUMMARY. of 131. Field Ambulance
(Erase heading not required.)

Place	Date	Hour	Summary of Events and Information	Remarks and references to Appendices
HONEBCKE	5/7/17.		Major Davy (2i/c in command) went on leave. Pay day. all O.R paid 17. O.R under treatment.	
	6/7/17		Medical & foot inspection — Bn. Informed child. 19. O.R. under treatment.	
	7/7/17		Unit proceeded to having one and took part in manœuvres of 115. Brigade. March in made 5.45 a.m — worked till at 6.4 m returned at 4.30 P.m. Captain J O/c Irish Ambulance at A.D.M.S. office taken over the training one in a Reflee of that part of him to be taken by 38 Divin late as for "push". 21. O.R. under treatment.	
	8/7/17.		Sunday: Religious service & Pushia work only. 26. O.R under treatment.	
			A.Q.P.M.S 38' Div visited the unit. 26 O.R. under treatment	
	9/7/17		A.D.M.S. inspected P.B + T.U. men. 35. O.R. under treatment.	O H Kinly astah Lt Col o/c. 131. Field Ambulance

Army Form C. 2118.

WAR DIARY
or
INTELLIGENCE SUMMARY of 131 Field Ambulance
(Erase heading not required.)

Place	Date	Hour	Summary of Events and Information	Remarks and references to Appendices
HONERGHEM	10/7/17		Conference of Regimental Medical Officers and M.O's i/c St. Germain Substations at 129 F.A. Capt Reynolds attended from this F.A. – he will be i/c of this F.A. bearer dressing post. 296 R. under treatment.	
	11/7/17		Conference of Quartermasters at 131 F.A. to meet A.D.M.S. Visited A.D.M.S and accompanied him to the D.D.M.S. XIV Corps and Canada Farm – from unit to Widely to take over the site later on during the push.	
	12/7/17		Divisional Field day. Replica of what is to happen later on. Ground laid out accordingly. On site at HONERGHEM apart CANADA FARM and is staffed accordingly by Tent Subdivision. Bearer Subdivision with Command of Capt. Reynolds join in Manoeuvres with bearer of 129 & 130 F.A. He works under Command of Capt. Roe 129 F.A. Breakfast 4.30 AM – dinner bottle cold – retired at 8 P.M. Scheme worked very satisfactorily.	
	13/7/17		Quite work of keeping an Unit, licencing futol. night march – 1/2 hour in gas respirator. Order received from man of 11C. Brigade from LAIRES to STEENBECQUE area. 131 F.A. to be billeted at MOLINGHEM – just night of move.	

NTWhitelock
Lt Col
O/c. 131. Field Ambulance

WAR DIARY
or
INTELLIGENCE SUMMARY of 131 Field Ambulance

Army Form C. 2118.

(Erase heading not required.)

Place	Date	Hour	Summary of Events and Information	Remarks and references to Appendices
HONENGHEM	14/7/17		Routine work & Genl. training. O/c proceeded to R4 (115) Fiel Ambl — Send Cpn. inf. with temp. 103°. 19. O.R. made treatment.	
	15/7/17.		Pms. Genl. Cpn. evacuated to 57 C.C.S. Polishing party Capt. J.J. Daw & 1 N.C.O. proceeded to MOLINGHEM to meet billeting oprs. Capt. Irving. 21. O.R. made treatment.	
	16/7/18		HONENGHEM. (MOULINEL) Unit with its transport marched from MOLINGHEM (CHATEAU) at 7.15 A.M. (Reveille 4.30 A.M.) arrived MOLINGHEM at 11.30 A.M. — 11 mls. (2° in command major Davis returned from leave). Polishing party 1. Offn. & O.R. proceeded to CAESTRE his next Bivgac. (Billeting Offr) MOLINGHEM	
	17/7/18.		Unit with its transport marched from CAESTRE at 3.30 A.M. — reached CAESTRE 12.30 P.M. clearing HAZEBROUCK at 6.30 A.M.	
	18/7/18		The unit & transport reached from CAESTRE to ECKE about 2 mls. to rest for the day & night	
	19/7/18		Proceeded from ECKE to PROVEN area, no billet — bivouacked in a field. Unit on advanced party. 1. Offn. & 6. O.R. to CANADA FARM	

WAR DIARY or INTELLIGENCE SUMMARY of 131 Field Ambulance

Army Form C. 2118.

Place	Date	Hour	Summary of Events and Information	Remarks and references to Appendices
PROVEN AREA	20/7/17		Lt. Col. ECKE & Q.M. reached CANADA FARM at 12 noon with 2nd line A Park & on Tac. Subdivisions. The whole of the Tent Subdivision was entrained at 5.30 A.M. & 2 Officers followed at 6.30 by Car to take over part of CANADA FARM from 86 Field Ambulance. Took over command of C.M.D.S. at Canada Farm, now manned by No 3 & No 131 F.A's. A new type of gas smelling slightly of garlic is mentioned here nearly two weeks in use by enemy on 5th Army front. (Iron tent bolts retd.)	
	21/7/17		Patients admitted — 40, evacuated 35 — O.R. 1 Officer.	
	22/7/17		Of the above O.R. 1 was gassed & 34 shell wounds. 1 Officer, 1 child wound. Sunday. A board was held at 131 F.A. to investigate a case of Anthrax. President. Capt. Thompson 4.5th S. Member. Lt. Col. O'H Malt. Ord. & Lt. Col. W.B. Edwards. O.R. admitted 112, evacuated 90 — gassed 16 — shell wounds 74. Officers 5 — gassed 1 — S.W. 5	
	23/7/17		Icklepsa & Canton work. Pts admitted Officers 3 (shell wound) evacuated 3 O.R. 128 115. (SW. gassed — 57. S.W.) (M.T. Car driver — shortly instructed) M-Car ordered to and from XIV Corps school Bollezeele. O.K. Williamson U. Col. O/C 131 Field Ambulance	

Army Form C. 2118.

WAR DIARY
or
INTELLIGENCE SUMMARY. of 131. Field Ambulance
(Erase heading not required.)

Place	Date	Hour	Summary of Events and Information	Remarks and references to Appendices
Shul 28 A.18.G.17	24/7/17		A.D.M.S. visited unit for inspection of P.B. & T.B. men - men for inspection & D.M.S. - visited & inspected unit. 5 Officer & 211 O.R admitted. 115 OR 62. O.R. S.W 5 " 180 " evacuated 1 O.f games 2. two M.O's reported for duty.	
	25/7/17		Officer to Ammunition Reserve on 2. day (Capt Reynolds) & G.D. Sergt visited Canal bank to reconnoitre. 6. Officer games. 3 Officers games 290. O.R.f evacuated —— 236 O.R.f admitted 300 O R.f	
	26/7/17		word by A.D.M.S. He informed me that O/c 129. F.A. is the evacuation to 62 CCS the F.A's hopes. he is accordingly passed thro' the F.A's hopes. O/c noted of D.A.L. and obtained permission to get B.R.C & by means of motor for admission of patient article, to C.M.B.; Jimken (Red Cross) of obtains from C.S.Cap. 6 Cottage road.	
	27/7/17		Visited B.R.Com. in ambulance with stone Royal Society. A.D.M.S. orde.. "Motor field Ambulance ready to take up position & a laid down from 2. day at one hour notice" D. Knell notably Lt.fol O/c 131. Field Ambulance	

WAR DIARY or INTELLIGENCE SUMMARY. Of 131. Field Ambulance

Army Form C. 2118.

Place	Date	Hour	Summary of Events and Information	Remarks and references to Appendices
Sul. 28 A.18.D.17	28/7/17		O.B.M.S. 28' Welsh Division visited C.M.S. also O.B.M.S. XIV Corps. Enemy aeroplane flew low on C.M.S — dropping used flare by with machine gun fire. Officers admitted 7 O.R. " 218 Officers evacuated 7 O.R. " 137 80 gassed cases from 14' R.W.F. admitted — 9 where 74 in very slight and am kept for observation.	A.D. Homefan Con arising 38th Div.
	29/7/17		O.B.M.S. sent medical arrangements (scheme) + 2 addendum No 11 created. A.D.M.S came that M.O. i/c 38 Divisional Train & 30' D.A.C. was report on night of 30th for duty. Officers admitted — 4 O.R. " 157 " evacuated 4 O.R. " 210	
	30/7/17		M.O.'s 38 Divisional Train + 30. D.A.C. reported for duty — sent them to Canal Bank. Reaves 9, 129 & 130 F.A. during the day. They were put with our men at intervals on Canal Bank. Se Denier refuses for been sick. Lieut C.H.R.S. M.O. R. Parker from 29 & 29 Division also reported for duty at C.M.S. Sent R. Applied Capt. Brian Canadian Robert Lyon Lieut Lyon will Rendesons at S.S. the Him morning.	No. 2 F.A. Officer O.R. Buch, German 247. 748. 9. 112 No. 131 F.M. Germany Officer O.R. 52. 743. 134
	31/7/17		Allies attack began about 4AM Cars admitted to XIV C.M.S. from Zero hour 31/7/17 to 12 noon 1/8/17 Total 1845	A.D.S.S./Forms/C. 2118. O H Willarlab Lt Col O/C. 131. Field Ambulance

Confidential

War Diary

131 Field Ambulance
38 (Welsh) Division
for
August 1st - 1915

(Volume XX)

Aug 1919

Vol 21

14of 4 38

COMMITTEE FOR THE
MEDICAL HISTORY OF THE WAR
Date -5 NOV. 1917

Army Form C. 2118.

WAR DIARY
or
INTELLIGENCE SUMMARY of 131 Field Ambulance

(Erase heading not required.)

Place	Date	Hour	Summary of Events and Information	Remarks and references to Appendices
Shret 28 A.18.a.1.7	1/8/17		A very wet day. Camp is a quagmire. Very difficult for team work. additional	
	2/8/17		Weather like yesterday. Sent another M.O. to Canal Bank. Fifty horses sent down for a night's rest — to report again at Canal Bank at 6 A.M. M.O. first to Canal Bank.	
	3/8/17		In order to save pack wastage A.D.M.S. decide to have light cars treated in tramer has instead of pushing them to C.R.S. They will not go to Corps Dick Adducting Post. 38 division not from A.D.M.S. XIV Corps & A.D.M.S. 36 Division So two shuttle beam corm down for night's rest, go hybrid at Canal Bank terminus 6 A.M. 131 remain at	
	4/8/17		36 Stir's released by 20 Stir. C.M.D.S. 129 & 130. F.A. go to PROVEN. AREA.	
	5/8/17		CANADA FARM. K.and.- C.M.D.S.	
	6/8/17		Between 6 M.O's return to unit from Canal Bank, A Boche shell dropped in C.M.D.S. Compound – no casualties – several casualties by another shell in road in front of C.M.D.S. Capt. McMahon joined unit.	
	7/8/17		Amble M.O. — Lieut Parsons and Carleton sent to 129 & 130. F.A's – 2 M.O's –	
	8/8/17		M.O. — Lieut Rooke — evacuated to C.C.S. — ear trouble. Visited Field Cashier at PROVEN to draw pay. A good many shells fell in neighbourhood of about Camp.	

O H Mills O Leary Lt Col
O/C 131. Field Ambulance

WAR DIARY
or
INTELLIGENCE SUMMARY of 131. Field Ambulance

Army Form C. 2118.

(Erase heading not required.)

Place	Date	Hour	Summary of Events and Information	Remarks and references to Appendices
Shut. 28 A.18.a.1.7	9/8/17		A.D.M.S. visits camp — All lorries that were lent from Corps Supply for evacuation purposes to return to their headquarters.	
	10/8/17		M.O. detailed to 1/7 R.W.F. to replace one going on leave.	
	11/8/17		2 U.S.A. M.O.'s report for duty. arrange with No 3. F.A. to open an advance post. There is no need to keep 6th Ambulance open every night. Work being slackened.	
	12/8/17		R.E. Officer called to inspect road leading to & from C.M.D.S. — Surface is very rough for wounded patients — two loads of broken granite sent to place on & later rough roast tracks & put posts used for making roads.	
	13/8/17		Sch. Collecting Post is placed under control of O/c C.M.D.S. (i.e. O/c 131 F.A.) A.D.M.S. visits Camp.	
	14/8/17		P.A. Day. A.S.M.L. aspnl. with camp and presents military medal to L/Cpl Davies for gallantry near Individual Cross. Thu Football Medal also presented to Pte Simpson in ? julia Divisional Football Competition. member of R.A.M.C. team — Runner up in Julia Divisional Football Competition. two men from unit (131 F.A.) away on each Annual & Sp allotted -S. Medal leave.	

Mitchell, Robert, Lt/Col
O/c 131. Field Ambulance

Army Form C. 2118.

WAR DIARY
or
INTELLIGENCE SUMMARY. of 131. Field Ambulance

(Erase heading not required.)

Instructions regarding War Diaries and Intelligence Summaries are contained in F.S. Regs., Part II. and the Staff Manual respectively. Title pages will be prepared in manuscript.

Place	Date	Hour	Summary of Events and Information	Remarks and references to Appendices
Sheet 28. A.18.a.1.7	15/8/17		A.D.M.S. visited C.M.D.S. accompanied him to C.W.V.S. at MOUTON FARM. O/c. 4.M.A.C. reported himself for duty in view of Operation — 30. M.A.C. Cars on duty at C.M.D.S	
	16/8/17		2 day for 20 & 25' division — all operation obtained. 28 officers & 371 O.R. 20' Division 5 " 6 " 35' " } passed thru 131. F.A. 1 " 11 " Corps Troops	
	17/8/17		Orders received that 38' Div is to relieve 20' Div — movement to be completed on 19/8/17. 131. F.A. to go to Canal Bank & be attached to 130. F.A. who will be cleaning. Leaves 131. F.A. sent to PELISSER FARM to report to O/c 130 F.A. who has no H.Q. there.	
	18/8/17		Three horse Ambulances sent to 131. F.A. Horses & men to be retained by them to run the Corps Collecting Sick Post at Canada Farm. Capt Procell reports accordingly.	
	19/8/17		Sanitary Section work visit by A.D.M.S. 38' Division an officer from 129 is to run the Head Quarters — H. Camp	
	20/8/17		M.O. detailed to attend Sick at H. Head Quarters — H. Camp 9 off } admitted 96 O.R }	
	21/8/17		Capt Graham from R.A.M.C. evacuated hurts (scratches) to C.C.S. Capt Aspinall R.A.M.C. rejoined unit. 4 officers } admitted 95 O.R }	

N Mulhollich Lt Col
O/c 131 Field Ambulance

Army Form C. 2118.

WAR DIARY
or
INTELLIGENCE SUMMARY.
(Erase heading not required.)

131. Field Ambulance

Instructions regarding War Diaries and Intelligence Summaries are contained in F. S. Regs., Part II. and the Staff Manual respectively. Title pages will be prepared in manuscript.

Place	Date	Hour	Summary of Events and Information	Remarks and references to Appendices
Sept 28 A 18 a 17	22/8/17		Intimation received that Military medal granted to Sergt Sands, for good work done on 31st ult — during recent operations — DCM was expected. 3 Officers & 69 O.R. admitted	
	23/8/17		DMS 5th Army visited Camp, & expressed satisfaction. He took all ambulance cars to be kept in conjunction with the A.S.M.S — Work has been in progress for sometime, covering him with the A.S.M.S. Sent 6 OR Tank in team — A staff event — k 129 F.A. M.O. Capt. M.C. Paterson against wrote. 3 Officers & 145 O.R. admitted	
	24/8/17		10 Corps & Officers went to BAILEUL stopped on & stay with 1/2 way — ADMS visited Camp went to Trans/ft control 27 Div to examine division pan. On way back to Trans/ft control 27 Div to examine division pan, went to sidings A.S.C. (Divisional Train) with 3rd & 1st Inf'y. A staff notion to detail an officer to sidings. 84 O.R. admitted. 3 Officers N.C.O.'s & others — 2. of present M.D.N. at	
	25/8/17		visited A.D.M.S. Office re promotion of N.C.O.'s to uptece — 2. at present M.D.N. at C.C.S. 1 Officer. 54 O.R. admitted	
	26/8/17		(Sunday) Routine work	
	27/8/17 28/8/17		Visited PELISSIER FARM and accompanied A.D.M.S. to FUSILIER FARM D.S. CHEAP SIDE & SOLFERINO, SISING, concerning known "operation. 6 Officers & 49 O.R. admitted 6 Officers & DS. Band I/N.C.O & 26 men out to concert — where were realised in the afternoon. Acting D.D.M.S.	
	28/8/17 29/8/17		Sent 12 additional Stretcher bearers to Junshi A.D.S. They were realised in the afternoon. Acting D.D.M.S. FARM to do stretch work for day — hery wet & stormy day the Capt visited Camp, also A.D.M.S. 36 sick Division 3 (Bearer) returned from FUSILIER A.D.S. 3 Officer & others. 42 O.R. admitted M.O. (Capt. Cowan) 1 and unit 3. Officer 42 O.R. admitted	D. M. Millwood Lt Col O/c 131. Field Ambulance

2353. Wt. W2514/1454 700,000 5/15 D.D. & L. A.D.S.S./Forms/C 2118.

Army Form C. 2118.

WAR DIARY
or
INTELLIGENCE SUMMARY. 131 Field Ambulance.
(Erase heading not required.)

Place	Date	Hour	Summary of Events and Information	Remarks and references to Appendices
Shel. 28 A.18.a.1.7.	29/8/17		4 Outposts of known German operation and who did not receive a medal — although recommended for same. M.O. (Capt. Parry) rejoined unit from sick leave — another M.O (Capt Copp) reported — Corps ordered will be detailed later on. 55 Officers + 69 O.R. admitted.	
	30/8/17		Sat on M.O (Capt. Reynolds) to help M.O. Sanitation Sect. at ONDANK — to be continued every morning. M.O (Capt. Curson) arrived 28/8/17 - detailed to E.M.C. (D.I.M.S order) 1 Officer { 41 O.R.} admitted.	
	31/8/17		M.O. (Capt. Copp). detailed for duty with 9 R.H.A. 5th Army Brigade. M.O (Capt. (Carleton (from 129 F.A.) reports for duty. M.O. (Capt. M'Indoo) detailed for temporary duty with 122 R.F.A. Brigade. 1 Officer { 51 O.R.} admitted.	

A.G. Thompson Col
ADMS @ 38th Div.

N. Kirkpatrick Lt Col
O/C 131 Field Ambulance

140/2238

No. 131. 7 a.

COMMITTEE FOR THE
MEDICAL HISTORY OF THE WAR
Date —5 NOV. 1917

WAR DIARY
or
INTELLIGENCE SUMMARY of 131st Field Ambulance

Army Form C. 2118.

(Erase heading not required.)

Instructions regarding War Diaries and Intelligence Summaries are contained in F. S. Regs., Part II. and the Staff Manual respectively. Title pages will be prepared in manuscript.

Place	Date	Hour	Summary of Events and Information	Remarks and references to Appendices
Sheet 28 A 12 a 17	1/9/17		Augmented by R.A.M.C. trencher detachment to total 5 Officers & 60 O.R. of 13th C.C.S.	O.H.M.R.
			Bivouac until their new site at MOUTON FARM is ready.	
	2/9/17		Sunday. Routine work.	
			Detached our M.O. (Capt Parry) to actively supervise Sand advance Salvage Coy.	R.H.M.R
	3/9/17		Camp visited by Col Inyan Cdt. A.D.M.S. 38 (Welsh) Division — has asked Cavly. Corps	R.H.M.R
			6 Officers & 60 O.R. from No 13. C.C.S. reported as arranged. E. & O. as on 1/9/17.	O.H.M.R
	4/9/17		O/C. goes on 10 days leave and Captain S.H. Parry.	
	5/9/17		}	
	6/9/17		} Routine work.	
	7/9/17		}	
	8/9/17		}	
	9/9/17		Advanced party proceeded to PANAMA CAMP near PROVEN.	
			28440 Pte J.J. Parkin; 28348 Pte J.H. Evans G/A of the Field Ambulance awarded Military Medal.	
			R.C. Service at CARDOEN FARM. Our C/E at CANADA FARM.	
	10/9/17		131 Field Ambulance landed one Bearer Section to 61 Field Ambulance at Epton Bigby,	
			1 R and 1/2 the dy 131 Field Ambulance for XIV Corps from Bearing Station at CANADA FARM.	
	11/9/17		131 Field Ambulance at E.a.m. this day marched from CANADA FARM to PANAMA CAMP. Transport proceeded and at 6 a.m.	

J.C. Beeris Major

Army Form C. 2118.

WAR DIARY
or
INTELLIGENCE SUMMARY. of 131 Field Ambulance
(Erase heading not required.)

Instructions regarding War Diaries and Intelligence Summaries are contained in F. S. Regs., Part II. and the Staff Manual respectively. Title pages will be prepared in manuscript.

Place	Date	Hour	Summary of Events and Information	Remarks and references to Appendices
EECKE ESTAIRES	12/9/17		Captain & 2 O.R. Reynolds O.O.M.C & 1 2 O.R. proceeded this day in advance to EECKE. 131 Field Ambulance marched this day under Brigade arrangements to EECKE and remained there over night	
MORBECQUE	13/9/17		131 Field Ambulance marched this day under Brigade arrangements from EECKE to MORBECQUE area. Captain Reynolds and 2 O.R. proceeded this day in advance to the new site for billeting duty at ESTAIRES.	
ESTAIRES	14/9/17		Captain Reynolds and 20 O.R. proceeded this day to new Headquarters at FORT RONPOU. 131 Field Ambulance marched to ESTAIRES.	

J.C.Barr. Major RAMC

Army Form C. 2118.

WAR DIARY
or
INTELLIGENCE SUMMARY of 131. Field Ambulance
(Erase heading not required.)

Instructions regarding War Diaries and Intelligence Summaries are contained in F. S. Regs., Part II. and the Staff Manual respectively. Title pages will be prepared in manuscript.

Place	Date	Hour	Summary of Events and Information	Remarks and references to Appendices
ESTAIRES Sheet 36. H 7. d. 63	14/9/17		O/C. 131 Field Ambulance returned from leave, joining unit billets for night at ESTAIRES	O.H.M.R.
	15/9/17		Unit marched from ESTAIRES at 2.30 P.M. reaching site at FORT ROMPO. (map ref Sheet 36. H 7.d. 63) at 4.30 P.M.— remain parked. Site was to taken on turnover. A.D.S. at HOUPLINES and BRICK STACK are taken on tonight on M.O. with 21 or 25 men being part of each A.D.S.— and details as required for detached posts. O/C M.O's been quite of men q 2. 3d Wess. FA.	O.H.M.R.
	16/9/17		Took over Field Ambulance site — (mq. of an stabs) at FORT ROMPO. from 2/9. 3/9 West. F.A. Visited A.D.S. at HOUPLINES and BRICK STACK.	O.H.M.R.
	17/9/17		Conf. of O/C's F.A. at A.D.M.S. office at 2.15 P.M. O/C 131 F.A. sick when him temporad. A.D.M.S. intends going on leave on 19th	O.H.M.R.
	18/9/17		Carefully inspected the new site, found that there was room for many improvement, the site required much cleaning.	
	19/9/17		By Col R.H. Pile- Robert took over temporarily duties of A.D.M.S. vice A.D.M.S. proceeding on leave. Major J.C. Burns assumed command of 131 Field Ambulance.	
	20/9/17		Lieut M.Y. Fenton R.S.R. his duty took on medical change of 16 P.W. Z and was struck off on strength S.O.C. 38' (Math) Gibson visited the unit	
	21/9/17		acting A.D.M.S. visited the Field Ambulance for inspection of Kitchens P.B. and T.U. men. Visited A.D.S. at the BRICK STACK.	
	22/9/17		Lt. Parker U.S.R. was detailed for the inspection and medical charge of numerous details in the area	
	23/9/17		C.M.E. farewell at Church Hut at 10.30 a.m. From C.M.E. in Dump room at 3.30 p.m. visited A.D.S. at NEUNE HOUPLINES	

J.C. Burns Major R.A.M.C.

Army Form C. 2118.

WAR DIARY
or
INTELLIGENCE SUMMARY.

of 131 Field Ambulance

(Erase heading not required.)

Place	Date	Hour	Summary of Events and Information	Remarks and references to Appendices
FORT ROMPOU	23/9/17		Capt. M. Gittani R.A.M.C. proceeded to a Portuguese Battalion forming this Division in order to assist and advise the medical officer.	
	24/9/17		Visited A.D.S. BRICK STACK. Fresh improvement had been carried out which added materially to the comfort & safety of the personnel stationed there. Capt. M. Roberts R.A.M.C. reported for duty.	
	25/9/17		D.D.M.S. XI Corps visited the unit & there very much pleased with what he saw.	
	26/9/17		The improvement to the main approach road was commenced. Two officers and 12 O.R. attended a demonstration at 129 Field Ambulance. It proved Pressident demonstration to men of the Thomas Splint in cases of fracture of the femur.	
	27/9/17		Pay the day at 2 p.m. Progress was made with the new Incinerator and Cook house.	
	28/9/17		A.D.M.S. inspection of proposed P.B and T.U men. Progress made with construction of new road at entrance to Station.	
			# Col. Mill. Roberts returned from Divisional Headquarters.	
	29/9/17		Capt. F.A.C. Reynolds return from leave in England.	
			Relgious Service C of E at 10.30 a.m at YMCA Hut BAC ST MAUR.	
	30/9/17		Divisional Service held at Hay's Train Room 5.15 p.m.	
			Capt: Reynolds relieves Capt M'Mullen at HOUPLINES + D.S.	

W. Thompson Capt RAMC
3 S "
OC/on

M.Burns Major RAMC

Confidential
16
Col. 191

W.O.&99

War Diary
1st Field Ambulance
38 (Welsh) Division
for
October 1st 1917

Volume XXIII

COMMITTEE FOR THE
MEDICAL HISTORY OF THE WAR
Date -8 DEC. 1917

Army Form C. 2118.

WAR DIARY
or
INTELLIGENCE SUMMARY. of 131. Field Ambulance

(Erase heading not required.)

Instructions regarding War Diaries and Intelligence Summaries are contained in F.S. Regs., Part II. and the Staff Manual respectively. Title pages will be prepared in manuscript.

Place	Date	Hour	Summary of Events and Information	Remarks and references to Appendices
Sheet 36. H.7.d.6.3	1/10/17		Sent M.O. (Capt. McMillan) to relieve M.O. (Capt. Spilsbury) attached to Portuguese Troops. — Latter returned to unit. Admission 26 O.R.	
	2/10/17		D.M.S. & D.A.D.M.S. 1st Army, Gen. Thompson & Lt.Col. Davidson accompanied by A.D.M.S. & D.A.D.M.S. 38 held division visited unit. — I proceeded with party to JOURLINES & BRICK STACK A.D.S. The General appeared pleased with what he saw. Admission 17 O.R.	
	3/10/17		Routine work. Men of good education required as Candidates for Commission with the Infantry (Daily orders this day) Admission 1 Officer (Sent to 129 a. There is no accommodation for Officers at 131 F.A.) 19 O.R.	
	4/10/17		Visited A.D.S. at BRICK STACK — good progress with new work. M.O. (Capt. Richards) detailed to take on temporary medical charge of Heavy Artillery group during absence of their M.O. (Capt. Newton) 23 O.R. admitted.	
	5/10/17		A.D.M.S. visited unit for inspection of P.B. men. Conference of M.O.'s Admission at 131 F.A. + D.M.S. proceeded. M.O. detailed (Capt. Richards) to 17.R.W.F. (vice Capt. Gwin wounded) & Shock Shingle of unit. 15 O.R. admitted.	

O H Willocks Lt. Col.
O/C 131. Field Ambulance.

WAR DIARY
or
INTELLIGENCE SUMMARY of 131 Field Ambulance

Army Form C. 2118.

Place	Date	Hour	Summary of Events and Information	Remarks and references to Appendices
Sheet 36 H.7.d.6.3.	6/10/17		Sergt. Major returned from leave. Order received to put clock back by 1 hour. O.R. 12 admitted.	
	7/10/17		Winter time adopted by British armies in France at 1.A.M. this day — 1.A.M. Keeping 12 m.n. — 6/7 wise. Routine work. Sunday. Religion service. 11.0 O.R. admitted.	
	8/10/17		Conter (131 F.A.) reopened. Arrnat. given by 13 + 14 bdh. Bats. Application made to A.D.M.S on telephone re O.R. 131 F.A. 17. O.R. admitted.	
	9/10/17		S. Majr (Edward). H.T. attached sent on leave. S.A.S.C. hate sent to base when applied for. 5 T.U. men joined unit to replace 5 A.S.C. 36. O.R. admitted.	
	10/10/17		5 A.S.C. men sent to base in ambulance with order received. 6. men with slight wounds of Company attached to O/c 123 F.Coy R.E. front. I.M.O (Capt. McMillan) proceeded on leave; ~~returned on leave~~ 6. O.R. admitted.	
	11/10/17		Pay day (2 P.M.) A.A.Q.M.G. 38 Division visited Camp. M.O.(Lieut Bush) detailed to closely inspect of billets 112 Brigade. 8 T.M. billets noted. LtCol ~~Slott~~ O/c 131 Field Ambulance 6. O.R. admitted.	

Army Form C. 2118.

WAR DIARY
or
INTELLIGENCE SUMMARY of 131 Field Ambulance
(Erase heading not required.)

Instructions regarding War Diaries and Intelligence Summaries are contained in F. S. Regs., Part II. and the Staff Manual respectively. Title pages will be prepared in manuscript.

Place	Date	Hour	Summary of Events and Information	Remarks and references to Appendices
Sheet 36 H.7.d.63	12/10/17		A.D.M.S. visited camp for inspection. P.R. men. Routine work. 24 O.R. admitted	
	13/10/17		Routine work.	
	14/10/17		Maj. Gen. Mackade, G.O.C. 38 Division visited unit — He was accompanied by a General Officer, U.S.A. and others. F.A. to relieve Personnel Jurisd. for Auxiliary R.A.M.C. Officers. Ordered O/C 129 & 130 F.A. to choose Personnel for Bench Work A.D.S. (letter signed unit) Lieut. Buck relieved Capt. Parry of Bench Work A.D.S. 17 O.R. admitted.	
	15/10/17		Instructions received for Major S.C. Davis to proceed to England. 12 O.R. admitted.	
	16/10/17		For the 2'9 in Command of the unit Major S.C. Davis proceed to England for home service. A.S.M.S instructions. 31 O.R. admitted.	
	17/10/17		Conference of O/C's F.A. 28 Div. at A.D.M.S. Offices. 28 O.R. admitted.	
	18/10/17		Visited A.D.S's & R.A.P. at TISSAGE. Dynamo notified — Electric light re-established at new kitchen & Catham complex at M.D.S. M.D.S.	O. Muirhead, Lt Col. O/C 131 Field Ambulance

Army Form C. 2118.

WAR DIARY
or
INTELLIGENCE SUMMARY of 131. Field Ambulance
(Erase heading not required.)

Instructions regarding War Diaries and Intelligence Summaries are contained in F. S. Regs., Part II. and the Staff Manual respectively. Title pages will be prepared in manuscript.

Place	Date	Hour	Summary of Events and Information	Remarks and references to Appendices
Sheet 36 H.7.d.63	19/10/17		A.D.M.S. inspection of P.B. men. Finished band instr. and a plays during afternoon. An excellent performance. 10 O.R. admitted.	
	20/10/17		A.D.M.S. & D.A.D.M.S. visit unit and accompany me to trenches to inspect them.	
	21/10/17		M.O.(Capt Parry) at TROUPLINES relieved (by Capt Spilsbury) S-M Seconds R.C. attended two leave. Sunday Routine work. 1 Offr. & 28 O.R. admitted.	
	22/10/17		Visited TROUPLINES A.D.S. and TISS + C.E. R.A.P. Satisfactory progress made at both places as to construction work. 3 O.R. & Portugue admitted.	
	23/10/17		Routine work. 1 Offr. 20 O.R. & 1 Portugue admitted.	
	24/10/17		Visited BRICK STACK A.D.S. & SQUARE FARM R.A.P. over to TISS+CE R.A.P. walked to blockhut forward A.D.S.'s put up at TROUPLINES A.D.S. — upland Comdg with view to establish forward A.D.S.'s. But A.D.M.S. advising dwellyard of SQUARE FARM. Called on Town Major of ARMENTIERES and discussed with him possible site in the town for M.D.S. 12 O.R. 4. Portugue admitted.	
	25/10/17		Pay day. Money drawn at LA GORGUE all men of M.D.S. & A.D.S. R.A.P's and various detachments paid. 1 Officer [admitted] O.H.Hillabold. Lt Col 20 O.R. O/c 131. Field Ambulance. 2 Portuge.	

Army Form C. 2118.

WAR DIARY
or
INTELLIGENCE SUMMARY. of 131 Field Ambulance

(Erase heading not required.)

Instructions regarding War Diaries and Intelligence Summaries are contained in F.S. Regs., Part II. and the Staff Manual respectively. Title pages will be prepared in manuscript.

Place	Date	Hour	Summary of Events and Information	Remarks and references to Appendices
Sheet 36 H.7.d.63	26/10/17		O.K.m.S. visits unit to inspect P.B. men.	
	27/10/17		M.O. (Capt: McMahon) rejoined unit from leave, & transferred to 129 F.A. Shick H Shingt of this unit evacuated; 1 Offr. S.O.R. and 1 Portuguese admitted.	
	28/10/17		Sunday. Religious Service and Routine work. 1 Offr. admitted 13 O.R. 2. Portuguese	
	29/10/17		2. wounded German prisoners admitted — interviewed by intelligence Offr (Capt Stanley) and evacuated & afterwards to S.I.C.C.S.	
	30/10/17		visited A.D.S. at POPERINGHE and SQUARE FARM and R.A.P at TISSAGE — work proceeding satisfactorily. A.td to Infantry — 80 all O.R. in the unit to be reclamped — B. imps Fn — 73 153.	
	31/10/17		Total Strength of unit = 177. 07 Men 7 at R.A.P.s on clamps to Inf. Regts. W.E 7 Remaining 17 — Clamped A. 7/10 1670 B. 7/10 17 172 Routine work.	

A.J. Thompson
O.M.M. Dolark Lt. Col.
OC 131 2nd Ambulance

Confidential
Vol 24

War Diary
131 Field Ambulance
38th (Welsh) Division
for
November 1/30 1917

(Volume XXIV)

Army Form C. 2118.

WAR DIARY
or
INTELLIGENCE SUMMARY. of 131. Field Ambulance
(Erase heading not required.)

Place	Date	Hour	Summary of Events and Information	Remarks and references to Appendices
Sheet 36 H.7.d.63	1/4/17		Capt:s Morell, Tillie and Henry. R.A.M.C. reported for duty & taken on strength of this unit. 14 Aeroplane guarded from this date. 7. O.R. and 1. Belgium admitted.	
	2/4/17		D.A.M.S. expected. Not forthcoming. Coy: of Divisional M.O.'s at 131.F.A. at 3 p.m. P.R. men inspected by A.D.M.S. 6.O.R. admitted.	
	3/4/17		Sent M.O. (Captain Parry) to last and demonstrate A.A.S. to Capt. Morell. O.R. 25. Pct. 3. admitted	
	4/4/17		Sunday. Religion services and routine work. Visita A.D.M.S. 1 Off. 9. O.R. admitted	
	5/4/17		Visited & inspected A.A.S. at BRICKSTACK and HOUPLINES also R.A.P.'s at SQUARE FARM and TISSAGE- was accompanied by Capt's Henry & Tillie. R.A.M.C. to instruction. 0 Off. 1. O. R. 43. Pvt. 2. admitted.	
	6/4/17		Attended demonstration on "Jump line" at H.Q. 113. Brigade. Sent M.O. (Capt. Henry) to relieve M.O. (Pvt. Markham) in charge of 11. S.W.R. the latter Office taken on strength of this unit. Capt. Tillie relieved Lt. Pank at Brickstack. A.A.S.	

Army Form C. 2118.

WAR DIARY
or
INTELLIGENCE SUMMARY of 131 Field Ambulance

(Erase heading not required.)

Instructions regarding War Diaries and Intelligence Summaries are contained in F.S. Regs., Part II. and the Staff Manual respectively. Title pages will be prepared in manuscript.

Place	Date	Hour	Summary of Events and Information	Remarks and references to Appendices
Sheet 36 H.7 d 63.	7/11/17		Routine work. Officer 4. O.R. 57 admitted.	
	8/11/17		Visited Steenkerke & Protestock A.D.S. and Squadron from R.A.P. Arrangt. E.M.O. at later (Capt. J. Davis) as to arrangets. for parts recd. at an early date. 12 attached stretcher bearers sent to Squadron farm & Woodland area Post. also 36. Stands. 12 Reserve bearer post to HOOPLINES & BRUCHSTRAAT Posts.	
	9/11/17		O.R. 21. Pnt 6. and 5 German Prisoners (wounded) admitted wounded. 5 inch. Sodium admitted.	
	do day.		A.D.M.S. inspected P.R. main Protestock & spoke that Steenkerke had been hit — wind a inspected — recently being Protestock. ay Infants to M.S.G, passed to R.E. — attempts no immediate stays. Infants to M.S.G, passed to R.E. Stretcher out by cart 16 or kept out.	
			O.R. 26. 1 Pnt. admitted.	
	10/11/17		M.O. (Capt. Spetan) at Hooplines attend by Capt. Morell. Div. Band played during afternoon & evening. Officer 2. O.R. 14 admitted.	
			C.R.E. inspected Protestock & Woodstock to hold the stock which is dangerous.	

WAR DIARY
or
INTELLIGENCE SUMMARY of 131 Field Ambulance

Army Form C. 2118.

(Erase heading not required.)

Instructions regarding War Diaries and Intelligence Summaries are contained in F. S. Regs. Part II. and the Staff Manual respectively. Title pages will be prepared in manuscript.

Place	Date	Hour	Summary of Events and Information	Remarks and references to Appendices
Sheet 36 H.7.d.63	11/11/17		Sunday. Religious service & routine work. Sent M.O. (Lt. Markham) to relieve M.O. (Capt. Inskeep) who is sick - gone on leave. O.R. 19 - Part 2 admitted.	
	12/11/17		Quarters (First Fleet) kept open on leave. Officer 1. O.R. 16. Part 1 admitted.	
	13/11/17		Maj. Gen. Alexander V.C. (temporarily commanding 32 Division) visited us to say he was very pleased with what he saw. Visited us in afternoon. War Graves Comm to say he was very pleased with what he saw. Lt Col S. XI Corps & A.D.M.S. with Rev D. Astins, impulse limit - staying very pleased. O.R.E. O/c visited 17th Pst's. No stock in any dangerous spot. Permit to find men to take it tomorrow. O.R. - 17 admitted.	
	14/11/17		2 M.O's Capt Spiderson & Just Brooke (U.S.A) sent to attend a 10-day course of instruction at BETHUNE - accompanied by one N.C.O (Capt Turner). Sent M.O. (Capt Paymeth) to relieve M.O. (Capt Wallace) at -19. W.St. Pioneers While Latter goes on leave. A.F.S. Orrstock facially shelled never direct hits Officer 2. O.R. - 37 admitted.	(1) A.T. Millerseck Lt Col O/c 131 Field Ambulance

Army Form C. 2118.

WAR DIARY
or
INTELLIGENCE SUMMARY. of 131. Field Ambulance
(Erase heading not required.)

Instructions regarding War Diaries and Intelligence Summaries are contained in F. S. Regs., Part II. and the Staff Manual respectively. Title pages will be prepared in manuscript.

Place	Date	Hour	Summary of Events and Information	Remarks and references to Appendices
Sheet 36. H.7.d.63	15/4/17.		Orve Droball match with "CORPS Twsps" - result 131.F.A. won by 1 goal to nil. O.R. admitted 18	
	16/4/17.		A. Sm. S. inspects P. B. men. Stock at A.D.S. - Shown dsn. - I felt free from worm (rabling); no damage done. 1 Offrs. 20 - O.R. 1 Pont" admitted.	
	17/4/17.		Visited W/th A.D.S. Satisfactory work going on. Offrs. 1 - O.R. 12. Pont 1 - admitted.	
	18/4/17		Interchanged M.O's at A.D.S. Sunday Rubicon temis & routine work. O.R. 19 - Prisoners - 2 admitted.	
	20/4/17		In accordance with A.D.M.S. instruction - 12. O.R. sent to ZELOBES to take down a large barn that & brings it here. Found a Cellar at ARMENTIERES. CHAPELLE which has evidently been used as APS by R.A.M.C. long before advent of this unit to the neighborhood. S/- will be an useful adjunct to BRICKSTACK A.D.S. especially when Cettu is shelled. (4 German Wounded (prisoners admitted (Telgrd. day 19/4/17) (O.R. 26 admitted yesterday 19/4/17) (1) Armeth Roberts Lt. Col O/c. 131. Field Ambulance
			O.R. 12. admitted	

Army Form C. 2118.

WAR DIARY
or
INTELLIGENCE SUMMARY. of 131 Field Ambulance
(Erase heading not required.)

Instructions regarding War Diaries and Intelligence Summaries are contained in F. S. Regs., Part II. and the Staff Manual respectively. Title pages will be prepared in manuscript.

Place	Date	Hour	Summary of Events and Information	Remarks and references to Appendices
Sheet 36 H.7.d.6.3	21/4/17		A.T. match between 130 & 131 Field Ambulance – result a win for latter – 1 goal to nil. 2 O.R. detailed to work for M.O. 10th S.W.B. — 19 O.R. admitted. 1 Pnr.	
	22/4/17		Pay day – unable to draw money. XI Corps having closed their office & XV Corps had not taken over. O.R. 19 admitted.	
	23/4/17		Drew money from Field Cashier – M.D. & A.D. paid and various detachments.	
	24/4/17		2 M.O's (Capt Sifiani and [?] [Park?]) with Corp Tunnel returned from course of instruction at BETHUNE. 19 O.R. } admitted 6 Pnr. }	
	25/4/17		Sunday. Religious Service & routine work. A.T. match with 114 Coy. R.E. 131.F.A. won by 1 goal to nil.	
	26/4/17		Routine work.	

O.K.Killingate [?] Lt Col
O/C 131 Field Ambulance

2353 Wt. W2544/1454 700,000 5/15 D. D. & L. A.D.S.S./Forms/C. 2118.

Army Form C. 2118.

WAR DIARY
or
INTELLIGENCE SUMMARY of 131 Field Ambulance

(Erase heading not required.)

Place	Date	Hour	Summary of Events and Information	Remarks and references to Appendices
Sheet 36 H.7.d.63	27/11/17		M.O. I/c ADS relieved — Capt Parnel at BRICKSTACK by Capt Spidan " Fillis " HOUPLINES " by Pvt Brooks (USA) F.A. — visited ADS's.	
	28/11/17		Routine work. A football match V. 16th R.W.B. Match 131.3 goals to one goal. Quartermaster (Pvt Flint) attend rum team.	
	29/11/17		First & Quartermaster Sheet leave unit leave unit to proceed to 47 General Hospital at TREPORT	
	30/11/17		Adm S. P.O. & T.B. over. ADS Dined with going then instead of Pvt Brooks Exchanged M.O's at HOUPLINES	(1) Promulgated Lt Col O/c 131 Field Ambulance

Confidential Vol 25

War Diary
131 Field Ambulance
38 (Welsh) Division
for
December 1st - 31 - 1917

Volume XXIV

Army Form C. 2118.

WAR DIARY
or
INTELLIGENCE SUMMARY.
(Erase heading not required.)

of 131 Field Ambulance

Instructions regarding War Diaries and Intelligence Summaries are contained in F.S. Regs., Part II. and the Staff Manual respectively. Title pages will be prepared in manuscript.

Place	Date	Hour	Summary of Events and Information	Remarks and references to Appendices
Sheet 36 H.7.d.63	1/12/17		Sent an M.O — Lieut Roothy U.S.A. — to 13th Welsh to relieve Captain Buchan. Latter joining this unit. M.O at Morphia A.D.S. relieved. 9 O.R admitted.	
	2/12/17		Sunday. Routine work & religious services. 19 O.R. } admitted. 1 Public }	
	3/12/17		Sent an M.O (Capt Spicer) to relieve M.O. (Capt O'Donnell) to "B" Welsh. (for the day only.) C.R.S. at MERVILLE Closed. O.R — 12 } admitted Pub — 2 }	
	4/12/17		2nd Anniversary of unit leaving homestile to France. Celebrated by dinner and Concert, &c O.R. 15 } admitted. Pub — 1 }	
	5/12/17		D.D.M.S. VI Corps and A.D.M.S. 38 Division - visited & inspected unit M.D.S. & A.D.S. O.R 17 } admitted. Pub. 12 }	

O.K.Mill Wotely Lt Col
O/c 131 Field Ambulance

2353 Wt. W2514/1454 700,000 5/15 D. D. & L. A.D.S.S./Forms/C. 2118.

WAR DIARY or INTELLIGENCE SUMMARY

Army Form 2118.

131 Field Ambulance

(Erase heading not required.)

Instructions regarding War Diaries and Intelligence Summaries are contained in F.S. Regs., Part II. and the Staff Manual respectively. Title pages will be prepared in manuscript.

Place	Date	Hour	Summary of Events and Information	Remarks and references to Appendices
Sheet 3b. H.7.d.6.3	6/12/17		Sent M.O. (Capt. Sploan) to relieve M.O. 16 Welsh. M.O. from MDS relieving M.O. at HOUPLINES A.D.S. Also sent M.O. from HOUPLINES A.D.S to relieve M.O. 10th S.W.B. at SQUARE FARM. Returned M.O. from 130. to relieve HOUPLINES (temporary). Payday – MDS and all outlying detached parties. O.R. — 11 } admitted. Pat — 1 }	
	7/12/17		A.D.M.S. visit and to inspection of P.A.S. DR — 15 } evacuated Pat — 3 } Leave — 1 } O.C. (Lt.Col. Rekills Rhets Club) proceeded on leave England 5th-22nd Dec. T/Capt Snofany Rand took charge Aunit. W.O.h way joined for duty from No.7 Rem Hosp. Le Dépot.	
	8/12/17		Lt Markham rejoined from Army Tirne School proceeded to Houplines A.S.b where all gents, No hent. K/19 & 24 Bat hig. It wents Seperations from Amy School. He was relieved by Capt. W.J. Garryshone. 1 Officer, Not. 2 J admitted.	

2353 Wt. W2544/1454 700,000 5/15 D.D. & L. A.D.S.S./Forms/C. 2118.

Army Form C. 2118.

WAR DIARY
or
INTELLIGENCE SUMMARY. of /31. Field Ambulance

(Erase heading not required.)

Instructions regarding War Diaries and Intelligence
Summaries are contained in F. S. Regs., Part II.
and the Staff Manual respectively. Title pages
will be prepared in manuscript.

Place	Date	Hour	Summary of Events and Information	Remarks and references to Appendices
	9.12.17		A.D.M.S. + D.A.D.M.S. visited Unit half [?] 10 o'c. clearing	
			Visited Reserve Attg. after seeing down supp Ammunition. Cpl went for of.	
	10.12.17		Patients admitted O.R. 19 Potts no. 3.	
			Commenced carrying 40 gallons water daily to Officers Club &c. Schwart 20 gals in ulterate days to M.D.S.	
	11.12.17		Patients admitted O.R. 13 Pvt. 9 Trench 2	
	12.12.17		Patients admitted O.R. 16. ST G [?] took work received for vehicles	
			New hospital Marquee (accomodates 30) completed	
	13.12.17		Patients admitted O.R. 10 Pvt 3	
			Capt. O.C. Wundle Road took over medical charge 5th Rif. R.D.S. vice Capt. J.M.B. Sony Moved to S.E. C.C.S.	
			Pte. admitted O.R. 19	
	14.12.17		Lieuts J.P.B + E.I Ryan to A.D.M.S.	
			THO Sown Wicens for No 3 last D.A.C.	
			Sergt. gottb D.R admitted to Unit	
	15.12.17		Patient admitted O.R. 12.	Stretcher Party from R.A.P making Klos 4/6 V. Evans Capt OC 31 F Amb

2353   Wt. W2544 1454 700,000 5/15 D D & L.   A.D.S.S./Forms/C. 2118.

WAR DIARY
or
INTELLIGENCE SUMMARY.
(Erase heading not required.)

of 131 Field Ambulance

Army Form C. 2118.

Place	Date	Hour	Summary of Events and Information	Remarks and references to Appendices
Field	16/12/17		Parade Service as usual. Parties work. Patients admitted {Offrs. nil, OR. 5, Sgt. 2 wounded}	
	17/12/17		Parties work. Officers nil. OR. 15 sick 1 wounded. {admitted}	
	18/12/17		Meeting of ADSMS with MDOs of 38th Bank & R.N. Div. Capt. R. Kingcote leave T.F. and Capt. W.A. Ivens R.A.M.C. T.F. joined for duty. Taken in strength. Officers nil {admitted} OR. 8	
	19/12/17		2 Officers & 42 OR. of 10th Aust. Fd. Amb. (3rd Aust. Divisn referred to bhq on & ADSs at Amphine & Poncholick 10ff & 50 OR. proceeded to later - available 16 hours) Off. nil, OR. 10 sick 11 wounded {admitted}	
	20/12/17		ADSs at Hospitalize & Poncholick with all RAPs & have been handed over the day to 10th Bns & Fd. Amb. Capt. C.J.B. Brockan RAMC returned Transport to 131 & Aust. officers nil, OR. 16 sick & {wounded} {admitted}	
	21/12/17		ADS. Bois Grenier, all personnel kits other than 131 Fd. Amb. removed & Lt. de ADSMB Inspection & useful was. Off. 1 and {admitted} OR. 12	W. Ram Capt. 131 Fd [illegible]

WAR DIARY
or
INTELLIGENCE SUMMARY

(Erase heading not required.)

Army Form C. 2118.

of 131 Field Ambulance

Instructions regarding War Diaries and Intelligence Summaries are contained in F.S. Regs., Part II. and the Staff Manual respectively. Title pages will be prepared in manuscript.

Place	Date	Hour	Summary of Events and Information	Remarks and references to Appendices
	22/12/17		Lt Col R.A. Mills, returned from leave and proceeded to view R.E. trust in round during absence of Col A.D. Hampson RAMC. O/R — nil {returns} O/R — 15 sick, 2 wnd	
	23/12/17		Private owners & orderlies work as usual. Capt R Howard joined M.O. i/c 15"R.W.F. in stress of through flu P.U.O. sick. Capt. R. Dufresne RAMC TF returned to headqrs at A.D.S. Bois Prieux. O/R 1 sick {admitted} O/R 6 sick {admitted}	
	24/12/17		Capt W.J. Allen RAMC took over temporary medical charge of # # # # # # O/R nil O/R 16 sick & 1 wnd {admitted}	
	25/12/17		Xmas day - horses men greatly enjoyed themselves nil O/R nil O/R 3 wnd {admitted}	
	26/12/17		Capt Sir Kenneth Russell reported for duty from 2/1 Fd. Amb. to take in reliefs O/R nil O/R 14(5) (10) {admitted}	
	27/12/17		United man cooks attended to him Rest Sounds at South 30/G7 as a Q. hdgrs rendered 3/30 subject to K.131 O/R nil O/R nil	EoMar 23 Captain 6/C 131 Field Amb

Army Form C. 2118.

WAR DIARY
or
INTELLIGENCE SUMMARY.

of 131 Fd Ambulance

(Erase heading not required.)

Instructions regarding War Diaries and Intelligence Summaries are contained in F.S. Regs., Part II. and the Staff Manual respectively. Title pages will be prepared in manuscript.

Place	Date	Hour	Summary of Events and Information	Remarks and references to Appendices
Field	27/12/17		Orders 1/thn Fd Amb. ordered 9 a.m.. All patients (29) evacuated to Fd Amb. Any advance to rear to 29th Fd Amb. Stretcher Bde Bearer A.D.S. not forward.	
	28.12.17		A.D.M.S. inspection of unfit men. Cch parade as usual. Camp patigues	
	29.12.17		Unit moved to new site at 36/P.17.a.8.4.	
	30.12.17		Camp fatigues. Whole building cleaned out. Receiving room & wards begun. Capt. Ellis handed Kruid relieved by Capt. N.E. Harris M.O. i/c 11th CMB to base and is struck off strength of the 131 Fd Amb.	
	31.12.17		A.D.M.S. visited Fd. Amb. Receiving room & wards ready to receive patients.	

O H Mills Cooke Lt. Col.
Acting A.D.M.S.
3rd (Welsh) Division

G Somm
Capt A.D.M.S.

Confidential

Vol 26
36

War Diary
131 Field Ambulance
38th (Welsh) Division
for
January 1/31 1918

(Volume XXVI)

COMMITTEE FOR THE
MEDICAL HISTORY OF THE WAR
Date -4 MAR 1918

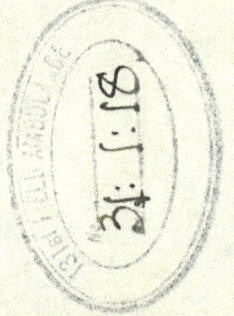

Army Form C. 2118.

WAR DIARY
or
INTELLIGENCE SUMMARY.
(Erase heading not required.)

of 131 Field Ambulance

Instructions regarding War Diaries and Intelligence Summaries are contained in F. S. Regs., Part II. and the Staff Manual respectively. Title pages will be prepared in manuscript.

Place	Date	Hour	Summary of Events and Information	Remarks and references to Appendices
Field 9.17 a.E.4	1.1.18		Ord Rout opened for admission of sick wounded. 16 O.R. [admitted]. Civilian.	
			One W.O. does ordinary sick round – another holds inspection parad at Sailly hop Room. Sheer pen horse to report to 24th Cavalry section at 9 a.m. staff & nagen horse with F.S. wagon at Salvage Dump Sailly. 10 men report always from troutt in R.A.P. Patients admitted O.R. 15.	
	2.1.18		Pay for transend. Visited A.D.M.S. Barn Suieur & new work being done attaye hum R.A.P. Patients admitted O.R. 27.	
	3.1.18			
	4.1.18		Inspection fungit nun by A.D.M.S. all N.C.O. & men hated at Divisional Bath. Patients admitted Officer 2. Other Ranks. 15.	
	5.1.18		T/Capt B. Adam awarded M.C. Mccan ant Hospital pullen completes Capt Stew retained Capt Stonyold at A.D.S. Pts admitted – 24 O.R. Pts admitted – 19 O.R. Natural str of trays.	
	6.1.18		Capt Stonyvale Rawle took over medical charge of 11 W.B. vice Capt Stichnell to 24th Deerm to strenth of attempt. Pts admitted – 22 O.R. Pts admit 1 off. 14 O.R.	
	7.1.18			
	8.1.18			
	9.1.18		S/L P.R. Spence detached to attend 1st Army School of Instruction of men (19 ccs) Pts admitted D.T.O.R.	

E. Adam
Capt RAMC

Army Form C. 2118.

WAR DIARY
or
INTELLIGENCE SUMMARY.

(Erase heading not required.)

87 Div. 1st/3rd West Riding Field Ambulance

Instructions regarding War Diaries and Intelligence Summaries are contained in F. S. Regs., Part II. and the Staff Manual respectively. Title pages will be prepared in manuscript.

Place	Date	Hour	Summary of Events and Information	Remarks and references to Appendices
Not Shet 36.C.	10.1.16		M.O. of 36th Fd. Amb. (1st/1st W.R.) visited the Fd. Amb. HdQrs. A.D.S. 131 Fd. Amb. to take over area allotted by F.A. Corps in back area. Traced sub ground & guide arranged for 131 Fd. Ambulance. Phoned – O.R. 17	
Map 62.618	11.1.16		Inspection of unit on A.D.M.S. HdQrs 12 Division 5 & Officers 36 Fd. Amb. inclu. 131 Fd. Amb. Officers M.O.s Held by 36" Fd. Amb. to proceed at Rueberque (RV to 76) by 38th D.A.D.S. Hospital accommodation & all offices including a bearer attended conference of O.C.'s at A.D.M.S. Office 26 Admn. O.R. 16.	
	12.1.16		Also admitted O.R.II Packing wagons – 3 loads owing to this precaution. Advance parts of 16 Officer & 20 O.R. of 36 Fd. Amb. reported at Sailly (M.D.S.) Advance parts of 1 officer & 75 O.R. of 36 Fd. Amb. reported at M.D.S. Proceeded to A.D.S. Boro Grenier same evening.	
	13.1.16		Advance party 131 Fd. Amb. Capt. E.C.A. Reynolds 70 O.R. proceeded at 6 A.M. this day to rail at Rueberque together with all supp. stores. Capt. Rees marched personnel of 36" Fd. Amb. to M.D.S. from A.D.S. Boro Grenier which was handed over to 36 Fd. Amb.	
	14.1.16		Pts. of 38th Division transferred to 130 Fd. Amb. which remained at Estaires. Infra troops other formations remain. H.M.S. and remaining patients handed over to 36 Fd. Amb. Unit marched to Puteo Bergues – horse transport with remaining 2 loads moved independently an hour before personnel.	

2353 Wt. W25H/1454 700,000 5/15 D. D. & L.   A.D.S.S./Forms/C. 2118.

Army Form C. 2118.

WAR DIARY
or
INTELLIGENCE SUMMARY. 67 /. 131 Field Ambulance
(Erase heading not required.)

Instructions regarding War Diaries and Intelligence
Summaries are contained in F.S. Regs. Part II.
and the Staff Manual respectively. Title pages
will be prepared in manuscript.

Place	Date	Hour	Summary of Events and Information	Remarks and references to Appendices
Hosp Out 36.A	15.1.18		Filled up sections — no returns. Pte admitted OR 2. Pte have to collect a Roller in hospital left. Draw nails to clean to C.C.S. the 7th Batt presents 113 Brigade.	
K.22.6.9.c.			Capt. Forbes proceeded to 1st Army Gas School for 6 days instruction in Practice Gases rain — not friendly with water.	
	16.1.18		1/c admitted OR 5. WORK nailed aids. Horse him earth floors. DADS even to other talcum furnished + DADOS	
	17.1.18		Run at 1.30 a.m. ASC MT MT changed ATB wrote fine side of horse lines a foot deep in water. Recommendation for continuous front with unchequered Post cut three breakfast in front of mound — road to Louville in the morn. Ambulance cars to Maurut before arms or Beaufargin. Capt C.J.R. Buchan took over temporary medical charge of 19th Welch Regt.	
	18.1.18		Inspection Durfit men by ADMS, Capt EW Army proceeds on leave from 19.1.18 – 2.2.18 Sick parade at Maurokaype collected.	
	19.1.18		O/C (Lt Col Mc Iroit) man unit off — 6 inch shells — 14 aeroplanes to take a atter of ADMS — to Armes Command, MO Capt Buchan called of Staff of Unit (Capt J.R. Inch) — L.O.R. admitted	
	20.1.18		Isaac wick Hooded. Accom to Hospital "Skallet" by official. Sunday Palegean Service. J.C.R. admitted	

O Cmulosley Lt 131 Field Amb

Army Form C. 2118.

WAR DIARY
or
INTELLIGENCE SUMMARY. Of 131 Field Ambulance

(Erase heading not required.)

Instructions regarding War Diaries and Intelligence
Summaries are contained in F. S. Regs., Part II.
and the Staff Manual respectively. Title pages
will be prepared in manuscript.

Place	Date	Hour	Summary of Events and Information	Remarks and references to Appendices
Mahhud 36.A K.22.6.8.8	21/4/16		Attended conference at A.D.M.S. - to discuss possibility of reducing transport of F.A. apart to 15 tent. wall frigerton. O R 13 admitted	
	22/4/16		1st womel. Arrive Mobile plaque V.C. batty 122 R.F.A. - went to your each field James U.S.A. taken an strength of unit. O.R. 9 admitted	
	23/4/16		[struck through] Reconnaissance accommodate to Hospital in case of all army lengths of in the L. Comm. 2 N.C.O's proceeded to Army R.A.M.C school instruction at 22 C.C.S. O.R - 5 admitted	
	24/4/16		Inspection of unit men by A.D.M.S O.R 4 admitted daily	
	25/4/16		Route work C.O. proceeded at 9.30 am for pollutes by Outreach officers 1 } admitted O.R 3	O.K. mile 010 lub Col [signature] O/c 131 Field Ambulance

Army Form C. 2118.

WAR DIARY
or
INTELLIGENCE SUMMARY of 131 Field Ambulance
(Erase heading not required.)

Instructions regarding War Diaries and Intelligence Summaries are contained in F. S. Regs., Part II. and the Staff Manual respectively. Title pages will be prepared in manuscript.

Place	Date	Hour	Summary of Events and Information	Remarks and references to Appendices
Gul 36.A	26/1/18		Route work. Deemenza and S.E. of ESTAIRES (in advance of XIS O.R. 5. admitted.	
K.22.6.f	27/1/18		Signaling upper limbs O.R. 3 admitted. Team (25 OR) detailed to convert run-forward sports – result nits but 1st man in was no 131 F.A. O.R. 3. admitted.	
	28/1/18		Rugby match (training sports) c 129 F.A. xxxxxxxxxxxxxxxxxxxxx referred M.O. detailed transport details pick at signal school at VIEUX BERQUIN O.R. 7 admitted	
	29/1/18		Polyard match (Rugby) c 129 F.A. played – Result 131. 1 goal. 129 – Nil O.R. 11 admitted	
	30/1/18		Brown match (Assoc.) c C. Batty 122 R.F.A. c 129 R.F.A. played – both played at townail. ½t -2. Extra -20 min – both played 9t townail. R.F.A. won O.R. 11 admitted	
	31/1/18		A.D.M.S inspected unit. man yesterday's drawn match replayed. R.F.A won by 1 goal to nil. O.R. 7 admitted. Pay day	

Aly Thompson Col
A.D.M.S. 38 Div
O/C 131 Field Ambulance
(1) KATHRN Asbestos L. Col

2353 Wt. W2514/1454 700,000 5/15 D. D. & L. A.D.S.S./Forms/C. 2118.

40/2784.

No. 131. F.A.

COMMITTEE FOR THE
MEDICAL HISTORY OF THE WAR
Date 8 APR 1918

Army Form C. 2118.

WAR DIARY
or
INTELLIGENCE SUMMARY. 131st FIELD AMBULANCE

(Erase heading not required.)

Instructions regarding War Diaries and Intelligence Summaries are contained in F.S. Regs., Part II. and the Staff Manual respectively. Title pages will be prepared in manuscript.

Place	Date	Hour	Summary of Events and Information	Remarks and references to Appendices
Map Sheet 36.A K.22.6.88	1/2/18		Interchange of 113 & 114 Inf Brigades. Sent 2 Ambulance wagons to carrying posts. Arrive I Match C. Smith 121 A.F.A.— Later was by I. Good. Regt. Medic. attached to 130 F.A. A. D.M.S instruction f 25/1/18 — O.C. recommends Sjt on 16/1/18 Mynd put in today.	
	2/2/18			
	3/2/18		Sunday. Religious service. Site visited by D.D.M.S to Corps & A.D.M.S 38 (Welsh) Division. Divisional Spirit — Tug of War. W.O. against Divisional H.Q. scratched. Capt Parry attend for leave.	
	4/2/18		A.D.M.S visited unit. O.C. recommends VIEUX BERQUIN area for permanent field Ambulance site — report accordingly sent in. A.D.M.S instructs R.M.O.s of Brigade.	
	5/2/18		Sent M.O. to do Company duty with 10th Welsh during absence on leave of their M.O. Other med. M.O. to do duty of with 15. Welsh.	
	6/2/18		Reconnoitre ERQUINGHEM area in accordance c A.D.M.S instruction.	
	7/2/18		A.D.M.S inspected Lewis men.	
	8/2/18		Asst A.D.M.S & A.D.M.S at EPINETTE to inspect site for F.A. Instruct Lt Col David Prodie awarded Belgian CROIX DE GUERRE Nampuh quit presence Oct 13	

Army Form C. 2118.

WAR DIARY
or
INTELLIGENCE SUMMARY.
(Erase heading not required.)

131st FIELD AMBULANCE

Instructions regarding War Diaries and Intelligence Summaries are contained in F. S. Regs., Part II. and the Staff Manual respectively. Title pages will be prepared in manuscript.

Place	Date	Hour	Summary of Events and Information	Remarks and references to Appendices
Mofshurt 36.A. K.22.6.8.	9/9/18		General Shunt. Tug. of War V R.A.C. – @ 13.F.A. won by 6y. 2 pulls to nil. Only 10 p&s to be kept in F.A. – consisting of Men likely to be soli in 4 days from adv.	
	10/9/18		Sunday – Religion Serve & routine work.	
	11/9/18		Visited Enquinghem. in S.S – 6 Confere. of A.T.S.M.F. Officers. of O/c. F.A. O/c. 2/2 went F.A. usbd PUREBEQUE. ssc. arranged attach on to marked adop.	
	12/9/18		attended lectur. at BRUAY – (Army School –	
	13/9/18		All the unit bathed. An assumed party consisting of S.M.O. and a S.O.R. proceeded to look our A.T.S at STOUPLINES and BRICKSTACK.	
	14/9/18		Unit (an assumed Parks as attack whholi) moved to his area handing on "F.A." Transport marched independly present att to 2/2 Wenst F.A. 131 F.A. bed. 122. R.F.A. Tug of War (Strinined Strok).	
	15/9/18		Received orders to take over Command of 41 Stating Hospital.	

WAR DIARY
or
INTELLIGENCE SUMMARY

131st FIELD AMBULANCE

Army Form C. 2118.

Instructions regarding War Diaries and Intelligence Summaries are contained in F.S. Regs., Part II. and the Staff Manual respectively. Title pages will be prepared in manuscript.

Place	Date	Hour	Summary of Events and Information	Remarks and references to Appendices
14[?]	14/7/16		Assumed Temporary Command 131st Field Ambulance vice Lieut. Col. R.H. Mills-Roberts. Orig. T.D. Route to 41 Stationary Hospital	J. Mus. Capsidone J.M. 12/7/16
ERQUINHEM	17/7/16		Religious Services. Routine Duties. Capt. FREW RAMC + 3 O.R. returned from 1st Army School of Instruction. Visited A.D.S. at HOUPLINES & BRICKSTACKS. BRICKSTACK area heavily shelled.	J.M.
	18/7/16		1/Lieut BUGBEE MORC USA took over Medical charge 122 Bde. R.F.A. vice 1/Lieut. McROME to England. Visited BRICKSTACK A.D.S. which was again shelled. Roads around all shew up unable to get out. Ambulance Car for BRICKSTACKS A.D.S. extricated with difficulty + brought	J.M.
	19/7/16		Took F. ERQUINHEM — BRICKSTACK's area heavily shelled. Visited R.A.P. at SQUARE FARM - WELLINGTON AVENUE. A.D.M.S. inspected new unit for work in forward area.	J.M.
	20/7/16		Under orders from A.D.M.S. BRICKSTACKS A.D.S. was evacuated at 6 P.M. 1 N.C.O. + 8 O.R.	J.M.

Army Form C. 2118.

WAR DIARY
or
INTELLIGENCE SUMMARY. 131st FIELD AMBULANCE
(Erase heading not required.)

Instructions regarding War Diaries and Intelligence Summaries are contained in F. S. Regs., Part II. and the Staff Manual respectively. Title pages will be prepared in manuscript.

Place	Date	Hour	Summary of Events and Information	Remarks and references to Appendices
ERQUINGHEM	20/2/16		remained Brickstacks & from relay Post. New MDS established in cellars at I.1.d.7.5. Sheet 36.	J.R.
		10.40/pt	reported to 122 Bde RFA for hints to training into new R. Commission.	
	21/2/16		Visited RAP at WELLINGTON AVENUE with Bearers. ADMS held conference of all MO's of the R division at Dressing Station at ERQUINGHEM. Personnel of Ambulance, less Capt. FREW + 140R who remained at Collecting Station at ERQUINGHEM, proceeded to WATERLAND'S CAMP. B.21.c.2.2. Sheet 36.	J.R.
WATERLAND'S CAMP.	22/2/16		DDMS XI Corps, accompanied by DMS (30th Div) inspected Collecting Station at ERQUINGHEM + New MDS at I.1.d.7.5. (Sheet 36.) Court of Inquiry touching the death of Civilian killed in a street accident held at Collecting Station ERQUINGHEM. Capt. FREW R.A.M.C gave evidence.	pt.

WAR DIARY or INTELLIGENCE SUMMARY.

131st FIELD AMBULANCE

Army Form C. 2118.

Instructions regarding War Diaries and Intelligence Summaries are contained in F.S. Regs., Part II. and the Staff Manual respectively. Title pages will be prepared in manuscript.

(Erase heading not required.)

Place	Date	Hour	Summary of Events and Information	Remarks and references to Appendices
WATERLANDS CAMP.	23/1/18		Visited nearests on I.10.7.5. (Sheet 36.) Work proceeding satisfactorily.	32A
	24/1/18		Hon. Lt. & Qm. H. WAY R.A.M.C. found unfit for work in forward area left for Base. Mr SHEPP MORE O.S.A. relieved Capt. LORIMER R.A.M.C. of medical charge of 14th R.I.J.	A.1
	25/1/18		Captain J.C. SPROULE R.A.M.C. arrived & take over Command from M'Innes.	33 Rev. Ceremene
	26/1/18		Took over command of 131 Field Ambulance yesterday. The morning spent in the day was spent inspecting WATERLANDS CAMP. This camp is very dirty and requires complete overhaul & much re-construction. In the afternoon visited the Collecting Post at ERQUINGHEM and the new "VICTORY A.D.S." and the A.D.S. at HOUPLINES. These were all in a good condition & everything was highly satisfactory. CAPTS. DINGWALL & BADENOCH R.A.M.C. reported for duty. This brings the M.O.s up to full strength. Visited A.D.M.S. about several routine matters. May/June. Heavy frost last night.	

James C Sproule
Capt. R.A.M.C.
O.C. 131 F.A.

Army Form C. 2118.

WAR DIARY
or
INTELLIGENCE SUMMARY.
131st FIELD AMBULANCE
(Erase heading not required.)

Instructions regarding War Diaries and Intelligence Summaries are contained in F. S. Regs., Part II. and the Staff Manual respectively. Title pages will be prepared in manuscript.

Place	Date	Hour	Summary of Events and Information	Remarks and references to Appendices
WATERLANDS CAMP	27/2/18	—	Work progressing. A.D.M.S. 38th Division visited Camp. D.A.D.M.S. 38th Division was present at a conference to make some medical arrangements for coming small festival. Visited Collecting Post at EROUINCHEM &c.	
	28/2/18	—	Drew pay at MERVILLE for men front war O.C. 2 M.A.C. Visited VICTORY A.D.S. BRICKSTACKS and SQUARE FARM. Went on to HOUPLINES A.D.S and paid men.	
		6 pm	By appointment met G.O.C. 115 Infantry Brigade + discussed some operations with him. Paid men at EROUINCHEM. 1 N.C.O. and 12 men from 129 F.A. + 1 N.C.O. + 20 men from 130 F.A. reported here for duty to-day. Work progressing favourably.	

James Elphinstone
Capt. R.A.M.C.
O.C. 131 Field Ambulance

W Humphrey
Col. 38 Divs
A.D.M.S

140/2849

131st. Field Ambulance.

June 1918

COMMITTEE FOR THE
MEDICAL HISTORY OF THE WAR
12 MAY 1918
Date

WAR DIARY or INTELLIGENCE SUMMARY

Army Form C. 2118.

131st FIELD AMBULANCE

Place	Date	Hour	Summary of Events and Information	Remarks and references to Appendices
WATERLANDS CAMP. Sh. 36 N.W. B2 c 2.2.	1/7	—	CAPT. REYNOLDS R.A.M.C. returned from leave last night. Received instructions from A.D.M.S. 38th Division to evacuate BRICKSTACKS Excel. are encampment. This unit to be fit to relay post. Commenced checking all stores and equipment. Started Collecting Post at ERQUINGHEM. Sent from wheeled stretchers from 129 Fd. and from 130 field ambulance. Had those up to VICTORY A.D.S. to hand on to SEVERE FARM. Rep. G.O.C.	See App. I
	2/7		Opposite Capt. Royne. A.S. 131 Fd.A. Work in camp progressing well. Went to ERQUINGHEM in morning to see Bearer attention to A.D.S. at HOPOINT'S and on to TREES DUMP. Went on to VICTORY A.D.S. and Dad Hd all arrangements near complete. (App. I) Day cold. Very hot last night. Rain came to-day.	
	3/7		Colonel MACDONALD R.A.M.C. (Can.) Here A.D.M.S. Office reports to the B. hatred engagement. At last night not after a lunch. Men stayed much advance in trenches. Engaging for At Etna MOOR. 2 A.D.I.S. 38th Division asked to make some arrangements. Wasserfalling Post sent out. The two new necharifement apparatus working. Bearers reported in Premiere tsight as asked about This time went suppose to whom it was hands. Tomorrow morning bearers to vote. See G.O.C.	

Army Form C. 2118.

WAR DIARY
or
INTELLIGENCE SUMMARY.
(Erase heading not required.) **131st FIELD AMBULANCE**

Instructions regarding War Diaries and Intelligence Summaries are contained in F.S. Regs., Part II. and the Staff Manual respectively. Title pages will be prepared in manuscript.

Place	Date	Hour	Summary of Events and Information	Remarks and references to Appendices
WATERLANDS CAMP.	3/7/16	—	Received instructions from A.D.M.S. (101) to take medical charge of MENEGATE CAMP. New is an Entrenching Battalion in this camp about 1300 strong. New arranged for morning sick to be seen at 8 A.M. daily. Detailed Capt FREW R.A.M.C. to relieve Capt DUNN D.S.O. M.C. D.C.M. R.A.M.C. M.O. 2nd R.W.F. the latter officer is proceeding on leave.	
	4/7/16		Lieut H.C. Fellon M.O.R.C. detailed to report to O.C. M+F Camp LINGHEM on 6th in relief of Capt WHITE R.A.M.C. who is proceeding to a course of instruction at the R.A.J Army Corps School.	
			Ten new (recruits) arrived & were taken on the strength. Sent Carpenter to Houplines A.D.S. A.D.M.S. 38th Division visited A.D.Ss.	
			Produced gas-proof pack outside main Entrance. Visited HOUPLINES and VICTORY A.D.s. Attended a lecture at SAILLY on the "Good function as Englands Day Crew & damb by Col Bulpus — D.A.D.M.S. 12th Division (Capt R.G.M. N.R. and 35th Division visited Camp. D.D.M.S. XIII wrote. Lunch at Billeting food. Medical advanced dressing station at HOUPLINES and CHAPELLE d'ARMENTIERES. Day fine &	
	5/7/16			
	6/7/16	3.45	Lieut C.H. FILTON M.O.R.C. proceeded to LINGHEM. Two N.C.Os proceeded to the first Army Rest Camp School for the South Grove. G.O.C. 38(Welsh) Division visited the Camp. New gas proof door on HOUPLINES R.D.s finished Co.	

Army Form C. 2118.

WAR DIARY
or
INTELLIGENCE SUMMARY.
(Erase heading not required.)

131st FIELD AMBULANCE

Place	Date	Hour	Summary of Events and Information	Remarks and references to Appendices
WATERLANDS	7/7/18	—	Lieut Gen Sir J.P. DuCane K.C.B. (XI Corps Commander) accompanied by D.D.M.S, X Corps, A.D.M.S, + D.A.D.M.S. 38th Division inspected Headquarters, Collecting Post and A.D.Ss of the Field Ambulance. On report of General made on sanitary inspects of HOULBECQ E Camps sent in report. Hay fires fatigue parties burning the	
	8/7/18		different grass moved round through the Collecting Post in the heart of the Wood. Were welcomed by Chief Gas Mess many at SAILLY. Visited Collecting Post, tent on Camp, & officers S well. Deep Ss are making a new entrance into Vicinity A.D.S. New experience arrange plan of Stretcher A.D.S. There appeared to be fire ground cases Wagons word through the Collecting Post.	App II detached App III Appx with Report of A.E.Ss
	9/7/18		Day Inst to that Collecting Post. Inspected the Sanitary arrangements of Camp on the Vicinity A.D.S Ditto. 38 Division note Waterlands Camp. Cat of S.Ds 12 mes Reports reported to duty, six deviled sick. Casino. Not at right.	
	10/7/18	—	Twenty one cases of Influenza (Landsquarts) through the Audit Pick nothing the past of two expt 4 Gas. This morning Influenza aspected & reported & were admitted (?) has died, remainder passed on to CCS Had a confidence with my H.Q. & F.M. R.A.P. (Newmarket Roland.)	
		After Noon	Received Memo from H.Q. R.A.E. to Evacuate trench huts at FERINGHEM and all harvest of ground at WATERLANDS. All Evacuation to hand over Beds at NOUVEL HOSPITAL also observed at camp hospitals to hand over Beds at NOUVEL HOSPITAL	

Army Form C. 2118.

WAR DIARY
or
INTELLIGENCE SUMMARY.
(Erase heading not required.)

Instructions regarding War Diaries and Intelligence Summaries are contained in F.S. Regs., Part II. and the Staff Manual respectively. Title pages will be prepared in manuscript.

Place	Date	Hour	Summary of Events and Information	Remarks and references to Appendices
WATERLANDS CAMP		10.30 P.M.	Who had hardly arrived were to proceed tomorrow morning. Meeting party of M.C.O. and 17 men reported to 130.7.9.	
		1 P.M.	Attend approval of O.C.S 2nd Echelon B.M.M Seventeen plans/advance (?) troops operation and referred the nurses attention before. Go.	
	11/30		O.R.S. at MOUNT HOSPITALS now augmented men on to 130 Pt. Which O.R.S "VICTORY" and Entrants in relation to First Instructio is M.O.40. Made the equipment of VICTORY and ERBURNENFER up to 400 Stretchers 50 OPERATORS each. Ten to peace-known. Through following hot in who up it goes, the morning 52 which 38 was wounded. With last number of officer and 29 O.R. men Stretcher came from forward made his camp to-day.	
	12/30		Capt DIXON + Staff Sergeant to me meeting to arty at our C.P.S. Russ NORA 9 O.R. WELCH/CUL, BECKER, REID & JULIO to proceeding on board of SAN JAMES R.P.C.V. attended a.m. S. Board at THOENGEN CAPT ROBERTSON (M.O. to 18° R.Nf.) Brown. Sent two privates for duty at the hot smith. Number & c350 Stretchers on the past 24 hours 62 of which 16 mere general. Station to be well taken will use Morfene. Nest as	

2353 Wt. W3141/1454 700,000 5/15 D.D.&L. A.D.S.S./Forms/C.2118.

WAR DIARY
or
INTELLIGENCE SUMMARY.

Army Form C. 2118.

Instructions regarding War Diaries and Intelligence Summaries are contained in F.S. Regs., Part II. and the Staff Manual respectively. Title pages will be prepared in manuscript.

(Erase heading not required.)

Place	Date	Hour	Summary of Events and Information	Remarks and references to Appendices
WATERLANDS CAMP	12.3.16	5 a.m.	Went out with A.D.M.S. 38" (Welsh) Division and visited ADS R.A.P. in FLEURY SWITCH also "VICTORY" and HOUPLINES A.D.S. Visited BRAUWERM Collecting Post. Pte McCULLAGH R.S.C. driver of an Ambulance was killed to-day by a shell wound received while proceeding through ESTAIRES. Ford Car badly damaged with probably have to be evacuated. Received wire from A.D.M.S. to issue all MATCHES immediately. Crash to Evacuated. Received wire from A.D.M.S. to issue all MATCHES immediately. Crash to handed with great care to O.R.s and issued accordingly. & in camp going on well. 19 cases passed through the Collecting Post 3 of which were gassed. Day fine but it looks like rain tonight.	
	12.3.16		Went round the Headquarters and Collecting Post. Received information from A.D.M.S. that HOSPICE ERQUINGHEM would be evacuated to Boulogne to-day after it was to be kept over as an A.D.S. and the A.D.S. in the MAIRIE evacuated. Also had a telephone message marvellous in this camp within the next few days. 41 cases passed through the Collecting Post for 24 hrs, 3 of whom are gassed. Those 19 were gassed. Day fine.	
	13.3.16		Received information from A.D.M.S. that armour operation was to be carried out on the night 14/15/16 in area INCANDESCENT TRENCH (at N.W.I.11a). Arranged to have two MGs at M. Collecting Post. Reinforced VICTORY ADS by an mine Ambulance with a second complete its garrison of 1 Officer 15 O.R. two visits Ambulances me had Ambulances at BRICKSTACK also MAIRIE FARM. Stay post reinforced with team stretchers & stretchers also MAIRIE FARM. Arrived 24 at MAIRIE, stretchers from the 29 P.A. and that two to RATTLE & R.M.F. Capt Barry C. Kirman & Bunche visited Collecting Post with me. Also A.D.S. visited.	

Army Form C. 2118.

WAR DIARY
or
INTELLIGENCE SUMMARY.
(Erase heading not required.)

Instructions regarding War Diaries and Intelligence Summaries are contained in F. S. Regs., Part II. and the Staff Manual respectively. Title pages will be prepared in manuscript.

Place	Date	Hour	Summary of Events and Information	Remarks and references to Appendices
WATERLANDS	15/3/18		Day fine. Thirty one cases passed through casualty post of which 16 were wounded, of the latter number 19 were wound gassed.	
	16/3/18	12pm-10pm	Zero.	
	16/3/18	12.0	Four cases arrived at A.R.S. One ambulance (motor) were sent up for cases at BRANDHOEK and hrs/g Gr the cases back to A.D.S. This saving much labour. All cases brought through VICTORY A.D.S. by 11.20 a.m. Two wounded prisoners passed through.	
		6 am	Stretcher message cart to A.D.S. Giving number of casualties. Took A.R.S. & collecting post. all cleared except one case.	
		9 a.m	Made reconnaissance of foot path along both sides of the canal, between ERQUINGHEM and PONT de NIEPPE Bridges, and reported to A.D.M.S. El. Chaco Evacuated in 15 foot Dyke at 5. 9 a.m. Alley tile. & o	
	17/3/18		One ambulance (motor) turned out for shelling action, 2 Second got small hole in petrol tank. Both sent to refaid to workshops. Third Evacuated and manned A.D.S. which also sun out take lorries in the Hospice de NINVE has been damaged. Then AD/MS 36 Div. has, and arranged that, in case ERQUINGHEM Keep no Man's after Boro with to Evacuate via PONT de NIEPPE & WATERLANDS Camp and to relay foot with me ambulance A/c in ERQUINCHEM. & o	

2353 Wt. W2514/1454 700,000 5/15 D. D. & L. A.D.S.S./Forms/C. 2118.

WAR DIARY or INTELLIGENCE SUMMARY

Army Form C. 2118.

Instructions regarding War Diaries and Intelligence Summaries are contained in F. S. Regs., Part II. and the Staff Manual respectively. Title pages will be prepared in manuscript.

(Erase heading not required.)

Place	Date	Hour	Summary of Events and Information	Remarks and references to Appendices
WATERLANDS CAMP.	16/7/18		Visited new activity post in ERQUINGHEM area. VICTORY A.D.S. 62 men evacuated through Walking post in last 24 hours to 9 a.m. this morning of which 38 were wounded. Lieut Reynolds Reynolds interviewed by A.D.M.S. 30th Division. DDMS Corps wishes collecting post. Day fine. Rain in evening.	
	19/7/18		Received instructions from A.D.M.S. that starting from to-day Motor HOPKINS A.D.S. would evacuate cases to PONT de NIEPPE & cases from there by M.A.C. Slight cases to be cleared from this by horse ambulance to L'ESTRADE. Slight cases sick from No 131 F.A. A.D.S. will be cleared to 129 F.A. STEENWERCK by horse ambulance of No 131 F.A. Cases from VICTORY A.D.S. as hitherto. Received information that the D.M.S. Second Army has issued instructions to No 2 C.C.S. Nos 1 & 2 AUSTRALIAN C.C.S. to accept casualties from the left side of XV Corps area at any time. If this is so it should be notified by wire to A.D.M.S. Office. {No 6 at LILLERS & MyJ at Palma by wire while Lewis train working in this Division. {No 21 at HAUBERSQUERQUE. For Bachelorsqueart. A.D.M.S. visited Board at ERQUINGHEM. A.D.S. cases passed through McCall during first of which 26 were wounded. One died. Day very wet. Etc.	
	20/7/18		Sixteen cases passed through collecting post of which five were wounded. Morning very wet. Etc.	

WAR DIARY
or
INTELLIGENCE SUMMARY.

(Erase heading not required.)

Army Form C. 2118.

Place	Date	Hour	Summary of Events and Information	Remarks and references to Appendices
AD.	21/7/18	8:00	Visited Collecting Post and A.D.S. Met M.O. of 10 S.W.B. (Lieut HANSON M.O.R.C.) and talked over some medical operations with him. Had opened WATERLANDS Camp yesterday as a Hospital to receive slight cases which would be fitter in four days. Also to receive Ear, Eye, Nose & Throat patients. Since cases passed through the Collecting Post of which 26 were Evacuated. Seven patients remaining in hospital last night. Go	App IV
	22/7/18		101 cases were dealt with yesterday including 91 wounded. Visited DADMS 38th Division to inquire about some equipment; also A.D.C. 129 F.A. about same. A.D.M.S. 1 AA & QMG 38th Division unaffected camp. This Range worked and never from VICTORY suffering from Lachrymatory Gas. All evacuees are very slight & will be retained. Day fine.	
	23/7/18		Got orders pushing to keep to one at Collecting Post. Also know from VICTORY Pos. all slightly at XV Corps Gas School. This went men part Sent down from VICTORY Pos. all slightly suffering from Shell gas near Locksystem. Day fine. 69 patients passed through the Collecting Post during the day 56 Evac. Go	
	24/7/18		Divine Service for both Offrs & Protestants. Received instructions that 5th R.F. Warwickshire Regiment I not accounted for 23rd and that 51 Offrs. 1,133 O.Rs were to be taken in. Allotment Inps. Officers to travel to 51 R.W.S. Extract from tel. no 179 at 17.3.18 Appendix. Commanding Offr R.A.M.C. Army Service Corps. Capt. J.C. SPROULE to be actg. Lieut. Col. whilst commanding No.131 Field Ambulance 3/8/18. T.Capt. G.W. PARRY to be actg. Major whilst Commanding no.76th Ambulance while C.O. R.M.C. is absent. (See orders to all to work whole extent in appendix IV) 50 cases were passed through in last twenty four hours extracted [illegible]	

WAR DIARY
or
INTELLIGENCE SUMMARY.

(Erase heading not required.)

Army Form C. 2118.

Place	Date	Hour	Summary of Events and Information	Remarks and references to Appendices
WATERLANDS CAMP	25/7/16	—	Morning fine, a little mizzen in the afternoon. Four men of this unit went sick & were sent to O.C.S. to-day. Billy Lewis returned sick & was sent through Collecting Post in last 24 hrs. Remaining in S.A. last night 17. Wrote M.O. of 2.R.W.F. that we evacuated men in morning at VICTORY A.D.S. at 8.30am. He replied that he would. Remaining 19.	
"	26/7/16	From —	Met M.O. of 2.R.W.F. and Fusiliers sent Medical arrangements to operate. Wrote Square from him, Fd 1.2.&.6. BRICKSTACKS Relay Post. Offrd Bugts officers were armed HOLLEBECKE MEDICATE Camp with A.D.M.S. MAJOR PARRY RUNS, R.H.& re report to R. WAR OFFICE on execution of contract. Seven of this Unit evacuated & C.E.S. two men overseas received from 38 M.G.C. Remaining in Infield 8.6.	V
"	27/7/16	—	Four R.A.M.C. recruits duty men received from 19th R.W.F. Districts 58 "Dunsean" invited Camp. May Hn & Col. M.S.Wilkinson Collecting Post Construction work is going on & will soon be finished. The Cellar has been sandbagged & it is fit in for running the Crickets with it. G.O.	
"	28/7/16	—	Operation mentioned in Appendix IV took place this morning. The motor ambulance cars all to go up as far as GLEN FIELD and have a Lightest Carriage was used. Went to VICTORY A.D.S. at 4am & supposed that all came except of had permitted to Collecting Post. Received through Collecting Post & fired 5 wounded men. Paid men of unit. Got oral from A.D.M.S. that Reg were there await orders to-night. Made arrangements as contained in Appx V. O.D.F.E. Got orders to dump Rats at 9.45. Evening wet, the	

2353. Wt. W2544/1454. 700,000 5/15 D. D. & L. A.D.S.S./Forms/C. 2118.

WAR DIARY
or
INTELLIGENCE SUMMARY.
(Erase heading not required.)

Army Form C. 2118.

Place	Date	Hour	Summary of Events and Information	Remarks and references to Appendices
WATERLANDS	29/74	—	Got orders from A.D.M.S. last night, to hand over VICTORY A.D.S. etc to 130 F.A. and to move from WATERLANDS Camp to STEEN WERCK to take Relief received by 129 F.A. Loaded up and handed over VICTORY and Bell Pat arriving at STEEN WERCK at 4.30 p.m. Received orders to attend a conference at A.D.M.S. Office at 2.30 p.m. At the conference A.D.M.S. Explained move of unit. All supplies Kit has been dumped. Capt Reynolds Ram. C. left for England on completion of contract. Capt Davies Ram. C. promoted to Major. Left relieving party at waterland	
		2.30 pm	Received orders when relieving unit arrives to hand over site at STEEN WERCK to advanced party of 103 F.A. this unit 6 to be attached to 115 Inf. Bde. Saw Staff Captain & arranged for billeting tomorrow night. Wagons transit ready for road. 6p.	
STEEN WERCK	30/74	12.20 midnight	Received Order from A.D.M.S. that 131 Fd. would be attached to 113 Inf. Bde. & not 115 Bde.	
		2.30 pm	Received order from 113 Bde. giving instructions as to Entrainment	
		4.0 pm	Unit left STEEN WERCK at 6.30 a.m. & marched via NEUF BERQUIN and MERVILLE to HAVERSKERQUE where it is billeted for the night Major J. E. Davies Ram. C returned from 19th Welsh Regt. 1 Rank & Rem for convoit received. Day very wet & disagreeable (Capt Dingwall R.A.M.C. reported. at from Bns to the reserves returned)	

Army Form C. 2118.

WAR DIARY
or
INTELLIGENCE SUMMARY.

(Erase heading not required.)

Instructions regarding War Diaries and Intelligence Summaries are contained in F. S. Regs., Part II. and the Staff Manual respectively. Title pages will be prepared in manuscript.

Place	Date	Hour	Summary of Events and Information	Remarks and references to Appendices
HAVERSKERQUE	31.3.18	—	Unit in Billets here. Copies of operation orders will be entered in next month's diary.	

Received Approvile
Lieut Col. Ramsé
OC 131 Field Ambulance

A.G. Stranfrey
Col.
ADMS. 38thDis

2353 Wt. W2344/1454 700,000 5/15 D. D. & L. A.D.S.S./Forms/C. 2118.

SECRET

Medical arrangements issued in accordance with 115 Brigade Order no. 215 para. 16.

DISPOSITIONS

(a) Concrete dug-out at I.16.a.75.95.
12 Regimental stretcher bearers will be posted here with 6 stretchers.
3 squads of 2 stretcher bearers will follow the attacking platoons to point of assembly.
The remaining three squads will remain in dug-outs.
Pte. PROBERT will remain in dug-out and will act as Senior S.B. and deal with emergencies.

(b) Advanced R.A.P.
All stretcher cases will be brought to the Advanced R.A.P. at I.9.d.5.0. The M.O. 17th R.W.F. and his staff will be stationed here and will receive all stretcher cases. Six relay stretchers will be kept here. 8 stretcher bearers will be posted here for evacuation duties between this point and SQUARE FARM. 2 pairs of wheelers and 4 stretchers will be brought to this point. Cases will be evacuated from here to SQUARE FARM.

(c) The M.O. at SQUARE FARM has received instructions to receive all walking wounded and direct them to VICTORY A.D.S. I.1.d.7.6.
(I.1.d.7.6.)

METHOD OF EVACUATION

(a) Walking cases will go direct to SQUARE FARM via LEITH WALK. The M.O. i/c SQUARE FARM R.A.P. has been instructed to notify "HARVEY" B.H.Q. regarding all walking cases that pass through, giving the number and name of each case.

(b) Stretcher cases. These will be brought straight down to the advanced R.A.P. at I.9.d.5.0. S.B's will take the LEITH WALK route till they reach the trench in front of the DISTILLERY leading to the sentry on building called LILY POST 1. and proceed to the advanced R.A.P. Cases will leave the Advanced R.A.P. by one of two routes.

1. If the LILY ROAD is safe, they will carry cases by wheeled stretchers to SQUARE FARM.
2. If the LILY ROAD is unsafe, cases will be carried to LEITH WALK, and along that route to SQUARE FARM.

(c) Stretcher Bearer party at SQUARE FARM (I.9.a.9.5.) consisting of 8 men and four wheeled stretchers will convey stretcher cases to BRICKSTACKS.

(d) Relay post at BRICKSTACKS (I.8.b.3.7.) consisting of 8 men and two wheeled stretchers will convey stretcher cases to VICTORY A.D.S.

(e) A.D.S. at VICTORY (I.1.d.7.5.) manned by 1 M.O. and 10 O.R. One Horse Ambulance and 2 motor ambulances to convey wounded to Collecting Post at FROUINGHEM.

James E. Sproule
Capt. R.A.M.C.
O/C 131st Field Ambulance

28/2/18

Copies for information to
Headquarters 115 Infantry Brigade
A.D.M.S. 38 Division
O/C 17 R.W.F.

Map 36N at 1/10,000

Appendices II & III

Detached and filed with Plans. — under.

Advanced Dressing Stations

Victory A.D.S. and Hopkines A.D.S.

SECRET.

APPENDIX 4

Medical Arrangements issued in accordance with 175th. Brigade
O., O.O. 7691 d/d 18/3/18
Map Sheet 30 N.W.1/20,000

1. DISPOSITIONS.

(a) Twelve regimental stretcher bearers with 3 stretchers
    blankets etc., will be posted in the front line at I.21.q.6.
    and will clear all casualties to the ADVANCED R.A.P.

(b) ADVANCED R.A.P., (I.20.d.3.0).
    All stretcher cases will be brought to the Advanced R.A.P.

    The M.O. 10th. Bn. O.T.R. and his staff will be stationed
    here. 24 stretchers, 3 wheeled stretchers and 60 blankets
    will be kept here for use as ordered by M.O. 10th. OTRSR
    6 regimental stretcher bearers will be stationed here and
    will take patients on wheeled stretchers to WELLINGTON Relay
    Post.

(c) WELLINGTON RELAY POST (I.14.d.3.9) 1 N.C.O. and 9 R.A.M.C.
    bearers with 6 stretchers and 3 wheeled stretchers and 18
    blankets will evacuate to BRICKSTACKS RELAY POST.

(d) BRICKSTACKS RELAY POST, (I.8.q.9.7) Consisting of 1 N.C.O
    and 9 bearers 3 wheeled stretchers 6 stretchers and 24
    blankets.
    Patients will be conveyed from here to VICTORY A.D.S.

(e) VICTORY A.D.S., I.1.a.7.6) Manned by 1 N.C.O. and 14 other
    ranks. One horsed ambulance and two motor ambulances to
    convey wounded to ENGLEBELMER Collecting Post.

(f) The N.C.O. i/c WELLINGTON R.A.P. has received instructions to
    receive all walking wounded and direct them to VICTORY A.D.S.

(g) SQUARE FARM (I.20.a.7.8. 1 N.C.O. 4 men and 2 wheeled
    stretchers. Evacuation to VICTORY A.D.S. by trench or road

2 METHOD OF EVACUATION

(a) WALKING CASES will proceed along the road from BURNT FARM
    (I.20.d.3.7.) to the subsidiary line near battalion H.Qrs.
    (I.20.a.8.6.) from thence along the subsidiary line to
    WELLINGTON R.A.P. From thence to BRICKFIELDS RELAY POST by
    road and then by road to VICTORY A.D.S.

(b) LYING CASES
    Along front line and communication trenches to ADVANCED R.A.P.
    From there by hand and wheeled stretcher along road to
    I.20.a.8.6. to subsidiary line. From this
            (i) If safe by road and wheeled stretcher to
                WELLINGTON RELAY POST
            (ii) If road is unsafe, by stretchers bearing along the
                subsidiary line to WELLINGTON RELAY POST.
    From thence along road by wheeled stretchers to BRICKSTACKS
    RELAY POST and from thence by Motor Ambulance, wheeled
    stretcher on road or stretcher carried in trenches is
    possible.

Secret

Medical arrangements issued in accordance with 115 Brigade
B.7166× 23/3/18

Map 36 N.W. 1/20,000.

Dispositions.

(a) Two squads of stretcher bearers will accompany the attacking party
(b) R.A.P. will be situated in a concrete dug-out at I.9.d.5.0.
    The M/O 2nd R.W.F. and Staff will be stationed here. Six stretchers,
    12 blankets and 5 pairs of wheeled stretchers will be kept here for
    use between this point — I.10.a.5.9. and GLENFIELD
(c) R.A.M.C. Relay Post at I.9.c.4.6. (GLENFIELD) manned by 1 N.C.O.
    and 6 O.R. with 2 pairs of wheels 6 stretchers and 12 blankets.
    If possible an ambulance stationed here.
(d) BRICKSTACKS RELIEF POST I.9.b.3.7. manned by 1 N.C.O. and 9 men with
    6 stretchers and 2 pairs wheeled stretchers.
(e) VICTORY A.D.S. (I.1.d.7.6.) manned by 1 M/O, 17 O.R., 50 stretchers,
    100 blankets, 1 Horsed Ambulance and 2 Motor Ambulances (1 to be as
    in (c) above.)
(f) 10 stretchers and blankets will be stored at EVELYN (I.16.b.2.4.)

Evacuation.

(a) Walking cases: Will proceed direct to VICTORY A.D.S. via:- LEITH WALK
    and LILLE ROAD or if the latter is unsafe by LEITH WALK to SQUARE
    FARM and thence by BRICKSTACKS WALK to VICTORY A.D.S.
(b) Lying cases.
    These will be carried to I.10.a.5.9. where they will be taken
    over by the first Regimental Relay and if possible carried on wheeled
    stretchers to Advanced R.A.P.
    From Advanced R.A.P. they will be carried on wheeled stretchers by
    Regimental stretcher bearers to GLENFIELD.
    If conditions permit they will be taken from here in a motor
    ambulance. If this is unsafe they will be carried by R.A.M.C. bearers
    by hand on wheeled stretchers to BRICKSTACKS from where they will
    proceed
        (1) By ambulance to VICTORY A.D.S.
        (2) By wheeled stretchers to VICTORY A.D.S.
        (3) Carried by trench and post to VICTORY A.D.S.

140/2900-

131st Field Ambulance.

COMMITTEE FOR THE
MEDICAL HISTORY OF THE WAR
Date 6 JUN 1918

Confidential.

War Diary
of
No. 131 Field Ambulance.

From 1st April 1918
To 30th " 1918

(Volume 29).

Army Form C. 2118.

No. 131
FIELD AMBULANCE.

No. 4 3/18
Date 30/4/18

WAR DIARY
or
INTELLIGENCE SUMMARY.
(Erase heading not required.)

Place	Date	Hour	Summary of Events and Information	Remarks and references to Appendices
HAVERSKERQUE	1-4-18	—	Held inspection of gas respirators, Iron rations, identity discs, foot drill dressings,	
	2/4/18		Well kitted of all the men of the unit. Horse transport entrained at DEN BECQUE at 8 pm	
		9:30 p.m.	and personnel at 9:30 p.m. Train left at 10.45 p.m. Arrived DOULLENS at 9:30 a.m.	
			reported to officer i/c detraining and was ordered to join 115 BRIGADE. Fed marched	
			men out of station & gave them breakfast.	
		11:20	Received Brigade order saying that 115 BRIGADE was moving to HEDAUVILLE.	
			Marched for two via DOULLENS - ALBERT road. Advanced party went on to arrange	
			billets. On arrival at FORCEVILLE received information from billeting party that there	
			were no billets available at HEDAUVILLE. Rode forward & reported to Staff Captain 115 Bde	
			and was told to billet for the night in FORCEVILLE. Reported arrival to A.D.M.S. 38th Div.	
			Three Ambulances reported here 38 M.T. Coy.	
	3/4/18	6:30 a.m.	Received orders from Albert that 131 Field Ambulance was to move to vicinity	
			of CLAIRFAYE. Reconnoitred ground and found empty P of W Camp	
		8:00	at CLAIRFAYE.	
		10 a.m.	Unit marched off to CLAIRFAYE arriving 9:30 a.m.	
			Established A.D.S. at HEDAUVILLE to Capt Dingwall R.A.M.C. Sent two	
		1:30 p.m.	Clerks to Walking Wounded Collecting Post & two to Kris Cross Dressing Station at	
			CLAIRFAYE	

Army Form C. 2118.

WAR DIARY
or
INTELLIGENCE SUMMARY.
(Erase heading not required.)

No. 131 FIELD AMBULANCE.
No. ...113/A...
Date ...30/4/18...

Instructions regarding War Diaries and Intelligence Summaries are contained in F.S. Regs., Part II. and the Staff Manual respectively. Title pages will be prepared in manuscript.

Place	Date	Hour	Summary of Events and Information	Remarks and references to Appendices
CLAIRFAYE			Unit on trek. Medical Inspection of men.	
	3/4/18	8 am	A.D.M.S. inspected this morning. Day very wet. Visited A/C. 36 F.A. who is running the walking wounded Collecting post and our A.D.M.S. 12th Division also visited lying wounded collecting station to. Received order that Division is to be held in readiness to move at 1 hours notice. Everything is ready. got small quantities of kill dressings packed in sandbags so that within 5 minutes would be ready available. Visited A.D.S. at HEDAUVILLE. Much gun fire going on all through the day. Visited the 150 F.A. and arranged about accommodating sick and wounded if this Division So.	
	4/4/18		Visited A.D.S. at HEDAUVILLE and saw our officers to arrange with him together the would adopt in case of emergency. Nothing fresh to. Visited M.O. 19th WELSH REGT and RE Coys in same village and saw that their Evacuation of sick was working satisfactorily. Received orders from A.D.M.S to say that also 15th Bde were	
		1:25pm	A.D.S and proceed at 36 + 37 F.A. were to be withdrawn and that this Unit remained till further orders.	
		4pm	Received Brigade order saying that Brigade would move to TOUTENCOURT and HERISSART to day. Zero to be notified later. Sent two horse ambulances	

WAR DIARY
or
INTELLIGENCE SUMMARY

Army Form C. 2118.

No. 131 FIELD AMBULANCE.

Place	Date	Hour	Summary of Events and Information	Remarks and references to Appendices
CLARAFAYE	7.4.18	—	To march with Brigade. The H.D. Horse which was evacuated on 4th is reported from the Base to have B.9. Contagious Stomatitis. All the remainders were examined by C.A.D.V.S 38th Division and placed in isolation.	
"	8/4/18	—	Received orders from ADMS to make reconnaissance of the LEALVILLERS - HARPONVILLE - ARQUEVES - TOUTENCOURT area. Went around the area & submitted scheme of evacuation. *And Sqn. Piéce Ramb. Evacuated (sick) to CCS. to-day. Day very wet & unpleasant, &c	
	9.4.18		Out in morning making reconnaissance of ground around LEAVILLERS TOUTENCOURT and HARPONVILLE. Extract from V Corps order: "the right supporting Division is now the 38th Division. xxx Brigades will be prepared to assemble as follows 115 Bde. between HEDENCOURT and SENLIS with a view to holding the MILLENCOURT - ENGLEBELMER LINE between W.I.C. and the Corps southern boundary, off holding the Corps right in order to be able to send a made reconnaissance of part of this front in order to and a report to N.D. M.S. SENLIS was being shelled & it was unfavourable to search the town for billets &c	App I

WAR DIARY or INTELLIGENCE SUMMARY

(Erase heading not required.)

Army Form C. 2118.

No. 131 FIELD AMBULANCE.

No. 4-3/8
Date 30/4/18

Instructions regarding War Diaries and Intelligence Summaries are contained in F. S. Regs., Part II, and the Staff Manual respectively. Title pages will be prepared in manuscript.

Place	Date	Hour	Summary of Events and Information	Remarks and references to Appendices
CLAIRFAYE	10/4/18		Received 38 Div. wire detaching 131 Field Ambulance to 113 Bde. Sent two Ford Ambulances to meet 113 Brigade after Brigade from RUBEMPRE to HARPONVILLE. Received admin. orders & instructions and 113 Brigade orders with reference to the move. Clerks sent to V Cpl's Workshop wounded and lying wounded Collecting stations sent to V Cpl's Gas Centre. DADOS came with reference to BELLE EGLISE in afternoon & 4 A.S. POSTS MO Capt. to Salvage. Arranged to send Bus to BELLE EGLISE in afternoon & 4 A.S. POSTS MO Capt. and Sgt. & G. P. DAVIES C.A.M.C. reported for duty. The troops who straggled in over the past 48 hours	Appendices I, II
			Had arrived in Brigade area with 16 36 Field Ambulance on arrival a battle during this invasion by 12th division. There is a unit not connected to office and 88 B.M.at BOOZINCOURT and this unit called from front line and Reserve Battalion & train to Ambulance with patient to CLAIRFAYE	
			At SCAMS to the L/Offr. and S.B. on duty after hour with one group. Cars to Evacuate them via WARLOY to CLAIRFAYE. Hy lost out some ambulances	
			Running Posts 3) "Junior members" to BUZINCOURT and SENLIS	
	5.30		As arrived 131 Bde. to BUZINCOURT and SENLIS	
	4p.p 90		issued Route 131 Field Ambulance Order No.3.2. Capt. Dee Pando Intelligence	Appendix IV
			Rank will be of Lewis ARMS worked ramps & Extreme Medical Officers	

WAR DIARY
or
INTELLIGENCE SUMMARY
(Erase heading not required.)

Army Form C. 2118.

No. 131 FIELD AMBULANCE.
No. ...11/3/18...
Date ...30 Sept/18...

Place	Date	Hour	Summary of Events and Information	Remarks and references to Appendices
CLAIRFAYE	11/9/18	8 p.m.	Parties proceed to A.D.S. BOUZINCOURT 1 officer 2 NCOs 2 Runners 1 Cook 20 ORS	
	12/9/18		SENLIS — 1 " 1 " — 8 " Cqs	
	12/9/18		Whence proceeded to BOUZINCOURT A.D.S. about 11 p.m. Heavy shelling intermittently between midnight	
			and 3 a.m. and again from 5 a.m. to 6 a.m. No casualties. Number wounded passing	
			through this A.D.S. 8 Officer Cases, 11 Walking Cases & 12 Sick	
			Visited A.D.M.S. 1 DC. 29 Field Ambulance	
	13/9/18	11 a.m.		
		3 p.m.	Visited A.D.S. at CARNOY & found all quiet. Had no to R.D.S. at BUZINCOURT A.D.S. V.	
			and decided to form this into a Rear Post. Consisting of 1 NCO. 1 Cook & 20 O.R.	
			Saw & organised M.D.S., also saw their R.M.P. about 80 yards away. Arranges	
			with them to use their R.M.P. and Mr Allan to take charge of Rear Post.Two Left	
			2d stretchers & 100 blankets for same. Notified A.D.M.S. 1 N.Z. Brigade & Charge	
			Also arranged to work on the lines in relays at Standing at HEDAUVILLE	
			A.D.S. at BUZINCOURT. Gave instructions with regard to A.D.M.	Appendix VI.
			Precautionary measures against effects of Mustard gas. Received from about 38" Division	Appendix VII.
			Warned etc NZ. 1 up & NZ FAs. A.DL at SENLIS moved to V 10.e.5 (kept yard him old A.D.S.)	
	14/9/18		Q.C. 37 M.T. Coy visited unit re ambulances. He is going to evacuate the MANISTRY which	

Army Form C. 2118.

No. 131 FIELD AMBULANCE.
No. 1
Date. 31/1/18

WAR DIARY
or
INTELLIGENCE SUMMARY.
(Erase heading not required.)

Instructions regarding War Diaries and Intelligence Summaries are contained in F. S. Regs., Part II. and the Staff Manual respectively. Title pages will be prepared in manuscript.

Place	Date	Hour	Summary of Events and Information	Remarks and references to Appendices
MARIAYE	14/4/18		was sent in a few days ago and now on last leave. It will if possible replace this by new C.M.M. Also said he would send back the oxygen cylinders hitherto by hospital convoy.	
	15/4/18	9.30am	A.D.M.S. inspected the medical arrangements viz the forward area collar at 129 Field Ambulance (Lieut Col Ross M.C. RAMC) on way back and had a conference about evacuation of gases in this area. Spent day arranging a new system of arranging communication with them. The ambulances arose & staying in commencement in last 24 hrs up to 9am this morning Very very sick and misty. Evacuated in last 24 hrs up to 9am this morning 12 sick + 210 wounded. Recommended scheme of evacuation to 143 Bde Capt PORTER M.C. C.A.M.C. proceeded to Senlis A.D.S. in relief of Capt LUCE WALL R.A.M.C. Post posts of evacuation visited and extra cellars found in BEAUCOURT and SENLIS. This will allow wounded to be kept in comparative safety in case of further town being heavily shelled and evacuation of wounded being impossible. The full scheme to be continued in afternote VIII which was forwarded to to A.D.M.S. See Sent ambulance was engined last night by a hyre backing into its radiator. Visited C.C. 107 F.A. (Lieut Col. HEMPHILL R.A.M.C.) Also OC 36 F.A.	Appx VII See VIII App VIII

WAR DIARY
or
INTELLIGENCE SUMMARY.
(Erase heading not required.)

Army Form C. 2118.

No. 131 FIELD AMBULANCE.

Place	Date	Hour	Summary of Events and Information	Remarks and references to Appendices
CLAIRFAYE	1/4/18	—	Went around R.A.P.'s and A.D.S. of 103 Brigade. At the Kings Arabs and working on strengthening it. Called Capt Porter M.C. R.A.M.C. Ascended to No 3 Canadian Stationary Hospital. Capt Deryes C.A.M.C. Evacuated to No 3 Canadian General Hospital. Drivers Douglas from 10 Workshops Y Corps lent a return trip to A.D.M.S. twenty reinforcements secured to-day. Took them to the different centres. No	
	2/4/18	—	war at Barn Post and R.A.P. Proceeding well. Sent £10 to Rev. C. Crofts Fund for R.A.M.C. Prisoners of War. This is a voluntary subscription of the Officers, N.C.O.s and men of the Unit. Returned motor cycle to D6 Y Corps M.T. Coy Workshops which was drawn from him on 8/9/18.	
		3pm	A.D.M.L. Conference of Field Ambulance Commanders. The following points were discussed :- (1) Gas cases and tricks (2) Sanitation of area (3) Mobility of transport of field Ambulances (4) New Filts (5) Evacuation of Wounded. Morning fine afternoon wet.	
			Admitted up to Gen (Incl 10 for) Sick 1 OR 17	
			Wounded — 16	
			2 Ys.	

No. 131 FIELD AMBULANCE
No. A3/8
Date. 21/4/18

Army Form C. 2118.

WAR DIARY
or
INTELLIGENCE SUMMARY.
(Erase heading not required.)

Instructions regarding War Diaries and Intelligence Summaries are contained in F. S. Regs., Part II. and the Staff Manual respectively. Title pages will be prepared in manuscript.

Place	Date	Hour	Summary of Events and Information	Remarks and references to Appendices
CLAIRFAYE	18/4/18	9 a.m.	1 Officer and 2 O.R. Wounded and 20 Sick passed through F.A. in last 24 hrs.	
			Visited R.A.P. at BOUZINCOURT and saw Regimental M.O.S. Arranged to help them to fit up	
			a cellar as an Emergency dressing room. Found two cellars for Bearer Post reserve. Visited A.D.S.	
			SENLIS. Saw Signals at both places & they say they will take Signal message to call	
			Ambulance at any time. This will cost the numerous between SENLIS and 113 Bde H.Q.S.	
			Saw Bde Major 113 Bde re Evacuation of wounded. Inspected Sanitation of several camps in	
			area paying particular attention to water supply. Day cold & some rain.	
			~8pm. Received a Signal message from 113 Brigade "Prisoners from BUZINCOURT" that enemy	
			precautions.	
	19/4/18		2 O.R.S. killed received through this F.A. this morning. Cases Evacuated in last 24hrs 34 Sick	
			and 1 wounded, including 3 cases of Trench feet and one general case. Visited P.6. 10	
			11 Divisary Section with A.D.M.S. and D.D.M.S. where for estimating amount needed	
			H water. Morning cold with showers of rain. Weather was colder in the last night. Dr. U.S.	
			Lt. 16 Lt/Mn Co	
			Not actual in running. Hot Engines kept visible and M.O.s 113 and 115 Bde in afternoon	
	20/4/18		to arrange for further Visited Bouzincourt Studio &c	

WAR DIARY or INTELLIGENCE SUMMARY.

Army Form C. 2118.

No. 131 FIELD AMBULANCE.

(Erase heading not required.)

Place	Date	Hour	Summary of Events and Information	Remarks and references to Appendices
Cassel 1918	21/4/18	—	Encamped in East 20 Cos. turned out. POB Sub 2nd OR Conference at 2.30 P.M. officer i/c & Commandant. Field medical arrangements and plan of Evacuation via 131 F.A. Visited Lieut W.M. Kerr Rance & Lieut G.R. Wilson Reserve Office to duty. Lieutenants f/Webster, Smith & dural up Active & Light.	
	22/4/18	9 am	Evacuated in East 24 hrs officers nil OR ORs 19 Wounded 11	App X
		9.30am	Major H. Davies R.A.M.C. went up the line opened his trench Camus medical arrangements attached East Prev Kam & 1/6 if 1 Officer and 6 OR. to locate the walking wounded accepting test. Two lorries were supplied by Devron to convey the cases to WARLOY. Was able to find their way to the walking wounded post by means of the white tape. Reserve equipped with term officer at Commencement function including Lumbosacral OR. Succeeded 1 off 9 NCOs 91 OR. Caus. for esate to evac. 100 Stretcher 18 Walking Stretcher 140 Buses ca 6 15 Minor Points Ordinary Splints	

Army Form C. 2118.

No. 131 FIELD AMBULANCE.
No. ..2/5..
Date ...31/4/18...

WAR DIARY
or
INTELLIGENCE SUMMARY.
(Erase heading not required.)

Instructions regarding War Diaries and Intelligence Summaries are contained in F. S. Regs., Part II. and the Staff Manual respectively. Title pages will be prepared in manuscript.

Place	Date	Hour	Summary of Events and Information	Remarks and references to Appendices
Hanford	29/4/18	5.30am	ZERO	
		9.30 "	Went round + found everything working well. Walking wounded were arriving at last at 10 p.m. + lying cases were arriving at 129 F.A. when it was needed at 11 p.m.	
			Rang up 4 D.D.S. + to Lieut WSILLIGHTON RAMC (No 1527) reported to me as O.M.K but (he was at 129 F.A.) reported back to Base officer in the Convent + the surgical team	
29/4/18	1.15am	Lieut 20. catechised moved up to Baron officer in the Convent + the surgical team	
		3.15 am	Lent up Res + car + dressings on One lorry was required	
		3.20 am	Received wire from the adjusting amb.lance for 13th Bde Relieving the F.O.C 129 F.A. who took over	
		8.10am	Lent 20 more lorries up to bearer officer	
		6.30am	Wanted out to go around Lieut Rt 129 C.A. Everything reported to be working well	
			At Walking wounded Post Everything was cleared. I knew returned to 129FA	
			Met Bearn officer at 6.30 am. It had there so far as I could ascertain about 7 cases to clear. 4 officers + infantry hat to received. a lot of cases in coming from 10 S.W.B. and 19th Welch Regt without any stretchers. It is supposed to be ale to bring cases down during the day	
		7.30	Ambulance cars sent up to BOUZINCOURT as at a time as required when shell fire is ceasing	

Army Form C. 2118.

No. 131 FIELD AMBULANCE.
No. ....
Date ...2/4/18...

WAR DIARY
or
INTELLIGENCE SUMMARY.
(Erase heading not required.)

Instructions regarding War Diaries and Intelligence Summaries are contained in F. S. Regs., Part II. and the Staff Manual respectively. Title pages will be prepared in manuscript.

Place	Date	Hour	Summary of Events and Information	Remarks and references to Appendices
Clairfaye	23/4/18		Casualties in Rank & Honours to members slightly	
		6.30 a.m.	Sent two medical officers to 127th to help ale 127th F.A.	
			Bearer officer thinks a few more cases may filter down during the day to Orchard & Major buildings on BOUZINCOURT-SENLIS Road to be called on when required.	
		2 p.m.	Capt. J.H. BANKES RAMC reported to A.D.M.S. office	
			Lieut. A. Carr M.B.R.E. relieved Lieut. Mortland RAMC. He is to Rest for one day.	
			Evacuated via road 34 lying up to sitting up. O.R. 4 Sick 22 wounded.	
			along CLAIRFAYE	
		4 p.m.	Bearer officer reports "Gues to night will between 15 walk from BOUZINCOURT to car stand at V.12.C.0.1. He has had a steady stream of stretcher cases & evacuation by car was quite easy from Advanced R.A.P. Withdrew to Bearer Cases Evacuated about 400	
	24/4/18	5 a.m.	Enemy counter attacked but no party off. none known taken.	
		9 a.m.	Bearer officer thinks that everything is quiet that he has had nothing to do all right. Of Casting Wounded pot refuse no ones since 3 a.m. yesterday morning.	
		2 p.m.	Withdrew officer and all extra bearers working L in the Advanced R.A.P. H.Q.M.S. & Howard (Capt Rec to Rank) Visited Camp.	
	25/4/18	10.30 a.m.	Met A.D.M.S. 38th Division at CLAIRFAYE and wished all the Advanced Evacuation	

Army Form C. 2118.

No 131
FIELD AMBULANCE.
No............ 43/18
Date......... 25/4/18

WAR DIARY
or
INTELLIGENCE SUMMARY.
(Erase heading not required.)

Instructions regarding War Diaries and Intelligence Summaries are contained in F. S. Regs., Part II, and the Staff Manual respectively. Title pages will be prepared in manuscript.

Place	Date	Hour	Summary of Events and Information	Remarks and references to Appendices
CLAIRFAYE	25/4/18		Horse and hand pick. Returned at 10.30 am. Checked part of the equipment of the Field Ambulance with Major of Standing units Advance & Medical Units (one git.)	
			Morning fine. They November & Wonder Horses on the afternoon	
	26/4/18		O.R.6 Stoff and 6 wounded Evacuated in the last 24 hrs up to 9 am t-day, to	
			Went still mostly retreat Lost this morning houses 25 am now are	
			myself Evacuated in last 24 hrs 12 oth November 1 Officer 32 O.R. sick OR. 7 Oth 3	
	27/4/18		Questionnaire and Hon Lyf G.A. COLLIER R.A.M.C. reported for duty Recent order from	
			A.D.M.S., to station in I.A. all cases which could be evacuated in 6 days. See no previous	
			van in afternoon. Received instructions to Evacuate car no 48 to	
	28/4/18		Having service for C/S, R.C.s & Other Protestant Religions at Church parades	
			Evacuated in last 24 hrs 1 Officer 7 O.R. Sick 7 O.R. wounded	
	29/4/18		Visited R.A.P. at BOUZINCOURT and A.D.S. at SENLIS made some arrangements with M.O. 105/V/3	
			Received R.A.M.C. arrangements re operation which will be Appendix 1 in next months diary	
	30/4/18		Morning wet Arranging R.A.Us on Road from aux am cut in BOUZINCOURT	

James Sproully
Lieut Colonel
O.C. 131 Field Ambulance

140/2983.

COMMITTEE FOR THE
MEDICAL HISTORY OF THE WAR
Date 9 JUL 1918

No. 131 F.A.

May 1918

Army Form C. 2118.

No. 131
FIELD AMBULANCE.
No. 3/1/18
Date 31/1/18

Nov 30

WAR DIARY
or
INTELLIGENCE SUMMARY.
(Erase heading not required.)

Instructions regarding War Diaries and Intelligence Summaries are contained in F.S. Regs., Part II. and the Staff Manual respectively. Title pages will be prepared in manuscript.

Place	Date	Hour	Summary of Events and Information	Remarks and references to Appendices
CLAIRFAYE	1.5.18		ADMS held a conference of Field Ambulance Commanders yesterday. R.A.M.C. order No 119 received. Small raid by 17th RWF last night. 15 Wounded were evacuated. One of the Field Ambulance N.C.O bearers (Cpl GREEN HAUGH R.A.M.C.) was killed.	App. I App. I (a)
		9am	Made another reconnaissance of the MARTINSART sector of the line. Handed over Evacuation of BEUZINCOURT and SENLIS to 129 Field Ambulance. Evacuation in East 24 Bn. OR 35 cR. 918 wounded.	
		4.5.18	Took over Evacuation of the MARTINSART area from 129 Field ambulance. The R.A.P.S are on the edge of AVELUY WOOD and the stretcher parties are dug in beside them. Relink are carried from the actual casualty to Q 32 a 2.3.5 where the wounded are placed on which brings the Patient to Q 32 a 8.9 There is a car standing at this point which brings the Patients to HEDAUVILLE. Six Men of each. Two officers and 2 NCOs and 20 Bearers with 2 foot wheeled stretchers and two motor ambulances returned.	O.b.H. II
			Lieut D G McINOR M.O.R.C. left for duty with 17th RWF in relief of Capt RICHARDS R.A.M.C. Copies of provisional Evacuation Scheme forwarded to 112 & 114 Bdes. Casualties last 24 hrs Officers sick 1, OR Sick 4 wounded 4, Remaining in Hospital 3 sick and one wounded 40	

(19929) Wt W33581/362 60,000 12/7 D. D. & L. Sch. 52a. Forms/C2118/15

Army Form C. 2118.

WAR DIARY
or
INTELLIGENCE SUMMARY.
(Erase heading not required.)

Instructions regarding War Diaries and Intelligence Summaries are contained in F.S. Regs., Part II. and the Staff Manual respectively. Title pages will be prepared in manuscript.

Place	Date	Hour	Summary of Events and Information	Remarks and references to Appendices
CLAIRFAYE	3/5/18	6.30am	Actually 38th Division called here and picked me up. He inspected the system of evacuation in the front area. Abolished the Bearer post in ENGLEBELMER and arranged to dig at new dugout into the bank at Q.32 d.2.8. Picked huts for 50 stretchers for 130 Field Ambulance who are coming here tomorrow. Admitted in last 24 hrs OR 11/Sick 1 wounded. Remaining in Hospital 3/Sick 1 wounded.	
	4/5/18	—	Conference at HQ11 Wing of Field Ambulances Commanders. The M.O. is to take over the Cuthbert Appendix III. evacuation of the Divisional Front. 50 Bearers from 130 Field Ambulance are to be attached and two Ambulance Cars. For the event practice operations were carried over the course from 129 Field Ambulance. Inspected new post for M.D.S. with R.E.S at HEDAUVILLE. Went around lines. Lieut G.H. WILSON R.A.M.C. proceeded to duty with "W" RFC in relief of Lieut Heard. M.O. R.C. admitted in last 24 hrs 13/Sick, 2ll/wounded. Remaining 2/sick, 1/wounded. Capt T.H.	
	5/5/18	10am	Visited Front area at BAIZINCOURT (picked out sites/action in accept heavy)	
			Barnes R.A.M.C to be acting helper. Admitted 26 (wounded) Evac 20 19 wounded. Remaining 10 (wounded). Visited Adv. A.S. 50 men from 130 FA. reported for duty.	
		6.0pm	Visited Adv HQ 11 Wing. Arranged scheme for evacuation to Div. factive direction.	

Army Form C. 2118.

WAR DIARY
or
INTELLIGENCE SUMMARY.
(Erase heading not required)

Instructions regarding War Diaries and Intelligence Summaries are contained in F. S. Regs., Part II. and the Staff Manual respectively. Title pages will be prepared in manuscript.

Place	Date	Hour	Summary of Events and Information	Remarks and references to Appendices
Clairfaye	14/5/16	—	Took over all evacuation routes of the forward divisional area, &c. Drew "Elephant" from RE & picked up some near HEDAUVILLE to dig it in. Started work on this in the afternoon. B.M. Senior Officers were in the forward area all day. Arranging ADS. & places for bearer squads. Attended ADNS conference of Regimental M.Os. Sent names to division. Admitted 32 sick, 12 wounded. Evacuated 32 S, 10 W. Died R. Duty! Remaining in Hospital 9.	App IV
	15/5/16	—	Work. Extension of a dugout in the sunken road S. of BOUZINCOURT. Call Bennett relieved at SENLIS by Lieut Slape. Am making an Elephant dugout on the VARENNES—HEDAUVILLE road near the latter place in case anything happens to the ADS. at HEDAUVILLE. Borrowed 36 Pickets and 200 Hurdles from O.C. 129 F.A. also 9 pro Mills Jerves who he visited forward review in the MARTINSART SECTOR. Found ADN.S at his office &c. Evacuation in case of active operations in his sector. DADOS. 38th Division called. No 48727 Pte S.S. JENNINGS RAMC, awarded the Military Medal. No 48909 Pte (A/Cpl) E.B. THOMAS Rawcl. awarded ter. the Military Medal. Admitted 23 sick, 7 wounded. Evacuated 21 sick, 5 wounded. Died R. Remaining 11 &c.	

WAR DIARY or INTELLIGENCE SUMMARY

Army Form C. 2118.

(Erase heading not required.)

Place	Date	Hour	Summary of Events and Information	Remarks and references to Appendices
Claudoye	8/6/18	—	Went over back between BOUZINCOURT and MARTINSART. 2DAYS. 38th division reliefed camp.	App V
			Received 114 Brigade Operation Order No 174 from MGRS.	App VI
			Received Scheme for Evacuation of Casualties in the event of active operations, put equipment up	App VII
			An Enc in cord of this time took so laid down in App VII. Basevics 3" mortars & was notified that 28 men were crossing by trans from No 130 7A, 3rd OR 129 that Sworn regime personnel officer nearer however by 7pm 7 mgs 24 Borks RAMC handed	
			No 129 Field ambulance. Capt NJ Snow appointed as OC B octa rice there St Claudio Renno have been wanted to relieve him for duty at 7am to fin no 2 ametta wounded. Class 2	
			CR 8, CR sigh 30. Examer officer wounded & Obs. Sick 33 Wounded oc. 2 duty 2	
			Remaining 6 — sick 1.	
	19/6/18		Reinforcement & Reinf. Officers HER wounded 24OR evacuated sick 1 officer 39OR wounded. OH R. to duty 2. Remaining 6 DQ	
			Men posted as chickba laying for an direction to capture enemy high back RANCY Wood. Re towns in chickeness of extra ammunition and equipment use obtained from NOs 129 and 130 field ambulanes	Appendices VIII
		8 am	Field ambu reported to carry walking wounded cases	

WAR DIARY
or
INTELLIGENCE SUMMARY.

Army Form C. 2118.

(Erase heading not required.)

Instructions regarding War Diaries and Intelligence Summaries are contained in F. S. Regs., Part II. and the Staff Manual respectively. Title pages will be prepared in manuscript.

Place	Date	Hour	Summary of Events and Information	Remarks and references to Appendices
HEDAUVILLE	night		Were kept busy until 4am. Also walking wounded before Mashers. The walking wounded kept area also marched out with Sgr. Wards.	
		11.20	First cases arrived from ENGLEBELMER - MARTINSART Sector.	
		12.25	Bearer Officer from BOUZINCOURT Sector reports that all is quiet and that he saw the sister on arrival. This second ambulance was directed on to the Wt.	
			Both posts sending evacuation supplies to the proceeding normally.	
		2pm.	Sent up 2 motor amb. to MARTINSART sector. No orders for Bearer wounded.	
		2.6pm	All was quiet.	
		3.30	Walking wounded post returned. Had many to shelter. It was to be sent to eject about 98/83 hours. The A.D.S. Bearer Officer from BOUZINCOURT about normal.	
			Cars returned as there was no casualty coming through the sector.	
		5.15	Walking wounded post closed as none had been coming through to send. Cars left after back stores went to CHERPYE.	
		6pm	Posts MARTINSART still stand as few cases coming through. Capt Smith A.M.C. took in charge post for the night. Arranged to bearers to be relieved at Bearer posts during the night.	

Army Form C. 2118.

WAR DIARY
or
INTELLIGENCE SUMMARY.
(Erase heading not required.)

Instructions regarding War Diaries and Intelligence Summaries are contained in F. S. Regs., Part II. and the Staff Manual respectively. Title pages will be prepared in manuscript.

Place	Date	Hour	Summary of Events and Information	Remarks and references to Appendices
	10/5/18		Distribution Ambulances 2 ENGLEBELMER Sectn	
			2 HEDAUVILLE ADS	
			3 CLAIRFAYE (BPn)	
			" " H/qrs (motor)	
			3 " (Dieds in reserve)	
			Cycles 1 BOUZINCOURT	
			1 HEDAUVILLE	
			1 CLAIRFAYE (H/qrs)	
		9pm	Evacuated up to present 80 s/ung 102 sitting.	
			Evacuation in last 24 hours by USes this morning Officer 2 Sub nil remaining	
			OR 53 sick NY wounded. Evac areas	
			OR 21 " 25 "	
			S duty 21 "	
			Remaining 26 sick & wounded.	
	11/5/18	9 am	Visited ADS at HEDAUVILLE and found that the right had been quiet and only 14 cases passed through. Visited Waitwart sectn. Medical Officer reported quiet night. Visited Regimental M.Os and found all quiet having quiet during night.	

Army Form C. 2118.

WAR DIARY
or
INTELLIGENCE SUMMARY.
(Erase heading not required.)

Instructions regarding War Diaries and Intelligence Summaries are contained in F. S. Regs., Part II. and the Staff Manual respectively. Title pages will be prepared in manuscript.

Place	Date	Hour	Summary of Events and Information	Remarks and references to Appendices
Vaudage	11.5.18		Pratze on Squad attack R.A.P. with 6 Sketches and 8 Standards. Patrol Sergeants at Posts	
			Officers Lent out Rifle Grenades on landing party. Each squad to lose time Guerrilla 16 Standards	
			and then Down to Battle Jumper where attackers Presentor 6 men. Detachment sent to	
			CLEARY. Reinforcements at HEDAUVILLE to Elbouin on 2 Lewis Detachment 1/f	
			Ambulances 1. Haultmont aux	
			1 Molainville units 1 Molainville	
			1 Mr Molainville (not to run to Bouzincourt) 1 Bouzincourt	
			When 2 Officers, 7 Runner and 1 Ambulance obtained to 1/29 Field Ambulance	
			Gas. BSM's say island sent to Ulf Service Field Ambulance for his appointment	
			Casualties during action on Nov. 6 Above Thur 28 Ja. 9 hrs. 129 P.M. wounds	
			also 2 hrs. 30 Field Ambulance	
				Killed	3	W
			Admit up to 9 P.M.	3	6
			Evacuated	2	6	27	90	183
			Died			27	183
			Duty			6
			Remaining			1
				26.4

(A9175) Wt. W2358/P.560 60,000 12/17 D. D. & L. Sch 512. Forms/C.2118/15

WAR DIARY or INTELLIGENCE SUMMARY.

Army Form C. 2118.

(Erase heading not required.)

Instructions regarding War Diaries and Intelligence Summaries are contained in F. S. Regs., Part II. and the Staff Manual respectively. Title pages will be prepared in manuscript.

Place	Date	Hour	Summary of Events and Information	Remarks and references to Appendices
Clanderys	12/5/18	9 am	Officers 38 Div. / Other ranks 38 Div. S W / S W Admitted 2 — 20 13 Evacuated 2 — 15 6 Died — — — 2 Remaining 31 - 9 Visited MEDAILLE & SENLIS with Gas Officer 38th DIVISION Capt Richards Reunb. returned from 43 CCS, where he had been being for Specialist Divine service in the morning. Football match v 36 FA. in afternoon	App. viii
	13/5/18		Medical arrangements 36th Div Defence Scheme received Officers / Other ranks S W / S W Admitted 1 — 20 8 Evac. 1 — 15 9 Died — — — — Duty — — 10 — Rem. — — 26 7 Recce reconnaissance of ground for defence scheme. Called at adjmt office re Adjms	

Army Form C. 2118.

WAR DIARY
or
INTELLIGENCE SUMMARY.
(Erase heading not required.)

Instructions regarding War Diaries and Intelligence Summaries are contained in F. S. Regs., Part II, and the Staff Manual respectively. Title pages will be prepared in manuscript.

Place	Date	Hour	Summary of Events and Information	Remarks and references to Appendices
Claytyle	13/5/18		No. 106 Field Ambulance called + showed him the scheme of Evacuation in this area.	
			The following appointments were made to-day:	
			No 25909 Pte (A/Cpl) Thomas E.B. M.M. to be A/Sgt with pay from 30/3/18) D.Que 4/1050/2405	
			" 48719 Pte (A/Cpl) Matthews S. " " " " 21/4/18) A.10.C.8	
			No 48330 Pte (L/Cpl) Blackett A.E. to be A/Cpl with pay from 13/5/18) A/Gal Cons men	
			No 48768 Pte (L/Cpl) Judson H. " " " " 13/5/18) No 13.	
			The following men was wounded No 24723 Pte Arthur GRIME R.A.M.C.	
			HEAVY rifle was sheel to-day with M.S. Knapoot + MARTINS ART Sects was also busily.	
	14/5/18		D.A.D.M.S. Division visited MARTINSART Sects and saw Evacuation from front system.	
			06 No 106 Field Ambulance arranged to visit this Secto tomorrow.	
			Officers O.R.	
			Admitted 8 W 26.14	
			Evac 25 10	
			Died — 1	
			Duty Room present 12 i	
			17 10	Cay force

WAR DIARY
or
INTELLIGENCE SUMMARY.
(Erase heading not required.)

Army Form C. 2118.

Place	Date	Hour	Summary of Events and Information	Remarks and references to Appendices
Clayfaye	15/8/15	—	26, 106 Field Ambulances moved the front part of the Divisional area	
			No USU 24 Bn (R.H. Brigade) (a) Horse Lines evacuated to G.S. and suffering from	
			C.W.C.	
		12:30 am	Conference at room of Office of Field Ambulances Commanders. Subjects discussed	
			1. Sites for Field Ambulances	
			2. Number of Stretchers in each Brigade	
			3. Use of Contents of M.V.A. in Gassed cases no ambulances present	
			4. Defence of Field used to 107 F.B. (up to stop in our lines not done)	
			5. Use of Motor-transit lorries in Gassed cases	
			6. Evacuation of P.W.O. cases	
			7. Entrenchments	
			8. Filling up with ambulances with { a. Warm leg fluid	
			{ b. Thomas arm splint	
			{ c. Morphia Dosage Tablets	
			{ d. Bruntly Mentha Splint	
			{ e. Roll of Board Splints	
			For. F W O	
			Enac. 35. 10	
			Admitted 26 O Dustuppi 1. S Running N-S	

Army Form C. 2118.

WAR DIARY
or
INTELLIGENCE SUMMARY.

(Erase heading not required.)

Instructions regarding War Diaries and Intelligence Summaries are contained in F. S. Regs., Part II. and the Staff Manual respectively. Title pages will be prepared in manuscript.

Place	Date	Hour	Summary of Events and Information	Remarks and references to Appendices
Contay	10/5/16			
			Officers 8	
			Ranks 117	
			Evac 4	
			Duty 5	
			Remaining 15 4	
			Both Harponville & Contay sent sample. Capt HORNER M.R.C. reports for duty.	
11	11/5/16		D.A.D.M.S. 38th Division visited BOUZINCOURT Sector. Visited No 105 Field Ambulance and saw the huts which said he handed over to us on relief. Arranged with No 106 Field Ambulance that his relieving party would be here by 6 p.m. on 19th and that we would use their posters.	Appx IX
			Officers Other Ranks	
			S W S W	
			Admissions — 1 35 13	
			Evac — — 30 13	
			Duty 2 3	
			Remaining 18 1	

WAR DIARY
or
INTELLIGENCE SUMMARY

Army Form C. 2118.

(Erase heading not required.)

Place	Date	Hour	Summary of Events and Information	Remarks and references to Appendices
Neuville	13/5/18		OR's S.W	
		casualties	— 1 22-21	
		Sick	1 16-20	
		Duty	4 —	
		Raw	21. 2.	
			Joined 21 Suss Ambulance Oden. No 26	
			United O.B.Co. found all well. Heavy rain during the afternoon &	Opp x
	14/5/18		During the night there was a lot of gunfire. Some small attacks made on enemy posts with complete success.	
		ca 11 am	71th Ambulance visited two men final arrangements for handing over.	
			2NCOs and 220Rs of 130 Field Ambulance returned to his own unit.	
			No 59739 Pte A.L.W. Lewis evacuated to military hosp.	
			Lieut KERR R.A.M.C. proceeded on M.D. to British Red Cross hospital Markham Rouen & succeeding to England on expiration of contract	
		4 pm	Handed over CHARTREUSE CAMP to 127 Field Ambulance (Major David R.A.M.C)	
		6 pm	Relief commenced was completed by 9.30 pm	

Army Form C. 2118.

WAR DIARY
or
INTELLIGENCE SUMMARY.
(Erase heading not required.)

Instructions regarding War Diaries and Intelligence Summaries are contained in F. S. Regs., Part II. and the Staff Manual respectively. Title pages will be prepared in manuscript.

Place	Date	Hour	Summary of Events and Information	Remarks and references to Appendices
Clairfaye			ORS S W	
			Admitted 27 29	
			Evacuated 26 28	
			Died - 1	
			Duty 6 1	
			Remaining 16 1 (Hands transferred to 129 2A)	
Contaye	20/4/16		Unit marched out at 5 am. going via TOUTENCOURT to HERISSART.	
			ORS S W	
			Admitted 29 26	
			Evacuated 30 26	
			Duty 2 -	
			Remained 13 1	
HERISSART		5pm	Arrived office moved here. Horse ambulance sent of march after 113 Bde when coming from five this morning	
			Received orders for refuse of Brown five system. Detailed MO & 2 Rank ORs for duty with A.P.M. tomorrow.	App XI

WAR DIARY
or
INTELLIGENCE SUMMARY.

Army Form C. 2118.

Place	Date	Hour	Summary of Events and Information	Remarks and references to Appendices
Louisset	20/4/18		Admitted — Offrs 5, S 8, W 7, ORS 9, S 1, W —	
			Duty — 1, —, 1, 7, 1, —	
			Remained — 1, —, —, 7, 1, 40	
	21.5.18		114 & 115 Bdes came out of line last night. Arranged for ambulance wagons to follow 115 Bde & notes to 129 F.A. to arrange for 114 Bde.	
			Lt. Jones and Cpl. S. Howells R.A.M.C. sent to Third Army School of Cookery.	
			Received telegram to say that "38th Division will have one hours notice from 6 am to 10 am. daily. At 2 hrs notice for remainder of day". Received several cases from other formations.	
			115 Bde. went to 2nd Rest Bivouac and one Offr sick. Me is so slightly gassed Offr.	
	22/4/18		Admitted — Offrs 2, S 1, W —, ORS 16, S 1, W —, S.W. 6	
			Evac — 1, —, —, 8, —, —, 6	
			Duty — —, —, —, 1, —, —, 1	
			Di Rest St — 1, —, —, 4, —, —, —	

Army Form C. 2118.

WAR DIARY
or
INTELLIGENCE SUMMARY.
(Erase heading not required.)

Instructions regarding War Diaries and Intelligence Summaries are contained in F. S. Regs., Part II. and the Staff Manual respectively. Title pages will be prepared in manuscript.

Place	Date	Hour	Summary of Events and Information	Remarks and references to Appendices
HERISSART	21/5/16		A.D.M.S. Conference of Field Ambulance Commanders. Several cases of gas evacuated to Y Corps Gas Centre. M.O.s sent to see sick at 10 S.W.B. and 2nd R.W.F. The M.O.s of these	
	22/5/16		had Battalions are both sick. Holding party sent to TOUTENCOURT. Major Gen Sir J. Murray Irvine	
			R.A.M.C. Third Army inspected No Hospital Billets etc this morning. Capt. HORNER	
			U.S.M.O.R.C. detailed as M.O. to 10th S.W.B. D.D.M.S. V Corps (Lt. Denis Murray Callaghan) and	
			the A.D.M.S. 38th Division (Col. A.J. Thompson) accompanied the D.M.S. on his inspection this morning.	
			Lieut. Hearn U.S. M.O.R.C. sent for temporary duty at 38 C.C.S. Holding party returned from	
			TOUTENCOURT. Major J.E. DAVIES R.A.M.C. returned to U.K. on 14 days leave Dr.	
	24/5/16		A.D.M.S. Board. 10 men were our out sick to Cols.	

	38th Divn			Other formations		
	Officers	O.Rs		Officers	O.Rs	
	S.	W.	S.W.	S.W.	S.W.	
admitted	1	20	2	1	9	
sick		28		1	10	
Duty		1		1	Do	

	25/5/16		A.D.M.S. Conference at which C.O.s 129 & 130 Field Ambulances submitted a scheme for clearing the	
			front line in case of certain eventualities. V Corps Commander is inspecting the 115 Brigade on 29th.	
			Relieved for the afternoon. Day fine.	

WAR DIARY
or
INTELLIGENCE SUMMARY.
(Erase heading not required.)

Army Form C. 2118.

Place	Date	Hour	Summary of Events and Information	Remarks and references to Appendices
HERISSART	25/9/18		28th Division other formations	
			Officers ORs Officers ORs	
			S W S W S W S W	
			Admitted 3 — — 12 — 3 — —	
			Evac. 3 — — 9 — 1 — —	
			Duty — — — 1 — — — —	
			Rem. — — — 11 — 3 — 6	
	26/9/18		Divine service this morning. Capt WRIGHT MO & RC 28th Division was sent to Divisional Rest Station to-day. Capt RICHARDS RAMC of the unit was Evacuated to C.C.S. yesterday.	
			28 Div other formations	
			Officers ORs Officers ORs	
			S W S W S W S W	
			Adm. 1 — — 25 — 1 — —	
			Evac. 1 — — 14 — 1 — —	
			Des. — — — 7 — — — —	
			Duty — — — 3 — — — —	
			Rem. — — — 3 — — — 6	

Army Form C. 2118.

WAR DIARY
or
INTELLIGENCE SUMMARY.
(Erase heading not required.)

Instructions regarding War Diaries and Intelligence Summaries are contained in F. S. Regs., Part II. and the Staff Manual respectively. Title pages will be prepared in manuscript.

Place	Date	Hour	Summary of Events and Information	Remarks and references to Appendices
HERISSART	2/8/18	—	Capt HORNER M.R.C.V.S.A. transferred to 105 S.W.B. on move and struck off the strength. Capt Richards R.A.M.C. and "Lieut Hanson M.R.C.V.S. have both been evacuated from C.C.S. to Base.	
		3 pm	Depot Commander inspected 115 Brigade. Brigade marched past Army Commander Gen Sir JULIAN BYNG. Parade state 3 officers, 149, 125 O.R. (R.A.M.C.) 1 W.O, 14 O.R. (A.S.C.) 3 Ambulance Wagons 4 G.S. Wagons, 3 G.S. wagons limbered, 1 Maltese Cart, 2 water carts and 34 horses.	

	38th Division			Other Formations		
	Officers		O.R.S		Officers	O.R.S
	S	W	S	W	S W	S W
Admitted	1	—	9	—	— —	2 —
Evacuated	—	—	5	—	1 —	2 —
D.O.S.	1	—	—	—	— —	— —
Duty	—	—	1	—	— —	1 —
Remaining	—	—	15	—	— —	2 —
Day fine						6

WAR DIARY
INTELLIGENCE SUMMARY.
(Erase heading not required.)

Army Form C. 2118.

Place	Date	Hour	Summary of Events and Information	Remarks and references to Appendices
Herissart	29/5/16	—	Lecture by Col Grey C.B. Consulting Surgeon Third Army on the splints used in the front area in war.	
			38th Division Other Formations	
			Officers O.R.s Officers O.R.s	
			S. W. S. W. S. W. S. W.	
			Adm — 11—0 — 3 —	
			Evac — 9 — — 2 —	
			Duty — 5— — 1 —	
			Rem — 12 — — 3 — 6.	
			Walking wounded intra Divisional Collecting Station moves from CLAIRFAYE to Pos VILLERS to-day. Conference of D.A. Commanders at 130 Field Ambulance after lecture there by Col Grey C.B. ADMS.	
	30/5/16		38th Div Other Formations	
			O.R. Off. O.R.s	
			S. W. S. W.	
			Admitted 16 1 3 —	
			Evac 11 — 2 —	
			D.R.S. 4 2	
			Rem. 13 2. 6	

Army Form C. 2118.

WAR DIARY
or
INTELLIGENCE SUMMARY.
(Erase heading not required.)

Instructions regarding War Diaries and Intelligence Summaries are contained in F. S. Regs., Part II. and the Staff Manual respectively. Title pages will be prepared in manuscript.

Place	Date	Hour	Summary of Events and Information	Remarks and references to Appendices
HERISSART.	30.5.18	7pm.	Out looking for site for Field Ambulance All 1pm. Reconnoitred PUCHVILLERS & VAL DE MAISON districts. Received RAMC Order No 52. "Lieut McIVOR MORC U.S.A. evacuated to CCS with fracture of Radius	APX XII
			38th Division	
			Officers OR Other formations Officers ORs	
			admitted 1 5 W — — —	
			— 12 6 — — 6 —	
			Evacuated 1 11 6 — — Y —	
			D.R.S. — — — — — — —	
			Died — — 1 — — 1 —	
			Remaining — 13 — — — 6 —	
	31.5.18	—	aDaily weekly bath Lila hut ; 16 men to be seen at it morning fires. O.C. incoming unit visited the ambulance rear hutts occupied	
			James Sperrin Lt Col RAMC O.C. 131 Field Amb

140/30 76.

131st F.a.

June 1918

COMMITTEE FOR THE
MEDICAL HISTORY OF THE
7 AUG. 1918

Army Form C. 2118.

Vol 31

WAR DIARY
131st FIELD AMBULANCE
INTELLIGENCE SUMMARY.
(Erase heading not required.)

Instructions regarding War Diaries and Intelligence Summaries are contained in F.S. Regs., Part II. and the Staff Manual respectively. Title pages will be prepared in manuscript.

Place	Date	Hour	Summary of Events and Information	Remarks and references to Appendices
HERISSART	1.6.18	—	D.A.D.M.S. V Corps inspected Hospital yesterday. No. 130 Field ambulance called his morning with reference to handing over the unit at ST POL. O.C. 145 Field Amb called and saw billets. He is sending an advanced party on Monday. Major T. E. DAVIES recd. awarded to Military Cross. Cross admitted 17. Evacuated 17. D.R.S. 6. Remaining 11. Saw A.D.M.S. with re. Transport will start tomorrow (Sunday) night and Tent Division will go by train on Monday from ACHVILLERS. Day fine. ho. Divisional Horse jumping Competition "Bobby" ridden by myself got 4th place. Tent Subdivision left and transport left HERISSART at 7 p.m. and marched via CANDAS to ST POL. Train arrangement cancelled. ho.	A No. 1
	2.6.18	3.30	Arrived at ST POL, 38 patients taken over from 130 Field Ambulance. the Divisional Rest Station is here and is actively evacuated. Patients are all doing well. ho.	
	4.6.18	—	Visited Divisional Reinforcement Camp and Baths Supplies arranged dressing Station. Remainder of 130 20 and 1 F.A. marched out and are this morning.	
	5.6.18	—	Visited H.Q. M.O.T.O.N. Saw morning O.C. Col. Dupois & new asked hire from HERISSART Veterinary officer inspects Horses Day fine	

Army Form C. 2118.

WAR DIARY
or
INTELLIGENCE SUMMARY.
(Erase heading not required.)

Instructions regarding War Diaries and Intelligence Summaries are contained in F. S. Regs., Part II. and the Staff Manual respectively. Title pages will be prepared in manuscript.

Place	Date	Hour	Summary of Events and Information	Remarks and references to Appendices
ST LOT	6.6.18	—	Remained Off 4/6 OR 1 75	
			Admitted 4 25	
			Adm. trans. from 130 Ja 2	
			Evacuated 2 7	
			Duty 11	
			Rem 3 74	
			Day fine. Visited MAISON PONTHIEU. Arranged for inoculation of Battle supplies. &c.	
"	7.6.18		Remained Off 3 OR 74	
			Adm 10	
			Evac 8	
			Duty 14	
			Remaining 3 62	
			Day fine. &c.	
			Divisional Band played for patients this afternoon.	
	8.6.18		Admitted 10 Discharged or Transferred 10 Remaining 3 Officers 58 ORs &c.	

Army Form C. 2118.

WAR DIARY
or
INTELLIGENCE SUMMARY.
(Erase heading not required.)

Instructions regarding War Diaries and Intelligence Summaries are contained in F. S. Regs., Part II. and the Staff Manual respectively. Title pages will be prepared in manuscript.

Place	Date	Hour	Summary of Events and Information	Remarks and references to Appendices
ST. LOT.	9.6.18	—	A.D.M.S. 28th Division visited unit and inspected men for his medical Board. D.D.M.S. Cavalry Corps (Col MORGAN D.S.O A.M.S.) visited camp. All men of unit had a bath at AUXI-LE-CHATEAU. Wing sports at MAISON PONTHIEU. Major Davis Leave returns from leave.	
			Admitted o.R 1	
			offrs 8	
			Remaining 3 58	
			bed 1 4	
			Duty 2	
			Rem. 3 60 ls	
	10.6.18		Day fine but cloudy. offr o.R	
			Remaining 3 60	
			Admitted 3	
			Transfer A.Ds. 1 3	
			Evac — 3	
			Duty 1 19	
			Rem 3 44. les	

Army Form C. 2118.

WAR DIARY
or
INTELLIGENCE SUMMARY.
(Erase heading not required.)

Instructions regarding War Diaries and Intelligence Summaries are contained in F. S. Regs., Part II. and the Staff Manual respectively. Title pages will be prepared in manuscript.

Place	Date	Hour	Summary of Events and Information	Remarks and references to Appendices
ST LOT.	11.6.17	—	Visited D.D.M.S. Cavalry Corps n/w of Bolen Dieufoits. Promised to let me have it this afternoon for use tomorrow morning. Visited Parks at MAISON PONTHIEU, saw R.C. Divisional Reception Camp. Could not find sufficient water well to get water supply from.	
			R.A.S. officers	
			Remained 3 44	
			admitted 4	
			Evac. 3	
			Duty 3	
			Rem. 3 45	
		5pm	Received orders for Headquarters Tent Subdivision to proceed to VALHEUREUX (S.E. of CANDAS) to arrive by tomorrow morning. The whole village Parks to be taken over for the division.	Apt T
		10pm	Headquarters Tent Subdivision marched out. Night fine but very cold.	
	12.6.17	7.30am	Arrived at VALHEUREUX. Took over site for D.R.S. Capt. W.H. ARMISTEAD R.A.M.C. reported (Servant) Hut. Commenced preparing site for D.R.S. Arrival to take over the Strength D.R.S. at ST LOT opened for reception of patients. 130 O.R. admitted 2 off 130 O.R. Oris 2 off 4 O.R. Remaining 8 off 550 O.R. Sn.	

Army Form C. 2118.

WAR DIARY
or
INTELLIGENCE SUMMARY.
(Erase heading not required.)

Instructions regarding War Diaries and Intelligence Summaries are contained in F. S. Regs., Part II. and the Staff Manual respectively. Title pages will be prepared in manuscript.

Place	Date	Hour	Summary of Events and Information	Remarks and references to Appendices
VALHEUREUX	13/6/18	—	Visited ADMS as our O.C. Major Thompson DADG 38th Division returned with me to see about billeting & Battle Surplus which moves up here on 16th. Camp will be ready to take in patients tomorrow. Admitted 1 Off. 6 O.R. Discharged 2 O.R. Remaining 4 Officers 22 O.Rs fro.	
	14/6/18		Advance party of Battle Surplus arrived few. Arived rehich	
			Offr. O.R.	
			Patients Remaining 4 22	
			Admitted 1 7	
			Evacuated — 6	
			Died — 1	
			Remained 5 22 J.S.L.	
	15.6.18		Arranging camp for Battle Surplus which is due tomorrow. O/C Detachment reports that one here has picked up a nail so unable to travel. Notified D.A.D.V.S. & he promised to have the horse attended to. Night very cold. Admitted 17, Transfers from 130 F.A. 6. Evacuated 18, Duty 2, Remaining 5 Officers 25 O.Rs fro.	
	16.6.18	—	Detachment & unit found Headquarters from F.A.T. Battle Surplus arrived Leut Coffee 9o. a a Coy 9 38th Division visited Camp. Patients remaining this morn 2 Off 1 30 O.R. J.S.L.	

Army Form C. 2118.

WAR DIARY
or
INTELLIGENCE SUMMARY.
(Erase heading not required.)

Place	Date	Hour	Summary of Events and Information	Remarks and references to Appendices
VAL HEO REUS	7.6.18		A.D.M.S. visited camp, inspected arrangements for patients and picked new billets for men. Admitted 22 O.R. direct & as transfers 13. Evacuated 10. Remaining 2 Off. 65 O.Rs. Day fine.	
	13/6/18		Admitted 30 Offrs 34 O.Rs. Enac. 2 Off. 40 O.R. to duty 13 O.R.S. Remaining 30ff 67OR. Rain in evening turning night fro.	
	15.6.18		O.D.M.S. Conference. Subjects discussed 1. Distribution of Ambulances on 25th inst 2. Small units on loan from 130 Field Amb. 3. Patients to be sent to CAWDRS station by men collected here by us daily. 4. Care of Thermometers 5. Kit clips for Thomas Splints	
			G.O.C 38th Division visited & inspected camp and billets of Batts. Surplus to Admitted 3 Off. 20 O.R. Euac. 2 Off. 40 O.R. duty 12. Remaining 3 Off 6 7 O.R. Wet in morning but cleared up in afternoon.	

Army Form C. 2118.

WAR DIARY
or
INTELLIGENCE SUMMARY.
(Erase heading not required.)

Instructions regarding War Diaries and Intelligence Summaries are contained in F. S. Regs., Part II. and the Staff Manual respectively. Title pages will be prepared in manuscript.

Place	Date	Hour	Summary of Events and Information	Remarks and references to Appendices
VALHEUREUX	20/6/18	—	A.D.M.S. visited camp. Got 7 extra tents from 130 Field Ambulance. Admitted 1 off 45 O.Rs. Evacuated 1 off. Remaining 3 off. 640R. Day showery. ks	
"	21.6.18		Admitted 35 O.Rs. Evacuated 1 off & 20 O.Rs. Duty 17 O.R. Remaining 3 off & 690 O.Rs. ks.	
"	22.6.18		Admitted 2 officers and 38 O.Rs. Remaining 4 officers 132 O.Rs. Duty 11 O.R. Visited A.D.M.S. and A.D.V.S. also 130 Field Ambulance. Capt R.C. WILSON RAMC(T) returned to duty with this unit. Day fine with high wind. D.D.M.S. V Corps visited camp. ks	
"	23.6.18		Admitted 1 off 37 O.Rs. Evacuated 1 off 2 O.Rs. Remaining 1 officer 131 O.Rs. Duty 1 officer 37 O.R. A.D.M.S. (Lieut Col J.E.H. Davies D.S.O. RAMC) inspected. Water officer from V Corps Hqrs and adjutant to C.R.E. 38th Division inspected camp in order to find out the water supply. At present all water is derived from CANDAS by means of one 50 gallon water lorry and three horse water carts. It is proposed to have one or 400 gallon water lorry and also to sink a shaft for water. Day fine hot cold. ks	
"	24.6.18		Sick Parade. Admitted 4. Evacuated sick 2 and 20. Remaining 30 officers 117 O.Rs. Inspected camp with Commandant. Morning fine afternoon wet. ks	
"	25.6.18		Sick admitted 1 off 70 R. Evac 1 off Duty 22 O.R. Remaining 3 off 1020 R. Lecture at Clairfaye afterwards A.D.M.S. had Conference of R.M.Os. Agent for Patents. ks	

(39753) Wt. W2355/1361 600,000 12/17 D.D.&L. Sch 532a. Forms/C2118/15

WAR DIARY
or
INTELLIGENCE SUMMARY.

Army Form C. 2118.

(Erase heading not required.)

Place	Date	Hour	Summary of Events and Information	Remarks and references to Appendices
VALHEUREUX	26.6.18		Into admittia 5 off. 16 O.R. Evac 5 off. Discharged 19 O.R. Remaining 3 off. 99 O.R.	
			An broad epidemic of influenza seems to be raging again. The main feature of the attack were, sudden onset accompanied by a high temperature in some cases reaching 105° F. Constipation. Patients all looked very flushed. About six hours after the onset agonising pains in the backs of the legs, the back and back of neck set in, these were accompanied by headache vomiting & bleeding from the nose +the some cases. The temperature fell by a crisis on the third day & the patient was able to be about again and at light duty in four days time.	
			Cinema this afternoon. Concert this evening for patients. ↓a	
	27.6.18		Admitted 39 O.R. Evacuated 2, to duty 3 off. 2 O.R. Remaining 10 off. 129 O.R.	
			Camp visited by Lieut Col. L.C. Lito M.O. A.M.C. 38th Division. Arrangest to take 36 cases in to-day from 129 & 130 Field Ambulances. Received 15 Extra hints yesterday to enlarge Hospital if necessary. Eleven of the Q.R. reported from 129 F.A. to	
	28/6/18		Admittes 30, Evacuated 3, to duty 17. Remaining 10 offices 148 O.Rs. Day beautifully warm. O.C. 33 Sanitary Section visited Battle surplus camp. Another concert arranged for this evening. ↓a	

Army Form C. 2118.

WAR DIARY
or
INTELLIGENCE SUMMARY.
(Erase heading not required.)

Instructions regarding War Diaries and Intelligence Summaries are contained in F. S. Regs., Part II. and the Staff Manual respectively. Title pages will be prepared in manuscript.

Place	Date	Hour	Summary of Events and Information	Remarks and references to Appendices
VALHEUREUX	24.6.18	—	Admitted 6. Transfers 25. Evacuated 2., to duty 20 remaining 153. Visits adm/s about one routine incurred. Arranged to take 24 patients daily. Day firs. No.	
	26.6.18		Remaining in Hospital to-day 2 officers and 172 O.R.	

James Sproule
Lieut/Col Rank.
O.C. 131 Field Ambulance

140/2131

Army Form C. 2118.

WAR DIARY
or
INTELLIGENCE SUMMARY.
(Erase heading not required.)

Place	Date	Hour	Summary of Events and Information	Remarks and references to Appendices
VALHEUREUX	1.7.18	—	Admitted: 21 OR Transfers 20ff 23OR Evacuated 2 Discharges 46 Rem 4 off 159 OR. Camp visited by the G.O.C. 38" Division and ADMS 38" Division. Day fine. Canadian Corps Sports.	
	2.7.18		Capt ARMISTEAD R.A.M.C. returned from 130 FA. Rev HAMLIN JONES CF. admitted for duty. Rev DAVIS C.F. to 114 Bar for duty yesterday. Admitted 14 OR. Transfers 36 OR. Evacuated 1 to aug 10 from 14 OR Remaining 3 officers 165 OR. DDMS. 38" Division and Brigadier Major 115" Bde visited camp.	
	3.7.18		Admitted: 19 ff. 22 OR (chiefs exanema) Transfers 31, Evacuated 3 to aug 28 Remaining 4 officers 184 ORs. Day fine. "April 20" (Col Davies R.S.O.) and O.C. 129 FA (ChanColonel Jones D.S.O.M.C.) visited camp. The former came over for A.D.M.S Beard.	
	4.7.18		Admitted: direct 6 to transfers 10 128 OR. Evacuated RR 2 aug 25 OR Remaining 5 officers 190 ORs. Day fine	
	5.7.18		Admitted (direct) 4, to trans fro 18. Evacuated 1, to July 20, Rem 5 officers 197 OR Camp inspected by D.D.M.S. V Corps. Visited No 3 Canadian Stat HC. No 29 CCS, No 38 CCS.	
	6.7.18		Admitted (direct) 8 to Transfers 20ff 20 OR's Evac 10R to aug 24 OR Rem 7 off 188 ORS.	

WAR DIARY or INTELLIGENCE SUMMARY

Army Form C. 2118.

Place	Date	Hour	Summary of Events and Information	Remarks and references to Appendices
VOLKARINX	2/7/18		Draw two heavy and one LD horse to make up to full strength. Visited OC 26 M.C.	
			Admitted (direct) 7, Transfers 15, Evacuated 3. 2 Aug. 30. Remaining 5 officers 176 OR.	
			Lieut Hurd RAMC left for temporary duty with #13 RMF in relief of Capt Robertson Heart Sp.	
	3/7/18		Admitted (direct) 2, Transfers 21, Evacuated 17, 3 Aug. 30. On duty 10 officers 220 OR. Remaining	
			6 officers 1, A. adml. 3rd Divsion (Col Thompson CMG DSO and..) inspected	
			Hospital. Lent rain in evening &c.	
	4/7/18		Admitted (direct) 6 or transfers 10, To duty 24. Remaining 5 officers 180 ORs.	
		2.30pm	ADMS conference of Field Ambulance Commanders subjects discussed:-	
			1. New Cap Station Depot at TALMAS	
			2. Disposal of clothing at ADS during active operations	
			3. Promotion of NCOs of this Unit	
			4. Dental cases	
			5. Fresh Vegetables for Rations	
			6. No 129 & No 130 FA. to transfer cases to D.R.S. & not to keep any patient who	
			cannot walk.	
			7. 50 cases sent to 130 FA (34 sent 16 at present at 129 FA)	

Army Form C. 2118.

WAR DIARY
or
INTELLIGENCE SUMMARY.
(Erase heading not required.)

Instructions regarding War Diaries and Intelligence Summaries are contained in F. S. Regs., Part II. and the Staff Manual respectively. Title pages will be prepared in manuscript.

Place	Date	Hour	Summary of Events and Information	Remarks and references to Appendices
VILLERVAL	9/7/18	—	8. Sme arrangements went ahead in case p/active operations. Rain during evening &	
	10/7/18		Admitted (Sick) 4 as transfers 1 officer 9 O.Rs. to duty 2 Officers 30 O.Rs. Remained 4 Officers 151 O.Rs. 28 men sent by train to CANDAS to secure to 38 FA. Rain during Evening. Concert 4.	
	11/7/18		Admitted (sick) 3 O.Rs. (as transfers) 1 offr. 40 O.Rs. Evacuated 5 O.Rs. to duty 18 O.Rs. Remaining 5 Officers 171 O.Rs. Reception Camp and Field Ambulance visited by G.O.C. and A.A. & Q.M.G. 38th Division. Evening Wet 4.	
	12/7/18		Admitted (sick) 4 as transfers 12. to duty 21 Remaining 5 Officers 160 O.Rs. to.16 A.D.M.S. office. Bath Company started trying to hang at VAL HEUREUX. Received permanent sentry men to camp. Received water during first week = 50 lts. Pack horses overnight last two days. This morning parents to cinema in afternoon 4.	
	13/7/18		Admitted (sick) 4 Transferred 8 Evacuated 1 Transfers by lorries 1 offr. 4. to duty 16 O.R., remaining 5 Officers 155 O.Rs. Rain in morning. Refresher drill during requisite for one hour daily) has been carried out during last two days 4.	

(19975) Wt. W29371/P580 6000000 12/17 D. D. & L. Sch 53a. Forms/C2118/13

Army Form C. 2118.

WAR DIARY
or
INTELLIGENCE SUMMARY.
(Erase heading not required.)

Place	Date	Hour	Summary of Events and Information	Remarks and references to Appendices
VALHEUREUX	14.7.18	—	Sgt Major EDWARDS A.S.C. returned from leave to Eng (and Cass admitted (sick) Officer and 2 O.R. to Transfer 10. Evacuated 3, discharged to duty 13. Remaining 6 Officers 154 O.R. Rain was heavy and of rain during the day. No Bicycle articles were obtained from No 29 Field ambulance. Sent six men to CANDAS to draw out water supply. Rambs (30th Division) Order No 75 received received. Medical Defence Scheme for middle aisti 1 Corps Front (name proto) received not.	
	15.7.18	—	Admitted 2 Officers 30 O.R. Rothnefogles 190R Evacuated 1. to duty 16 Remaining 8 Officers 159 O.R. Tu. Received Preliminary Orders to move from VALHEUREUX to TOUTENCOURT. Went to see ADMS in afternoon. Heavy Thunderstorm & rain during the night. Admissions 6 O.R. Transfers 10th O.R. Canada 2, to duty 15 O.R. remaining 9 Officers 157 O.R. called on O.C. 29 Field ambulance (Lieut Col A.J. JONES DSO. M.C.) Day fine but sultry to.	App I App II
	17.7.18		Returned 300 Blankets to No 21 M.A.C. Capt E Witt MC (Canh.) 3 am disinfector arrived to disinfect Blankets of patients. Received Orders to say that Unit might have to move to site now occupied by 129' Field Ambulance	

WAR DIARY
or
INTELLIGENCE SUMMARY.
(Erase heading not required.)

Army Form C. 2118.

Instructions regarding War Diaries and Intelligence Summaries are contained in F. S. Regs., Part II. and the Staff Manual respectively. Title pages will be prepared in manuscript.

Place	Date	Hour	Summary of Events and Information	Remarks and references to Appendices
	17.7.18	—	O.C. Gas centre at CLAIRFAYE will send one officer (2nd/Lieut Wall) and two clerks there tomorrow morning. Held meeting of men with reference to Divisional Sports on 23rd inst. Got entries for all the competitions. Admitted (sick) 4, Evacuated 13, Transferred 2 to duty 2 officers 9 O.R. Remaining 9 officers and 162 O.R.	
	18/7/18		Very heavy thunder and hail storm about 8 p.m. this evening. Hail stones as large as pigeons eggs fell much damage done to crops. No A.D.M.S. visited camp and held his weekly inspection given formal parade. No. 21 M.A.C. (Capt Elliott M.C. R.A.M.C.) visited camp & saw hospital. C6 38th Div Supplies Col visited camp. Received R.A.M.C. order No 56. Admitted sick Transfer received 1 officer 130 O.R. Evacuated 30 O.R. Duty 1 officer 60 O.R. Remaining 7 officers 166 O.R. Showery during day.	App III

Army Form C. 2118.

WAR DIARY
or
INTELLIGENCE SUMMARY.
(Erase heading not required.)

Instructions regarding War Diaries and Intelligence Summaries are contained in F. S. Regs., Part II. and the Staff Manual respectively. Title pages will be prepared in manuscript.

Place	Date	Hour	Summary of Events and Information	Remarks and references to Appendices
VALHEUREUX	19/7/18	—	Called on A.D. 43 C.C.S. also O.C. R.P.C.S. Day fine. Admitted 1 Officer and 5 O.R.s. Transferred to 20 C.H., Evacuated 2 O.R., Remaining 10 Officers + 70 O.R. Transferred to Paris Depot 2 O.R. To duty 2 Officers 8 O.R.s Remaining 5 Officers 150 O.R. Both Aeroplane returned Brigades. Sent home Ambulances with them.	
	20/7/18		Two officers of 129 Field Ambulance report to take over Divisional rest Station. DADOS 38th Division called. Admitted 46 O.R. Transferred 10 O.R., Evac. 4 O.R. Remaining 5 officers 169 O.R. Visited No 3 Canadian Stationary Hospital. Saw several interesting surgical cases.	
	21/7/18		Advance Party of 129 Field Ambulance arrived at this site. Hospital and patients handed over to 129 Field Ambulance. Loaded Equipment. Received orders for move tomorrow. Evacuated 70 O.R. Discharged to duty 1 Off 10 O.R. Remaining (handed over) 4 Officers 161 O.R.s	
	22/7/18	5.30am	Unit left VALHEUREUX and marched via HERISSART and TOUTENCOURT to O.27.B.8.9. Reported arrival in person to A.D.M.S. Very good camp consisting of 11 NISSEN Huts and several smaller buildings. Visited gas cents. Medical Arrangements in the Event of the Division leaving and taking over No 57 Received.	Apps IV. V.
	23/7/18	—	Day very wet. Visited gas cents.	
	24/7/18	—	Showery during day.	

WAR DIARY or INTELLIGENCE SUMMARY

Army Form C. 2118.

Place	Date	Hour	Summary of Events and Information	Remarks and references to Appendices
02 & 9	25/7/18	—	A.D.M.S. held a conference of all Medical Officers of the Division. Several subjects were discussed. Showery during day. &c.	
	26/7/18	—	Bath and clean change of clothing for all men in the Field Ambulance. Remained Sor., admitted 10 O.R. to D.R.S. C.O.R. Remaining 70 R. Showery during the day. Heavy showers all day. Received notification for draft to report at base f/3 or 9 Division hubs. &c.	
	27/7/18	—	Horse noises hub around. Visited augment in VARENNES – HARPONVILLE road where it is proposed to have an A.D.S. Made further reconnaissance of that area. Found suitable hacks for evacuation of walking cases & found places in Echo A.D.S. Visited 51st F.A. at CLAIRFAYE	
	28/7/18	—	Made reconnaissance of ACHEUX village and fixed up a place to establish a sick collecting post if required. Received Routine Order NO J.B. Sent two officers (Major PREW & Capt JINGWALL) to take over the Gas Centre and Walking wounded Collecting Post from 6th " Field Ambulance tomorrow. Day fine	appt
	30/7/18	—	Made reconnaissance of the "Broad Line System from FORCEVILLE to BEAUSSART and out report to R.D.M.S. Sent 1 N.C.O. and four men in Lutter 27C. at ACHEUX to form a entrainocoring post Medical Inspection room for 11th Bde. H/qrs	

Army Form C. 2118.

WAR DIARY
or
INTELLIGENCE SUMMARY.
(Erase heading not required.)

Instructions regarding War Diaries and Intelligence Summaries are contained in F. S. Regs., Part II. and the Staff Manual respectively. Title pages will be prepared in manuscript.

Place	Date	Hour	Summary of Events and Information	Remarks and references to Appendices
ACHEUX	30.7.16	—	Two will be under the M.O. 9th Battalion in ACHEUX.	
		10 am	Bro Centre taken over.	
		10 pm	238 cases have passed through the Centre, mostly yellow x 2. A few cases of Shrapnel.	
	31.7.16	—	Visited Medical Inspection Room at ACHEUX and found that everything was going well. The M.O. i/c (S.W.B.) had sent his morning sick. Visited the Centre and found that a few cases were still coming in. Arrangement of A.D.M.S. the FOLLOWING day was that accompanying walking sick patients 66, 26 M.A.C. called. Day fine.	

Ronald Morris
Lieut Col RAMC
no. 131 Field Ambulance

SECRET   *Appendix*   Copy No. 3

38th (Welsh) Division.

R.A.M.C. Order No. 55.   14th July 1918.

---

1. The 21st Division will relieve the 38th (Welsh) Division in the line on the 17th, 18th and 19th July, reliefs to be completed by the morning of the 19th inst.

2. O.C. No. 129 Field Ambulance will hand over all medical posts in the forward area to O.C. No. 63 Field Ambulance, relief to be completed by 10 a.m. on the 18th, from which hour O.C. No. 63 Field Ambulance will be responsible for the evacuation of the line.

3. O.C. No. 129 Field Ambulance will return all stretcher bearers, cars, and wheeled stretcher carriages at present attached to him to their respective ambulances. On completion of the relief he will proceed with his ambulance to BEAUQUESNE and occupy the site vacated by O.C. No. 63 Field Ambulance, N.8.a.9.1.

   O.C. 130 Field Ambulance will hand over the Corps Gas Centre, the Walking Wounded Collecting Post at CLAIRFAYE, and the transport lines at RAINCHEVAL N.17.d.8.8. to O.C. No. 64 Field Ambulance, relief to be completed by 10 a.m. on the 18th inst.
   On relief O.C. No. 130 Field Ambulance will proceed with his ambulance to PUCHEVILLERS and occupy the site vacated by O.C. No. 64 Field Ambulance N.21.d.2.1.
   An interchange of sites will take place on the 18th between the holding parties of No. 64 Field Ambulance at HERISSART and No. 130 Field Ambulance at TOUTENCOURT.

4. Receipts for all stores and equipment handed over will be taken and two copies forwarded to this office.

5. All details of reliefs will be arranged direct between the Os.C. concerned.

6. O.C. No. 131 Field Ambulance will continue to carry on the D.R.S. at VALHEUREUX for the present.

7. On arrival in new area, O.C. No. 129 Field Ambulance will arrange to collect sick of 115 Brigade and adjacent units.
   O.C. No. 130 Field Ambulance will arrange to collect sick of 113 and 114 Brigades and the units in the neighbourhood.

8. The office of the A.D.M.S. will close at O.22.d.1.6. on the 18th inst. and re-open at BEAUQUESNE on the same day.

Field Ambulances and A.D.M.S. 21st Division will please acknowledge.

                               Sgd. A.G. Thompson, Colonel,
14.7.18.   A.D.M.S., 38th (Welsh) Division.

Distribution

129 Fd. Amb.	'G'	D.A.D.V.S.
130 " "	'Q'	D.A.D.O.S.
131 " "	Dv. Train	Signals
D.M.S.	S.S.O.	A.D.M.S. 21st, 17th, 63rd Div.
D.D.M.S.	27 M.A.C.	War Diary and File.

Appendix I

38th (Welsh) Division.

Amendment to R.A.M.C. Order No. 55

Para. 3.
    Cancel lines 4 and 5 and substitute the following:-
"he will proceed with his ambulance to TOUTENCOURT and occupy the site at present held by a party of No. 130 Field Ambulance. On relief this party will proceed to HERISSART and take over the site at present held by a party from No. 64 Field Ambulance".
Cancel lines 13, 14, and 15.

                      Sgd. A.H.Spicer Major R.A.M.C.
14.3.19.   for A.D.M.S. 38th (Welsh) Division

A.D.M.S. No. C.3/16.

Appendix II

38th (Welsh) Division.

MEDICAL DEFENCE SCHEME FOR MIDDLE SECTOR V CORPS FRONT (MESNIL Sector)

For Medical arrangements for the present front line see A.D.M.S. No. C.8/1 dated 8.6.18.

O.C. No. 129 Field Ambulance will be responsible for clearing the line in any of the situations hereunder described.
R.A.Ps. will be selected by Regimental Medical Officers in collaboration with the Os.C and their situation and map reference will be given to O.C. No. 129 Field Ambulance with whom they should keep in constant touch.

O.C. No. 129 Field Ambulance will keep in constant touch with all R.M.Os. and Brigade Headquarters and will have a runner attached at each of the latter. He will select for himself relay posts and car posts along the routes of evacuation, and be prepared with alternative routes should enemy activity necessitate them.

For the purpose of clearing the line, O.C. No. 129 Field Ambulance will have attached to him all the bearers of No. 130 Field Ambulance and 50 of the bearers of No. 131 Field Ambulance. All the cars (less two) of these two ambulances will also be attached to him.

(a) PURPLE SYSTEM.
   O.C. No. 129 Field Ambulance will evacuate ENGLEBELMER.
Suggested R.A.Ps. In the neighbourhood of Brigade Headquarters at P.24.d.3.3. for the left; in the neighbourhood of P.36.a.9.1. for the right.
Collecting Post will be at HEDAUVILLE P.34.a.4.2.
Advanced Dressing Station will be at O.27.b.8.9.
Main Dressing Station will be at RAINCHEVAL N.18.d.central.
Routes of evacuation will be either by tracks if the weather permits or by the HEDAUVILLE-VARENNES-LEALVILLERS road by horsed ambulance or motor ambulance to the A.D.S. and thence by the TOUTENCOURT-RAINCHEVAL road to the M.D.S.

Walking wounded will be by marked out overland tracks to the A.D.S. and thence by overland route to the Corps Walking Wounded Post at RAINCHEVAL.

O.C. No. 129 Field Ambulance will send one Tent-Sub-Division and as much of his transport as possible to a site outside PUCHEVILLERS, and prepare a M.D.S. there.

O.C. No. 130 Field Ambulance will move his gas centre to RAINCHEVAL N.18.d. central. He will load as much of his transport as possible and collect it at the site of his present transport lines N.17.b.7.4.

(b) INTERMEDIATE SYSTEM.

   In the event of this being held O.C. No. 129 Field Ambulance will hold on to ENGLEBELMER with a skeleton party.
   Suggested R.A.Ps will be at Q.19.b.7.4. on the left, and on the right about Q.31.b.8.6.
   The rest of the arrangements will be as for the present front line.
   In the event of a withdrawal behind the PURPLE LINE, the probable route of withdrawal for the ambulances will be towards Fme.DU ROSEL at M.16.a.5.0. and LA VICOGNE for both 129 and 130 Field Ambulance.

                     Sgd. A.G. Thompson, Colonel
14.7.18.   A.D.M.S. 38th (Welsh) Division.

SECRET.   Copy No. 3
                       38th (Welsh) Division.

                       R.A.M.C. Order No. 56.
_____

1. R.A.M.C. Order No. 55 is cancelled.

2. The 17th and 63rd Divisions will relieve the 38th Division in the line
   reliefs to be completed by 6 a.m. on the 19th instant.
   The dividing line between the two Divisions will be BLAKE ALLEY,
   17th Division taking over South of the line, 63rd Division taking
   over the NORTH.

3. No. 129 Field Ambulance will arrange to hand over all his posts
   to O.C. of an ambulance of 63rd Division by 5 p.m. on the 18th
   but will leave one officer at ENGLEBELMER and two squads of
   Bearers at the R.A.Ps. until the Divisional relief takes place.
   O.C. No. 129 Field Ambulance will then concentrate his ambulance
   at his present Headquarters. On the 19th instant he will proceed to
   HERISSART and relieve the holding party of 21st Division.
   He will leave a holding party at his present site until relieved
   by No. 131 Field Ambulance. On the same day he will send two officers
   to report to O.C. No. 131 Field Ambulance at VALHEUREUX.

   On the 21st inst. he will send two tent-sub-divisions to take over
   the Divisional Rest Station at VALHEUREUX.

4. On the 18th inst. O.C. No. 130 Field Ambulance will move his Headquarters
   and transport lines to TOUTENCOURT, leaving sufficient personnel
   to carry on the Gas Centre and Walking Wounded Post at CLAIRFAYE
   until relieved of this duty.
   He will have 43 other ranks of No. 131 Field Ambulance to assist him.
   On and from the 19th inst O.C. No. 130 Field Ambulance will be
   responsible for clearing the Brown Line and for this purpose
   he will get in touch with 113 Brigade and the Medical Officers
   of the Battalions of that Brigade.

5. On the 18th inst. O.C. No. 131 Field Ambulance will send
   one officer and two clerks to the Gas Centre at CLAIRFAYE.

   On the early morning of the 22nd inst. O.C. No. 131 Field
   Ambulance will proceed to the site at present occupied by No. 129
   Field Ambulance at O.27.b.8.9.

6. Receipts for all stores and equipment handed over will be taken
   and two copies forwarded to this office.

7. All details of reliefs will be arranged direct between the Os.C.
   concerned.

8. On arrival in the new area Os.C. Field Ambulances will arrange to

   collect the sick of the Brigades and Divisional Units in their
   immediate area.
9.
The office of the A.D.M.S. will remain at the present site.
10. On completion of relief 38th Division will be in G.H.Q. reserve
    and will be V Corps Right Supporting Division.
    The 38th Division will be at the following notice to move:-
              Midnight to 5 a.m.   1 hour.
              Remainder of day and night   9 hours.

                                                         (P.T.O.)

Field Ambulances and A.D.M.S. 17th and 63rd Divisions will please acknowledge.

                              Sgd. A.G.Thompson,
                                        Colonel
                A.D.M.S. 38th (Welsh) Division.

17.7.18.

Distribution as for R.A.M.C. Order No. 55

Appendix III

Officer Commanding
    131st Field Ambulance.

You will be exchanging Ambulance sites with O.C. No. 129 Field Ambulance on Monday next 22nd instant at TOUTENCOURT. Definite orders will be issued shortly.

Your 50 stretcher bearers at present attached to No. 130 Field Ambulance will go to TOUTENCOURT, and will be rationed by you on and from the 22nd inst.

Sgd. A.H.Spicer Major R.A.M.C.
15/7/18   for A.D.M.S. 38th (Welsh) Division.
No. M 9/78

38th (Welsh) Division.

ADDENDUM TO R.A.M.C. ORDER NO. 56.

Para. 3. After "Posts" Line 1. add -

" except HEDAUVILLE which will be taken over by an Ambulance of the 17th Division.

Sgd. A.H.Spicer Major, R.A.M.C.
17.7.18. For A.D.M.S. 38th (Welsh) Division.

No. 131
FIELD AMBULANCE
133/13/18
Date 17/7/18

App IV

SECRET   38th (Welsh) Division.

MEDICAL ARRANGEMENTS IN THE EVENT OF A DIVISIONAL MOVE.

The Division is now in G.H.Q. Reserve and is at One hour's notice to move from midnight to 5 a.m. and 24 hours' notice the rest of the day.   In the event of this notice comong through:-

1. Os.C. of all Field Ambulances should immediately clear all cases unfit to return to their Units to C.C.S.

2. The O.C. Field Ambulance at HERISSART will embus or entrain with the the Brigade in that area.
   He will immediately Telephone the A.D.M.S. and the D.D.M.S. Corps the number of cases he has remaining at D.R.S.
   He will hand over the D.R.S. to a Holding Party detailed by the Vth Corps.

3. O.C. Field Ambulance at TOUTENCOURT will embus or entrain with the Brigade there.

4. O.C. Field Ambulance at site O.27.b.8.9. will embus or entrain with the Brigade holding the Brown Line.
   He should immediately hand over this site to Holding Party of 63rd Division.
   He should also immediately notify the A.D.M.S. 17th Division and hand over the Gas Centre to Holding Party of that Division.

5. The O.C. of each Field Ambulance will render to this office immediately a return showing:-
   1. Embussing Strength
   2. Entraining Strength.

In the event of the Division embussing, Os C. Field Ambulances should take as many Stretchers as possible and also sand bags full of extra Dressings in addition to Shell Haversacks, etc.

Embussing points and Groups are as under:
                      Head of Bus Column.
              For move North.   For move South.

Brown Line Brigade.   (Group C.)   N.27.d.6.8.   T.2.b.8.4.
TOUTENCOURT Bde.   (Group B.)   N.27.d.6.8.   T.2.b.8.4.
HERISSART Bde.   (Group A)   T.3.a.0.8.   T.8.c.0.5.

   Entraining Points:-
Brown Line Brigade   (Group A.)   CANDAS
TOUTENCOURT Brigade   (Group B.)   DOULLENS
HERISSART Brigade   (Group C.)   DOULLENS.

Field Ambulances to acknowledge.

                    Sgd.   A.H.Spicer, Major,
                            for Colonel
21/7/18.   3 Fd. Ambs: A.D.M.S. 38th (Welsh) Division.
            3 Brigades
            38 Div. 'A'   38 Div. 'G'   D.D.M.S.

app V

SECRET.   38th (Welsh) Division.   Copy No. 3.

            R.A.M.C. Order No. 57.   22nd. July 1918.

1. O.C. 130 Field Ambulance will hand over the Gas Centre and the walking wounded Collecting Post at CLAIRFAYE to O.C. 64 Field Ambulance on 25th July 1918.

   Advanced Party will be sent by the 21st Division on the 23rd inst.

2. Details of relief will be arranged by the Os.C. concerned.

   130 Field Ambulance & A.D.M.S. 21 Division to acknowledge.

                    Sgd.   A.H.Spicer Major,
                                for Colonel,
22/7/18.   A.D.M.S. 38th (Welsh) Division.

Distribution
   129 F.A.   38th Sigs.   D.D.M.S.
   130 F.A.   D.A.D.V.S.   D.A.D.O.S.
   131 F.A.   Div. Train   ?.S.O.
   D.M.S.   'G'   A.D.M.S. 21, 17, 63 Div.
   27 M.A.C.   'Q'   War Diary & Flde

Appendix VI

38th (Welsh) Division.   Copy No. 3

R.A.M.C. ORDER NO. 58   29th July 1918.

1. O.C. 131 Field Ambulance will take over the Gas Centre and the Walking Wounded Collecting Post at CLAIRFAYE (O.29.b.5.6.) with sufficient personnel on Tuesday, July 30th 1918, from O.C. 64th Field Ambulance.

   Relief to be completed by 10 a.m.

   An advance Party will be sent to-day, July 29th.

2. Details of relief will be arranged by the O.s.C. concerned.

O.C. 131 Field Ambulance and A.D..S. 21st Division to ACKNOWLEDGE.

Sd. A.G.Thompson, Colonel,
A.D.M.S. 38th (Welsh) Division.

29/7/18.

Distribution.
129 F.A.   27 M.A.C.   D.A.D.V.S.
130 F.A.   38th Sigs.   D.A.D.O.S.
131 F.A.   'G'   S.S.O.
D.D.M.S.   'Q'   A.D.M.S. 21st Div. 17 & 63 Divs.
D.M.S.   Div. Train.   War Diary and File.

140/3700

1313th F. A.

COMMITTEE FOR THE
MEDICAL HISTORY
Date 5 OCT 54

Aug. 1948

26 131 2ⁿᵈ Aug JH 33

WAR DIARY
or
INTELLIGENCE SUMMARY.
(Erase heading not required.)

Army Form C. 2118.

Instructions regarding War Diaries and Intelligence Summaries are contained in F. S. Regs., Part II. and the Staff Manual respectively. Title pages will be prepared in manuscript.

Place	Date	Hour	Summary of Events and Information	Remarks and references to Appendices
O.S.+S.D.	1.8.18	—	Visited Corps qr Cmte. a few patients are still coming in. All the clothing of the patients is being dis-infected and returned to D.A.D.S. and O.C. Baths. W/c to more but moves but had required new Jr section. D.D.M.S. V G who called and inspected the camp. Admitted 19ff 20O.R, to C.C.S. 12 (wounded), to D.R.S. Duty 5, Rem. 19ff 196O.R.	App I
"	2.8.18	—	A.D.M.S. 38th Division held his usual Medical Board here. Day very wet. Received R.A.M.C. order No 59. Admitted 12, to C.C.S. 3, to D.A.S. 1ff 5O.R, Duty 1 1, Rem. 100O.R.	
"	3.8.18	—	Admitted O.R. 10 sick 1 wounded; Evacuated 3 sick 1 wounded; Evacuated Sept 3 Convalescing 6. Visited No. 51st Field Ambulance and 8 O.R., 16 sick to Sept 3 Convalescing 6. Wet in morning. Afternoon fine. Personnel Sports saw over his camp. D.A.D.M.S. 38th Division and Educational Officer also C.O. 10th S.W.B. called also. to D.R.S. O.R. 5 Remaining	
"	4.8.18	—	Admitted 13 sick 1 wounded. Evacuated O.R. 8 wounded 5 sick. to D.R.S. Visited Gas Cas.ties. Very few cases coming through. O.R. 9. Division Horse Show day fine.	
"	5.8.18	—	Sent advance party to 51st Field Ambulance. Visited Gas Cas.ties. No cases coming through. Visited A.R. under Construction in VARENNES-HARPONVILLE ROAD. Arranged for handing over of Gas Cas.ties. Advance party 1/30 Field ambulance arrived at this site. Lt Col Davies & Lt Col to 2.A. called inspected site. Admitted 2 officers sick and 12O.R sick and 2 O.R wounded. Evacuated O.R. 3 sick 2 wounded; to D.R.S 1 Officer + 5O.R sick to Sub.div Sept 2 O.R. Remaining 1 Officer 10 O.R. (sick) Received orders for move tomorrow.	App II

Army Form C. 2118.

WAR DIARY
or
INTELLIGENCE SUMMARY.
(Erase heading not required.)

Instructions regarding War Diaries and Intelligence Summaries are contained in F. S. Regs., Part II. and the Staff Manual respectively. Title pages will be prepared in manuscript.

Place	Date	Hour	Summary of Events and Information	Remarks and references to Appendices
O3a & 2.B.	6.8.18	—	Left O27 b 8 9 and marched to V Corps LYING WOUNDED STATION (O.30 & 2.B.) Cases are sent from here by M.A.C. cars to C.C.S. Handed over V Corps Gpo Cushi. Admitted 22 sick, 3 wounded. Evacuated 1 off 5 O.Rs. to D.R.S. 16 O.R. Remaining 14 O.R.	
	7.8.18		A.D.M.S. 17th 21st and 38th Division visited Camp. Town Major CLAIRFAYE called. Admitted 2 off 15 O.R. Evac 2 off 9 O.Rs. To D.R.S. 6 O.R. Remaining 12 O.R.	
	8.8.18		A.D.M.S. Conference of O.Cs. Field Ambulances. Subjects discussed were
1. A stamp (temporary?) was raised to Field ambulances for winter quarters
2. Meeting accommodation for winter quarters
3. Returns of American Troops
4. Discharge of homeshoes. As regards this it was stated that influx homeshoes could not be carried in luxuries but is or enough for two packs a hoof
5. Accidental Injuries
6. Heating of Ambulances
7. Supply of Stretchers	

WAR DIARY
or
INTELLIGENCE SUMMARY.
(Erase heading not required.)

Army Form C. 2118.

Instructions regarding War Diaries and Intelligence Summaries are contained in F. S. Regs., Part II. and the Staff Manual respectively. Title pages will be prepared in manuscript.

Place	Date	Hour	Summary of Events and Information	Remarks and references to Appendices
	30/6	—	8 Restart of trench fat.	
			9 Hair cutting	
			10 Each 9 a. to have hair 20 ft glasses forceps	
			11 Issue of Br. Brait to personnel	
			12 Arrival of slight gassed cases	
			13 Increase in senior of patients	
			14 No of patients to D.R.S. if telephoned to agent by 1 pm daily	
			15 Use of Ford cars for evacuation of forward area.	
			Extra took over gas centre from 52 Fa Field Amb. & a hay note box	
			Tiphted for temporary aug.	

Strength   80 div   other formations

	Off	OR		Off	OR
	S	W	S	W	
adm.	1	38	10	3	2
Duc	1	23	9	3	2
D.R.S.		6			
Section Depot		1			
Duty		5			
Remain		12	1		

WAR DIARY
or
INTELLIGENCE SUMMARY.

Army Form C. 2118.

Place	Date	Hour	Summary of Events and Information	Remarks and references to Appendices
Div H.S.	9/9/18	—	Weekly held weekly head [Capt?] Robertson Regt reports in duty are taken on the strength of the unit.	
			25th Div
			Off ORs S W S W
			Adm 27 – 25 1 10 7
			Evac 12 32 1 8 7
			D.R.S 6 1
			Section S/Sgt 1
			Remaining 20 2 3	K.
	10/9/18	—	Attended meeting of stock committee at No 3 C.C.S. Admitted 2 officers and 57 O.R. Evacuated 29 off 26 O.R. died 1 O.R. 6 days S.O.P. O.R.S. 24 O.Rs. Remaining 27 O.R. 4 day private Co.	
	11/9/18		Handed over to Major J. S. Davies. M.C. Rank 6 Graded Reserve [LCC?] 11/9/18. [signature]	

Army Form C. 2118.

WAR DIARY
or
INTELLIGENCE SUMMARY.
(Erase heading not required.)

Instructions regarding War Diaries and Intelligence Summaries are contained in F. S. Regs., Part II. and the Staff Manual respectively. Title pages will be prepared in manuscript.

Place	Date	Hour	Summary of Events and Information	Remarks and references to Appendices
O.30 62 E	11.8.18		Took over charge of the unit from Lt Col W.L Staub R.A.M.C. granted leave to U.S.	
			Nell 11.9.18	
			Admitted 86 O.R. Evacuated 30 O.R. To Eng. L.O.R. To D.R.S. 20 O.R.	
			Remaining 11 O.R.	
			The D.D.M.S. 2nd Corps inspected Gypo Wound Clearing Station. Grading and Walking Wounded Station.	
			He recommended that blood transfusion be performed upon suitable cases at the Gypo Wounded Clearing Station.	
	12.8.18		Admitted 1 officer and 49 O.R. Evacuated 32 O.R. To D.R.S. 12 O.R.	
			Remaining 1 officer and 16 O.R.	
	13.8.18		Took Major Corenne called. Weather fine and very hot.	
			Admitted 3 officers and 24 O.R. Evacuated 1 officer and 14 O.R. To D.R.S. 1 Officer	
			15 O.R. Remaining 1 Officer 11 O.R.	

WAR DIARY
or
INTELLIGENCE SUMMARY.

(Erase heading not required.)

Army Form C. 2118.

Place	Date	Hour	Summary of Events and Information	Remarks and references to Appendices
0306.2.8	14.8.18		Admitted 51 O.R. Evacuated 29 O.R. To DRS 1 officer, 12 O.R. Remaining 18 O.R. His de Roy MORC stuck off Return Kingston alongwith 129 Field Ambulance.	
	15.8.18		Capt Robertson and Mrs W M Kerr were sent to 56 CCS for Temporary duty. Admitted 2 officers and 35 O.R. Evacuated 2 officers and 16 O.R. To DRS 10 O.R. Remaining 24 O.R.	
	16.8.18		ADM S held weekly Board and inspected Camp and Horse Transport. A boiler arrived a/c Gas Enks trolley for the disinfection of gassed clothing. Admitted 2 officers and 40 O.R. Evacuated 2 officers and 18 O.R. To DRS 20 O.R. Remaining 25 O.R.	
	17.8.18		DDMS inspected, Keys Wounded Collecting Station, Gas Enks and Walking Wounded Collecting Posts. Weather is very fine. Admitted 1 officer and 35 O.R. Evacuated 16 O.R. To DRS 1 officer and 23 O.R.	
	18.8.18		Admitted 25 O.R. Evacuated 13 O.R. To DRS 13 O.R.	
	19.8.18		Admitted 28 O.R. Evacuated 13 O.R. To DRS 14 O.R.	

WAR DIARY
or
INTELLIGENCE SUMMARY.

Army Form C. 2118.

Place	Date	Hour	Summary of Events and Information	Remarks and references to Appendices
03.0.C.2.8.	20.6.18		ADMS held conference of Ambulance Commanders. Subjects discussed were :—	
			1. Pairs of Stoke Batchs to keep on carrying Bearers overnight.	
			2. All Cases of Dysentery are to be sent immediately to CCS	
			3. Five packsaddles are to be issued to the Ambulance for the transport of materiel on the forward area.	
			4. The Medical Arrangements on the event of Active Operations in this area.	
			5. The 131 Field Ambulance is to form a MDS in HEDAUVILLE. Major O'Brien with the Tent Sub Division of A Section left this evening for Hedauville and formed the MDS there, but this MDS is not to function until further orders are received. Written verbal Line. Capt Dingwall relieved Major Fres at the Gas Gate and Major Ridolfi with one tent Subdivision reported tonight in readiness to take over this Dying Wounded Station	

Army Form C. 2118.

WAR DIARY
or
INTELLIGENCE SUMMARY.
(Erase heading not required.)

Instructions regarding War Diaries and Intelligence Summaries are contained in F. S. Regs., Part II. and the Staff Manual respectively. Title pages will be prepared in manuscript.

Place	Date	Hour	Summary of Events and Information	Remarks and references to Appendices
			Visited Netherwitt and arranged for the New MDS Que with Major Burke RAMC. Relieved RAMC odr No 61.	App 3.
			Admitted 18 OR. Evacuated 9 OR TO DRS 6 OR	
21.8.18			Major Rothuell RAMC with one tent subdivision opened the rest for Offrs. last night. The MDS at Netherwitt all in readiness to function as such.	
			Captn OC Irvin RAMC reported from No 3 CCS. The D.D.M.S visited "Lying wounds Collecting Station" and the DADMS & Capts. visited in the Afternoon to enquire about Capt. Ironside.	
			Admitted 67 OR Evacuated 54 OR TO DRS 14 OR	
22.8.18			Visited the M.D.S Netherwitt this morning. It commenced to receive sick at 6.0 am this morning, Evacuated every day by 5 MAC cars obtained there.	
			8 OR men admitted suffering from wounds caused by "Trap" land mines and 12 OR suffering from wounds caused	

WAR DIARY
or
INTELLIGENCE SUMMARY.
(Erase heading not required.)

Army Form C. 2118.

Instructions regarding War Diaries and Intelligence Summaries are contained in F. S. Regs., Part II. and the Staff Manual respectively. Title pages will be prepared in manuscript.

Place	Date	Hour	Summary of Events and Information	Remarks and references to Appendices
			by burying woollens fraks.	
			The Orderly Room and the A.T.D. Officer transferred to the Gas Cadre	
			Left At Wilson RAMC (acting) the M.D.S. Irquenville for duty	
			and Capt W H Armistead RAMC T. to the Gas Cadre.	
			At 2.0 P.m the M.D.S. at Hedauville was withdrawn and reformed	
			at the Corps Lying Wounded Station, Acheux.	
23.8.18			ADMS held weekly Board and DDMS visited the Corps Lying Wounded	
			Station. Received instructions connection with 38 Division Order No 213	App IV
			Admitted 2 officers and 71 O.R. Evacuated 2 officers and 44 O.R. to D.R.S.	
			34 O.R.	
24.8.18		8.0 Am.	Received orders to form M.D.S. at Hedauville.	
		9.0 Am	M.D.S. at Hedauville opened and ambulance directed to CCS	
			and "Walking wounded Collecting Station" by M.A.C.	
			Received RAMC o/ans No 62 & 63	Apps V & VI
			Recce ADMS mobile tins to Regimental medical officers in the event of the	

Army Form C. 2118.

WAR DIARY
or
INTELLIGENCE SUMMARY.
(Erase heading not required.)

Instructions regarding War Diaries and Intelligence Summaries are contained in F. S. Regs., Part II. and the Staff Manual respectively. Title pages will be prepared in manuscript.

Place	Date	Hour	Summary of Events and Information	Remarks and references to Appendices
			Before making a rapid advance.	
	25.8.18	2.0 am	Received orders to move west to Hartenwart and from the MDS there	App. III
W3.B.87		6.0 am	MDS at Hartenwart established and opened and was visited by the ADMS	
			The tops Gaolenke was handed over to the 129 Field Ambulance.	
		12:0 am	The MDS at Hartenwart was moved to Bonzincourt, having been trying	
			in charge and assisted by Capts Bingwall. Evacuation from the	
			Hartenwart MDS and the Bonzincourt MDS done by MAC cars and	
			Walking Wounded taken by lorries to the Corps Walking Wounded Station	
			Headquarters in the Chateau at Hartenwart.	
			Admitted 3 officers and 127 O.R. Evacuated 2 officers and 130 O.R.	
			To IDRS 22 O.R.	
			Prisoners of War admitted 6 O.R.	
	26.8.18	5.0 pm	Headquarters and MDS moved from Hartenwart to the vicinity of	
			La Boiselle, and remained the night there awaiting orders.	
			Capt. AC Arthur and one tent sub division with equipment sent to	
			the Chateau at Contalmaison and assisted as the 130 F Field Ambulance	

WAR DIARY
or
INTELLIGENCE SUMMARY.
(Erase heading not required.)

Army Form C. 2118.

Place	Date	Hour	Summary of Events and Information	Remarks and references to Appendices
			ADS which was established here. Weather fine	
			Major D Friar with an hint out shirts and equipment still carrying on	
			the MDS at Bouzincourt.	
			Admitted 8 officers and 107 O.R. Evacuated 8 officers and 101 O.R.	
			To 129 Field Ambulance 6 O.R. Duty 1 O.R.	
X.16.G.8.2	27.8.18	8am	Operation opened the MDS at Enclinameer Chateau and Hallignalis	
			Horse Transport and remainder of personnel moved from Za Boiselle	
			and reformed at Enclinameer Chateau	
			Major Friar RAMC moved his MDS from Bouzincourt to	
			Za Boiselle when he is awaiting orders.	
			The ADMS and ADMS visited the MDS at Contalmaison.	
			Admitted 13 officers and 262 O.R. Evacuated 258 O.R. and	
			13 officers. To Duty 4 O.R.	
	28.8.18		The transport was sent to Za Boiselle from Contalmaison on	
			account of enemy shelling and change of work. and	
			Admitted 20 officers 532 O.R. Evacuated 20 officers and 519 O.R.	

Army Form C. 2118.

WAR DIARY
or
INTELLIGENCE SUMMARY.
(Erase heading not required.)

Instructions regarding War Diaries and Intelligence Summaries are contained in F. S. Regs., Part II. and the Staff Manual respectively. Title pages will be prepared in manuscript.

Place	Date	Hour	Summary of Events and Information	Remarks and references to Appendices
N.16.C.8.2.	29.8.18		Detachment under Major Fred R.A.M.C. reported Headquarters from La Boisselle. Admitted 4 officers and 62 O.R. Evacuated 6 officers and 58 O.R.	
	30.8.18		The M.D.S. was visited by the D.D.M.S. V Corps and the A.D.M.S. Admitted 5 officers and 116 O.R. Evacuated 5 officers and 115 O.R.	
	31.8.18		Capt S Robertson R.A.M.C. and Capt W.M.Kerr R.A.M.C. reported for duty from 56 C.C.S. Admitted 13 officers and 254 O.R. Evacuated 13 officers & 250 O.R.	

140/3259

COMMITTEE FOR THE
MEDICAL HISTORY OF THE WAR
Date 8 NOV 1916

131st F. Amb.

WAR DIARY or INTELLIGENCE SUMMARY

Army Form C. 2118.

131 / A Auth
961 34

Place	Date	Hour	Summary of Events and Information	Remarks and references to Appendices
X.16.8.2 (57c)	1.9.18		Admitted 1 officer and 33 O.R. Evacuated 1 officer and 26 O.R. Duty 5 O.R.	
	2.9.18		Died 2 O.R. Prisoner admitted 19 O.R. Capt P.C. Nixon R.A.M.C. left to do Enquiry duty with the 14th R.W.F. relieving Lieut G.R. Nixon who returned here for a rest.	
	3.9.18		Admitted 18 officers and 205 O.R. Evacuated 18 officers and 205 O.R. Died 9 O.R. Duty 1 O.R. Admitted 19.0.12 prisoners of war. Captain R.A.M.C. Rome left to do Enquiry duty with the 16 R.W.F.	
T9.C.6.1 (57c)			The unit moved from Cateau Station to Old German Hospital (T9 C61) and opened a new MDS there. Evacuated close to before by MAC to Centre. Admitted 10 officers and 210 O.R. also 2 O.R. prisoners of war. Evacuated 8 officers and 213 O.R. Died 1 officer, 7 duty, 1 officer. Lieut van den Rome left to do Enquiry duty with the 16th R.W.F.	
	4.9.18		Major D. Rees R.A.M.C. unit Lieut Robertson established a MDS at U.2.C60 (57c) this MDS was opened at 3:15 PM and was evacuated clear, wheels by MAC. Capt S. Robertson R.A.M.C. returned to duty, were at MDS U.2C60 (57c) MAC. Admitted 6 officers and 82 O.R. Evacuated 6 officers and 81 O.R. Died 1 O.R. Capt E. Dagnall R.A.M.C. proceeded to act on leave.	
	5.9.18		The MDS at U.2.C.6.0 was handed over to an Ambulance of the 21st D.I. and Major D. Rees with his Col. Robertson returned to Headquarters at T9 C61. Lieut G.R. Nixon R.A.M.C. returned to his Battalion (14 RWF). Admitted to officers and 176 O.R. Evacuated to officers and 176 O.R. Admitted and evacuated 1 O.R. prisoner of war.	
	6.9.18		Capt P.C. Nixon R.A.M.C. returned to unit from Enquiry duty with the 14 RWF. Lieut van den Rome returned similar from Enquiry duty with the 16 RWF. Capt D.A. Homer M.O.R.C. USA a few days M.O. for duty to 21 C.C.S.	

Army Form C. 2118.

WAR DIARY
or
INTELLIGENCE SUMMARY.
(Erase heading not required.)

Instructions regarding War Diaries and Intelligence Summaries are contained in F. S. Regs., Part II. and the Staff Manual respectively. Title pages will be prepared in manuscript.

Place	Date	Hour	Summary of Events and Information	Remarks and references to Appendices
78.C.6.1.	6.9.18 (cont)		Admitted 2 Officers and 137. O.R. Evacuated 2 Officers and 136. O.R. Died 1. O.R.	
	7.9.18		Capt. W.H. Ancotal R.A.M.C took over permanent medical charge of the 10th Batt. and others off Strength. Lieut. Garell M.O.R.C. taken on the strength from the 130th Field Ambulance. Lieut W.M.Kerr R.A.M.C attached for temporary duty with the 100th Field Ambulance. Admissions and evacuations nil. Attended conference with ADMS office.	
	8.9.18.		Weather cold and windy. Admitted 15. O.R. Evacuated 15. O.R.	
	9.9.18		ADMS visits the unit. Received orders to move at once 115 Brigade to Icekele. Evacuated Brigade headquarters and received Allied instructions. Admitted 10. O.R. Evacuated 10. O.R.	App. 1.
	10.9.18		Received Brigade order No 266 with Administrative instructions to accompany same. Major D Faus R.A.M.C proceed to U.K. on leave. The unit left the German Hospital at 78.C.61 and marched with the 115th Lt Brigade to Icekele where a camp was made. Admitted 1 Officer and 15. O.R. Evacuated 1 Officer and 15. O.R.	
P.31.C.7.7.	11.9.18		Moved to 129th Field Ambulance A.D.S at Pira. 3 NCOs, 60. O.R and 5 m.to Ambulances sent for duty to the 129th Field Ambulance. Admitted and evacuated 15. O.R. Evacuated of casualties. Admitted and evacuated 15. O.R. Colonel 9C Stead R.A.M.C. returned from leave.	

Army Form C. 2118.

WAR DIARY
or
INTELLIGENCE SUMMARY.
(Erase heading not required.)

Instructions regarding War Diaries and Intelligence Summaries are contained in F. S. Regs., Part II. and the Staff Manual respectively. Title pages will be prepared in manuscript.

Place	Date	Hour	Summary of Events and Information	Remarks and references to Appendices
LECHELLE	12.9.18	—	Arrived back from leave last night and reported arrival to A.D.M.S. Went over post ambulance which had taken place during the month. Visited Coys walking wounded collecting post and Coys lying wounded collecting post. A.D.M.S. held his weekly medical board at this camp. Visited No. 129 Field ambulance and his site. Admitted and Evacuated G.O.R.s.	James of spirits Lt Col Lane
"	13.9.18		Day cold but fine. ADMS 38th Division visited camp. Visited 130 Field ambulance saw their new site. Admitted sick 65 wounded. Evacuated 58 Remaining S. ho.	
"	14.9.18		D.D.M.S. v Coys visited camp also a 51st Sanitary Section. Sent 20 men to help OC. 130 F.A. in construction work at his new site.	
			admitted 29 43	
			Evac. 29 68	
			Died 4	
			Duty 6	
			1 Quadrone of French Mission at 38th Div Evacuate to C.C.S. ho	
	15.9.18	—	wounded	
			admitted sick 22 14	
			Evac 22 11	
			Died 2	
			Duty 1 Jay Sine ho	

Army Form C. 2118.

WAR DIARY
or
INTELLIGENCE SUMMARY.
(Erase heading not required.)

Instructions regarding War Diaries and Intelligence Summaries are contained in F. S. Regs., Part II. and the Staff Manual respectively. Title pages will be prepared in manuscript.

Place	Date	Hour	Summary of Events and Information	Remarks and references to Appendices
LEALVIE	16.9.18		Good deal of aeroplane activity during the night. Until further orders. 129 Field Ambulance and later accompanied by M.A.I.H.S. 39th Division made arrangements the country around F.M.S and also a site for a walking Wounded Collecting Post if should be required. Day fine. Admitted 89 sick 30 wounded Discharged 29 " 28 " Died — " 1 " To duty — " 1 "	
	17.9.18	3 am	Avery severe wind storm accompanied by rain & lightning swept over the country this morning. Admitted 22 sick 12 Wounded Evacuated 21 10 Died — 2 Remaining 1 — Withdrew personnel from 130 Field Ambulance. Received orders No. M.50/05 A.16.9.18. to make arrangements to establish W. Wounded Collecting Post near FRUANCOURT.	App. II
		5 pm	Arrived at ERVANCOURT VII a. 2.2 and established Post.	

Army Form C. 2118.

WAR DIARY
or
INTELLIGENCE SUMMARY.
(Erase heading not required.)

Instructions regarding War Diaries and Intelligence Summaries are contained in F. S. Regs., Part II. and the Staff Manual respectively. Title pages will be prepared in manuscript.

Place	Date	Hour	Summary of Events and Information	Remarks and references to Appendices
Near ÉQUANCOURT VII a 2.2.	18/9/18	6 a.m.	Everything ready. Camp visited by A.D.M.S. 38th Division. All available Motor ambulance cases evacuated at disposal of O.C. 129 Field Ambulance, who is clearing the line. Arranged to have use of the following horse ambulances:	
			2 from 130 F.A.	
			3 " 129 F.A.	
			3 " 131 F.A.	
			2 " 53 F.A.	
			2 " 51 F.A.	
			2 " 53 F.A.	
			4 " 21 Division (2 pair)	
		6.30.	Zero hour	
		7.25	Walking wounded began to arrive.	
			In evacuation of lying cases to the Corps main dressing station the following motor ambulances were used.	
			3 from 17th Division	
			3 " 21st "	
			3 " 38 "	
			4 " (known)	
			Use was made of empty ammunition lorries returning from the line to convey walking wounded to the Corps Walking Wounded Dressing Station. An officer was detailed by Corps for the duties of supplying & towing lorries. (App.1)	
		9.30.	Wounded arriving quickly. Asked M.A.C. for 6 Cars, these arrived at 9.30 a.m.	

Army Form C. 2118.

WAR DIARY
or
INTELLIGENCE SUMMARY.
(Erase heading not required.)

Instructions regarding War Diaries and Intelligence Summaries are contained in F.S. Regs., Part II. and the Staff Manual respectively. Title pages will be prepared in manuscript.

Place	Date	Hour	Summary of Events and Information	Remarks and references to Appendices
Order ERVILLERS	18/3/18	10.20 a	D.A.Q.M.G. & D.A.Q.M.G. 38th Division visited camp also a.d.M.S. 21st Division.	
		4.30 p.m	All camp cleared. A.D.M.S. 63 Division called.	
		6 p.m	Number Wounded cleared from this camp (including overflow from lying wounded, i.e. 9 Ja.) Lying 255 Walking 1134 Total 1389.	
		9 p.m	Attacked again.	
		10.30	Wounded men commenced to arrive	
		12 (midnight)	A.D.M.S. 32nd Division called. During the night the Boy-aid Arrived slowly. &	
19.3.18		6 a.m	Number of wounded cleared from this camp at 7.24 two Lying 249 Walking 1528 Total 1807 (including 61 P.O.W.)	
		10 a.m	D.A.Q.M.G. 38th Division called.	
		11 a.m	Received (31st Div.) Advanced train received. Lying 293 Walking 1822 Total 2115	
		4 p.m	Left ERVILLERS and marched to LECHELLE. Camp Evacuated	App III

Army Form C. 2118.

WAR DIARY
or
INTELLIGENCE SUMMARY.
(Erase heading not required.)

Instructions regarding War Diaries and Intelligence Summaries are contained in F.S. Regs., Part II. and the Staff Manual respectively. Title pages will be prepared in manuscript.

Place	Date	Hour	Summary of Events and Information	Remarks and references to Appendices
LECHELLE	28.9.18	—	Attached personnel returned to their units. Refilled dressings etc. issued. Visited Camp. Visited ADM.S at his office on present situation of Camp. Day cold and showery. Sick returns: Admitted 21 149 Evacuated 21 144 Sick 8 Duty 0 1 Remaining 1 No. 1 No. Camps aar no. 67 received.	App. IV.
	29.9.18	—	Rey. pur. tak. over. Visited M.O. of 114 Bde. and told them to means of evacuation of patients and to send on the 7a. to Army's dressing St. Wounded Admitted 26 39 Evac. 18 37 To DRS (Sick) 6 1 Died 1 Duty 2 Remaining 21 R. on P. 3d Division visited Camp Co.	

WAR DIARY
or
INTELLIGENCE SUMMARY.

Army Form C. 2118.

(Erase heading not required.)

Place	Date	Hour	Summary of Events and Information	Remarks and references to Appendices
LECHELLE	22/9/18	—	114 Infantry Brigade moved to LECHELLE to-day. Lieut CASSELL M.O.R.C. USA sent to 130 Field Ambulance. Lieut KERR R.A.M.C. from 130 F.A. to this unit for duty. Admitted Sick wounded 6 Evac 1 4 to D.R.S. 5 Remaining 2 1	
	23/9/18	—	Visited 16, 130 Field Ambulance and attended the funeral of 16, 15th Field Ambulance. Afternoon went Capt. SINGLETON R.A.M.C. returned from leave. Reconnoitred 39th Division at his office is nearing the line. He next time that Division goes into the line. Visited 16, 53 F.A. and No. 99 F.A. Col Purdy R.A.M.C. and Lieut-Col RANE reported for temp duty. Arranged to go around line with 16. 99 (Lt Col MORRIS DSO R.A.M.C.) tomorrow morning. wounded Admitted sick 15 Evacuated 6 7 D.R.S. Remaining 21 1 do	

Army Form C. 2118.

WAR DIARY
or
INTELLIGENCE SUMMARY.
(Erase heading not required.)

Instructions regarding War Diaries and Intelligence Summaries are contained in F.S. Regs., Part II. and the Staff Manual respectively. Title pages will be prepared in manuscript.

Place	Date	Hour	Summary of Events and Information	Remarks and references to Appendices
LECHELLE	24.9.18	—	Met around 3.30 Divison HQ and made medical arrangements for Repatriation. Visit received by Divisional gas officer, Major Joyfeis.	
			O.R.'s	
			admitted 14 wounded	
			Evacuated 13 — 1	
			N.Y.D.(N) (syph) 2 — 1	
			Duty 2 — 1	
			Draft of 9 R.am.C. reinforcements arrived from Base.	
	25.9.18	—	Capt. A.C. Wilson R.am.C. (T) attached to 2st Bn R.P.A. in relief of Lautier who is proceeding on leave. Day cold.	
			O.R.'s	
			admitted 9ck 5 wounded 6	
			Evacuated 5 — 6	
	26.9.18	—	Visited 86, 63 FA. who at present is to go to a station of the Evacuation of the line. Arranged to go around his pacts at 9am. tomorrow morning. Visited 3 cases Isaac. X ray taken. Major M.J. Van Kauch returned from leave to U.K.	
			admitted 9ck 1 wounded 2	
			Evac — 2	

WAR DIARY or INTELLIGENCE SUMMARY.

Army Form C. 2118.

(Erase heading not required.)

Instructions regarding War Diaries and Intelligence Summaries are contained in F. S. Regs., Part II. and the Staff Manual respectively. Title pages will be prepared in manuscript.

Place	Date	Hour	Summary of Events and Information	Remarks and references to Appendices
LECHELLE	27.9.18	—	Spent at G.O.C.'s conference at Divisional Headquarters. Afterwards A.D.M.S. Conference of M.O.'s and Field Ambulance M.O.'s. Different tactical situations discussed. Day fine. Made preliminary preparations for a move at an early date. Sid.	
	28.9.18		Left LECHELLE and moved with 114 Bde to SORREL & GRAND priorim. 115 Bde on arrival. Made reconnaissance of area occupied by 115. Bde. Returned to do not. Day fine. Received about No M.58/52 a 29.9.18	App V.
	29.9.18		Received 115 Bde Oran No 275. Had interview with G.O.C. 115 Bde. Given (1 M.G.O. and 12.O.R.) posted to each Battalion of 115 Bde yesterday. Runner posted to Signals to-day. The Medical orderly sent to Divisional Headquarters for duty. Visited No 59 American Field Hospital which is stationed at VILLERS FAUCON with an A.D.S. at ST EMILIE. Visited 54 Field Ambulance also M.D.S. and A.D.S. in same village as American Field Hospital. 54 Field Ambulance have now put a large car dump in EPEHY and run a FORD car up to RONSSOY. Cases are evacuated from their M.D.S. by M.A.C. cars. Visited 06. 129 Field Ambulance. Made reconnaissance of area around EPEHY and MALASSISE FARM. Found & suitable places for A.D.S. and post for Bearers. Sid.	App VI.

Army Form C. 2118.

WAR DIARY
or
INTELLIGENCE SUMMARY.
(Erase heading not required.)

Place	Date	Hour	Summary of Events and Information	Remarks and references to Appendices
SORREL LE GRAND	30.9.18	—	Night very wet and stormy. Under canvas last night. Medical arrangements in connection with 38 Div near No 23S. Looked around EPEHY for more accommodation. Day wet.	App VII

30. 9. 18.

James Sprowle
Lieut Colonel
O.C. 131 Field Ambulance

10/3/41

COMMITTEE FOR THE
MEDICAL HISTORY OF THE WA.
Date   12 JAN 1918

No. 9/6 Vol 7 131 Jth Ambce

Army Form C. 2118.

WAR DIARY
or
INTELLIGENCE SUMMARY.
(Erase heading not required.)

Place	Date	Hour	Summary of Events and Information	Remarks and references to Appendices
SOREL le GRAND	1.10.18	—	Made reconnaissance of medical arrangements of 33rd Division. Visited A.D.S. in PEZIERE. Visited O.C. 130 Field Ambulance at FINS. BULGARIA asks for unconditional peace.	
	2.10.18	—	Day fine. G.O. Visited A.D.M.S. 38th Division also O.C. 130 Field Ambulance. Made reconnaissance of FINS - GOUZEAUCOURT road. Rain in afternoon.	
RONSSOY	3.10.18	—	115 Brigade moved at 3 p.m. to the neighbourhood of RONSSOY and bivouacked. Units the night. Field ambulance less Mot. lor. ambulances 5 G.S. wagons, 3 lumbers, 2 water carts + 1 Maltese cart moved in rear of brigade and bivouacked in trench at F8a central. Visited O.C. 2/3 NORTHUMBRIAN Field Ambulance and made arrangements to evac. of 38th Division to be evacuated by him in accordance with A.D.M.S. instructions. Reports arrived to 115 Bde. night quiet.	Apt T
"	4.10.18	7 a.m.	115 Brigade moved to BONY. Bearers attached to Battalion followed their Battalion. Bearer Officer, Major W.D. FREW R.A.M.C. established his Headquarters with Car post of 2/3 NORTHUMBRIAN Field Amb. Bearers made reconnaissance of BONY. Apt T Distant. 38th Division called	

Army Form C. 2118.

WAR DIARY
or
INTELLIGENCE SUMMARY.
(Erase heading not required.)

Instructions regarding War Diaries and Intelligence Summaries are contained in F. S. Regs., Part II. and the Staff Manual respectively. Title pages will be prepared in manuscript.

Place	Date	Hour	Summary of Events and Information	Remarks and references to Appendices
RONSSOY	4.10.18	3.30pm	D.A.D.M.S visited BONY and surrounding area. Received 20 buses from 129 3.A. Attached motor Ambulances for duty with 2/- NORTHUMBRIAN F.A. Clinic situated E.15.a. Wires begun.	
			P.A.s. Received following 30" Div Telegram - "Pending further instructions movements of Field Ambulances will be controlled by above A.D.S. 2 Ambulances will remain in	
		10.50pm	present site pending further orders. Medical 30" Division 115 Brigade frontally relieving 150 Bde to-night. 113 Brigade moving up to BONY to-night.	
5.10.18		—	115 Inf Bde took over from 150 Inf Brigade this morning. Both factors out and 2nd	
"			Div Cavalerie	
		08.00	A.D.M.S & D.A.D.M.S. 37" Division called visited forward areas. Made reconnaissance of LE CATELET + vicinity N.y.R. Visited Bde M.yro & saw R. & Evacuating plans of Evacuation. Saw wounded and arranged to change A.D.S. tomorrow to somewhere in the vicinity of HONNECOURT. Found car hot in LE CATELET.	
6.10.18		05.20	Made reconnaissances of HONNECOURT LE TERRIERS district. Arranged to establish advanced car post at the latter A.D.S. at S.w.a. (nr.HONNECOURT) Visited 113 & 115 Bdes & saw P.O.C.s. Arranged to switch over Evacuation at 18.00 hrs. Cases came through in short time. Left some cars in LE CATELET during night & one	

Army Form C. 2118.

WAR DIARY
or
INTELLIGENCE SUMMARY.
(Erase heading not required.)

Instructions regarding War Diaries and Intelligence Summaries are contained in F. S. Regs., Part II. and the Staff Manual respectively. Title pages will be prepared in manuscript.

Place	Date	Hour	Summary of Events and Information	Remarks and references to Appendices
HONNECOURT 6.10.18 S.W.A. Sheet 57.B		21.00	Received information that RICHMOND C/128 is missed. Night quiet. No.	
	7.10.18		We combined M.D.S. (No 53 Fiels Ambulance) opens at FINS at 7 a.m. to-day & closes at the same hour at X.H.Q. (VILLERS GUISLAIN).	
	8.10.18	00.00	Zero. 112 Brigade attacked. Walking cases started to arrive at LE TERRIÈRE App II at M.H.S. and Lying Cases 02.00. Large Ambulances were pushed up to less and later in the day the F.RD Ambulances were pushed up to AUBENCHEUIL aux BOIS. Cases were at first evacuated to 129 F.A. at EPEHY and at	App II
		07.000	switched off to C.M.D.S. A.D.S. moved up to A TERRIE and FORDS ran up R.A.Ps upwards 4/600 casualties were evacuated during the day. A large proportion of the cases were lying cases. Walking wounded were sent down in empty ammunition lorries. The fighting was very successful and the division advanced capturing 361 prisoners. A.D.S. pushed up to AUBENCHEUIL aux BOIS at 18.00.	
		16.00	Clear of cases.	
		18.00	A good many wounded Germans coming in. Received fair Rank reinforcements.	

Army Form C. 2118.

WAR DIARY
or
INTELLIGENCE SUMMARY.
(Erase heading not required.)

Instructions regarding War Diaries and Intelligence Summaries are contained in F. S. Regs., Part II. and the Staff Manual respectively. Title pages will be prepared in manuscript.

Place	Date	Hour	Summary of Events and Information	Remarks and references to Appendices
AUBENCHEUL			Through today a section of No. 30 L.a. took over the rear a.d.s. while the front one was being established.	
			Received orders from 113 Bde to be prepared for an early move. Orders for the morning.	
	9.10.18	—	Only thirty have been passed through during the night. Visited S.O.S. 114, 15" & 113 Bdes. Made reconnaissance of forward area with Brigand 31" Division, 23" Division moved through 38" Division this morning on a line WARLINCOURT – SERAIN pursuing enemy back.	
WARLINCOURT		15:00	Left AUBENCHEUL En route for WARLINCOURT where unit was billeted for the night. Ourselves returning to the town.	
	10.10.18	09:00	115 Brigade moving to BERTRY and Bde moving to TROIS VILLERS. 114 Bde moved to CLARY tonight.	
BERTRY	09:30		Unit moved to BERTRY. Opened an A.D.S. in old German hospital tent at CLARY. 115 Bde only got to CLARY last night and 113 to just N of WAMBAIX COURT. Recce reconnaissance of forward area up 1 kilometre W of Le CATEAU. Roads very quiet. A.D.M.S. 20 A.B. at L. 38" Division called. Visited Brigades.	

Army Form C. 2118.

WAR DIARY
or
INTELLIGENCE SUMMARY.
(Erase heading not required.)

Instructions regarding War Diaries and Intelligence Summaries are contained in F. S. Regs., Part II. and the Staff Manual respectively. Title pages will be prepared in manuscript.

Place	Date	Hour	Summary of Events and Information	Remarks and references to Appendices
BERTRY	10.11.18	09.0	Visited 113, 114 & 115 Bdes & 06. 115 Bde did a rehal of move to Capo Encampements across Nat. Everything possible done for the comfort of the Soldiers who have been left in the territory. Evacuated Cycle Camp. Arranged with Mayor to issue handbills this evening. Lieut KERR R.A.M.C. detailed as M.O. to Capo P.O.W. cage. Visited Brigades & 129 F.A. Ordered & 86, 91 FA. to select site. No 62. 19th Field Amb. Two Amt. is at present running a M.D.S. for 17th, 23rd & 38th Division in BERTRY.	
BERTRY	11.10.18	—	Found orders for 130 Field Ambulance. Enemy shelling BERTRY this morning. Receive Brigade orders saying that 38th Division was relieving 33rd Division in the line to right and that 114 Bde (Hqrs at TROISVILLES) would be in the line, 115 Bde in Reserve (Hqrs at TROISVILLES) and 113 Bde in reserve (Hqrs at BERTRY.) (No Davis D.D.O. Rawl.)	App III
		09.00	Rawl 6 D6. BD. P.A. arrived & 6% over site.	
		12.00	Divisional Hqrs came to BERTRY. Received Rawl 6. order No 58	App IV
		14.00	Left BERTRY en route for TROISVILLES arriving at 3 p.m. Opened Adj. and Saw O/C attachment 101 F.A. who is to place. Arranged with him that his bearers would stay in this to right and that bearers give him any help that is required.	

WAR DIARY
or
INTELLIGENCE SUMMARY.
(Erase heading not required.)

Army Form C. 2118.

Place	Date	Hour	Summary of Events and Information	Remarks and references to Appendices
TROISVILLES	17/10/18		This arrangement was made on account of the 33 Division attacking at 5pm. Received 114 Brigade Order cancelling relief of Bn. of 33rd Division to night. Received 33rd Div. Recce. Order No 69. Afternoon wet.	App Y.
	18.10.18	—	Now ordered. Emergements of line held by 33rd Division again this morning. Arranged to post bearers and take over all advance of Mts. line from 16.00 his. Bearers posted. 1/5 Bde. relieved 100 Inf Bde. on the line to right.	
		1400	114 Infantry Brigade came to TROISVILLES as Brigade in support APM & BADMS 38th Division around a.m.	
	14.10.18	—	Went around line. C.6. 130 Field Ambulance called and marked out buildings as hospitals. Walking wounded collecting posts. Received memo from RAMC stating that M.D.S. would be opened at MONTIGNY at 9 hrs on 15th and that the M.D.S at CLARY would close at the same hour on same day. All walking cases sent to be sent on returning Empty lorries to WALINCOURT direct if possible.	
			N.C.M.T. ruled as long traffic routes known blocked...	
	15.10.18	—	Cases admitted up to midnight for last 24 hrs. 15 sick. 31 wounded. Admis from 00.01 hrs 15 to 23.59 15th; 25 sick 56 wounded. ADMS conference. Enemy shelled back	

Army Form C. 2118.

WAR DIARY
or
INTELLIGENCE SUMMARY.
(Erase heading not required.)

Instructions regarding War Diaries and Intelligence Summaries are contained in F. S. Regs. Part II and the Staff Manual respectively. Title pages will be prepared in manuscript.

Place	Date	Hour	Summary of Events and Information	Remarks and references to Appendices
TROISVILLES	16.10.18		area with mustard gas during the night. Cases admitted on last 24 hrs up to 23.59 hrs 16 inst. **30** inst. 192 wounded. Of the latter 120 were gassed. Lieut G. Tenton MORC m.o. 16 121 Bde R.F.A. was wounded during the night. Capt Craigmile R.amb. started temporarily to 121 Bde. Evacuate amount of enemy shelling during the day. Capt B. Wilson R.amb. returned from leave & will proceed tomorrow as M.o. to 121 Bde RFA on relief. Many of the civilians in this village are sick and are being attended to. Day quiet & ground very muddy.	
"	17.10.18		Capt Wilson R.amb. returned to 121 Bde R.F.A. in relief of Lieut Tenton R.amb. Reliefs. Their went to 122 Bde RFA in relief of Lieut Briscoe M.O.R.C. who proceeded to 130 Field Ambulance. A great deal shelling of back area with mustard gas. The ambulance car who hit by a shell. R.amb. only woman that is to evacuate the driver was slightly wounded. Another R.amb. orderly was wounded yesterday. MORC visited medical posts. ~~front banks~~ MORC departed for temporary duty. Evacuos during past 24 hrs. 24 hrs 36 wounded of which 20 were gassed.	

Army Form C. 2118.

WAR DIARY
or
INTELLIGENCE SUMMARY.
(Erase heading not required.)

Place	Date	Hour	Summary of Events and Information	Remarks and references to Appendices
TROISVILLERS	18/9/18	—	Went round line in morning. Relieved Mann posts. Visited I.A. 966th Division which is evacuating the line on our right. 114 Brigade is relieving 115 Bde. to right 113 Bde (19.R.W.F.) is relieving 9Bn G.G.'s Regt. 115 Bde returned to billets in TROISVILLERS. A.D.M.S. Conference to arrange medical details for coming operations. It was arranged that the I.A. should have every available ambulance car placed at its disposal. The number of ambulances available at present is 3 FORDS and 11 forgicars. Conference again at 12 hrs to arrange matters. 113 Bde allocation of Fld.'s/Bde R.A.P. Evacuation in last 24 hrs 42 sick, 7/4 wounded. &c. Received Corps medical arrangements for operation. Conference at D.D.M.S. office of I.A. Ammunition. It was arranged that Ammunition column attending fort should be formed in TROISVILLERS and hot cocoa &/or being tea here would be sent to 129 F.A. at BERTRY to be drunk. Lorries would be provided by Corps for this purpose. &c.	App VI
		16.00	Extra squads of bearers were posted. Everything ready. &c.	

(39175) Wt W235/P369 500,000 12/17 D.D. & L. Sch. 612. Forms/C2118/15

WAR DIARY
or
INTELLIGENCE SUMMARY.
(Erase heading not required.)

Army Form C. 2118.

Place	Date	Hour	Summary of Events and Information	Remarks and references to Appendices
TROISVILLES	20.10	02.10	for 17th & 18th Divs. Two hour Barrage opened on line of railway N. of LE CATEAU (between MONTAY & NEUVILLY) which was held strongly by Enemy. Our troops lay to cross the river before the attack. Rain & mist. First objective carried as planned & troops advanced to second & final objective which lines approx N & S. 1/4 mile E. of AMERVAL. Evacuation forward worked well. 4 cases were got from the line forward through quickly. Extra motor ambulances were got from 129 & 130 Fas.	
		08.30	One lorry sent to 129 Fa. to convey to wounded from BERTRY to WALINCOURT	App VII
			Accd. was sent at 15.00 hrs. final objective reached.	
			Evacuated during day.	
			Sick wounds.	
			Officer 26 16 } all lying cases.	
			Other ranks 29 18	
			P.O.W — 13	
			O.C. of F.A. called at lorry our line of evac. Sub. situation report known	App VIII
			On 19th ? General refugees were evacuated from MONTAY.	

Army Form C. 2118.

WAR DIARY
or
INTELLIGENCE SUMMARY.
(Erase heading not required.)

Instructions regarding War Diaries and Intelligence Summaries are contained in F. S. Regs., Part II. and the Staff Manual respectively. Title pages will be prepared in manuscript.

Place	Date	Hour	Summary of Events and Information	Remarks and references to Appendices
TROISVILLES	21.10.18		114 and 113 Brigades are being relieved in the line to-day by 115 Bde. The relief will, so far as possible, be carried out in daylight. Sick to report a.d.s. in MONTAY. This is in the old Boche hospital at the entrance to the village from to CATEAU.	
"	22/4/18		Unit relieved in line by XIX Field Ambulance. Handed over billets to this F.a. Found no sick in village.	
"	23/4/18	07.30	33rd Division attacked this morning. Good progress made. Reconnaissance of FOREST district. XIX F.a. have an A.D.S. there. No 115 Bde is in front of this village an R.A.P. of this F.a. was sent forward at 14 hours (also there at 16 hrs). Two Ram: C bearer squads attached to No 10th F.W.B. were wounded to-day. Two cars from 129 Wess Z.a. & two from 130 F.a. reported for duty. Evacuated 1 officer 35 o.r. sick nil " 4 " wounded	App IX
"	24/4/18	—	Headquarters remainder of F.a. moved to FOREST. Got in touch with forward Evacuation carried out by XIX F.a. (B.Du) FOREST shelled in afternoon. Evac sick nil Officers " 50 O.R. 5	

Norman
nt. Officer

Army Form C. 2118.

WAR DIARY
or
INTELLIGENCE SUMMARY.
(Erase heading not required.)

Instructions regarding War Diaries and Intelligence Summaries are contained in F. S. Regs., Part II. and the Staff Manual respectively. Title pages will be prepared in manuscript.

Place	Date	Hour	Summary of Events and Information	Remarks and references to Appendices
FOREST	28/10/18	—	Three horses wounded this morning by shell fire, one had to be destroyed. Arms Office moved to RICHEMONT. Received Ramb order NO.7.	App X
		16.20	Receive information that adv. to Cancelled. The 129 F.A. + Adv. Res + saw off for new H.Q.	
			Evacuated Sick — 1 Offr. 83 ORs	
			" " " — 12 "	
	29.10.18	—	O.C 129 Field Ambulance E arrived at FOREST. Made reconnaissance of POIX du NORD and ENGLEFONTAINE. There are many civilians in each town and the latter is under heavy shell machine gun fire. This field ambulance moved to MOULIN de MARPLAS leaving handful at FOREST. Car loading post in charge of X IX F.A. at MAISON PAUL JACQUESLAND cars run up to the R.A.P. at POIX du NORD. DADMS 99th Division visited A.D.S. 33rd Division attacked enemy this morning capturing about 400 prisoners with small casualties. 3 wounded	
			Evacuated officers 4 Sick — 27	
			ORs 46 — 76	
			Received Medical arrangements for Clearing Huts	App X1

Army Form C. 2118.

WAR DIARY
or
INTELLIGENCE SUMMARY.
(Erase heading not required.)

Place	Date	Hour	Summary of Events and Information	Remarks and references to Appendices
MOULIN de HARPIES	27/10/18		Enemy dropped a few shells around A.D.S. killing one Infantryman (Stretcher bearer) wounding one Pte. L. Corp. Blunt & Cpl .... R.A.P.	
			Pte car left in POIX du NORD. Comd. & DADMS called. GOC 38th	
			Division called. Slight angle in evening.	
			Evacuated Sick 18 ORs	
			Wounded 5 Officers 63"	
"	28/10/18		Went around line with A.D.M.S and D.A.D.M.S and visited R.A.P.s. Pte CHATFIELD and Pte TATE A.S.C. attached to this unit awarded the Military Medal. Received memo	app XII
			from A.D.M.S re Economy in air stretchers. Received new Sunbeam ambulance NO +.	
			27 M.A.C. is now located at MONTIGNY. Returned our ambulance to 129 Fld Amb having 6 days 23 hours run	
		0900+1	to replace WOLSELEY Evacuated.	
			Evacuated Sick 3 ORs	
			Officers 27 "	
			Wounded 1	
	29/10/18		During the last two days several civilians have been evacuated from ENGLEFONTIEN. French mission are evacuating 20 this morning. Arrangements have been made to convey them from PAUL JACQUES FARM to FOREST. 114 Bde relieve 115 Bde to-day.	

Army Form C. 2118.

WAR DIARY
or
INTELLIGENCE SUMMARY.
(Erase heading not required.)

Instructions regarding War Diaries and Intelligence Summaries are contained in F. S. Regs., Part II. and the Staff Manual respectively. Title pages will be prepared in manuscript.

Place	Date	Hour	Summary of Events and Information	Remarks and references to Appendices
MOULIN DE MARPLAS	2.10.18	—	2nd visited Regimied No.3 and went around the line. 115 Bde carried out a successful raid this morning at 8 ho capturing about 20 prisoners. Two men of 1/4 Cheshire Changing Crate taken on ration strength	
			Evacuant Sick 1 Officer 38 ORs	
			Wounded 5 " 95 "	
			P.O.W 3 wounded sick 1 Civilian	
"	30.10.18		Enemy threw some gas over during the night but here were no casualties Lieutenant Muir Evacuated during day	
			Sick 2 Officers 93 ORs	
			Wounded — " 20 "	
			Airraid 6 sick were wounded	
			Received wire from a.d.m.s. re system of labelling Gassed cases	App XIII
"	31.10.18	—	went around A.D.S. Everything is still being carried sitter.	

James Sproule
Lieut Colonel
O.C. 131 Field Ambulance.

160/3491

COMMITTEE FOR THE
MEDICAL HISTORY OF THE WAR.
Date 11 JAN 1919

131st F.A.

Nov 1918

Army Form C. 2118.

WAR DIARY
or
INTELLIGENCE SUMMARY.
(Erase heading not required.)

131st Aunt
Vol 3

Instructions regarding War Diaries and Intelligence Summaries are contained in F. S. Regs., Part II. and the Staff Manual respectively. Title pages will be prepared in manuscript.

Place	Date	Hour	Summary of Events and Information	Remarks and references to Appendices
MOULIN DU HARPES	1/11/18	—	West Wood of this district Regimental Aid Posts & Car Park. ENGLEFONTAIN was being heavily shelled. Nine Civilians admitted to Hospital one in future to be notified daily to A.D.M.S. Two instructions issued re informal Voluntary Cases Evacuated. Sick 1 Officer 54 ORs Wounded 2 " 27 " Civilians 6 sick 1 wounded P.O.W. nil	Apps I + II
			Day fine.	
	2/11/18	—	115 Brigade relieved 114 Brigade. Before of O.C.s Field Ambulances. Arrangements made for coming of section B Co.s the spent at ESNES. Established our loading post at Proverty in ENGLEFONTAINE Evacuated Sick 1 off 19 ORs Wounded 1 " 24 " Civilians 1 sick 7 wounded P.O.W. NIL.	App III

Army Form C. 2118.

WAR DIARY
or
INTELLIGENCE SUMMARY.
(Erase heading not required.)

Place	Date	Hour	Summary of Events and Information	Remarks and references to Appendices
Do.	3/11/18	—	Two motor ambulances were put out of action (temp) by shell fire in POIX. Went around this made final arrangements for coming operations. Formed nucleus for an A.D.S. at the BRASSERIE, ENGLEFONTAINE and a walking wounded collecting post at PAUL JAQUES FARM. Got all available ambulance cars from 129 & 130 Field Ambulances (9 large & 5 small cars) arranged to clear walking cases by these ambulances and returning empty lorries to FOREST. Borrowed 20 Stretchers to act as bearers from 86.129 Field Ambulance. Stock of stretchers = 150 Blankets = 450. Two of shirts = 20. Shell dressings 1000. Thin dressings = sufficient for 1000 cases. 300R. 1 off. 450R. 1 Evacuated during day. Sick — Wounded 1 — Received Brigade order for the operation. We are our four objective, the first to be taken by 115 Bde., the second third by 113 Bde. the final objective by 114 Bde. Major J.E. Davis M.C. R.a.m.c. succeeded on leave to Lt.	App. IV

WAR DIARY
or
INTELLIGENCE SUMMARY.
(Erase heading not required.)

Army Form C. 2118.

Place	Date	Hour	Summary of Events and Information	Remarks and references to Appendices
Do.	4.11.18	5.30am	Cars were fitted to commence with two at BRASSERIE one pen at PONT TAQUES FARM and three in reserve. Proceeds all futue.	
		6.15	Very heavy barrage opened. First wounded arrived at 6.55 hrs. Lying cases were at first conveyed in the Ford ambulances to the A.D.S. the reserve cars being taken into use. As the road leading to BRASSERIE was seven from here to nine later on when the first objective was taken the large cars were pushed forward and at 9.30 hrs the A.D.S. at BRASSERIE was opened and the A.D.S. at the MOULIN de HARPIES closed. Use was made of P.O.W. Every movement down from the line. Wounded came in steadily during the day. Trial of vehicles was needed without much opposition at 17.0 hrs and 1st Bde advanced 4000 yards beyond their final objective. Lieut Cance M.C. No 16 to "THB" was killed. Lieut Crawhall R an C was detailed for duty in his place. O.C. XIX F.A. Called + as 33rd Division was passing through our Division at 6 hrs tomorrow, arranged to let him have part of BRASSERY for night. Statement of Casualties Etc seen in App. Received R an C Order NO 92. + answer first.	V / VI

Army Form C. 2118.

WAR DIARY
or
INTELLIGENCE SUMMARY.
(Erase heading not required.)

Place	Date	Hour	Summary of Events and Information	Remarks and references to Appendices
	4.11.18	7.00	Capt Hobson had 6 refused for temporary duty. Same to W.C.P. at PAUL JACQUES FARM. Sent 1 Officer + 30 OR to 38 Div Reception camps yesterday	
	5.11.18	—	Moved our surplus stretchers to No 19 Field Ambulance. Got in touch with Regimental M.O.s and officers who are now in Eastern side Youved Brigades are in close reserve. Arranged Evacuation of any from wounded. A.D.M.S. office moved to LOCQUIGNOL. 130 F.A. arrived here remained for the night.	
			Wounded — 9/10	
			Evacuated sick — 9/10	
			26 ORs	
			28 ORs	
	6.11.18		The roads through the FORET DE MORMAL are very bad for motor transport. Received instructions to close ORS at BERRY. Evacuated cases to CCS. Received medical arrangements.	
			Maps as app VIII	app VII
			Sent 1 NCO and 19 other ranks for duty at 21 CCS in relief of similar party of 130 Field Ambulance	app. VIII

Army Form C. 2118.

WAR DIARY
or
INTELLIGENCE SUMMARY.
(Erase heading not required.)

Instructions regarding War Diaries and Intelligence Summaries are contained in F. S. Regs., Part II. and the Staff Manual respectively. Title pages will be prepared in manuscript.

Place	Date	Hour	Summary of Events and Information	Remarks and references to Appendices
Do.			Evacuated Sick 1 Officer 31 ORs	
			Wounded —	
			Civilians 1	
			Got prisoners back from BERTRY. P.O.W. 216	
Do	7.11.18	—	Evacuated upto past 24 hrs. Sick 3 Officers 105 ORs	
			Wounded — " — "	
			Received orders from A.D.M.S. to get in touch with No. 130 Field Ambulance and to move to BERLAIMONT at daybreak tomorrow morning the Infantry to open a walking wounded Collecting post near the main lorry route. Visited road & bridge and found out traffic routes. Unit ready to move off at 6 hrs tomorrow. Received Route situation order No Y3	Appendix IX
BERLAIMONT	8.11.18	6.30	Advance party consisting of 2 Officers, 2 drivers, Cook, 1 Clerk, 1 S.D.O., Urinager, Junction flags, Cooking Utensils (Soyers stove) & medical comforts established at BERLAIMONT at 8 hrs. The wounded are to be brought from each to the 10 CP. Heig: y two bridges and the route has been marked from each to the 10 CP. Heig: Jan 30 "Turner" passing Hazeigh. Main party arrived at 12 hrs.	

Army Form C. 2118.

WAR DIARY
or
INTELLIGENCE SUMMARY.
(Erase heading not required.)

Instructions regarding War Diaries and Intelligence Summaries are contained in F. S. Regs., Part II. and the Staff Manual respectively. Title pages will be prepared in manuscript.

Place	Date	Hour	Summary of Events and Information	Remarks and references to Appendices
BERLAIMONT	8/11/18	—	Armd officer joined at AULNOYE this morning. Capt HERBERTSON R.A.M.C. proceeded to 130 Field Ambulance for duty. V Corps Main Dressing Station opened at BERLAIMONT at 17.20. Called on O.C. 130 Field Ambulance who has now moved his Headquarters up to Pol de VIN. made arrangements as far as his A.D.L. at WASSIGNIES. Enemy reported to be retiring quickly. Received return from A.D.M.S. to keep in close touch with 130 F.A. Evacuated during past 24 hrs.	App X
			Sick — Officers 23 ORs	
			Wounded 2 " 76 "	
			P.O.W 2	
"	9/11/18		Visited Pol de VIN. Major BANKS R.A.M.C. called with reference to a site for a Corps Walking Wounded Post. Called at A.D.M.S. office	
			Evacuated Sick 2 Officers 89 ORs	
			Wounded — " 32 "	
			day wet	

WAR DIARY
or
INTELLIGENCE SUMMARY.

(Erase heading not required.)

Army Form C. 2118.

Place	Date	Hour	Summary of Events and Information	Remarks and references to Appendices
BERLAIMONT	10/11/18		Arranged with No. 130 Field Ambulance to clear the sick of 115 and 114 Brigades. Evacuated 35 sick. 2 Wounded.	
Do.	11/11/18	11.00	Armistice with Germany signed and hostilities cease. All Bandsmen attached to this unit from Battalions of 115 Bde were returned to their units. All R.A.M.C. personnel attached to Battalions of 115 Bde were withdrawn. CAPT O'HEARA R.A.M.C. 129 Field Ambulance returned to temporary duty.	
			Col O'Meara R.A.M.C. proceeds for duty as M.O. to 19th Welsh Regiment. Capt. ROBERTSON R.A.M.C. joins this unit from 16th Bn. R.W.F. Receive instructions from A.D.M.S. to take officer units of 17th Div left behind	App x 1
	12/11/18		at BERLAIMONT. No. 15 advanced Depot of medical stores is moving to CAUDRY. Reconnoitred area around AVLNOYE for a J.A. site. Conference at A.D.M.S. office. Lieut.Col. Jones D.S.O. M.C. R.A.M.C. Deputy A.D.M.S. points discussed were :- 1. Each Division is to evacuate its own sick by Divisional cars to C.C.S. 2. Divisional flying cars will resort to 131 F.A. once daily, & by arrangement with	

WAR DIARY
or
INTELLIGENCE SUMMARY.

(Erase heading not required.)

Army Form C. 2118.

Place	Date	Hour	Summary of Events and Information	Remarks and references to Appendices
AD	12/11/18		27 M.A.C. will be put on their Ambulances at BERLAIMONT.	
			(III) All cases taken into F.A's will be sent on the ard lorries of the F.A. taking them in.	
			(IV) 129 F.A. will form A.D.R.S.	
			(V) A.C.C.S. will open shortly at LE QUESNOY. Urgent cases only to be sent	
			(VI) Dental Cases. 129 F.A. Sunday, Nov [date] Tues 5 Vacancies per day. 130 F.A. Mon Wed Fri 131 F.A. Tues Thurs Sat	
			(VII) F.A.'s responsible for medical attention of Civilians.	
			(VIII) O.C. F.A's responsible for sanitation of area around them.	
			(IX) 129 F.A. will take all walking cases	
			(X) D.R.S. cases will be known as transfers	
			Admission — Evacuation — Sick — , Officers 26 O.Rs. wounded. — 1	
	13/11/18		Evacuated sick = 19 O.R.S. Cases to I.R.S. anti those likely to be well in three days. Third Army Ophthalmic centre will open at SOLESMES on 15th inst. Started checking surplus stores. Heavy frost during the night. A.D.M.S visited the Field Ambulances	App XIII

WAR DIARY or INTELLIGENCE SUMMARY

Army Form C. 2118.

Place	Date	Hour	Summary of Events and Information	Remarks and references to Appendices
AULNOYE	14.11.18	—	Moved his the morning and occupied buildings opposite the railway station. Capt COLLIER R.A.M.C. returned from leave to U.K.	
	15.11.18		Evacuated sick 13 ORs. Daycase. Foggy frost in the morning.	
	16.11.18		Busy with equipment. Evacuated 2 officers 14 ORs sick. Capt ROBERTSON proceeded to GUARDS DIVISION for duty. Frost still continues.	
	17.11.18		Evacuated sick 22 ORs 2 civilians. Unit attended Armistice Thanksgiving Church Parade. Very cold day. Visitor 130 Field Ambulance. Evacuated 2 officers and 22 ORs all sick.	App XIII App XIV
	18.11.18		Evacuated 22 sick. Daycase + Frosty. Special Order of day by Army Commander Received instructions re escaped prisoners of war etc.	
	19.11.18		Done rain to day. Admitted 24 sick. (6 CCS 12 DRS 12)	
	20.11.18	—	Admitted 7 (6 CCS 10, DRS 7.)	
	21.11.18		Admitted 27 (6 CCS 9 DRS 8)	
	22.11.18		Frosty again tonight. Suggested list of equipment for use at A.D.S. and W.A.C.P. for 1000 patients as attached	XV

2353 Wt. W3544/1454 700,000 5/15 D. D. & L. A.D.S.S./Forms/C. 2118.

Army Form C. 2118.

WAR DIARY
or
INTELLIGENCE SUMMARY.
(Erase heading not required.)

Instructions regarding War Diaries and Intelligence Summaries are contained in F. S. Regs., Part II. and the Staff Manual respectively. Title pages will be prepared in manuscript.

Place	Date	Hour	Summary of Events and Information	Remarks and references to Appendices
AULNOYE	22/11/18	—	Admitted 26 sick (CCS 18, DRS 8).	
			23/11/18 Inspection and presentation of medals to 115 Bde by G.O.C. 38th Div. 4 recipients decorated. Got a German allowance from 151 Coy R.E. New medical arrangements for 114 Bde. Admitted 28 sick (1st CCS, 13 to VRS). 1 civilian evacuated.	
	24/11/18		Church Parade ADMS (Lieut Col J.E.H. DAVIES DSO RAMC) called. Major J.E.H. DAVIES H.C. RAMC of this unit arranged tea to M.C. Admitted 26 sick (to CCS 12 to VRS 14)	
	25/11/18		Explained demobilisation & election scheme to the units. Examined mining of 10" S.W.B. 2 R.W.F. & this unit.	
			Admitted 3 officers 26 ORs (to CCS 2 offrs 13 ORs)	
	26/11/18	—	Admitted 2 officers and 18 ORs (to CCS ORs) 18 ORs	
			Evac. 2 "	
	27/11/18	—	Admitted 1 officer 9 ORs. Evacuated at Evacuees. (ay org out	
	28/11/18	—	Admitted 1 off 29 ORs (to CCS 1 off 16 ORs, to DRS 13 ORs)	
	29/11/18	—	Admitted paid visit 20 ORs (to CCS 1 off 15 ORs to DRS 4 ORs). Lice meins sent to interview	
	30/11/18		Very cold. Heavy frost during night.	

James Alprenne
Lieut Col RAMC
O.C. 131 Field Amb

Army Form C. 2118.

WAR DIARY
or
INTELLIGENCE SUMMARY.
(Erase heading not required.)

Instructions regarding War Diaries and Intelligence Summaries are contained in F. S. Regs., Part II. and the Staff Manual respectively. Title pages will be prepared in manuscript.

Place	Date	Hour	Summary of Events and Information	Remarks and references to Appendices
AULNOYE	1.12.18	—	Sent N.C.O. and two O.R. to report to 123 Coy R.E.	App I
	2.12.18	—	Arranged to go and see new site on 5th inst. when Divl. met representative of R.E.'s and fix up details of alterations required in billet. Admitted 2 Officers and 19 O.R.s	
			Int Corpl minor S.S.M. EDWARDS A.S.C. Sent for interview. Admitted 16 sick all O.R.s. Met G.S.O.1. 30th Div. with reference to this keeping his Hd Qrs visiting AULNOYE tomorrow. Arranged for attendance of medical officers of the Hqrs & the 35th M.G.C.	
	3.12.18		Unit paraded for Inspection by H.M. the King. Admitted 20 O.Rs (to V.R.S. 5" Evacuated 15) Day wet.	
	4.12.18		Admitted 12 O.Rs (to V.R.S. 5 Evacuated 7)	
	5.12.18		Admitted 18 O.Rs (to V.R.S. 4 Evacuated 14)	
	6.12.18		Admitted 1 Officer 21 O.Rs (to O.Rs 5 O.R.S. to Col. 1 Off 16 O.Rs.) Warned to have 85 mules ready for demobilisation as miners. This order was cancelled later and Hondan to proceed.	
	7.12.18		Admitted 14 O.Rs (to C.C.1. 12 to V.R.S. 2) Day wet.	

WAR DIARY
or
INTELLIGENCE SUMMARY.

(Erase heading not required.)

Army Form C. 2118.

Place	Date	Hour	Summary of Events and Information	Remarks and references to Appendices
AULNOYE	8.12.18	—	Admitted 1 officer + 14 ORs To CCS 1 " 12 " To DRS — 2 Sent 14 men to be interviewed before demobilisation	
	9.12.18		Admitted 7 ORs To CCS 7 ORs	
	10.12.18		Major J.C. DAVIES M.C. R.A.M.C. returned from leave French Croix de Guerre awarded, for rescuing civilians, to No 480855 Pte C. RODGERS ⎫ 48346 " E EVANS ⎬ Ranks 48201 W.J. THOMAS ⎭ Reinforcements are to be announced from base so to bring unit up to Establishment Admitted 20 ORs Evacuated 13 ORs DRS 7 "	
	11.12.18	—	Admitted 1 officer 20 ORs Evac " 10 ORs DRS 10 ORs	

WAR DIARY
or
INTELLIGENCE SUMMARY

Army Form C. 2118.

Place	Date	Hour	Summary of Events and Information	Remarks and references to Appendices
AULNOYE	12/12/18	—	Twenty men sent for interview with view to demobilisation. Took over medical charge of 38th Bn M.G.C., 38th D.A.C. 333 & 336 Coy R.E.	
			Admitted Officer 1	
			" O.Rs 14	
			Evacuated O.Rs 10	
			D.R.S. 4	
			Bugh	
	13/12/18	—	Pte E. won the final match in the Division shoe winning a fair silver bugle presented by G.O.C. 38th Div. This and medals for the Runners.	
			Admitted 13 O.Rs	
			Evacuated 13 O.Rs	
	14/12/18	—	Four Gas cases sent for interview. S.S. Saunders to England for duty.	
			Admitted 12 O.Rs.	
			Evacuated 10 O.Rs.	
			D.R.S. 2 O.Rs.	
	15/12/18	—	Moved to have men ready for interviews tomorrow.	
			Admitted 15 O.Rs	
			Evac 11 O.Rs	
			D.R.S. 4 O.Rs	

Army Form C. 2118.

WAR DIARY
or
INTELLIGENCE SUMMARY.
(Erase heading not required.)

Instructions regarding War Diaries and Intelligence Summaries are contained in F. S. Regs., Part II. and the Staff Manual respectively. Title pages will be prepared in manuscript.

Place	Date	Hour	Summary of Events and Information	Remarks and references to Appendices
	16/1/16		Admitted 1 OR's Evac " OR's Very Cold	
	17/12/18		Granted 14 days special leave to U.K. on urgent family affairs. Handed over to Major J.E. Davis H.C. Dawl	
	18/12/18		Admitted 6 O.R's Evacuated 6 OR's	
	19/12/18		Admitted 4 OR's Evacuated 4 OR's DR's 2 OR's	
	20/12/18		Admitted 8 OR's Evacuated 7 OR's DR's 1 OR's	
	21/12/18		Lt Andrew visited and handed over to A/DMS. Admitted 5 OR's Evacuated 5 OR's.	
	22/12/18		Admitted 6 OR's Evacuated 5 OR's DR's 1 OR	
	23/12/18		Attended conference of OC's FA's AD DMS's office, and Chamont to details of move from the Aulnoye area.	

WAR DIARY
or
INTELLIGENCE SUMMARY.

Army Form C. 2118.

Place	Date	Hour	Summary of Events and Information	Remarks and references to Appendices
	24/12/18		Admitted 12 ORs / Evacuated 9 ORs / DRS 3 ORs. Preparations completed for the unit Xmas dinner.	
	25/12/18		Xmas Day. The Xmas dinner consisted of Turkey, pork, beef, various vegetables, abundance of beer, white wine &c. In the evening a concert was held. The unit spent a happy day. Hurst Xam and QMS.	
	26/12/18		A unit football match was played in the afternoon and in the evening a very successful concert was held.	
	27/12/18		Amounts of rations with Division ever small.	
	28/12/18		Admitted 12 ORs / Evacuated 12 ORs / DRS Nil. Half Sec. Ord. RAMC forwarded with the Divisional Rugby team to Paris to play a team representing France.	
	29/12/18		The unit were therefore moved from the Aulnoye Area to Poix du Nord. The Transport moved to Neuvilly. Admitted 3 officers / Evacuated 3 officers.	
Poix du Nord	30/12/18		Unit (minus transport) move from Poix du Nord to Solesmes.	

Army Form C. 2118.

WAR DIARY
or
INTELLIGENCE SUMMARY.
(Erase heading not required.)

Place	Date	Hour	Summary of Events and Information	Remarks and references to Appendices
Laby	31.12.18		The Transport under command of Capn Collin Rome moved from Neuvilly to Inchuveux. Day very wet. Casualties nil.	
			Unit (minus Transport) moved from Labry to Forgean Chateau by motor buses. The Transport moved from Inchuveux to Ramancourt. Casualties nil.	

JEDaho
Major Rome

140/55724

38 DIV

Box 2357

No 131 Field Ambulance

16/3

131 3rd Aust. Fld Amb
Vol 37

WAR DIARY
or
INTELLIGENCE SUMMARY
Army Form C. 2118

Place	Date	Hour	Summary of Events and Information	Remarks and references to Appendices
Jorpan	1/1/19		Visited all the Brigade units and arranged the evacuation of their quota. Lieutenants Grey and Loy went to Chatan and its pronto. The Tanque moved from headquarters to Albert. The ADMS and DDMS visited the unit. Admissions nil.	
	2/1/19		Admitted - nil. Evacuated - nil.	
	3/1/19		Capt W. Ormond RAMC attached to the 130th Field Ambulance for temporary duty. Admitted 1 officer and 2 ORs. Evacuated 1 officer and 2 ORs.	
	4/1/19		Huts and tent floors to improve tents were erected. Admitted and evacuated 3 ORs.	
	5/1/19		Admitted 2 ORs. Evacuated 2 ORs.	
	6/1/19		Major W.J. Fred and Rome returned unit from Paris leave. Admitted 2 ORs. Evacuated 2 ORs. Remaining N/Ks.	
	7/1/19		Admitted 6 ORs. Evacuated 2 ORs. Remaining 4 ORs.	
	8/1/19		Admitted 4 ORs. Evacuated 4 ORs. Remaining 6 ORs. Lt Col J.C. Grant Rome returned from leave and took over command of the unit. Jo Davis Major Rome.	

Army Form C. 2118.

WAR DIARY
or
INTELLIGENCE SUMMARY.
(Erase heading not required.)

Instructions regarding War Diaries and Intelligence Summaries are contained in F. S. Regs., Part II. and the Staff Manual respectively. Title pages will be prepared in manuscript.

Place	Date	Hour	Summary of Events and Information	Remarks and references to Appendices
Longueau Station	9.1.19	—	Admitted 30 ORs. Discharged 50 ORs. Remaining 50 ORs	
	10.1.19	—	Admitted 30 ORs Evac 40 ORs, 6 Duty 10R Remaining 30 ORs.	
	11.1.19	—	Admitted 60 ORs Evac 30 ORs Remaining 60 ORs.	
	12.1.19	—	Admitted 30 ORs Evac 40 ORs Duty 10R Remaining 40 ORs	
	13.1.19	—	Capt Dno G A Elem R.A.M.C. left the Unit to report to AUSTRAL HOUSE LONDON en route for RUSSIA. Admitted 50 ORs Evac 60 ORs Rem 30 ORs.	
	14.1.19	—	2nd Offrs move to OVERVIEW. Admitted 20 ORs Evac NIL Rem 50 ORs.	
	15.1.19	—	Admitted 20 ORs Evac 30 ORs Rem 4 OR. Capt 21 to report O.A.Sce	
	16.1.19	—	Admitted 50 ORs Evac 20 ORs Rem 7 ORs Adm't NIL	
	17.1.19	—	Admitted 7 ORs Evac 5 ORs sick 10R Rem 10 ORs	
	18.1.19	—	Admitted 3 ORs Evac 30 ORs Wast 30 ORs Rem 10 ORs	

Army Form C. 2118.

WAR DIARY
or
INTELLIGENCE SUMMARY.
(Erase heading not required.)

Instructions regarding War Diaries and Intelligence Summaries are contained in F. S. Regs., Part II. and the Staff Manual respectively. Title pages will be prepared in manuscript.

Place	Date	Hour	Summary of Events and Information	Remarks and references to Appendices
Aygun Aghem	19.1.19		Admitted 208 Evacuated 208 Ret. 1 O.R. Remaining 7 O.R's	
	20.1.19		Admitted 4 O.R's Evacuated 4 O.R's Remaining 9 O.R's	
	21.1.19		Admitted 5 O.R's Evacuated 5 O.R's Remaining 9 O.R's	
	22.1.19		Admitted 6 O.R's Evacuated 5 O.R's Remaining 10 O.R's	
	23.1.19		Admitted 3 O.R's Evacuated 3 O.R's Remaining 10 O.R's	
			Weather cold and dry. All roads frozen. The "first fort" Arrived. Football Championship of the Division was played today and was won by a team representing the 1st line Divisional Ambulances.	
	24.1.19		Admitted 4 Evacuated 4 Remaining 10 O.R's	
	25.1.19		Admitted 20R. Evacuated 3 O.R's Remaining 9 O.R's	
	26.1.19		Admitted 1 O.R Rem 10 O.R's Very cold & threatens snow.	
	27.1.19		Admitted 2 O.R's Evac 3 O.R's Rem. 9 O.R's Snow during night	
	28.1.19		Admitted 1 O.R Evac 1 O.R. Rem. 9 O.R's	
	29.1.19		Admitted 1 O.R. Evac Nil Rem 10 O.R's	
	30.1.19	—	Admitted 5 O.R's Evac 6 O.R's Rem 9 O.R's	
	31.1.19	—	Admitted 1 O.R. Evac Nil Rem 10 O.R's. Snow 1 foot	

James Sproule
Lieut Col RAMC
O/C 131 Field Ambulance

No. 131 Field Ambulance

Feb 1918

131 Fd Amb
Army Form C. 2118.
Vol 38

WAR DIARY
or
INTELLIGENCE SUMMARY.
(Erase heading not required.)

Place	Date	Hour	Summary of Events and Information	Remarks and references to Appendices
LONGEAU	1.2.19	—	Admitted 3 ORs. Rank to. Evac 2 ORs. Remaining 11 OR. Site Cold with heavy frost at night	
	2.2.19	—	Admitted 10R. Evac 3 ORs. Rem 9 OR.	
	3.2.19	—	Admitted 1 Off + 2 ORs. Evac 1 Off 2 ORs. Rem 9 ORs	
	4.2.19	—	Admitted 2 ORs. Rem 11 ORs. Took on ration charge of 255 PO W Coy. Sent 8 knows to Australian & Corps Stagnig Camp	
	5.2.19	—	Admitted 10R. Evac 3 ORs & 2 NS 6 ORs. Rem 30 ORs. Admitted 2 ORs. Remaining 5 ORs Weather mild. Snow at am.	
	6.2.19	—	Admitted 2 ORs. Evac 3 ORs. Rem 3 ORs. Remaining 4 ORs, also 4 POW admitted and evacuated. 10 Paw. from 255 Coy. employed on fatigues in Camp. HRH The Prince of Wales visited and inspected the Camp at 1030 hrs.	
	7.2.19	—	Admitted 4 ORs. Remaining 8 ORs. also 4 POW admitted and evac? Divre Troop. Pte Werner won Challenge Cup at Corps Boxing Tournament at Vaux. Cup presented by HRH Prince of Wales.	
	8.2.19	—		
	9.2.19	—	Admitted 1 Off + 3 ORs. Evac 1 Off + 3 ORs. Remaining 7 ORs, & 6 POW evacd. Were received. Cancelling Semi Final Corps Football Competition	

WAR DIARY
or
INTELLIGENCE SUMMARY.
(Erase heading not required.)

Army Form C. 2118

Place	Date	Hour	Summary of Events and Information	Remarks and references to Appendices
LONGUEAU	9/2/19	a.m.	3rd Army Ophtalmic Centre now at 18.C.6.8, Boullens. #1 Stat Hosp. now open at Poulainville. Four pairs H.O. Horses with their drivers sent to 33.0 by R. a.s.b. as per instructions of A.D.M.S. Miss Lena Ashwell's party entertained the Unit. Still hard frost.	
	10/2/19		Admitted 1, also 1 P.O.W. admitted Remaining 8. also 1 P.O.W. 10 P.O.W. employed on various fatigues. Weather still cold. Hereifter 3 O.Rs. to U.K. for demobilisation.	
	11/2/19		Admitted 1, Evacuated 3, Duty 1, Remaining 5- also 1 P.O.W. remaining and 3 admitted and evacuated All Ear, Nose + Throat cases to No.41 Stat. Hosp. Poulainville. A.D.M.S. 38th (Welsh) Division, Col. A.G. Thompson, 6 July. D.D.O. Army visited Unit and round Goodbye to the Officers, N.C.Os, + men We so going as D.D.M.S., 8th Corps. Weather same.	
	12/2/19		Admitted 1 (and died) 1, Duty 1, Remaining 4 and 1 P.O.W. One O.R. of 995 A.E. Coy accidentally killed in village. Died whilst in our hands, and was buried in Civil Cemetery, Longueau.	

WAR DIARY or INTELLIGENCE SUMMARY

Army Form C. 2118.

Place	Date	Hour	Summary of Events and Information	Remarks and references to Appendices
LONGUEAU	13/2/19		Admitted 2, Evacd 2, Duty 1, Remaining 3, Pas 1, Out. The 4 bro. HQ horses and their drivers returned from 33o bay Base Weather mild, a little thaw, but roads still bad for horse traffic.	
	14/2/19		Admitted 5, Evacd 1, Remaining 4. Capt Chinnochers and batman to 41 Stat. Hosp. for duty. Weather mild, but dull, general thaw.	
	15/2/19		Admitted 3, Evacd 4, Remaining 3. Works Parties preparation Football match played at Allonville. Revd B. Falwer York to Range (35 Gen ½ O. Ground very wet, unfit for playing. One O.R. Ranc. to No 40 Stat. Hosp. on Dental Course.	
	16/2/19		Admitted 3, Evacd 2, Remaining 4. also 1 P.O.W. evacd & remaining. 2 "Y" horses (1 Riding) (1 D.D.) sent to Boundon for instructions 5 O.Rs. Rank SJ 130 J Ault returned to their unit after leaving Played in Corps Final "Soccer" match.	
	17/2/19		Admitted 1, Remaining 5 also 1 P.O.W admitted & 2 evacuatin	

Army Form C. 2118.

WAR DIARY
or
INTELLIGENCE SUMMARY.
(Erase heading not required.)

Instructions regarding War Diaries and Intelligence Summaries are contained in F.S. Regs., Part II. and the Staff Manual respectively. Title pages will be prepared in manuscript.

Place	Date	Hour	Summary of Events and Information	Remarks and references to Appendices
Longuenon	18/2/19		Admitted 4 Evacuated 3 Remaining 6 also 2 P.O.W. admitted and Evacuated. Which Brise in arms Brown Hall and Ruffle. 2. 36 Divisional Services both autographed by H.R.H. The Prince of Wales - Gov.Cap.Capt.J.Gore Browne	
	19/2/19		Admitted and Evacuated 3 P.O.W. Hunt & Roberts Remaining 6. Capt W.H. Armitage R.A.M.C. left H1 Stationary Hospital for Temporary duty with No.43 C.C.S.	
			8 Heavy Draught Horses Class Z left unit to report to No 5 V.S. section for Cab in Amiens on 22.2.19.	
	20/2/19		3d unit A.D.M.S. Lieut Col Inman D.S.O R.A.M.C visited the unit twice during this period.	
			Admits Admitted 2 Evacuated 1 (L.Duty) Remaining 6 also 2 P.O.W admitted Remaining 2 O.R. admitted to be demobilised.	
	21/2/19		1 P.O.W. admitted 2 Evacuated 3 S/Sgt J/Sgt 1 Remaining 37 2nd Cpl. 4 also 1 P.O.W admitted 1.5 evac.P.O.W.	
	22/2/19		Admit.R. Admitted 1 Evacuated 1 Remaining 4 also 1 P.O.W admitted and Remaining.	
			2 Other Ranks left to be demobilised. Weather rather warm milder and many preparations Trench Ft.	
	23/2/19		Patients admitted 2 Officers + 2 Other Ranks, Evacuated 2 Officers + 2 Other Ranks Remaining 4. also 3 P.O.W admitted to be evacuated.	
			5 men available for the Army of occupation were this day transferred to 130 Field Ambulance and 5 men who were available for demobilisation were this day transferred to this Field Ambulance from 130 Field Ambulance.	

A7092 Wt. w.1285.19/M.1293. 750,000. 1/17. D.D & I. Ltd. Forms/C.2118/14.

Army Form C. 2118.

WAR DIARY
or
INTELLIGENCE SUMMARY.
(Erase heading not required.)

Instructions regarding War Diaries and Intelligence Summaries are contained in F. S. Regs., Part II. and the Staff Manual respectively. Title pages will be prepared in manuscript.

Place	Date	Hour	Summary of Events and Information	Remarks and references to Appendices
Longuenesse	24/2/19		Patients admitted 1 Remaining 5. 3 Horses Rehow T. left unit Tuesday proceeding to Forges to Tonne. Conference held at the A.D.M.S. Office all Medical Officers of the Division being present, the following subjects were discussed. Isolation from Returning from Leave. Inoculation with Stieing Vaccine. Isolation Apparatus – Venereal Centre. Use of LCB Tents – Inoculations against Typhoid. Dental Treatment – Evacuation Workshop.	
	25/2/19		Patients admitted 1 Officers 2 Other Ranks, Evacuated 1 Officer 2 Other Ranks Remaining 5 Other Ranks.	
	26/2/19		15 Horses Glass I proceeded this day to No 5 V.E.S. Mortries for the purpose of being handed over. Patients admitted 2 Evacuated 2 Remaining 5. also 1 P.O.W admitted and Remaining.	
	27/2/19		Patients admitted 3 Evacuated 1 Died 1 Remaining 6 also 1 P.O.W Remaining	
	28/2/19		Dispenser reports to No. 41 Stationary Isolation Hospital	

James Sproul Lieut Col RAMC
O.C. 131 Field Ambulance

160/3551

-7 JUL 1919

13t. F.A.

Aust. 1919

WAR DIARY
or
INTELLIGENCE SUMMARY.
(Erase heading not required.)

Army Form C. 2118.

Place	Date	Hour	Summary of Events and Information	Remarks and references to Appendices
LONGUEAU	1-3-19		Patients admitted British NIL. Remaining 5. 1 P.O.W. Admitted and evacuated and 1 Remaining. Summer Time commenced at 23.00 hours this day. Six O. Ranks left unit to be demobilised.	See Appendices No 1 & 2
	2-3-19		Patients 1 admitted 6 Remaining also 1 P.O.W. Remaining. Major Snow Shannon left unit though for the purpose of being demobilised. Weather exceptionally fine all day.	
	3-3-19		Patients NIL admitted 2 Evacuated 4 Remaining. also 1 P.O.W. evacuated NIL Remaining. One horse transferred to the 49 M.A.S. for destruction.	
	4-3-19		Patients NIL Admitted 1 to Duty 3 Remaining. also 2 P.O.W admitted Evacuated. Two N.C.O's and 5 O. Ranks sent this day as Guard at the Doctoral Polls G.H.Q.	
	5-3-19		Patients 1 admitted Evacuated 3 Remaining. P.O.W. 2 admitted Evacuated. Sent our collection of sick from 222 Railway	
	6-3-19		Patients 5 admitted 1 evacuated 3 Remaining. 2 "Drs" 2 L.t's 13 men attached left this day to the demobilised. Capt Dingwall returned.	
	7-3-19		Patients 2 admitted 5 Remaining	
	8-3-19		Patients NIL admitted 1 Duty 4 Remaining. 6 Rank Other Ranks and 3 Rank Other Ranks left unit this day to be demobilised. Capt Dingwall R.A.M.C. (T.F.) left unit this day to be demobilised.	
	9-3-19		Patients 2 admitted 2 Evacuated 3 Remaining. also 1 P.O.W admitted & Evacuated. Received Orders to bring equipment back from Blank & LONGUEAU & prepare for checking	
	10-3-19			

WAR DIARY
or
INTELLIGENCE SUMMARY.

(Erase heading not required.)

Army Form C. 2118.

Place	Date	Hour	Summary of Events and Information	Remarks and references to Appendices
Longueau	11-3-19		Patients 3 admitted 2 evacuated 4 Remaining also 1 POW admitted & Remaining	
	12-3-19		Patients 2 admitted 2 evacuated 3 Duty 1 Remaining also 1 POW admitted & Remaining	
	13-3-19		Patients 2 admitted 3 Remaining 1 POW to duty 1 Remaining. Weather exceptionally fine to-day	
	14-3-19		Patients Nil admitted 1 Evacuated 1 Remaining also 1 POW Remaining. Sent 3 light draught and 1 heavy draught Horses to No 49 in U.S. for standing over. 3 Admission and Discharge Books for Six months ending 31.12.18 were this day sent direct to the D.A.G. 24th Q 3rd Echelon. Capt Armitage Frank T.F. is to-day struck off the strength as from 11.3.19 and transferred to No 43 C.C.S. Capt (A/Major) HREW W/D Frank T.F. is demobilised and struck off strength as from 4-3-19. (Batt / Embar Ration)	
	15.3.19		Patients admitted 4 evacuated 2 Remaining 3 also 1 POW Remaining	
	16.3.19		Patients admitted 4 evacuated 2 Remaining 5 also 1 POW admitted & Remaining. Remaining 1 6 Rank & File Other Ranks left the unit this day for the purpose of being demobilised. Capt D G Dingwall is this day struck off the strength permanently as from 11.3.19 (Batt / Embarkation)	

Army Form C. 2118.

WAR DIARY
or
INTELLIGENCE SUMMARY.
(Erase heading not required.)

Instructions regarding War Diaries and Intelligence Summaries are contained in F. S. Regs., Part II. and the Staff Manual respectively. Title pages will be prepared in manuscript.

Place	Date	Hour	Summary of Events and Information	Remarks and references to Appendices
Torgueau	17.3.19		Patients admitted 3 Remaining 6 also 1 POW Remaining 2 Officers and 37 Other Ranks Rank reported this day en route for the Army on the Rhine and left later in the day to report to OC/MS 2nd Division for duty	
	18.3.19		Patients admitted 10fficer 16 OtherRank Evacuated 1 Officer 16 OtherRank Duty 3 OtherRanks Remaining 5 OR also 2 POW admitted Evacuated 1 POW Remaining -. Capt Hunter Rank reported from 17th Division enroute for the Army on the Rhine. No detained pending further enquiries Major J.S. Davis Rank proceeded on 7 days leave to United Kingdom.	
	19.3.19		Patients 2 admitted 4 Evacuated 1 Duty Remaining 2, also 2 POW admitted and evacuated Remaining 1. Orders received to arrange with OC 129 Field Ambulance to have a Central Medical Inspection Room at G/15Y for the 112 & 115 Infty Brigades	
	20.3.19		Patients admitted 2 Evacuated 1 Remaining 3 also 1 POW Remaining 2 Medical Officers reported enroute for the army on the Rhine and were despatched 3 Rank personnel left unit this day to be demobilised	
	21.3.19		Patients admitted 4 Evacuated 3 Remaining 4 also 1 POW Remaining	
	22.3.19		Patients admitted 2 Evacuated 1 Remaining 5 also 1 POW Remaining Temporary Sergeant A Sawbridge Leave	
	23.3.19		Patients admitted 1 Evacuated 1 Remaining 5 also 2 POW admitted Evacuated 1 Remaining	

Army Form C. 2118.

WAR DIARY
or
INTELLIGENCE SUMMARY.
(Erase heading not required.)

Place	Date	Hour	Summary of Events and Information	Remarks and references to Appendices
Longueau	24/3/19		Patients 2 admitted 2 Duty 5 Remaining also 1 OR to duty. Demobilisation leave resume normal movement.	
	25/3/19		Patients 6 admitted 4 Evacuated 7 Remaining. Of the 6 patients admitted 4 belonged to the 35 Bat[t?] MGC who had been accidentally wounded by a Pom Snell exploding	
	26/3/19		Patients 4 admitted 3 Evacuated 8 Remaining 1 Rank evacuated Sick 16 #1 Stationary Hosp. + is struck off strength	see appendix no 3
	27/3/19		Patients NIL Admitted 2 Duty 6 Remaining	
	28/3/19		Patients 1 Officer 2 OR admitted 1 Officer 10R evacuated 7 Remaining also 1 BOW admits + Remaining. Major J S Davies Returned from leave	
	29/3/19		Patients NIL admitted 1 to Duty 6 Remaining also 1 BOR Remaining. Major J S Davies Same in accordance with appendix No 3 is this day struck off the effective strength of this F.A. as taken on the Same are strength	
	30/3/19		Patients 4 admitted 2 Evacuated 8 Remaining also 13 OR admitted +14 Evacuated NIL Remaining. Owing to bad weather in the Channel, 4 Rank other Ranks who were on leave unit here enroute for disposal, have been detained.	
	31/3/19		Weather once again fine, where a mest agreeable after the Post ten days when it has been so cold.	Signed J G E Rand Lt 131 Fld Ambce

140/30550.

17 JUL 1919

131. 7. a.

April 1919

Army Form C. 2118.

131 7th Aug 19

Vol 41

WAR DIARY
or
INTELLIGENCE SUMMARY.
(Erase heading not required.)

Place	Date	Hour	Summary of Events and Information	Remarks and references to Appendices
KANTARA	1/4/19		Patients admitted 1 Officer 4 o'Ranks. Evacuated 1 Officer 4 o'Ranks. Duty 1 OR. Remaining 6 OR. Evacuation Football 38 Div v Sadre Group Competition - Same took 38 Mile by 8 goals to nil in the first round played this day at PONT-NOYELLES.	
	2/4/19		Patients admitted 5 Evacuated 5 Remaining 6	
	3/4/19		Patients admitted 1 Evacuated 2 Duty 1 Remaining 4. Capt J.E. Davies MC RAMC this day took over Medical charge of Gissy Area and to live with the 38 Div RA but remained on the effective strength of this unit.	
	4/4/19		Patients admitted 1 Officer 2 O Ranks. Evacuated 1 Officer 3 Ranks. Duty 2 O Ranks. Remaining 1 also 2 OR admitted & evacuated from the POW Coy. 48890 Cpl N & Jones RAMC taken on strength w.e.f. 29-3-19 from 38 D HQ. This N.C.O. is at present attached to SMO 38 Division for duty.	
	5/4/19		Patients admitted 2 Evacuated 2 Remaining 1 Nothing to report.	
	6/4/19		Patients admitted 5 Evacuated 5 Remaining 1 + OR (RAMC) left unit enroute for disposal. Nothing to report.	
	7/4/19		Patients admitted 5 Evacuated 4 Remaining 2. Capt P.B. Sharp RAMC taken on the effective strength from 29.3.19 and relieved Capt J.E. Davies MC RAMC at the 38 Div CRA. - keeps Davies returning to this unit for duty.	See appx 1

Army Form C. 2118.

WAR DIARY
or
INTELLIGENCE SUMMARY.
(Erase heading not required.)

Instructions regarding War Diaries and Intelligence Summaries are contained in F. S. Regs., Part II. and the Staff Manual respectively. Title pages will be prepared in manuscript.

Place	Date	Hour	Summary of Events and Information	Remarks and references to Appendices
Engheim	8/4/19		Patients Evacuated 4 Remaining 5 also 1 OR admitted & Remaining 2 Retainable Other Ranks transferred to the 2/5 Div Train & struck off the strength of this unit.	
	9/4/19		Patients Admitted 8 Evacuated 5 Duty 2 Remaining 6 Admitted 1 OR Evacuated 1 and Remaining 1. Nothing to report.	
	10/4/19		Patients Admitted 1 Officer 7 Other Ranks Evacuated 1 Officer 6 Other Ranks Duty 1 Remaining 6. OR Admitted & evacuated 2 Remaining 1. Returned to LoC Pontainville the equipment of "B" Section including 1 Ambulance Wagon 1 GS Wagon 1 Limber 1 Water Cart.	
	11/4/19		Patients Admitted 3 Evacuated 5 Remaining 4 also 1 OR Remaining. Lt Sharp RAMC struck off the effective strength of this unit and proceeded to report to HQ 2nd Army for duty with the Army on the Rhine.	
	14/4/19		Patients Admitted 5 Evacuated 2 Remaining 4. OR Admitted 1 Evacuated 1 Remaining 1. The LoC Other Ranks entrusted with the equipment of this Unit.	
	15/4/19		Patients Admitted 4 Evacuated 4 Remaining 4 also 1 OR Remaining. 6 Rank & other Ranks proceeded this day to the Concentration Camp awaiting for dispersal.	

Army Form C. 2118.

WAR DIARY
or
INTELLIGENCE SUMMARY.
(Erase heading not required.)

Instructions regarding War Diaries and Intelligence Summaries are contained in F. S. Regs., Part II. and the Staff Manual respectively. Title pages will be prepared in manuscript.

Place	Date	Hour	Summary of Events and Information	Remarks and references to Appendices
Lozovaia	14/4/19		Patients admitted 3 Evacuated 4 Duty 1 Remaining 5. RORs admitted 1 Evacuated 1 Remaining 1	
	15/4/19		Patients admitted 1 Evacuated 2 Duty 4 Remaining 4. RORs admitted 2 Evacuated 2 Remaining 1	
	16/4/19		Patients Admitted 2 Evacuated 1 Duty 1 Remaining 4 also 1 ROR Remaining. Under authority of A/dmg No 3 area 5 Janre O Ranks of this unit are this day transferred to 41 Stat Hosp permanently as from 13.4.19 — these O Ranks remain with this unit attached to 41 Stat Hosp for Temporary duty.	
	17/4/19		Patients Admitted 6 Evacuated 3 Duty 1 Remaining 6 also 1 ROR Remaining. I receive an application to return Sgt Regitrin on the C of E Establishment of this unit as Acting Quartermaster. No Quartermaster having been sent to replace Capt Callan gone.	
	18/4/19		Patients Admitted 2 Duty 1 Remaining 7 also 1 ROR Remaining. The W.O Ranks Rank who were attached to No 41 Stationary Hospital are this day transferred to that Hospital and struck off the strength of this unit. I report to the SMO 38 Div A/ the gradual increase of Patients being admitted suffering from Venereal Disease contracted in Armies District and report, than the Blue Lamp Room lectures that Officers and O Ranks may be aware of the existence of such places and therefore able to secure Prophylactic Treatment against the disease which is so	

A7093. Wt. W1285g/M1293F. 750,000. 1/17. D. D. & L., Ltd. Forms/C2118/14.

Army Form C. 2118.

WAR DIARY
or
INTELLIGENCE SUMMARY.
(Erase heading not required.)

Instructions regarding War Diaries and Intelligence Summaries are contained in F. S. Regs., Part II. and the Staff Manual respectively. Title pages will be prepared in manuscript.

Place	Date	Hour	Summary of Events and Information	Remarks and references to Appendices
LONGUEAU	18/4/19	cont	Precedent in this area. There tents have been established at the Army Rest Stn Annex, Hotel du Rhin, Relais Grenville, Longuau Chateau, and la Motte by using the pre divised huts of these places.	See Appendix 2
	19/4/19		Patients admitted 4 Evacuated 7 Remaining it also 1 P.O.W. Remaining. One sick patient admitted being surplus to the Cadre Establishment of the day transferred to 33 Stat Cas Base.	
	20/4/19		Patients Admitted 1 Officer 3 Other Ranks Evacuated 1 Officer 2 Other Ranks Remaining 5. P.O.W. 1 to duty. to France. Other Ranks to our unit. The day from the Repat Concentration Camp. Wants to dispersal.	
	21/4/19		Patients Admitted 2 Evacuated 2 Duty 1 Remaining 4	
	22/4/19		Patients Admitted 3 Evacuated 3 Remaining 4 also 1 P.O.W. admitted and evacuated. Lieut Col M. Greaves DSO RAMC S.M.O. 35 Div notifies that he has received orders to be demobilised and is known to England on 23/4/19 and Col 131 4th Amb to take over duties of S.M.O. 35 Div	
	23/4/19		Patients admitted 5 Evacuated 5 Remaining 4	
			Duties of S.M.O. 35 Division are this day taken over by Lieut Col Jespersle RAMC OC 131 4th Ambulance and the Office of the Same moves from la Motte to Longuau Chateau. Brig a. General sanctions retention of 9 N.C.O.s & 19 Other Ranks RAMC 2 N.C.O.s & 4 O.R. of the Ryl RAMC of the 6th of the Royal Army being surplus to Immediate Establishment. to complete Cadre Establishment. A. Mag. Lieut	

Army Form C. 2118.

WAR DIARY
or
INTELLIGENCE SUMMARY.
(Erase heading not required.)

Instructions regarding War Diaries and Intelligence Summaries are contained in F. S. Regs., Part II. and the Staff Manual respectively. Title pages will be prepared in manuscript.

Place	Date	Hour	Summary of Events and Information	Remarks and references to Appendices
Longueau	24/4/19		Patients Admitted 5 also 1 POW Admitted. Remaining 5 also 1 POW Admitted Remaining	
	25/4/19		Notification received from I Corps Group DDMS SMTO to the effect that in the event of Ladres of Field Ambulance entraining, Motor Ambulances and Motor lorries must be handed in to DADOS but lorry on the day the ladres entrain. Patients Admitted 2 Duty 1 Remaining 6. 1 POW Remaining discharged to duty	
	26/4/19		Patients Admitted 6 Evacuated 6 Remaining 6 also 1 POW Admitted Evacuated. Of the 6 Admitted 3 are suffering from severe wounds caused by the bursting of a bomb	
	27/4/19		Patients Admitted 1 Evacuated 2 Remaining 5	
	28/4/19		Patients Admitted 2 Evacuated 2 Remaining 5	
	29/4/19		Patients Admitted 4 Evacuated 4 Duty 1 Remaining 4. The German Delousor captured by 151 Fld Coy RE but remained with this Field Ambulance, was this day sent to DADOS 36 Div Pontruille for transmission to the Scotland Imperial War Museum. 149 Lyons St London S.W.	
	30/4/19		No event worthy of report.	

Jauwolfeuce
Mcolaure
AC 13/ Field Ambulance

3/5/19

Appendice No1   S.M.O. 38th Div.NoM58/138.

Reference 38 Div No540 of 3/4/19.

S.M.O.'s office closes at QERRIEU at 12.00. hours on the 7th of April
and will open at La Motte Brebiere at the same hour.
The 130th St John Field Ambulance moves from Bussy to La Moote Brebiere
on the 7th of April. This Unit will close on the 6th inst.
All Cases for evacuation will pass through the books of the 131st Field
AMBULANCE.
The 130th Field Ambulance will continue to look after the sick of the
Divisional Units North of the Somme.

                        (SIGNED) John E H Davies.
                                Lieut Col R.A.M.C.
                         S.M.O. 38th Welch Division.

4-4-19

Appendice NO 2

D.A.A.G.
38th Welsh Division.   A.D.M.S. No M.122/44

There has been a slight increase in the number of cases admitted to hospital suffering from Venereal Disease.
Could attention be drawn please, in Routine Orders or Otherwise that "Blue Lamp Rooms", where preventive treatment is given, are situated in:

      AMIENS. At the Army Rest Station near Railway Station.
      Glisy   AT the 38th D.A.C. Medical Inspection Room.
      Blangy At the Camp Medical Inspection Room.
      Longueau At the Chateau (131 Field Ambulance.)
      La Motte At the Nos 129 & 130th Field Ambulance.

Men should attend at these places at the earliest possible moment, if they have been subjected to the risk of infection.

      Lectures on the after effects of venereal Diseases have been given to most units. Further Lectures will be given at both GLISY and BLANGY by Capt J E Davies M C R A M C and Capt G W Riddell M C R A M C this week

      It is strongly recommended that as many as possible of both Officers and Men should attend these lectures.

                        (Signed) John E H Davies
                                  Lieut Col RAMC
18.4.19   S M O 38th Welsh Division.

ALL UNITS   38th Division NoA 1347.

      For information and communication to all ranks.

The Divisional Commander hopes that every facility will be given to all all ranks to attend the lectures above referred to.

                      Signed G P Thomas. Capt
22.4.19   For D A A G. 38 (WELSH) DIVISION

Table shewing number of cases treated in Blue Lamp Room Amiens of which only two have contracted Venereal Disease.

FEBRUARY

Day	Number treated	Day	Number treated	Day	Number treated	Day	Number treated	Day	Number treated
1	9	7	6	13	7	19	11	25	6
2	10	8	5	14	3			26	3
						20	8		
3	8	9	5	15	2	21	16	27	9
4	9	10	6	16	6	22	9	28	7
5	7	11	7	17	4	23	7		
6	6	12	6	18	16	24	8		

Total 211

MARCH

Day	Number treated	Day	Number treated	Day	Number treated	Day	Number treated	Day	Number treated
1	7	8	6	15	20	22	12	29	8
2	9	9	5	16	15	23	10	30	11
3	11	10	6	17	16	24	9	31	6
4	10	11	8	18	8	25	8		
5	7	12	7	19	10	26	6		
6	8	13	11	20	7	27	10		
7	9	14	8	21	9	28	6		

Total 283

APRIL

Day	Number treated	Day	Number treated	Day	Number treated	Day	Number treated	Day	Number treated
1	10	7	14	13	22	19	11	25	--
2	8	8	17	14	10	20	12	26	--
3	9	9	6	15	11	21	9	27	--
4	7	10	8	16	23	22	8		
5	12	11	7	17	8	23	10		
6	11	12	8	18	7	24	--		

Total 248

(6339) Wt. W160/M3016 1,500,000 10/17 McA & W Ltd (E 1898) Forms W3091.   Army Form W.3091.

Cover for Documents.

Nature of Enclosures.

131 Field Ambulance

Original WAR DIARY for month of May 1919

Notes, or Letters written.

G.O.C.,
　British Troops in France & Flanders

　　　　Herewith Original War Diary of the up-mentioned units, broken up on the respective dates shewn:-

129 Field Ambulance　　　　22/5/19
131 Field Ambulance　　　　22/5/19

　　　　　　　　A.H.T. Davis
　　　　　　　　Capt: R.A.M.C.
　　　S.M.O., 38th (Welsh) Divn

A.D.M.S.,
38th (WELSH) DIV.
No. T. 386
Date 22-5-19

131 Field Ambulance

WAR DIARY
or
INTELLIGENCE SUMMARY.
(Erase heading not required.)

Army Form C. 2118.

Place	Date	Hour	Summary of Events and Information	Remarks and references to Appendices
Longueau	1/5/19		Patients admitted 1 Remaining 4	
	2/5/19		Patients admitted 6 Evacuated 5 Remaining 5. Capt J C Davies MC have struck off the effective strength with effect on from 20-4-19 and shewn as transferred to No 41 Stationary Hospital but attached to this unit for rations	
	3/5/19		Patients admitted 3 Evacuated 2 Remaining 4 Patients "POW" Admitted 3 Evacuated 1 Remaining NIL Received this day from SM.O I Corps Group Ticket that under orders from DMS 1st Army B.T.1.F.M.F. that this Field Ambulance will shortly be broken up in France	
	4/5/19		Patients admitted 4 Evacuated 2 Remaining 6	
	5/5/19		Patients admitted 4 Evacuated 4 Remaining 6 Patients "POW" Admitted 2 Evacuated 2	
	6/5/19		Patients admitted 4 Evacuated 6 Remaining 8	
	7/5/19		Patients admitted 3 Evacuated 5 Duty 1 Remaining 5 Patients POW 2 admitted 2 Evacuated	

Army Form C. 2118.

WAR DIARY
or
INTELLIGENCE SUMMARY.
(Erase heading not required.)

Instructions regarding War Diaries and Intelligence Summaries are contained in F. S. Regs. Part II. and the Staff Manual respectively. Title pages will be prepared in manuscript.

Place	Date	Hour	Summary of Events and Information	Remarks and references to Appendices
Longuean	8/5/19		Patients Admitted 4 Evacuated 5 Duty 3 Remaining 1	
	9/5/19		Patients Admitted 1 Evacuated 1 Remaining 1	
	10/5/19		Patients Admitted 2 Evacuated 2 Duty 1 Remaining Nil	
	11/5/19		Patients Admitted 1 Evacuated 1 Remaining Nil. Allotment for 20 Rank Other Ranks to proceed to the Concentration camp this day unable to dispatch has been received, but any Man over fifty at the camp they entrust be sent, and to await further orders.	
	12/5/19		Patients Admitted 1 Other 1 O.Rank Evacuated 1 Other 1 O.R.R. Remaining Nil Presided at board of Enquiry re Absence of One Rame Other Rank of 130 Field Ambulance.	
	13/5/19		Patients Admitted 1 Evacuated 1	
	14/5/19		Patients Admitted 4 Evacuated 4 Visited Hd Qrs No 3 Area and sent a/o ms. Received Orders re handing in of equipment and arranged with 34ADS Poelcapelle and No 36 advanced Depot Medical Stores to hand the equipment on 17/5/19.	

Army Form C. 2118.

WAR DIARY
or
INTELLIGENCE SUMMARY.
(Erase heading not required.)

Instructions regarding War Diaries and Intelligence Summaries are contained in F. S. Regs., Part II. and the Staff Manual respectively. Title pages will be prepared in manuscript.

Place	Date	Hour	Summary of Events and Information	Remarks and references to Appendices
Longueau	15/5/19		Patients 1 Officer 3 OR admitted and Evacuated. 10 Releasable RASC HT men sent to report to DID Train enroute for demobilisation	
	16/5/19		32 Releasable Ranec men leave unit this day enroute to be demobilised. Return Railway Warrant will be given up minutes	
		7.54	[illegible] [illegible] to [illegible] Rendered in Advance Stores	
		11.54	One O.R. No. 5 men arrived. Sent to 38" Bri Train RASC (MT) Out to No V MT VRP also throw forge and one small ambulance + two Douglas motor cycles.	
			Bus sent Comps Link by M 1557 A 496 Sunbeam A5 9041 Ford 9675 sent on to the third section Division & Canteen fund to be handed to them to be handed to Army Hawke + Stewart on to the man at 9.70.50pm Capt T.W. [illegible] raised the Army rendering men of the Unit out of Equipment Etc OC 131 Field Amb.	

[signature]

Army Form C. 2118.

WAR DIARY
or
INTELLIGENCE SUMMARY.
(Erase heading not required.)

Instructions regarding War Diaries and Intelligence Summaries are contained in F. S. Regs., Part II. and the Staff Manual respectively. Title pages will be prepared in manuscript.

Place	Date	Hour	Summary of Events and Information	Remarks and references to Appendices
Little Bedwyn	19/5/19		I took over remainder of 131 Field Ambulance from Capt J Showden R.A.S.C. This consists of 7 O.R's. See war Diary.	
	27/5/19		The 7 O.R's were sent for Demobilisation & Say's the closing the Gods of the concentration Camp at Sorrisen unit.	Trew William Capt R.a.m.c.

www.ingramcontent.com/pod-product-compliance
Lightning Source LLC
Chambersburg PA
CBHW080817010526
44111CB00015B/2570